Archbishop Randall Davidson

Randall Davidson was Archbishop of Canterbury for quarter of a century from 1903 to 1928. Davidson was a product of the Victorian ecclesiastical and social establishment, whose advance through the Church was dependent on the patronage of Queen Victoria, but he became Archbishop at a time of huge social and political change. He guided the Church of England through the turbulence of the Edwardian period, when it faced considerable challenges to its status as the Established Church and helped to shape its response to the horrors of the First World War. Davidson inherited a Church of England that was sharply divided on a range of issues, and he devoted his career as Archbishop to securing its unity, whilst ensuring that its voice continued to be heard both nationally and internationally. A modest and pragmatic man, he was widely respected both within the Church and beyond, helping to find solutions to a range of political and ecclesiastical problems. This book explores Davidson's role within the Church and in the life of Britain more broadly during his time at Canterbury. It includes a large selection of documents that help both to reveal the Archbishop's character and to cast light on the way in which he carried out his demanding duties.

Michael Hughes is Professor of History and Head of Department at Lancaster University. He has published a book and numerous articles on Nonconformity in the twentieth century, as well as writing extensively on Anglo-Russian relations, with a particular emphasis on relations between Anglicanism and Orthodoxy (a subject with which Randall Davidson was particularly concerned). He was for many years a Lay Reader in the Anglican Church and has published five monographs and more than thirty articles in scholarly journals.

The Archbishops of Canterbury Series
Series editor: Andrew Chandler
University of Chichester, UK

Developed in association with Lambeth Palace Library archives, this series presents authoritative studies on the Archbishops of Canterbury. Each book combines biographical, historical, theological, social and political analysis within each archiepiscopacy, with original source material drawn from the Archbishop's correspondence, speeches and published and unpublished writings. The Archbishops of Canterbury series offers a vital source of reference of lasting importance to scholars, students, and all readers interested in the history of the international Church.
www.routledge.com/series/AARCHBISH

Archbishop Fisher, 1945–1961
Church, State and World
Andrew Chandler and David Hein

Archbishop Anselm 1093–1109
Bec Missionary, Canterbury Primate, Patriarch of Another World
Sally N. Vaughn

Archbishops Ralph d'Escures, William of Corbeil and Theobald of Bec
Heirs of Anselm and Ancestors of Becket
Jean Truax

Archbishop Pole
John Edwards

Archbishop Ramsey
The Shape of the Church
Peter Webster

Archbishop Howley, 1828–1848
James Garrard

Archbishop Randall Davidson
Michael Hughes

Archbishop Randall Davidson

Michael Hughes

LONDON AND NEW YORK

First published 2018
by Routledge

2 Park Square, Milton Park, Abingdon, Oxfordshire OX14 4RN
52 Vanderbilt Avenue, New York, NY 10017

Routledge is an imprint of the Taylor & Francis Group, an informa business

First issued in paperback 2019

Copyright © 2018 Michael Hughes

The right of Michael Hughes to be identified as author of this work has been asserted by him in accordance with sections 77 and 78 of the Copyright, Designs and Patents Act 1988.

All rights reserved. No part of this book may be reprinted or reproduced or utilised in any form or by any electronic, mechanical, or other means, now known or hereafter invented, including photocopying and recording, or in any information storage or retrieval system, without permission in writing from the publishers.

Notice:
Product or corporate names may be trademarks or registered trademarks, and are used only for identification and explanation without intent to infringe.

British Library Cataloguing-in-Publication Data
A catalogue record for this book is available from the British Library

Library of Congress Cataloging-in-Publication Data
A catalog record for this book has been requested

ISBN: 978-1-4724-1866-1 (hbk)
ISBN: 978-1-4724-1867-8 (pbk)

Typeset in Bembo
by Apex CoVantage, LLC

Contents

	Preface	vi
	Introduction	1
1	The making of an Archbishop	10
2	Archbishop Davidson and the Edwardian Crisis: a Victorian in a changing world (1903–1914)	34
3	Archbishop Davidson and the boundaries of Anglicanism (1903–14)	59
4	Archbishop Davidson and the First World War (1914–1918)	85
5	Archbishop Davidson and the development of the Ecumenical Movement (1918–1928)	111
6	Archbishop Davidson and the challenge of social and economic reform (1918–1928)	130
7	Archbishop Davidson, Church, and State (1918–1928)	147
	Assessment	166
	Documents	173
	Bibliography	215
	Index	225

Preface

Randall Davidson has intrigued me for many years. The man who served as Archbishop of Canterbury between 1903 and 1928 has featured on the periphery of a number of my previous research projects, yet has somehow remained, at least to me, a curiously elusive figure. Davidson is familiar to anyone interested in the fitful series of informal Anglican-Orthodox dialogues that took place in the late nineteenth and early twentieth-centuries. He also comes within the purview of students of Anglo-Russian relations, given his attempts to intervene on behalf of Russian clergy following the 1917 Revolution, as well as for his role in supporting the dispatch of aid to alleviate famine in Russia in 1918–19. Any historian who has studied the history of Britain during the First World War can similarly not fail to be aware of Davidson's sterling efforts to balance the demands of patriotism and the moral imperative to avoid an unreasoning hatred of the enemy. The Archbishop also naturally features in any history of the Church of England, not as a gifted theologian or charismatic preacher, but rather as a cautious yet well-regarded ecclesiastical bureaucrat who helped to guide the Church of England through 25 turbulent years of change and challenge.

And yet, despite George Bell's massive biography, first published in 1935, Davidson is not really a familiar figure beyond a comparative small number of Church historians. It is for this reason that I am grateful to Dr Andrew Chandler for encouraging me to write this book, which has given me the opportunity to try to better understand such an elusive quarry. I have come to Davidson from what is perhaps a rather unusual perspective: that of an international historian, whose interest in Davidson was prompted by my interest in understanding the Archbishop's attitudes towards the wider world, rather than as a student of the Church of England. And, as an historian of international history, I have long been interested in Davidson's 'pragmatism', which appears in these pages as a form of Realism rooted both in a belief in the virtues of compromise *and* a recognition of the challenge of uncritically applying a universal ethic to the recalcitrant world of human society. As someone who has down the years written a good deal on Russian Orthodoxy, I am also naturally inclined to make parallels between such ideas and the virtues of an apophatic theology sceptical about the extent to which divine revelation can serve as an unproblematic foundation for human action (although such a position is hardly unknown in the Western churches either). I have nevertheless endeavoured to keep these interests 'behind the scenes' in the text that follows – except perhaps in the conclusion – conscious that most readers will be more interested in a straightforward account of the 'life and times' of Randall Davidson.

I have taken every opportunity over the past few years to rummage through archives and libraries up and down Britain to help deepen my understanding of Davidson. The Reading Room staff at Lambeth Palace Library have been unfailingly courteous and cheerful as I ordered up a mountain of books and files. I have also benefitted greatly from the help of staff at the Borthwick Library (York), the Bodleain Library, the British Library, the British Library of Economic and Political Science, Lancaster University Library, the Library of Senate House (London), and the Sidney Jones Library (University of Liverpool). I am grateful to Sally Mills, who was once again kind enough to take the time to help turn my leaden prose into something more readable. I should also thank my colleagues at Lancaster for putting up with an increasingly irascible head of Department during the final stages of preparing this manuscript. The same goes for my wife, Katie. Once again, this book is dedicated to my parents Anne and John Hughes.

Introduction

In 1935, George Bell published his massive two-volume biography of Randall Davidson, who served as Archbishop of Canterbury from 1903 to 1928.¹ Bell had worked for many years as the Archbishop's Chaplain, and his biography was based on an exhaustive survey of the voluminous archival material, as well as first-hand knowledge of many of the people and events described in the book. He included numerous extracts from Davidson's private letters and memoranda, giving readers an insight into the character and outlook of the man who headed the Church of England for a quarter of a century, having previously served as Dean of Windsor and, successively, Bishop of Rochester and Winchester. Bell's biography was no simple exercise in hagiography, but it was permeated by the author's affection and admiration for his old mentor. It was also shaped by his friendship with the Archbishop's widow Edith, along with others who had known Davidson well, and expressed definite ideas about how they wanted him to be remembered.²

The picture of Davidson that emerges in the pages of Bell's book is an unambiguously positive one. The Archbishop was represented as a man of great personal integrity and industry, who tempered his ambition with a genuine sense of modesty, devoting his energies to defending the position of the Church of England in national life, whilst soothing away its internal divisions through the patient use of quiet diplomacy. Nor was such a portrait a controversial one. The journalist and *Church Times* editor Sidney Dark had already published a book in 1929 about *Archbishop Davidson and the English Church*, which praised Davidson as 'a great man' who was, in 'purity of character' and 'steadfastness of purpose', superior to most of his contemporaries in Church and State.³ The writer and social reformer Harold Begbie commended Davidson for exemplifying 'order, decency and good temper'.⁴ Few other writers showed any desire to challenge the image of an 'esteemed Archbishop'.⁵ When Davidson died in 1930, both published obituaries and private letters of sympathy paid tribute to a man who had throughout his life impressed those he met with his kindness and humility.

A few shadows inevitably appeared in some of the accounts of Davidson written by his contemporaries – often expressed as a kind of counterpoise to the paean of praise for his innate caution and decency. Dark suggested that the Archbishop lacked 'audacity', something which he attributed in part to the fact that he began life as a 'courtier' (Davidson had, as Dean of Windsor, been close to Queen Victoria). Begbie described the Archbishop as 'an admirable judge if an indifferent advocate'.[6] One former Anglican Bishop thought that Davidson had too often been 'led by circumstances'.[7] Bell himself acknowledged that there were occasions when the Archbishop's judgement deserted him, most notably towards the end of his career, when ill health and fatigue made him an increasingly detached figure. Davidson also naturally faced numerous criticisms throughout his long archiepiscopate, whether from Nonconformists angry at the privileged position of the Church of England in national life, or Anglo-Catholics irritated by his readiness to accept the right of Parliament to legislate in ecclesiastical matters. Such criticisms were, nevertheless, the exception rather than the rule. Even those who disagreed with him more often than not went out of the way to praise his generosity of spirit. Nor was Bell's positive account of Davidson simply a reflection of the close relationship between the two men. It is impossible, even after the passage of eighty years, not to admire his biography both as a model of scholarship and a vital source of information about the man who served as Archbishop of Canterbury for longer than any of his post-Reformation predecessors. All of which raises the question of why there is a need for any new assessment of the career of Randall Davidson.

The first answer, as anyone who has perused all 1,400 pages of Bell's massive account of Davidson will know, is that its sheer scale makes it a difficult read for all but the most determined. It is in many ways as much a work of reference as a biography. And, whilst generally full in its account of Davidson's life, Bell was at times notably discreet when discussing his subject's views on individuals ranging from Queen Victoria to David Lloyd George. He was also reticent when discussing such topics as the relationship between Davidson's sister-in-law Lucy Tait, daughter of Archbishop Archibald Tait, and Mary Benson, widow of Archbishop Edward Benson. Such discretion is quite in order when writing about a well-known figure, except in so far as their private life and opinions have ramifications for their public role (it is an approach followed throughout this book).[8] Of greater significance here, perhaps, is the question of Bell's interpretation of Davidson's long ecclesiastical career.

The Archbishop's erstwhile Chaplain began researching his book soon after Davidson's death. Whilst the idea that chronological distance creates the foundations of a nuanced perspective is often little more than a reflection of the historian's vanity, Bell certainly acted as a 'participant-observer' in many of the events he wrote about, to use one of the more tiresome phrases of modern sociology. Bell played an important role in shaping the Archbishop's policy on a variety of questions, most notably the various ecumenical initiatives that developed after 1918, in response to the horrors of the First World War. By the time he wrote his book about Davidson, Bell was himself an important figure in the Church of England, having been appointed Bishop of Chichester in 1929. Many of the issues that had concerned the Archbishop continued to preoccupy senior figures in the Church throughout the decade that followed. It should not therefore be a matter of surprise that the Davidson who emerges in Bell's book is very much Bell's Davidson.

None of this is to say that Bell was a prisoner of his own prejudices and beliefs (at least no more than any of us are). It is, rather, simply to note that his book was written in the tradition of authorised and semi-authorised interwar biographies of 'great men'. Such works generally assume that the correct way to recall a 'Life' is to trace how the individual subject navigated their way through the events they encountered in the course of their career. The very nature of biography requires a focus on the central character. Such a perspective is entirely reasonable, but perhaps requires a caveat that both author and reader should be aware of the danger that the agency of 'their' man or woman can easily be exaggerated, whilst the complexity and contradictions of history can too readily be lost through the simple act of concentrating on a single individual. It is certainly a caveat that the reader of this book should keep firmly in mind. Davidson himself was acutely aware that he was not master of all he surveyed. Like most of those who reach the top of any organisation – political, economic, or ecclesiastical – the Archbishop understood the limitations of his authority. His strength lay, indeed, in recognising that his most important role was to seek agreement between those who disagreed rather than trying to resolve divisions by imposing his own will.

Perhaps the main theme of this account of Randall Davidson's life is that he was (as Edward Carpenter has noted) essentially a Victorian in outlook,[9] who found himself responsible for guiding the Church of England through the perilous challenges of a multifaceted modernity. Davidson was born in 1848, the year when the revolutions that broke out across Europe briefly threatened the multinational empires whose roots stretched far back into the medieval period. He died in 1930, shortly after the Stock Market crash, which so damaged the global economy that it paved the way for the rise of Hitler and the growth of international tensions that exploded in the Second World War. Or, to focus more narrowly on literary landmarks, Davidson was born at a time when Charles Dickens' *Dombey and Son* was still being serialised, and died in the year that D. H. Lawrence first published *Lady Chatterley's Lover* (albeit not in Britain). None of this is to say that the Archbishop was born into a settled society with a common outlook on matters social and cultural. He was after all only 11 years old when Charles Darwin published his *Origin of Species*, destined to have a huge impact on the development of both scientific culture and religious belief in the decades that followed. Nor is it to assume that the Victorian era was a settled period of British history that endured until blown apart by the challenges of the new twentieth century: it was instead a time of massive social and economic development, ranging from industrialisation and urbanisation at home to the growth of the British Empire abroad. It is, however, indisputable that Davidson served as Archbishop during a period of great change in both the ecclesiastical and secular spheres. Much of his time at Canterbury was spent responding to the complex brew of shifting problems that emerged within the Church of England and more generally across British society.

The chapters that follow are organised both thematically and chronologically. The first chapter briefly reviews Davidson's career in the years before his appointment to Canterbury, examining how, from early in his ecclesiastical career, he was a member of the Victorian 'Establishment', his advance up the Church hierarchy rooted as much in the patronage of the Queen as in his own undoubted aptitudes and abilities. Although keen to look at the world from beyond the confines of his particular standpoint, Davidson imbibed from Archbishop Tait (whom he served as Chaplain) the idea that the Church of England was a National Church, whose senior figures had a responsibility to engage with social and political issues. He was nevertheless increasingly aware that the growing strength of Nonconformity meant that it was becoming impossible for the Church of England to assume its position in public life was unassailable. Whilst Davidson was most at home in private discussion with royals and politicians and Bishops, he was even before arriving at Canterbury convinced that the Church of England needed to be seen to earn its position as the Established Church. He was also aware that its internal divisions – flowing from the chasm between 'High' and 'Low' Churchmen that had developed following the rise of the Oxford Movement in the 1840s – could pose a danger to both its unity and authority. By the time he went to Canterbury in 1903, Davidson was already convinced that one of his most important tasks was to manage the tensions within the Church of England, whilst using his access to members of the political establishment to ensure that it continued to exercise influence in the corridors of power.

The next two chapters then examine Davidson's archiepiscopate during the years between 1903 and 1914. Chapter 2 examines his involvement in the major political controversies of the day – State control of education, the Parliamentary crisis of 1909–11, the Irish Home Rule crisis – during which the Archbishop worked hard to defend the influence of the Church of England, whilst seeking to broker compromise between senior political figures. His *modus operandi* was rooted in a belief that the Church needed to acknowledge the social and political changes embedded in the Liberal ascendancy, which followed the 1906 General Election, working with the grain of the times to prevent the Church's marginalisation as a site of authority in England and Wales. Chapter 3 then examines the internal tensions within the Church of England that Davidson had to deal with during his first ten years at Canterbury, ranging from the bitter divisions over Ritualism to debates about overseas mission work, as well as exploring the Archbishop's efforts to build closer ties between the provinces of the worldwide Anglican Communion. These challenges did not of course present themselves in neat sequential fashion. They instead formed part of the elusive yet tangible Edwardian Crisis, characterised by growing anxiety about threats to traditional patterns of authority and privilege, accompanied by an uneasy sense that the imagined certainties of the Victorian Age had been left far behind.

Chapter 4 examines Davidson's career during the First World War – a conflict traditionally seen as marking a kind of *caesura* in historical development, as the technological and social realities of total war blew away the assumptions and values of a more innocent age. The idea that the First World War represented a dramatic rupture has long been questioned by historians, not least because the Edwardian Crisis itself seemed to represent a break with the Victorian past, whilst in the years after 1918 the continuities with the pre-war years were in some ways as marked as the changes. The war nevertheless created new challenges for the Church of England, ranging from the need to supply chaplains at the Front and comfort to the bereaved at home, to the ethical conundrums raised by the use of poisonous gas and the demands for retaliation against German 'atrocities'. The familiar idea that the Church of England served as a kind of recruiting arm of the State, stridently endorsing the morality of the war, has become something of an historical cliché down the years. The reality was more complex, and Davidson himself took a quiet but determined lead in criticising the use of gas and the harsh treatment of conscientious objectors, even though he was fundamentally committed to the idea that Britain was fighting a virtuous war against tyranny.

Davidson continued to focus a good deal on internal Church affairs during the war, not least the on-going tension created by the commitment of some leading figures to a 'Modernism' that seemed to call into question many traditional doctrines. He also fretted about how a brutal war could have erupted between Christian nations who supposedly shared certain fundamental values. It is a cliché to suggest that the ecumenical movement was created by the First World War (its origins can be dated back much further). There is, though, no doubt that both the bloodshed and the shared experience of the trenches helped to fuel calls for the various denominations to work more closely with one another. Chapter 5 focuses on Davidson's role after 1918 in the burgeoning ecumenical movement. The Archbishop was committed to the principle of ecumenism, but much of his time was in practice spent trying to manage the tensions it created, since discussion of building closer relations with other churches at home and abroad necessarily raised questions about the nature of the Church of England itself. The final two chapters then consider how Davidson sought to maintain the national role of the Church of England in the final decades of his archiepiscopate. Chapter 6 examines how Davidson found himself increasingly at odds during the 1920s with a younger generation of clergy and lay people, led by the likes of William Temple and R. H. Tawney, who wanted the Church of England to use its influence to help place social and economic life in Britain on a new ethical foundation. Chapter 7 explores the growth of tensions within the Church of England leading up the debacle of 1927–28, when Parliament refused to approve the new Prayer Book, threatening to lead to a crisis in Church-State relations. At the heart of many of these developments was the nature of Establishment itself. Davidson himself was no Erastian, believing instead that the relationship of Church and State should be one of organic harmony, but he was also temperamentally unsympathetic to those who believed that the Church of England should use its position to call for fundamental social and economic reforms. One of the curiosities of

Davidson's life is, indeed, that he managed to be passionately committed to the principle of Establishment, whilst struggling to articulate both its character and its role in determining the Church of England's position in national life.

Davidson's reaction in the face of many of these developments often reflected his puzzlement at the position of those whose outlook on life was rooted in a passionate commitment to specific doctrines and practices. He was well aware that his defence of the comprehensive character of the Church of England made some look on him with suspicion as a latitudinarian, unwilling to set boundaries to the permitted beliefs of professing Anglicans. The charge was not altogether true – although there can be little doubt that the Archbishop's reluctance to support definite rulings on disciplinary and doctrinal issues was sometimes prompted by his concern that such action would only worsen division. Davidson's Anglicanism was not primarily a matter of doctrine. It was also shaped by a combination of reason and faith allied with an acute awareness of the past as a source of wisdom and a possible constraint on change. He was by instinct inclined to include rather than exclude. It was for this reason that he was ready to ordain William Temple in 1910 and consecrate Hensley Henson as Bishop of Hereford in 1918, even though their views on doctrine were seen by many as heterodox, and deeply inconsistent with traditional Christian (let alone Anglican) teaching on issues ranging from the Incarnation through to miracles. The fluidity of the Archbishop's vision of Anglicanism meant that he found it easy to support ecumenical initiatives, and discount doctrinal squabbles, since he was not convinced of the theological importance of the issues that so exercised many of his contemporaries. Any study of Davidson does, indeed, need to engage with the problem of defining the fine line that separates open-mindedness from lack of conviction. This book – like Bell's biography – suggests that Davidson's commitment to maintaining the Church of England as a broad Church was rooted both in pragmatism *and* a deeper sense that the Anglican tradition was one that should accommodate a wide range of outlooks and beliefs.

It is perhaps worth saying a few words about the vexed relationship between modernisation and secularisation, which has so preoccupied historians and theologians in recent years, and is a theme that inevitably recurs in the pages that follow. Davidson, throughout his 25 years at Canterbury, seldom fretted about the prospect of Britain ceasing to be a Christian nation – but he was intensely concerned about preserving the Church of England's place in a country where millions of men and women belonged to other denominations. He also understood that the changing temper of the times was transforming what might be termed the character of Christian culture. The decline of the rituals of the English Sunday, the development of cinema as a medium of mass entertainment, the growing circulation of popular newspapers – all these were both a hallmark and a source of the gentle retreat of Christianity from the heart of national life. The Church of England was not necessarily in decline, but it was confronting significant changes in the character of popular religion, even if these can be hard to delineate. The term *weltanschauung* – that nebulous 'spirit of the age' – is perhaps best avoided as a term of historical analysis since its content lies so much in the eye of the beholder. And yet the Britain of 1928, the year Davidson left Canterbury, was fundamentally different from the Britain of 1903 when he arrived. Some of the changes were objective: full adult suffrage, the growth of light industry and the consumer society, and the development of radio and other mass media. Others were less tangible, ranging from the rise of the 'flapper' to the appearance of fiction that dealt with issues of morality in ways that would have been almost unthinkable at the start of the twentieth century. It was through the changing contours of this landscape that Davidson had to guide the Church of England for quarter of a century.

Alert readers of this book will notice how hard it is to break free altogether from the shadows of Bell's massive biography of Davidson. Nor is this necessarily a problem given the very real strengths of his work. Bell was adept at identifying correspondence and memoranda of particular value. He was also generally fair-minded and balanced in his selection. There were nevertheless times when Bell edited particular documents in ways that distorted their significance (most frequently by removing some of Davidson's more impatient judgements about the people he met both within and beyond the Church of England). It is for this reason that I have in almost all cases – with the partial exception of Chapter 1 – returned to the original documents (whether in Davidson's own papers at Lambeth Palace or in other collections of archival and printed sources). Readers who are familiar with the academic literature will also note that I have tried, where possible, to locate Davidson's life and career within the scholarly debates that have flourished in recent years over such questions as the 'decline' of the Church of England and the putative growth of a secular society in Britain. I have, however, deliberately avoided dwelling on these debates within the text itself, mindful that many readers will not be familiar with the literature, and are in any case more interested in understanding both Davidson himself and his time as Archbishop. The work of scholars such as Simon Green, Callum Brown, Matthew Grimley, John Kent, Stuart Mews, and Melanie Barber has profoundly shaped my understanding of the religious landscape of early twentieth-century Britain. Their influence has hopefully received due acknowledgement in the references. The same is true of countless other scholars who have written on subjects ranging from the controversy over Ritualism through to the nature and significance of the ecumenical movement. Although this book is based on a large number of primary sources, it is also a work of interpretation and synthesis, designed to make accessible to a new audience a man – Randall Davidson – who has been largely forgotten except by those who have a particular interest in Church History.

The idea of 'Church History' is itself one that perhaps requires a brief discussion. One of the main themes in the scholarly literature over the past few decades has been to break down the idea that the history of religion in twentieth-century Britain can in some way be understood apart from wider social changes. Keith Robbins, Simon Green, and Matthew Grimley – along with many others – have devoted enormous energy to showing how the shifting landscape of religion in modern Britain has formed part of a complex tapestry of social, political, and cultural change. One of the most striking features of Davidson's time at Canterbury is, indeed, the extent to which the Archbishop recognised that the Church had to engage with a changing world or risk marginalisation. The following chapters in practice tend to divide between those that deal with 'Church' issues and others that consider 'social and political' questions. Such a distinction is, in a sense, misleading, even if it has the advantage of allowing the material to be presented in a way that makes it more accessible to readers who are not well versed in the subject. The bitter divisions over such issues as Ritualism and the revised Prayer Book erupted into the public domain precisely because the boundary between the secular and the religious was extremely fluid. The 'Protestant' character of the Church of England was for many Britons not simply a question of doctrine and ceremony. It was also a matter of national identity – something that encapsulated the meaning of British history over three centuries. The interaction between the porous spheres of Church, State, and Society is, indeed, a central theme throughout this book.

It is worth ending with a note on the origins of my own interest in Davidson, which developed out of a long-standing interest in two perhaps seemingly unrelated topics: the history of Anglican-Orthodox relations and the rise of a Christian Realist tradition that treats war as an inevitable if tragic aspect of the human condition.[10] Davidson is a familiar figure to anyone interested in relations between Anglicanism and Orthodoxy.[11] He also looms large in the consciousness of anyone who has studied the role of the churches in the First World War and its aftermath. Yet except for those who are specialists in the history of the Anglican Communion, Davidson seems a curiously elusive figure, despite occupying the See of Canterbury for quarter of a century. He seldom attracts more than a few references in political histories of the period, even though he was on close terms with generations of political leaders. And, whilst he was the most influential figure in the Anglican Communion over several decades,[12] he is even eclipsed in many histories of the Church, outshone by more charismatic or intellectually influential figures such as William Temple and Charles Gore. Davidson did not leave a clear 'legacy', precisely because his career was largely devoted to accommodating competing interests in an uncertain and changing world. He was not a heroic figure. And yet, as is perhaps too little realised, there is often great wisdom in focusing on immediate and practical objectives, eschewing the abstract and teleological in favour of the underestimated virtues of compromise and agreement. Davidson once praised Archbishop Tait for his 'half-conscious protest against the excited restlessness and fuss so familiar in modern clerical circles'.[13] Much of Davidson's own time at Canterbury was spent trying to bring order to a world of 'excited restlessness'.

Notes

1 The edition referred to throughout this book is George Bell, *Randall Davidson: Archbishop of Canterbury* (London: Oxford University Press, 1938).

2 For useful material about the writing of Bell's biography of Davidson, see Lambeth Palace Library, Bell Papers, in particular Vols 221 and 222, which contain extensive correspondence between Bell and Edith Davidson and Bell and Mary Mills (Davidson's secretary).
3 Sidney Dark, *Archbishop Davidson and the English Church* (New York: William Morrow, 1929), p. v.
4 Harold Begbie, *Painted Windows: A Study in Religious Personality* (London: Mills and Boon, 1922), p. 182.
5 Charles Herbert, *Twenty Five Years as Archbishop of Canterbury* (London: Wells, Gardner, Darnton, 1929).
6 Begbie, *Painted Windows*, p. 185.
7 Bell Papers 225, fos. 156–62, Knox, 'An Appreciation of Archbishop Davidson'.
8 For a discussion of the complex family lives of the Taits and Bensons, see Rodney Bolt, *As Good as God, as Clever as the Devil: The Impossible Life of Mary Benson* (London: Atlantic Books, 2011).
9 Edward Carpenter, 'Randall Davidson, The Last of the Victorians', in Carpenter (ed), *Cantuar: The Archbishops in Their Office* (London: Cassel, 1971), pp. 408–44.
10 See, for example, Michael Hughes, *Conflict and Conscience: Methodism, Peace and War in the Twentieth Century* (Peterborough: Epworth, 2008); Michael Hughes, *Beyond Holy Russia: The Life and Times of Stephen Graham* (Cambridge: Open Book Publishers, 2014).
11 See, for example, the discussion of Davidson's role in the Anglican-Orthodox dialogue in Bryn Geffert, *Eastern Orthodox and Anglicans: Diplomacy, Theology and the Politics of Interwar Ecumenism* (Notre Dame, IN: University of Notre Dame Press, 2010).
12 Stuart Mews, 'Randall Thomas Davidson', in *Oxford Dictionary of National Biography*.
13 Randall Davidson and William Benham, *Life of Archibald Campbell Tait: Archbishop of Canterbury* (London: Macmillan, 1891), 2 vols., Vol. 2, p. 563.

1 The making of an Archbishop

Early years

Randall Davidson was born in 1848 into a prosperous Edinburgh family.[1] His father ran a successful timber-importing business in Leith. His mother was the daughter of a prominent Borders family. Davidson later recalled that his mother's 'real absorption in the religious side of life' was 'a natural thing' that shaped the outlook of her children:

> I do not find it easy to explain the remarkable influence which my mother was able to exercise over and among us in all religious matters and in Bible teaching [. . .] I think her poetic temperament [. . .] gave her a power of putting things in a way that made them interesting at the moment and rememberable afterwards.[2]

Davidson was himself baptised into the Church of Scotland – his paternal grandfather and great-grandfather had been Church of Scotland ministers – but his upbringing was, according to his own reckoning, 'very undenominational [. . .] I have no recollection of receiving any teaching upon Churchmanship, either Episcopal or Presbyterian, the religion taught us being wholly of the personal sort, but beautiful in its simplicity and reality'.[3] Davidson never understood in later life the passion that matters of doctrine and liturgy exercised on so many who belonged to his generation – a reflection perhaps of his upbringing in a home where such things were deemed less important than a faith based on personal devotion and moral rectitude.

Davidson developed early in life a love of countryside and rural sports that stayed with him for the rest of his life (as Archbishop he continued to shoot and fish well into his seventies).[4] When his family moved in 1857 to a new home called Muirhouse, a large Gothic house surrounded by 200 acres of parkland, the young Randall spent much of his time shooting and riding his pony. He was taught at home until the age of 12, when he was sent away to a private school near Nottingham, before moving on to Harrow at the age of 14. The choice of Harrow does not seem to have reflected any great desire on the part of his parents to educate their son into the ethos of the British Establishment, for his father knew little of the values and cultures of the various public schools, but the decision was to play an important role in Davidson's life. He retained a strong loyalty to the school far into adulthood.[5] Davidson admired the new Headmaster, the Rev. Henry Montagu Butler, although some of his contemporaries were subsequently more inclined to recall Butler's penchant for using the cane.[6] He was still more influenced by his housemaster, the Rev. B. F. Westcott, later to become Bishop of Durham, and a man remembered by Davidson as 'the Prophet to whom we looked for intellectual guidance on every subject'.[7] Davidson was complimentary about the education he received at Harrow. His letters home discussing the sermons he heard in Chapel suggest he had little interest in abstruse theological questions, instead favouring more accessible addresses that focused on particular Biblical texts and their relevance for human conduct.[8] Davidson preferred, even as a schoolboy, to concentrate on the immediate and concrete rather than the mystical and remote.

The last year at Harrow was punctuated by an incident that had consequences for the rest of Davidson's life, when a friend accidentally shot him in the back whilst out shooting rabbits. Davidson spent months convalescing, and the accident left him with injuries that caused pain down until his death. He was cursed by ill health throughout his life – a weakness that was in part physical, but may also have reflected his perennial tendency to work himself into a state of nervous exhaustion. The shooting accident also had a more immediate effect, since it destroyed any chance of winning a scholarship to Oxford, although he still matriculated in the autumn of 1867 as a commoner at Trinity College. Davidson was already certain that he wanted to be ordained. It may be that the prospect of a clerical career – and the secure income it offered – appealed to a young man from a prosperous but not hugely wealthy upper-middle class background. His letters home from both Harrow and Oxford do, though, suggest that he possessed a faith that was strong if oddly unreflective in character.[9] Davidson was certainly largely oblivious to the great theological controversies of the day during his time at university (although he did show a lively interest in local ecclesiastical tensions and rivalries).[10] Neither the vexed questions posed by the legacy of the Oxford Movement, nor the challenge offered by Darwinism to traditional belief, evoked much interest in the mind of a young man whose faith was instinctive rather than cerebral in character. Whilst T. H. Green was already teaching at Oxford, Davidson was at university too early to come under his influence, or more generally the broad school of British Idealism that had such a powerful sway on a later generation of Anglican clergy (and indeed on some of Davidson's own contemporaries).[11] Nor is there much evidence that he had any real interest in philosophical questions more generally.

Davidson was frequently ill whilst at Oxford and graduated with a third class honours degree (something he regretted to the end of his life). It is indeed astonishing how quickly his career progressed in subsequent years, given the physical and emotional strain it must have placed on his health. Davidson travelled extensively after leaving university, visiting Italy and Switzerland, as well as starting his training for holy orders under the supervision of Dr Charles Vaughan at the Temple Church off Fleet Street (Vaughan had many years previously been Headmaster at Harrow).[12] Vaughan was sceptical of the value of theological colleges, and the training he gave to those planning a career in the Church typically involved a mixture of reading and sermon preparation, as well as a secondment to one of the less salubrious neighbourhoods of the capital.[13] Such a practical approach suited Davidson well, and many years later, when Bishop of Winchester, he spent considerable time organising the training of 'men who do not fit happily or easily into the life of an ordinary Theological College'.[14] The future Archbishop had little real interest in theology as an academic discipline (he never hid his lack of a theological cast of mind). He was familiar with the intellectual debates that preoccupied some of his Anglican contemporaries, but showed little interest in them, a pattern that was later repeated at Canterbury when he had to resolve passionate disputes on which he looked with a certain bemusement.

When Davidson was still at Oxford, he met the son of Archbishop Tait of Canterbury, Craufurd Tait, who was subsequently instrumental in arranging for his friend to serve as a curate in Dartford following ordination in March 1874. Davidson had whilst preparing for ordination also had the opportunity to travel once again, heading to Egypt and Palestine, a trip that fostered his lifelong interest in the Christian East.[15] Davidson's time in Dartford was, at least when he looked back many years later, among the happiest periods of his life. He worked with the sick, visiting smallpox patients, and offering care to those whose family were too scared to look after their relatives. At the age of 29, Davidson was well placed to embark on a successful career in the Church of England, set fair to obtain a living that would allow him to combine pastoral work with his love of country sports. Such a life might well have suited a man whose health was never good, but there was always in Davidson a streak of ambition which sat awkwardly with his modesty and caution. At the end of 1876, when Craufurd Tait announced that he planned to step down as his father's Private Secretary and Chaplain, the Archbishop asked his son to sound out Randall Davidson as a possible replacement (Archbishop Tait had known Davidson's father Henry since the two men were children in Edinburgh). The offer of the post was in due course made, and Davidson accepted without hesitation (before the formal offer was made, he tellingly fretted in a letter to his mother about his anxiety that he would be 'left out in the cold with nothing to look forward to').[16] His move to Lambeth Palace set him on a course that was to lead a quarter of a century later to Canterbury.

Chaplain to Archbishop Tait

Davidson first heard Tait preach when he was still at Oxford, writing to his mother rather dismissively of the Archbishop's 'slightly pedantic, rather dry and strikingly unattractive discourse'. His six years as Resident Chaplain at Lambeth Palace transformed his view of Tait ('a personality to be neither forgotten nor ignored').[17] There was a series of almost uncanny similarities in the two men's background, which may have accounted for the good relationship they built up, which was cemented still further when Davidson married Tait's daughter Edith in 1878. Both men had been born and raised in Edinburgh families with a strong Presbyterian tradition. They also both suffered from lifelong poor health and chronic pain. There was also a more elusive symmetry in their attitude towards religion in general and the Church of England in particular (doubtless in part reflecting Tait's influence on his young Chaplain). Neither man was a natural mystic or a gifted theologian. Both were deeply interested in political questions, devouring newspapers and journals, and cultivating relations with leading politicians. When Davidson finally went to Canterbury, in 1903, he followed Tait in identifying one of his principal tasks as the preservation of the influence of the National Church. The two men were both passionately committed to maintaining the Church of England's status as the Established Church, not so much as a defence of privilege, but rather because they viewed it as a fundamental element in the fabric of the nation. Gladstone once told the House of Commons that 'Take the Church of England out of the history of England, and the history of England becomes a chaos, without order, without life, and without meaning'.[18] Tait for his part agreed that the Church of England had always been

> a part of the history of this country [. . .] a part so vital, entering so profoundly into the entire life and action of the country, that the severing of the two would leave nothing behind but a bleeding and lacerated mass.[19]

It was a sentiment echoed by Davidson many times, albeit in more muted terms, during his long journey to Canterbury.

Much of the work carried out by Davidson at Lambeth Palace was very dull. Tait recalled a few years before his death how he had often

> seen [. . .] letters enough arrive [at Lambeth Palace] by a single post to fill a large basket. They have as soon as possible to be read and arranged [. . .] Many are of course routine letters, but each requires, none the less, an acknowledgement or reply [. . .] All these, and a hundred such cases, has the Chaplain to deal with.[20]

The Chaplain also had to arrange interviews, fend off callers, and generally manage the Archbishop's working life. Davidson excelled at the work. He later wrote in his two-volume biography of Tait that the Archbishop always put 'complete and unreserved confidence in his secretaries'. Such confidence brought both problems and benefits. Tait was inclined to be

> reckless about the time [and] engagements of his subordinates, and would keep us waiting in the most provoking manner on the chance of a spare three minutes for some signatures or directions, rather than hurry his movements in the least degree or cut a conversation short.[21]

The Archbishop's *modus operandi* nevertheless gave Davidson a chance to immerse himself in Church business, developing a detailed understanding of the concerns that had preoccupied its leading figures during recent years, including the protests against Ritualism that erupted in the period leading up to the passing of the controversial 1874 Public Worship Regulation Act (which led to the imprisonment of a number of Anglo-Catholic priests).[22]

Davidson wrote to his father soon after becoming Chaplain that his post meant he was 'now bound to see and do everything', describing how he drafted Tait's letters, and met with leading figures from Church and State on behalf of the Archbishop.[23] His letters home also show Davidson's acute ability to sum up the people he met in the course of his work. Tait valued the efficiency of his 'Chaplain-Secretary', assuring Henry Davidson that if his son's health remained good he had 'before him every prospect of great usefulness and eminence in the high profession to the work of which he gives himself with so much zeal and wisdom'.[24] Although his duties at Lambeth Palace were mostly carried out behind the scenes, Davidson became an increasingly familiar figure to senior figures in the Church of England, not least through the administrative role he played during the second Lambeth Conference of 1878. Whilst it was by no means certain that the position of Archbishop's Chaplain was destined to lead to greater things, the work was congenial enough to encourage Davidson to decline offers of other appealing posts, including the living at Maidstone. His decision was partly motivated by a desire not to take his wife Edith away from her father, particularly as Craufurd had died some years earlier, but it also reflected his reluctance to leave a position that was more varied and interesting than anything to be found in a country parsonage or suburban rectory.

Tait was determined to use his time in office to project the influence of the Archbishop of Canterbury beyond the purely ecclesiastical sphere. The legal scholar and politician James Bryce later wrote rather archly that Tait's lack of 'original power as a thinker' did not stop him becoming 'almost a model to his own and the next generation of what an Archbishop of Canterbury ought to be'.[25] The Archbishop's determination to assert his influence meant that he spent a good deal of time cultivating relations with leading politicians and members of the Royal Family. He also spoke regularly in the House of Lords, even though he lacked what Davidson referred to as 'lofty eloquence' and 'incisive repartee'.[26] Tait also made sure that he appeared regularly at major public occasions in order to emphasise the role of the Church of England in public life. The Archbishop was a fervent defender of the principle of Establishment – 'this distinctive connexion between the civil Government of the country and its ecclesiastical polity'[27] – which he conceptualised less as a matter of subordination of Church to State and more as a kind of organic embrace (the notion that Tait was an unabashed Erastian does not entirely stand up to close scrutiny).

Despite his role in promoting the Public Worship Regulation Bill, which he himself introduced in the House of Lords, Tait could be flexible on important ecclesiastical issues. When the Gladstone Government had previously introduced legislation disestablishing the Anglican Church in Ireland, in 1869, the

Archbishop focused his energy less on opposing the measure and more on working hard to ensure that it took place on the best possible terms.[28] Tait recognised that defending the interests of the Church of England could on occasion require accommodation with developments that might not be in its immediate interest, but which had too strong a political momentum to oppose. It was a philosophy of compromise that Davidson was later to follow during his own archiepiscopate. He came to understand, like his father-in-law, that maintaining the influence of the National Church required active engagement with the forces of social and political change.

A courtier-priest? Davidson as Dean of Windsor

In the months before Tait died, in December 1882, he told his son-in-law that he hoped to be succeeded either by Bishop Browne of Winchester or the more youthful Bishop Benson of Truro. The Archbishop was, however, anxious not to be seen to be influencing the choice of his successor. In the days following Tait's death, Davidson wrote to the Marchioness of Ely, one of the Queen's ladies-in-waiting, setting down the late Archbishop's views. It is not clear why Davidson chose to adopt such a course of action, given that Tait had been reluctant to make his views known, although he told Lady Ely that he was unwilling to take the responsibility of remaining silent (he concluded his letter by noting that 'now I have unburdened my soul').[29] The letter was duly passed on to the Queen, who summoned Davidson to visit her a few days later, when he repeated Tait's views about his possible successors. His knowledge of Church affairs impressed Victoria, who had already heard of his talents (the Dean of Windsor had just a few weeks earlier described him as 'most highly esteemed' when recommending him for the post of sub-almoner).[30] Her Journal entry shows that she was much 'struck' by the personality of her visitor, and believed that he could 'be of great use to me',[31] whilst in a meeting with Gladstone two days later she told the Prime Minister that Davidson was 'an admirable and charming person, thoroughly acquainted with everything concerning the Church and the Clergy'.[32]

Gladstone and the monarch did not agree about the appointment of Tait's successor as Archbishop. The Prime Minister favoured Edward Benson of Truro, who shared his own High Church views, whilst the Queen favoured Harold Browne. At Victoria's request, Davidson made a trip to Hampshire to inquire delicately whether Mrs Browne thought her elderly husband's health could stand up to the rigours of Canterbury. Gladstone nevertheless insisted on the appointment of Benson. Davidson was then instructed to go to Truro to discuss the offer of the post with the Bishop. He was also asked by the Queen to provide advice about the appointment of a new Bishop of Truro, to replace Benson, as well as the choice of a new Dean of Windsor to replace Gerald Wellesley. In the course of an astonishing few weeks, Davidson had won the trust of the monarch as an adviser on matters of major ecclesiastical appointments. Although one of his early biographers exaggerates Davidson's influence in the appointment of Benson, by suggesting that 'when an Archbishop's Chaplain may nominate an Archbishop he may well be expected to go far',[33] his star was clearly in the ascendant.

Davidson continued to serve as Benson's Chaplain at Lambeth Palace for a few months after Tait's death, but in May 1883, the newly incumbent Dean of Windsor, George Connor, died unexpectedly, after just a few months in the post. Victoria wrote to Benson asking for advice about a successor (she favoured either Davidson or William Boyd Carpenter). The Archbishop replied, praising Davidson as a man with 'a loyal nature' and 'very thorough knowledge of the clergy and others'. He also noted that his Chaplain's comparative youth should be no bar to appointment since it was combined with a pronounced 'carefulness of judgement'.[34] The Queen was persuaded, although Gladstone was not convinced: he told her Private Secretary that he had only been prevented from expressing his doubts because of the 'heavy artillery' that Victoria had been 'pleased to bring into the field'. The Prime Minister was, nevertheless, still confident that Davidson would make 'an excellent Dean'.[35] The Dean of Windsor was inevitably at the heart of the nexus of social and political relationships that defined the late Victorian Establishment, and the announcement of Davidson's appointment led to expressions of surprise in some quarters given his youth.[36] He nevertheless received numerous letters of congratulation, including one from his old housemaster Westcott, who wrote to remind his former pupil that he now had the responsibility of offering 'simple and direct counsel to those who have the heavy burden of sovereignty'.[37]

Davidson's six years at Windsor gave him an opportunity to develop a close relationship with Queen Victoria.[38] The Queen quickly became attached to her new Dean, invariably seeking his opinion on matters of ecclesiastical appointments, as well as turning to him for consolation on the death in 1884 of her youngest son Leopold (Duke of Albany).[39] She particularly admired her Dean's preaching – she frequently urged him to publish his sermons – and was shrewd enough to appreciate his broad Churchmanship which avoided the extremes of both 'High' and 'Low'.[40] Davidson was careful to adopt the tone of judicious respect that appealed to a monarch who was quick to take offence. His letters to her were models of discretion and cautious flattery.[41] Their private conversations often touched on 'general questions of this life and the next', and Davidson wrote in a memorandum whilst at Windsor that he had no doubt that Victoria's belief was 'definite as well as deep', and that 'religion [was] a potent force in her conduct'.[42] The monarch for her part fretted constantly about her Dean's health, noting on more than one occasion that Davidson 'works too much'[43] and repeatedly urged him to take more time away from his duties.

There were nevertheless times when Davidson was deeply frustrated by the Queen's behaviour, noting caustically on one occasion that 'there is a great deal more difficulty in dealing with a spoilt child of sixty or seventy than with a spoilt child of six or seven'.[44] The most serious rift in his relationship with the monarch followed her decision to publish a new volume of remembrances about her former ghillie John Brown (under the planned title *More*

Leaves from the Journal of a Life in the Highlands). Davidson warned her in a carefully worded letter that such a move would be unwise, given the ribald rumours circulating among some of her more plebeian subjects, who 'do not show themselves worthy of these confidences' (he did not tell her that he had discovered that obscene pamphlets on the subject were being sold in a number of bookshops). The Dean also privately thought the treatment of Brown 'ludicrously inappropriate'.[45] He offered to resign when Victoria demanded that he withdraw his words. A period of silence followed, but within a few weeks the Queen had become 'more friendly than ever', leading Davidson to note that Victoria 'liked and trusted best those who occasionally incurred her wrath provided that she had reason to think their motives good'.[46] The second volume of *Leaves* never appeared. Arthur Bigge (later Lord Stamfordham), who served as Private Secretary to Victoria in her final few years, wrote many years later that the Dean had been 'the hero of the hour' in averting significant damage to the reputation of the monarch. The incident showed that Davidson was already becoming adept at balancing the courtier's skills with a degree of plain speaking. He was throughout his long career remarkably adept at preventing differences on specific issues from turning into long-term personal disagreements.

Davidson was as Dean forthcoming when expressing his views about candidates for ecclesiastical positions. His time as Tait's Chaplain meant that he was familiar with the character and attributes of the leading figures in the Church of England. The letters he sent to Victoria typically offered firm judgements about both the quality of individuals and the impact their appointment would have on the balance between High and Low Churchmen on the Bench of Bishops. Davidson also carefully weighed the merits of candidates for particular posts. On the Bishopric of London becoming vacant in 1885, he counselled against one candidate who was primarily a 'preacher', and lacked the skills to run a large and complex diocese. When the Prime Minister Lord Salisbury nominated Henry Liddon as Bishop of Oxford, in 1888, Davidson sent the Queen a letter gently warning her against vetoing the appointment, since it was likely to anger senior High Churchmen who wanted better representation on the ecclesiastical bench. He instead counselled her to approach the issue obliquely, raising the question of whether Liddon's health could withstand the strain of such a position, since if he was unfit 'the difficulty of reconciling your Majesty's view with that of Lord Salisbury might be avoided without the need of facing the graver difficulties which that divergence involves'.[47] Davidson also played a significant role in the nomination of his old housemaster Westcott as Bishop of Durham, in 1890, a choice favoured by the Queen but viewed with some scepticism by Salisbury. Davidson was as Dean of Windsor able to exercise significant influence on the composition of the Church of England hierarchy, even though his role was largely invisible to the outside world.

Davidson maintained a close relationship with Benson during his time at Windsor, later recalling that the Archbishop was by temperament inclined to seek 'counsel and help from somebody else before dealing with the big questions'.[48] Benson for his part often treated the younger man as a confidante, lamenting how

> the singleness of the burden and solitariness of responsibility are strangely characteristic of this work – and with all thinking I do not see how on what friendly shoulders the burden is to be partly laid, or how the responsibility can really be shared.[49]

The detailed correspondence between the two men shows how Davidson sought to offer support. He gave Benson extensive advice during the furore that surrounded the prosecution of the Bishop of Lincoln prompted by the Church Association, in 1888–9, for allowing 'illegal' ritual practices in services at the cathedral (including lighted candles on the altar and observing the eastward position during Communion).[50] Benson corresponded regularly with Davidson about the complexities of the case, receiving in return reassurance that he was acting in a way that no 'fairminded men' could question.[51] Davidson himself took a definite public position, contributing a letter to *The Times* on 2 April 1889, in which he gently but firmly criticised 'the Ritualistic Party' for refusing to accept the jurisdiction of any ecclesiastical Court from which the ultimate appeal was to a secular Court (a position that he suggested would logically lead to Disestablishment). Davidson also made it clear in further letters to *The Times* that he recognised the need to assert authority within the Church of England,[52] whilst in private he spoke of the need 'to restrain and regulate High Church excesses and follies'. The Dean was nevertheless firmly convinced that the well-being of the Church meant that toleration was necessary to prevent tensions from erupting into open conflict. It was a policy that Davidson later followed both as Bishop and Archbishop when seeking to deal with the Ritual question, which had in one form or another dogged the Church of England since the rise of the Oxford Movement many decades before.

Davidson's readiness to express his views so publicly suggests that he saw himself as something more than a simple courtier-priest. He spoke regularly in Convocation, engaging with sensitive issues, including the question of establishing a committee to review the orthodoxy of the *Lux Mundi* essays edited by Charles Gore.[53] In a conversation with William Boyd Carpenter, by now Bishop of Ripon, Davidson even noted that he sometimes wanted 'to be unmuzzled by some more independent position where one could speak out freely what one felt instead of being [. . .] trammelled by the responsibility of not bringing "the Queen" into party politics'.[54] He was nevertheless instinctively more at home in a world of private discussions and discreet conversation. As Dean, he regularly met senior political figures including Gladstone and Lord Salisbury. He also became a *habitué* of London's Club Land, which provided him with further opportunities to become acquainted with the world of politics (Davidson's diaries and journals show that he regularly attended debates in both the House of Commons and the House of Lords). Davidson's wish to build relations with politicians partly reflected his temperamental fascination with public affairs and the intricacies of political life. It was also shaped by his conviction – which was later to become a defining feature of his archiepiscopate – that the Church of England could only justify its historic position by playing a constructive role in the public life of the nation. It was not for nothing that he had served for five years as Chaplain to Archbishop Tait.

Davidson's position as Dean of Windsor, along with his close relationship with Archbishop Benson, provided him with opportunities to exercise influence on a range of ecclesiastical issues. And yet, by the end of 1889, Davidson was clearly beginning to think of a move away from Windsor. Lord Salisbury had tentatively raised his name as a candidate for the Bishopric of Durham, to which Westcott was subsequently appointed, but the Queen later told Davidson that she had vetoed his name since 'she could not spare him'. The Dean's response was couched in suitably ambiguous terms, thanking the Queen for her kindness, but noting he was ready to serve 'whatever I should be called upon to do -here or elsewhere'.[55] Victoria was somewhat affronted by the reply, speculating archly in a letter to her Private Secretary Lord Ponsonby whether 'the Dean is at all an ambitious man'.[56] She also asked Ponsonby to make discreet inquiries about Davidson's position in the eyes of the Church. He duly did so, telling the Queen that Davidson was facing some criticism for staying in his 'quiet and comfortable' place, adding that the Dean himself wanted a Bishopric so that he could become more involved in 'social and national' affairs.[57] Victoria took the hint, writing to Benson early in 1890 that although she would be reluctant to lose Davidson, she accepted that his departure might be necessary 'for the good of the Church'.[58] Within 12 months, Randall Davidson had been appointed Bishop of Rochester.

Bishop of Rochester

Once the Queen accepted that Davidson's departure was inevitable, she threw her full weight behind his appointment to the Bench of Bishops, strongly pushing the case for his appointment to the See of Winchester when it fell vacant following the death of Harold Browne.[59] She was deeply irritated when Lord Salisbury rejected the suggestion, using the excuse that for questions of balance he wanted to appoint an Evangelical to Winchester, although the Prime Minister also thought that Davidson was too little known to be moved direct into such a prominent position ('his promotion would seem forced and unnatural').[60] Archbishop Benson, too, favoured Davidson's appointment to Winchester, but Salisbury persisted in his view, with the result that the Dean of Windsor was offered instead a choice of Worcester or Rochester. Davidson himself was able to follow these developments thanks to the indiscretions of Ponsonby.[61]

Davidson told the Queen's Private Secretary that he believed Lord Salisbury's remarks about his lack of experience were reasonable and that the Queen took an 'over-favourable' view of his abilities.[62] He opted to accept the See of Rochester which covered most of south London – the diocese of Southwark was not created until 1905 – and Davidson seemed genuinely excited at being responsible for a vast urban area, full of poverty, where 'Christianity is not in possession' (though he also found the prospect 'overwhelming').[63] He wrote to the Queen to thank her for her kindness, and assured her that he would be delighted to continue to serve her in any way she wanted (Davidson's wife Edith later wrote that he 'went through a time of agony' in deciding to leave his post as Dean).[64] In the years that followed, Davidson continued to travel regularly to Windsor and Balmoral, advising Victoria on ecclesiastical matters. His appointment to Rochester did not, however, meet with universal acclaim. Some Liberal newspapers looked unfavourably on a man who had made his career at the heart of the ecclesiastical establishment. The influential *Pall Mall Gazette* said he was a good 'organizer' but had an off-putting 'donnish' manner.[65] Another provincial paper snidely observed that if Davidson had not married the daughter of an Archbishop he would have thought himself lucky to get a 'fat Country living'.[66]

Davidson's choice of Rochester over Worcester seems odd, given the strain that responsibility for such a large and populous diocese was likely to put on his health, but he was swayed by a desire to be close both to Windsor and the political hub of London (he pointed out to Lord Salisbury that the areas included in the diocese of Worcester were 'to me, almost unknown'). He took up residence in two knocked together houses in Kennington – a setting almost as different from the gracious surroundings of Windsor as can be imagined – since he was (as he later noted to his clergy) determined to live 'at the central hub of our great whell'. Although most of Davidson's career had been spent a long way from the kind of urban squalor that now surrounded him, his curacy as a young man in Dartford had shown him at first-hand the challenges faced by the impoverished inhabitants of Britain's large towns and cities.

Davidson took an interest in practical social and economic questions when at Rochester, putting his name to motions calling for a decent standard of living for the working poor. He also wrote to Government ministers urging them to consult with clergy of all denominations when considering issues of poverty and deprivation. Davidson was, though, far from being a radical. He was instead more interested in identifying practical ways that the Church could help to relieve poverty in south London, encouraging the revival of an order of Deaconesses committed to working with the disadvantaged. He also gave support to clergy – many of them from the Anglo-Catholic wing of the Church – who organised societies and clubs designed to build closer relations with an impoverished and un-Churched working class. A few years after becoming Bishop, Davidson noted that issues of poverty could not be ignored by the Church, rejecting the idea that 'in any department of social life [...] we can safely brush aside even for an hour the consideration of what Christ would have us do'.[67] His comments certainly showed a commitment to Christian witness on issues of public concern, but they did *not* reflect any desire to challenge the economic and political institutions of late Victorian Britain, nor to engage with the kind of questions of social justice that were beginning to preoccupy a significant section of the Anglican clergy. Davidson did not join the Christian Social Union, founded in 1889 by Westcott and Henry Scott Holland, whose members sought to extend the spirit of Christianity to economic and social matters.[68] Nor did he share the Incarnational theology of members of the *Lux Mundi* group, which for some like Charles Gore provided a basis for treating the material world as a realm for fostering Christian values.[69] Davidson's views on social and economic questions instead reflected a more conventional position that Christian charity required the Church to do what it could to help ease the plight of the poor.

Davidson's health was bad throughout his years at Rochester (he later wrote that he had only been able to engage in 'active work' for 70 percent of the time). At one point he even seems to have thought he was dying, leading Benson to write urging him to maintain 'the most cheerful tones of a Christian man's thought under a great trial'.[70] Queen Victoria loaned Davidson a cottage at Osborne to recuperate on one occasion, noting in her journal that when he preached there he looked 'very transparent and ill'.[71] The Queen continued to consult her former Dean regularly on ecclesiastical appointments, including the controversial appointment of John Percival to Hereford (Percival favoured Welsh Disestablishment, and Victoria was furious when he was nominated by the new Liberal Prime Minister Lord Rosebery). Davidson believed the appointment 'an unfortunate one' given that the diocese of Hereford abutted the Welsh border. He was nevertheless convinced that the Queen should not veto the appointment, telling her new Private Secretary Arthur Bigge that she should consider writing to Rosebery, 'leaving on [him] the task of trying to reassure the Queen or else of accepting, after warning, the entire responsibility for whatever difficulties arise'.[72] It was typically adroit advice, designed to protect Victoria from being accused of thwarting the decisions of her ministers, whilst at the same time retaining her 'right to warn' (famously noted by Walter Bagehot as one of the most important elements in the monarch's prerogative powers). Davidson was later to become close to Rosebery, but he was in 1895 concerned that the Prime Minister was too inclined to appoint Bishops on Party political lines, and he advised Bigge to write expressing concern about the issue. Rosebery replied noting laconically that his predecessor, Lord Salisbury, had similarly overlooked Churchmen who did not share his political opinions.

During his time at Rochester, Davidson tentatively tried to develop closer relations with some of the Nonconformist denominations (he acknowledged that the Nonconformists had in the past often been more successful than the Church of England in keeping alive 'the smoking flax of personal religion' in the major cities).[73] He attended the funeral of the Baptist minister Charles Spurgeon, pronouncing the blessing at the graveside, a gesture that earned him some opprobrium in the High Church press.[74] There were, however, distinct limits to Davidson's embryonic ecumenical instinct. He was extremely wary of Lord Halifax's characteristically clumsy attempt in 1894 to engage in a round of personal diplomacy to secure the recognition of Anglican orders by Rome.[75] Davidson advised Archbishop Benson at length about how to respond to the difficulties created by Halifax's activities, which would have caused a public outcry if they had become more widely known. Davidson also corresponded with

Halifax himself at some length, noting that whilst he wanted Reunion 'with all my heart', he dreaded the 'Roman way of looking at things'. He also warned Halifax not to underestimate 'the strength and depth of the present Protestantism in England', noting that a mere recognition by Rome of Anglican orders would do nothing to overcome the deeper divisions with Canterbury.[76] The question became moot when Leo XIII issued the Papal Bull *Apostolicae Curae* two years later, declaring Anglican orders null and void, although the question of relations between Canterbury and Rome was once again to preoccupy Davidson and Halifax almost three decades later during the celebrated Malines Conversations. Back in 1894, the Bishop of Rochester remained convinced that the 'fundamental differences' between the two churches made any serious negotiations pointless.

Davidson's views on many issues facing the Church of England were set down in his *A Charge Delivered to the Clergy of Rochester* (1894), which represented his longest and most coherent *profession de foi* to date. Much of what he wrote reflected his desire to defend the Church of England as the National Church. Until he went to Rochester, Davidson had spent his career at the heart of the ecclesiastical establishment, working at Lambeth Palace as Chaplain to the Archbishop of Canterbury, and then as Dean of Windsor advising a monarch who was also Supreme Governor of the Church of England. In a speech in 1893, at a time when the clamour for Disestablishment in Wales was on the rise, he firmly defended the 'national character' of the Church of England, which he argued 'dates back to a time before England as a whole was a nation'.[77] His emphasis on the Church of England as the National Church echoed the views of Archbishop Tait, who when at Lambeth Palace had highlighted the importance of maintaining an organic union between Church and State, rather than treating Establishment as a simple assertion of the supremacy of the secular power over the ecclesiastical. In his *Charge to the Clergy of Rochester*, Davidson developed these ideas further, again attacking those who sought to deprive the Church of 'its national character', and argued that it alone had the resources to minister in such deprived areas as south London (he suggested, not very convincingly, that many of the Nonconformist denominations were retreating from such areas to the more prosperous suburbs). Disestablishment would, he argued, represent

> a deed of almost incredible folly and shortsightedness, a deed, the consequences of which, though unforeseen and unintended by its authors, would be in the highest degree prejudicial to religion, and therefore to the public good, a deed which we are bound as Christians and Englishmen to oppose to the uttermost.[78]

Davidson spoke from time to time of his 'liberal principles', but there was something rather 'Tory' about the vision of the National Church that he articulated whilst at Rochester. He was anxious to dismiss the importance of the squabbles over 'Ritualism', which had occupied such a 'large space' in recent history, precisely because they detracted the Church of England from its mission to articulate to the whole nation the 'principles of the Sermon on the Mount'. He defended Church schools against the threat of 'sectarianism' and demands for 'un-denominational' religious teaching. Davidson also articulated a distinctly Burkean vision of the role of statesmen at a time of political change and uncertainty:

> It is the part of the statesman to be wise to discern the time and resolute to redeem it – to look at the permanent, not the momentary and the passing, interests of the nation he is set to serve – to disregard if needs be the cries of partisanship, and the fleeting enthusiasms of the unthoughtful and the ill-informed – to let men share the fruits of his experience in public life and the lessons he has learned from history – to be a quiet guide and a firm leader in hours of popular perplexity or panic, or iconoclastic zeal, and to spurn the ignoble temptation to content himself with registering the currents of public opinion, and blindly executing the behests of a young democracy which has not yet learnt to weigh to the full significance of the votes it gives.[79]

Davidson was, whilst still at Rochester, already beginning to think hard about how a National Church, if it was to be worthy of the name, had to rest on something more than a simple claim to be the Established Church. His time in south London was instrumental in fostering his development into something more than a courtier-priest, responsible for offering advice and spiritual consolation to the monarch.

Bishop of Winchester

In early August 1895, Lord Salisbury wrote to Davidson offering him the See of Winchester (a move which the Queen had predictably pressed on the Prime Minister). Davidson's health was once again bad, and he hoped that life at the Bishop's residence at Farnham Castle might prove less stressful than the rigours of Rochester. The hope was perhaps rather forlorn, given both the size of the ancient diocese, and its inclusion of large urban areas on the south coast as well as the more leafy countryside to the north. Davidson spent much of the next few years on the routine yet tiring diocesan work of confirmations and ordinations. He also travelled regularly in order to visit as many parishes as possible. In his first few months at Winchester, the new Bishop gave his blessing to the foundation of a hostel for training young men for ordination (Davidson still fondly remembered his own informal training at the Temple). He personally approved the candidates and involved himself in the practical issues of running the hostel. Davidson's health flourished despite all these demands on his time. Farnham Castle was a beautiful mansion, surrounded by extensive parkland, and the peace of the buildings and grounds seemed to improve Davidson's ailments. His health was far better during his time at Winchester than it had been during the previous few years at Rochester.

Davidson was not spared from dealing with controversial issues whilst at Winchester, and within a few weeks of arrival, he was forced to confront the difficult questions of Ritualism and Episcopal authority, which had been comparatively quiescent during his time at Rochester. The subject was raised by the activities of Father Robert Dolling, an Anglo-Catholic priest who had devoted much of his life to working with the poor in Dublin and London, before moving to the south coast to run the Winchester College Mission in Portsmouth.[80] Dolling had been successful in raising the money for a new Church building, which had been completed just before Davidson arrived at Farnham Castle. At the opening, Dolling, wearing a biretta and cope, conducted the service in an atmosphere pungent with incense.[81] The Rural Dean who visited the Church to approve the licence told Davidson that the new building also contained an altar that was to be used exclusively for Masses for the Dead. After a series of meetings with Dolling, focusing a good deal on doctrinal questions about the nature of purgatory, Davidson determined that the services at St Agatha's did not sit 'in harmony with the Prayer Book'. Dolling duly resigned, attracting a great deal of public sympathy, given the widespread admiration for his work with the poor and marginalised. A petition with 5,000 signatures was presented to the priest calling on him to remain in his post.[82]

The case predictably attracted considerable interest in the national press.[83] A letter was printed in *The Times* claiming that Dolling had already decided to leave Portsmouth, and that Davidson's action in refusing a licence was only 'a stalking-horse', a claim that Dolling denied.[84] Davidson's correspondence with Dolling shows that the issue for the Bishop was primarily one of authority: the authority of the Prayer Book and the Bishop himself. His stance was widely welcomed by those on the Evangelical wing of the Church as well as some High Churchmen (many High Churchmen also disliked 'the Romish doctrine of Purgatory and its system of Masses for the Dead'). The Dolling case caused Davidson much anguish. He spoke truthfully when he told Charles Gore that he was committed to 'a wide elasticity as to individual opinion and practice'.[85] Davidson was nevertheless committed to the maintenance of order in the Church of England, and believed that Dolling was 'dealing absolutely at his will with the Prayer Book', taking positions that could not be brought within even the most comprehensive interpretation of the boundaries of Anglican teaching.

Davidson was also fated to play a significant role in the upsurge of controversy about Ritualism that erupted in Britain 1898–9, not least because he was fortunate (or unfortunate) enough to have resident in his diocese Sir William Harcourt, the Liberal politician and 'an Erastian undiluted' (to quote the words of Blanche Dugdale, niece and biographer of Arthur Balfour).[86] Harcourt often wrote to *The Times* criticising the Bishops for not enforcing discipline on High Church clergy who insisted on holding services at odds with the Book of Common Prayer.[87] Davidson also wrote to *The Times*, in August 1896, to defend the rights of Bishops to authorise the use of special services – though suggesting that every effort should be made to ensure these were in harmony with both scripture and the Prayer Book.[88] Davidson privately (and tellingly) told Harcourt that he was less concerned with aesthetic than doctrinal change – which was consistent with his treatment of Father Dolling – and he acknowledged the Bishops had sometimes been 'slack' in allowing too much 'liberty'.[89] He nevertheless suggested in his usual emollient way that it was important to treat the 'advanced' clergy fairly since this was the best way of ensuring their compliance: any concerns were best raised 'privately' and by 'personal influence', and should only be addressed 'publicly' if all else failed.[90] Harcourt's response was terse. He told Davidson that 'I am getting rather sick of the "good and earnest" men who violate the law and break their oaths', adding that he thought the Bishops were 'dilly-dallying' when dealing with 'the Halifax lot who are really Papists'.[91]

Davidson remained committed to his more cautious approach, writing to the Queen criticising Harcourt's 'violent and heated' letters to the press. On 9 February 1899, he spoke in the House of Lords, defending the Bishops, particularly against the charge that they had used their veto to prevent cases being taken to the Ecclesiastical Courts by plaintiffs infuriated at ritualistic excess. He also pointed out – rather elliptically – that many High Churchmen had won great popularity and respect by their work with the poor (Davidson noted ruefully that he had received ten times more letters attacking him than praising him for his behaviour in the Dolling affair).[92] Davidson continued to write to Harcourt in the months that followed, arguing that his campaign against Ritualism was doing more harm than good, since it only intensified the recalcitrance of clergy who were reluctant to accept that the forms of the services they took could be dictated by Parliament. The Ritual question continued to rage across Britain, leading the Archbishops of Canterbury and York to hold hearings about the lawfulness of using incense and processional lights, although the decision they arrived at (that such things were not lawful) did little to end the controversy.[93] It was an issue that was to confront Davidson within a few weeks of his own arrival at Lambeth Palace at the start of 1903.

Davidson's influence in the Church of England continued to be based in part on his relationship with Queen Victoria. The two corresponded regularly about ecclesiastical affairs down until her death at the beginning of 1901. He also continued to regularly visit both Windsor and Osborne House during his time at Winchester. Davidson was present when the Queen died, pronouncing a blessing at her passing, and subsequently helped to arrange many of the details of her funeral at Windsor. He was also instrumental in planning the Coronation Service of Edward VII, giving advice on questions of ceremony, as well as the correct way of managing the symbolic moments of the service such as the anointing of the new monarch.[94] Davidson was widely (though inaccurately) perceived to have the ear of the new King. The Archbishop of Canterbury, Frederick Temple, had always thoroughly disapproved of 'Bertie' (whose penchant for high living and sexual dalliance was no great secret). Judging from a private memorandum written by Davidson, many years later, he too had deep concerns about Edward's 'personal conduct'. Indeed, when the Coronation was initially postponed, after the King needed an urgent operation, the Bishop of

Winchester took advantage of his convalescence to impress on Edward the importance of dealing with 'the big issues and responsibilities of life'.[95] It is not clear how the King responded to such words. It is nonetheless striking that although Davidson had left Windsor more than ten years before, and was by his own admission never close to Edward, he continued to have a strong sense of himself as an adviser and counsellor to the Royal Family.

Frederick Temple had replaced Benson as Archbishop of Canterbury after the latter's sudden death in 1896.[96] The Queen had predictably pushed for Davidson to take Benson's place, telling Lord Salisbury that he had an unrivalled 'knowledge of all the members of the Church'.[97] Salisbury replied that for the general public 'who have not had [an] opportunity for knowing his merits, his rapid advancement is a cause of some perplexity', pointing out that if he were appointed to Canterbury there would be a sense that he had been given the post simply because of his royal connections. The Prime Minister added that if the 76-year-old Temple was appointed Archbishop, then after his death Davidson 'would be of a suitable age' to replace him (Davidson as ever diplomatically made it clear that he supported Temple's appointment).[98] Despite in effect being identified as heir apparent, Davidson was largely excluded from any influence over Church affairs at Lambeth Palace over the next few years, a strange experience for a man who had worked so closely with both Tait and Benson. Temple was by instinct a man who did everything himself (he was even reluctant to let his chaplains draft letters). The usually emollient Davidson noted many years later that Temple's age when he went to Canterbury meant that he found it hard to 'keep himself abreast of what was happening', adding that he would have been more successful 'if he had condescended to take counsel with one or two men'.[99] Davidson's deep knowledge of Church affairs, along with his royal and political connections, nevertheless meant that he continued to be a figure of considerable importance both in the Church and beyond. One of the reasons that men as different as Sir William Harcourt and Lord Halifax took so much trouble to correspond with Davidson was, indeed, that the Bishop of Winchester was seen as a man of influence and a future Archbishop.

Davidson played an important role in the fourth Lambeth Conference, which took place in 1897, a few months after Temple had become Archbishop, serving as Episcopal Secretary. Davidson believed that Temple had little interest or energy to deal with issues relating to the Anglican Communion beyond Britain. It was not something that could be said of Davidson himself. He had been closely involved in the organisation of the second Lambeth Conference, when serving as Tait's Chaplain, whilst at the third Conference in 1888 he had served as Assistant to the Episcopal Secretary. The growth of the British Empire in the closing decades of the nineteenth century had rapidly increased the Anglican presence in the new colonies. The older Anglican churches in the USA and the Dominions also continued to look to the Church of England in some elusive sense as a mother church (although this sentiment was combined with a very definite resistance to 'anything like a Canterbury Patriarchate').[100] The 1897 Lambeth Conference was organised around numerous committees which reported on subjects ranging from Church Unity to Industrial Problems. Around 150 Bishops attended the Conference, creating significant logistical and organisational challenges. Davidson was also called on to use his diplomatic skills to soothe away tensions created by Archbishop Temple's occasional lack of tact and judgement. Davidson's post as Episcopal Secretary helped him to extend his 'immense knowledge of all the members of the Church' (to use Queen Victoria's words) beyond the confines of the Church of England and across the whole Anglican Communion. Such knowledge subsequently proved of great value to him during his time at Canterbury, when he made the relationship between the Church of England and the other Anglican provinces a matter of priority, travelling abroad and corresponding at length with Bishops from around the world.

Archbishop Temple – at least by the time he went to Canterbury – showed little interest in political issues. Davidson's interest in such questions was by contrast greater than ever. As Bishop of Winchester, he sat in the House of Lords, which he attended regularly, speaking on a variety of topics. In 1899, he told the clergy of his diocese that Bishops should not 'be so exclusively local officers as to have neither time nor opportunity for interests which are larger still'. He added that Bishops in Parliament should not only speak on issues clearly within their sphere of concern, such as Church schools, but also on

> other matters which concern the social and moral health of our citizens and their children, say the protection of infant life from cruelty and wrong – or such amendment of our prison laws as shall make them remedial as well as punitive, – or provision for the cases of workmen who are injured in the discharge of duty – or enactments for checking commercial immorality – or arrangements for promoting the health of shop assistants.[101]

Davidson's speeches in the House of Lords were predictably well informed and meticulously prepared. George Bell notes in his biography that Davidson was generally an effective speaker in the House. The record of his speeches in Hansard certainly suggests that he was organised and methodical (if not strikingly powerful in his use of language). Most of the speeches he made whilst Bishop of Winchester were concerned with social issues, ranging from the welfare of shop assistants through to temperance reform. Davidson still relied whenever possible on using more private channels to exert influence. He remained an assiduous frequenter of London's Club Land – a good deal of his correspondence was written on Athenaeum notepaper – and he later wrote that it was in such settings as dinners at Grillions that he got to know politicians like Sir Edward Grey and Sir John Simon.

Davidson's *modus operandi* in seeking to influence political decisions whilst at Winchester can be seen in the field of education and, in particular, the status of Church-maintained schools (a topic that was to demand a good deal of his attention once he moved to Canterbury). Ever since the Education Act of 1870, there had been political tension over managing the division between fully funded Board (State) Schools and Voluntary Schools run by organisations such as the Church of England (most Voluntary Schools were Church of England schools, although a small number were run by other denominations, including the Roman Catholic Church). The Liberal Party typically favoured the Board Schools and, given the Party's strong support among Nonconformists, was wary of seeing public money spent on schools that gave denominational (typically Anglican) teaching. The Unionist (Conservative) Party favoured more generous funding for Voluntary Schools – but not at the price of seeing them lose their autonomy. The controversial 1902 Education Act made available State funding for Voluntary Schools *and* allowed them to retain the freedom to offer denominational education. Many Nonconformists bitterly objected to taxpayers supporting such teaching, and refused to pay rates, which led to dozens of imprisonments. Davidson was involved in the turbulent developments surrounding the introduction of the 1902 Act. In December 1901, at a time when it was already common knowledge that a new Education Bill was forthcoming, he wrote to Arthur Balfour, who was within a few months to become Prime Minister, suggesting that some form of compromise on all sides was likely to be needed. Davidson nevertheless made it clear that the Church had a clear expectation of greater financial support from the State for its schools.

Davidson subsequently played an important role in seeking to broker a compromise in which the Church of England accepted some diminution of its control over its schools – typically by allowing wider representation on the management boards – in return for funding. He wrote a number of memoranda on the subject, and maintained a detailed correspondence with Balfour, who was ironically himself little interested in the topic. Davidson sharply criticised the Baptist minister John Clifford, who led the campaign against the Bill, and sought instead to build bridges with more moderate Nonconformist leaders. He was also ready to support changes to the Bill designed to assuage Nonconformist concerns, as long as they did not undermine the principle of State funding for Voluntary Schools. Davidson in his public comments characteristically emphasised the areas of agreement between the two sides. He also repeatedly stressed, rather unconvincingly, that the real point at issue was the quality of education received by children (which he argued would be immeasurably improved with greater financial support). When the Bill came to the House of Lords, Davidson made one of his typically detailed speeches defending its provisions, whilst seeking to emphasise the practical benefits of the Bill. He also sharply criticised Clifford for his strident campaign of opposition. Davidson concluded his speech with a clear statement that 'this is an honest, straightforward, and courageous endeavour to grapple with a great and difficult problem in a way which will best meet the conflicting interests which anyone who has to deal with this subject has to meet'.[102]

Frederick Temple had spoken on the Education Bill in the House of Lords on 4 December 1902, but following his speech the 81-year-old Archbishop virtually collapsed, and had to be helped out of the Chamber. He died less than three weeks later. Davidson had for some years been the obvious successor. He was already on good terms with Arthur Balfour, who told Davidson that he intended to nominate him to the King, but the Prime Minister only (semi) formally put his views in writing on the last of day of 1902. Davidson told King Edward that he had 'mixed feelings' on being asked to move to Canterbury, given his sense of his own 'inadequacies'.[103] His words were both modest and disingenuous. Davidson was well aware of the challenges he would face, but he also believed he knew 'the ropes better than anyone', a claim with which it is hard to take issue.[104] The news of his appointment was received with little surprise in the press. The High Church *Guardian* noted a little acerbically that his appointment had been met, 'if not with enthusiasm at least with wide-spread satisfaction'. The *Daily News*, which had for some years had a particular aversion to Davidson, suggested that the new Archbishop owed his advancement up the Church to his experience as a 'clerical courtier'.[105] A few local newspapers similarly hinted that Davidson owed his appointment to connections at Court, rather than any great talent as a theologian or preacher (terms like 'courtier to the tips of his fingers' and 'clerical courtier' were commonly used).[106] More frequent, though, were articles like the one in the *Church Times* which praised Davidson's 'remarkable business capacities' and his great knowledge of the Church.[107] *The Times* noted that 'his fitness to lead the Bishops is beyond question', adding that he had taken a 'consistently moderate position' on issues of ecclesiastical controversy.[108]

Davidson was characteristically laid low with flu in the days after receiving news of his appointment, although he was well enough for the enthronement on 11 February, after which he gave a speech in Canterbury expressing hope that he would be able to build on the achievements of his predecessors.[109] His correspondence with Balfour over the next few weeks was full of discussion about Episcopal appointments (the minutiae of ecclesiastical appointments had enthralled him ever since he served as Archbishop Tait's Chaplain at Lambeth Palace many years before).[110] Davidson hoped that maintaining a balance on the Episcopal bench would minimise controversy between the various elements within the Church of England. It was in many ways a very 'Victorian' view of ecclesiastical politics. Over the next 25 years, the Archbishop had to confront far-reaching developments, both in the Church and across British society more broadly. Although his long ecclesiastical apprenticeship had provided him with valuable experience, he needed to come to terms with a changing world, in which many of the practices and assumptions of the past proved to be increasingly irrelevant and outmoded.

Notes

1 For some useful genealogical background, see Rev. Andrew Philip, *The Ancestry of Randall Thomas Davidson DD, Archbishop of Canterbury* (London: Elliot Stock, 1903).
2 Quoted in M.C.S.M. (Mary Mills), *Edith Davidson of Lambeth* (London: John Murray, 1938), p. 27. For a description of the informal character of the Davidson household at this time, see Lambeth Palace Library, Bell Papers 224, fos. 310–12, J.C. Gordon, Reminiscences of Davidson.

30 *The making of an Archbishop*

3. Bell, *Davidson*, Vol. 1, pp. 8–9.
4. For Davidson's interest in sport, see Stuart Mews, 'From Shooting to Shopping: Randall Davidson's Attitudes to Work, Rest, and Recreation', in Robert Norman Swanson (ed), *The Use and Abuse of Time in Christian History* (Woodbridge: Boydell and Brewer for Ecclesiastical History Society, 2002), pp. 385–99.
5. See, for example, his remarks in Randall Davidson, *The Inheritance of a Great Name: A Sermon Preached in the Chapter of Harrow School on Founders Day, October 11 1883* (London: Macmillan, 1883).
6. On Harrow during Butler's time, see Edward Graham, *The Harrow Life of Henry Montagu Butler* (London: Longmans, Green & Co, 1903).
7. On Westcott's time at Harrow, see *Life and Letters of Brooke Foss Westcott* (London: Macmillan, 1903), 2 vols, Vol. 1, pp. 173–300.
8. See, for example, Davidson Papers (henceforth D.P.) 1, fo. 141, Davidson to Father, 17 June 1866.
9. For an insight into Davidson's outlook at this time, see D.P. 2, various letters from Davidson to his family whilst at Oxford. For a useful discussion of the declining popularity of taking Holy Orders amongst young men from wealthy backgrounds during this period, see A.G.L. Haig, 'The Church, the Universities and Learning in Later Victorian England', *The Historical Journal*, 21, 9 (1986), pp. 187–201. For a wider discussion, see the same author's *The Victorian Clergy* (London: Croom Helm, 1984).
10. For a brief but valuable account of the Oxford Movement see P.B. Nockles, 'Lost Causes and. . . Impossible Loyalties: The Oxford Movement and the University', in M.G. Brock and M.C. Curthoys (eds), *The History of the University of Oxford* (Clarendon Press, 1997), Vol. VI, Part 2, pp. 195–207. For a more significant and rounded discussion, see Peter Nockles, *The Oxford Movement in Context: Anglican High Churchmanship, 1760–1857* (Cambridge: Cambridge University Press, 1997). For a useful collection of articles placing the Oxford Movement in a broader geographical perspective, see Stewart J. Brown and Peter B. Nockles (eds), *The Oxford Movement: Europe and the Wider World, 1830–1930* (Cambridge: Cambridge University Press, 2014).
11. On British Idealism generally, see Andrew Vincent and Raymond Plant, *Philosophy, Politics and Citizenship: The Life and Thought of the British Idealists* (Oxford: Blackwell, 1984). For a more focused discussion of the influence of Idealism within the Church of England, see Timothy Gouldstone, *The Rise and Decline of Anglican Idealism in the Nineteenth Century* (Basingstoke: Palgrave Macmillan, 2005).
12. On Vaughan see Trevor Park, *Nolo Episcopari: A Life of C.J. Vaughan* (St Bees: St Bega Publications, 2013).
13. For a discussion of Anglican theological training in the nineteenth century, see David Dowland, *Nineteenth-Century Anglican Theological Training: The Redbrick Challenge* (Oxford: Oxford University Press, 1997). For an insight into Vaughan's warm view of Davidson see, for example, D.P. 2, Letter 108, Vaughan to Davidson, 10 September 1873.
14. For Davidson's later reminiscences of the hostel he established at Farnham for young men preparing for ordination, see Bell Papers 221, fos. 209–13.
15. For Davidson's detailed and enthusiastic letters describing his experiences in the Egypt and the Holy Land, see D.P. 2, Letters 112–30.
16. D.P. 2, Letter 152, Davidson to Mother, 26 December 1876.
17. Davidson and Benham, *Life of Archibald Tait*, Vol. 2, p. 551. For brief portraits of Tait, see David L. Edwards, *Leaders of the Church of England, 1828–1978* (London: Hodder and Stoughton, 1978), pp. 123–43; Carpenter, *Cantuar*, pp. 334–59.
18. *Parliamentary Debates (Commons)*, 16 May 1873, col. 48.
19. Carpenter, *Cantuar*, p. 340.
20. Revd Wm Benham (ed), *Catherine and Craufurd Tait: A Memoir* (London: Macmillan, 1879), p. 537.
21. Davidson and Benham, *Life of Archibald Tait*, Vol. 2, p. 563.

22 On the Public Worship Act see G.I.T. Machin, *Politics and the Churches in Great Britain, 1869–1921* (Oxford: Clarendon Press, 1987), pp. 70–86; Carpenter, *Cantuar*, p. 345 ff.
23 Bell, *Davidson*, Vol. 1, p. 39.
24 Bell, *Davidson*, Vol. 1, p. 42.
25 James Bryce, *Studies in Contemporary Biography* (London: Macmillan, 1927), pp. 108–9.
26 Davidson and Benham, *Life of Archibald Tait*, Vol. 2, p. 583.
27 Quoted in Carpenter, *Cantuar*, p. 346.
28 Machin, *Politics and the Churches*, pp. 22–30.
29 *The Letters of Queen Victoria*, 2nd Series, Vol. 3, Davidson to Ely, 1 September 1882.
30 *Letters of Queen Victoria*, 2nd series, Vol. 3, Wellesley to Queen, 1 September 1882.
31 *Queen Victoria's Journal*, www.queenvictoriasjournals.org/home.do), 9 December 1882.
32 *Queen Victoria's Journal*, 11 December 1882.
33 Dark, *Randall Davidson*, p. 21. For a rather different view, see Arthur Christopher Benson, *The Life of Edward White Benson, Sometime Archbishop of Canterbury* (London: Macmillan, 1899), 2 vols., Vol. 1, p. 544 ff.
34 Bell Papers 237, fo. 14, Draft Chapter 3 of Volume 1 of *Davidson*, Queen to Benson, 4 May 1883; fos. 15-16, Draft Chapter 3, Benson to Queen, 6 May 1883.
35 *Letters of Queen Victoria*, 2nd series, Vol. 3, Gladstone to Ponsonby, 9 March 1883.
36 *Derby Daily Telegraph*, 23 May 1883; *Isle of Wight Observer*, 19 May 1893.
37 Bell Papers 237, fos, 19–20, Draft Chapter 3 of Volume 1 of *Davidson*, Westcott to Davidson, 11 May 1883.
38 For a recent discussion of Davidson's time as Dean, see Kate Hubbard, *Serving Victoria: Life in the Royal Household* (London: Chatto and Windus, 2012), pp. 275–91.
39 For Davidson's sermons following the death of the Duke of Albany, see Randall Davidson, *Three Sermons Preached in the Private Chapel of Windsor Castle* (London: Printed by Royal Command, 1894).
40 The Queen regularly praised Davidson's sermons in her journal as 'very fine' (16 March 1884), 'beautiful' (6 April 1884), 'excellent' (1 May 1885). On Victoria's own religious views see Walter L. Arnstein, 'Queen Victoria and Religion', in Gail Malmgreen (ed), *Religion in the Lives of English Women* (London: Croom Helm, 1986), pp. 88–128. For her use of patronage see Dudley W.R. Bahlmann, 'Politics and Church Patronage in the Victorian Age', *Victorian Studies*, 22, 3 (1976), pp. 253–96.
41 For Davidson's letters to Victoria, see D.P. 26 (various). For the letters from the Queen to Davidson, see D.P. 25 (various).
42 Bell, *Davidson*, Vol. 1, p. 83.
43 Benson, *Benson*, Vol. 2, p. 219.
44 Andrew Roberts, *Salisbury: Victorian Titan* (London: Faber and Faber, 1999), p. 318.
45 Bell Papers 237, fos. 50–2, Draft Chapter 3 of Volume 1 of *Davidson*, Undated Davidson Memorandum. It is perhaps unsurprising that this incident is one in which Bell was decidedly circumspect when deciding what material to publish in his biography of Davidson.
46 Bell Papers 237, fo. 11, Draft of section of *Davidson* headed 'The Queen and Dear Davidson'.
47 *Letters of Queen Victoria* 3rd series, Vol. 1, Davidson to Queen, 7 July 1888.
48 Bell, *Davidson*, Vol. 1, p. 103.
49 Benson, *Benson*, Vol. 2, p. 126. For the analysis of the 'intimate and devoted friendship' between Benson and Davidson by Benson's son, see Benson, *Benson*, Vol. 1, p. 585.
50 On the Lincoln Judgement see, Benson, *Benson*, Vol. 2, pp. 319–81.
51 Bell, *Davidson*, Vol. 1, p. 105.
52 *Times*, 9 April 1889.
53 For Davidson's private reflections on *Lux Mundi* – and his apparent scepticism about 'newfangled notions' – see D.P. 575, fo. 35, Davidson Journal entry 11 May 1890.
54 Bell, *Davidson*, Vol. 1, p. 152.

55 Bell Papers 237, fo. 89, Draft Chapter 3 of Volume 1 of *Davidson*, Davidson to Victoria, 23 December 1889.
56 Bell Papers 237, fo. 90, Draft Chapter 3 of Volume 1 of *Davidson*, Queen to Ponsonby, 24 December 1889.
57 Bell Papers 237, fo. 90, Draft Chapter 3 of Volume 1 of *Davidson*, Ponsonby to Queen, 28 December 1889.
58 *Letters of Queen Victoria*, 3rd series, Vol.1, Queen to Benson, 3 January 1890.
59 *Queen Victoria's Journal*, 27 August 1890.
60 *Letters of Queen Victoria*, 3rd series, Vol. 2, Salisbury to Queen, 3 October 1890.
61 D.P. 575, fos. 64–72, Davidson journal entry 5 October 1890.
62 Bell, *Davidson*, Vol. 1, p. 192.
63 D.P. 575, fo. 71, Davidson journal entry 5 October 1890.
64 Bell Papers 221, fo. 97, Edith Davidson notes for Bell.
65 *Pall Mall Gazette*, 16 October 1890.
66 *Sheffield Evening Telegraph*, 21 October 1890.
67 Randall Davidson, *A Charge Delivered to the Clergy of the Diocese of Rochester* (London: Macmillan, 1894), p. 50.
68 On the development of Christian Socialism see Alan Wilkinson, *Christian Socialism: Scott Holland to Tony Blair* (London: SCM, 1998). See, too, E.R. Norman, *Church and Society in England, 1770–1970: A Historical Study* (Oxford: Clarendon Press, 1976), p. 180 ff.
69 On Lux Mundi see Michael Ramsey, *An Era in Anglican Theology: From Gore to Temple* (Eugene, OR: Wipf and Stock, 1960), pp. 1–15. See, too, Ulrike Link-Wieczorek, 'Mediating Anglicanism: Maurice, Gore, and Temple', in David Fergusson (ed), *The Blackwell Companion to Nineteenth-Century Theology* (Oxford: Blackwell, 2010), pp. 280–300.
70 Benson, *Benson*, Vol. 2, p. 562.
71 *Queen Victoria's Journal*, 16 August 1891.
72 *Letters of Queen Victoria*, 3rd series, Vol. 2, Davidson to Bigge, 23 January 1895.
73 Davidson, *Charge Delivered to the Clergy of Rochester*, p. 36.
74 *Times*, 12 February 1892.
75 For Halifax's role in the attempt to secure recognition of Anglican orders, see J.G. Lockhart, *Charles Lindley, Viscount Halifax, 1885–1934* (London: The Centenary Press, 1936), pp. 38–91. See, too, Benson, *Benson*, Vol. 2, pp. 581–624.
76 Bell, *Davidson*, Vol. 1, pp. 232–33.
77 Randall Davidson, *Disestablishment: A Speech Delivered at a meeting held at the Corn Exchange at Rochester on June 8th 1893* (London, 1893).
78 Davidson, *Charge to the Clergy of Rochester*, p. 32.
79 Davidson, *Charge to the Clergy of Rochester*, p. 37.
80 On Dolling, see Charles E. Osborne, *The Life of Father Dolling* (London: Edward Arnold, 1903).
81 *Hampshire Telegraph and Sussex Chronicle*, 2 November 1895.
82 *The Hampshire Advertiser*, 14 December 1895.
83 See, for example, *Morning Post*, 10 December 1895.
84 *Times*, 11 December 1895; 12 December 1895.
85 Bell, *Davidson*, Vol. 1, p. 279.
86 Quoted in James Bentley, *Ritualism and Politics in Victorian Britain* (Oxford: Oxford University Press, 1978), p. 64. For an illuminating essay on the shifting and ambiguous character of 'Ritualism', and its place in the broader development of High Church and Anglo-Catholic sentiment, see J.E.B. Munson, 'The Oxford Movement by the End of the Nineteenth Century: The Anglo-Catholic Clergy', *Church History*, 44, 3 (1975), pp. 382–95.
87 *Times*, 18 July 1898.
88 *Times*, 26 August 1896.
89 D.P. 518, fos. 80–3, Davidson to Harcourt, 27 September 1898.

90 D.P. 518, fos 96–8, Davidson to Harcourt, 14 January 1899 (quotation fo. 96).
91 D.P. 518, fos. 99–103, Harcourt to Davidson, 15 January 1899 (quotations fos. 99, 102).
92 For Davidson's speech, see *Parliamentary Debates (Lords)*, 9 February 1899, cols. 265–80.
93 E.G. Sandford (ed), *Memoirs of Archbishop Temple by Seven Friends* 2 vols. (London: Macmillan, 1906), Vol. 2, pp. 290–308.
94 On the ecclesiastical input into the coronation of Edward VII, see Peter Hinchcliff, 'Frederick Temple, Randall Davidson and the Coronation of Edward VII', *Journal of Ecclesiastical History*, 48, 1 (1997), pp. 71–99.
95 D.P. 12, fos. 304–16, Davidson Memorandum, Easter 1913 (quotations fo. 310). For a valuable scholarly edition of this document, along with other very useful material about Davidson, see Melanie Barber (ed), 'Randall Davidson: A Partial Retrospective', in Stephen Taylor (ed), *From Cranmer to Davidson: A Church of England Miscellany* (Woodbridge: Boydell Press for Church of England Record Society, 1999), pp. 387–438.
96 On Temple's life and career, see Peter Hinchcliff, *Frederick Temple, Archbishop of Canterbury: A Life* (Oxford: Clarendon Press, 1998).
97 *The Letters of Queen Victoria*, 3rd Series, Vol. 3, Queen to Salisbury, 16 October 1896.
98 *The Letters of Queen Victoria*, 3rd Series, Vol. 3, Salisbury to Queen, 22 October 1896.
99 Bell, *Davidson*, Vol. 1, p. 292.
100 Bell, *Davidson*, Vol. 1, p. 300.
101 Randall Davidson, *A Charge Delivered to the Clergy of Winchester, September-October 1999*, (London: Macmillan, 1899), p. 10.
102 *Parliamentary Debates (Lords)*, 5 December 1902, col. 42.
103 D.P. 5, fo. 11, Davidson to King Edward, 9 January 1903.
104 Bell, *Davidson*, Vol. 1, p. 383.
105 *Daily News* reported in *Sheffield Daily Telegraph*, 9 January 1903.
106 *Cambridge Daily News*, 9 January 1903; *Daily News*, 9 January 1903.
107 *Church Times*, 16 January 1903.
108 *Times*, 9 January 1903.
109 *Times*, 12 February 1903.
110 For the detailed correspondence in 1903 between Balfour and Davidson on Episcopal appointments, see British Library Western Manuscripts, Balfour Papers, Add. Mss. 49788.

2 Archbishop Davidson and the Edwardian Crisis

A Victorian in a changing world (1903–1914)

The decade following Davidson's appointment to Canterbury was a troubled period in British history. When Queen Victoria died in 1901, Germany and the United States had already overtaken Britain as the world's leading industrial powers. The defeats in the South African War of 1899–1902 starkly revealed the limits to the country's military strength. The growth of the German navy seemed to threaten the sinews of Britain's imperial power. Closer to home, the controversies that erupted over the status of the House of Lords and Irish Home Rule raised the prospect of fundamental changes to the British Constitution (and indeed the geographical boundaries of the British State). The development of the Labour Party and growing calls for female suffrage reflected an increasingly vocal questioning of the social and economic status quo. In the literary sphere, writers like H. G. Wells raised important questions about the impact of technology on society, whilst journals such as the *New Age* published work marked by experimental form and a rejection of past certainties.

Although it is true that 'religion' continued to play a significant role in shaping both personal identity and public culture,[1] there was considerable unease across the churches that a large proportion of the working class population seldom went to church, or indeed even considered itself in any meaningful sense 'Christian'. A celebrated survey by the *Daily News* in 1904 suggested that less than 20 percent of Londoners attended church regularly (the figure was admittedly higher in the suburbs).[2] For Anglicans, the situation was made more fraught by periodic calls for Disestablishment, which not only threatened the status of the Church of England, but also raised the question of whether the National Church could in any meaningful sense claim to be national. Nor was this just a matter of its minority status in Wales and virtual absence from the religious landscape of Scotland and Ireland.[3] It also reflected deeper uncertainty about whether the Church of England could still command the allegiance of a majority of the residents of England itself.

It is perhaps too easy to overstate the extent to which the much-vaunted 'Edwardian Crisis' represented a fundamental break in the pattern of Britain's historical development,[4] for the continuities between the Victorian and Edwardian periods were in fact significant. The period between 1901 and 1914 was nevertheless experienced by many members of the British social and political establishment as a time of uncertainty, even as the familiar rituals of Country House parties and the London Season went on largely unchanged. Nor was the position of the Church of England in national life untouched by this sense of unease. When Davidson became Archbishop of Canterbury at the start of 1903, he faced two distinct challenges, which together dominated his attention in the years preceding the First World War. The first, which forms the focus of the current chapter, was the need to steer the Church of England through the contours of a changing social and political landscape. The second, discussed in the following chapter, was maintaining a sense of unity within the Church itself. Both tasks strained to the uttermost Davidson's capacity for hard work and his talent for forging agreement between people of radically different views.

Archbishop Davidson and the politics of educational reform

Almost no question created as much political passion in Edwardian Britain as the question of education. The 1902 Education Act introduced by Lord Salisbury's Unionist (Conservative) administration abolished the old system of School Boards, and placed all elementary schools under the control of new Local Education Authorities, effectively meaning that the running cost of denominational schools was paid through local taxation. The move was bitterly resented by many Nonconformists. Davidson became Archbishop a few months after the 1902 Education Act was passed, and he was inevitably drawn into the resulting controversy, although he behaved with his customary courtesy and restraint. In a letter published in *The Times*, in July 1903, he gently (and unfairly) chided the Baptist John Clifford and his supporters for being vague as to whether they favoured non-denominational religious teaching in schools or no religious teaching whatsoever.[5] A few months later, he published a further letter in which he argued more trenchantly that Clifford and other Nonconformists 'will not stop their warfare until they have completely disestablished the Church'.[6] He went on to defend the 1902 Education Act as 'an honest endeavour to deal fairly with a problem of singular complexity'. Davidson was probably wrong in seeing the campaign against the Act as part of a deliberate campaign for Disestablishment, but there was genuine outrage among many Nonconformists, and the Archbishop knew that such anger could easily fuel renewed demands for a change to the ecclesiastical *status quo*.

Davidson's public letters and pronouncements on the education controversy carefully sought to build consensus around the principle that reform was needed to raise educational standards. It was nevertheless inevitable that he often became the target for attack by Nonconformists bitter about the 1902 Act, particularly in Wales, where Anglicans formed a minority of the population. In a speech at Swansea, in November 1905, Davidson tried to calm anger by praising the Act for improving school funding. He nevertheless still faced a hostile response in the Welsh press, attracting criticism for supporting 'the assumption that the

State is bound to give privileges to one denomination at the expense of all the others'.[7] An editorial in the *Cambrian News* even caustically noted that 'We would no more attempt to reason with an Archbishop than with a bat, a mole or a log of wood'.[8] The 1906 General Election, which saw the return of a Liberal Government commanding massive support from the Nonconformist electorate, transformed the politics of education.[9] The *Church Times* noted that any attempt to take greater control of Church schools would encounter a 'stubborn resistance from Church people' (some leading Anglican lay figures like Hugh Cecil and Viscount Halifax had already bitterly criticised even the limited powers given to Local Educational Authorities over Church schools by the 1902 Act).[10] Repeal of the 1902 Education Act was, however, a priority for the new Liberal Government headed by Henry Campbell-Bannerman. Davidson, as Archbishop, faced the difficult task of defending a position that the newly elected Government was determined to reform.[11]

Davidson enjoyed good personal relations with many members of the new Liberal Government, largely built up during his frequent forays into London Club Land, or through his friendship with a previous generation of Liberal politicians such as Gladstone and Rosebery. The Archbishop was on excellent terms with Herbert Asquith, who replaced Campbell-Bannerman as Prime Minister in 1908, as well as Richard Haldane (who served as Secretary of State for War).[12] Indeed, Davidson had closer ties with members of the new Cabinet than he had with their Conservative predecessors, even though most were not practising Anglicans, and some like Haldane had few pretensions to any traditional form of religious allegiance. The Archbishop found it harder to deal with more radical ministers like David Lloyd George, who articulated a 'new' Liberalism committed to social and political reform, although Davidson was astute enough to realise that the Church of England could not ignore the growing popular appetite for change. Davidson noted ruefully a year before the outbreak of the First World War that Britain was moving into 'a thoroughly democratic age [...] rather suspicious of what we have been accustomed to regard as loyalty and patriotism and a proper historical pride'.[13] He nevertheless understood that it was it was impossible to turn back the tide.

Although Davidson was unhappy at the prospect of legislation designed to reduce the autonomy of publicly funded Church schools, he was also concerned by the violence of the language used by some Unionist politicians in opposing such a development. Some of them, for their part, did not trust the Bishops to fight sufficiently hard for their cause.[14] Davidson warned against suggestions that supporters of Church schools should refuse to pay taxes, as some Nonconformists had previously done in protest at the 1902 Education Act, writing in a letter to *The Times* that such people had lost all sense of 'historic proportion'.[15] He also expressed confidence that the new Government would behave fairly towards Church schools.[16] Davidson was therefore appalled when draft legislation was published that virtually seemed to expropriate school buildings that had been funded by the Church of England by handing full control of all elementary schools over to Local Education Authorities.

The Archbishop was given an early insight into the provisions of the new Bill by the Secretary of the Board of Education, Augustine Birrell,[17] and subsequently met the Prime Minister to express his concerns. Davidson was at first confident that he was more likely to change the Government's policy through the use of such confidential channels rather than more dramatic public proclamations. He nevertheless noted in a private memorandum that if the Bill took its planned form, then

> I could no longer abstain [. . .] from encouraging demonstrations or public meetings of protest on the part of the Church [and the Government] would have to reckon me among the unqualified opponents of the Government measure, their action having ousted me from the position of being among those who desire to co-operate with them towards a reasonable solution.[18]

As soon as the Bill was published, the Archbishop railed in a letter to *The Times* against the 'confiscation' of school premises and the effective destruction of denominational education.[19] His anger reflected the fact that he felt betrayed by Liberal leaders to whom he was personally close. In the weeks following publication of the Bill, the normally emollient Archbishop met frequently with Unionist politicians to discuss ways of defeating the legislation in the House of Lords. He had – not for the last time – overestimated his ability to influence policy from behind the scenes.

Once Davidson's initial anger wore off, he was torn between his opposition to the Education Bill and his reluctance to put the Church on a collision course with a Government that had so recently enjoyed a sweeping electoral victory. He told King Edward VII's Private Secretary in April 1906 that

> I have no desire [. . .] to identify myself with the sort of uncompromising Tory opposition which will be loud when Parliament meets again. On the other hand, I cannot in any way become an assenting party to provisions which will in my judgement be disastrous to our children religiously and educationally.[20]

A few days later, he told Edward himself that 'the Bill as it stands must be opposed outright, but I should always couple such opposition with a declaration showing that, if properly amended, Churchmen could accept it as the result of the recent election'.[21] The Archbishop was acutely conscious that the Church of England faced the danger of appearing out of touch with the popular mood. He was not convinced by the wisdom of staging public demonstrations against the Bill, as was suggested by many of its opponents, noting that 'I doubt whether that mode of demonstration is the most effective'.[22] Despite his earlier failures, the Archbishop still believed that opposition was best conducted by a patient campaign designed to win concessions from ministers. He feared that more public forms of protest would simply highlight differences with the Government, and give credence to the notion that the Church of England represented just one part of the nation.

The Education Bill continued to preoccupy the Archbishop for much of the next two years. He repeatedly expressed irritation that ministers in the Liberal Government were reluctant to make any concessions that might alienate their backbenchers. Davidson continued his round of 'shuttle diplomacy', meeting frequently with both Liberal and Unionist politicians, as well as discussing educational issues at length with his fellow Bishops. The Prime Minister (Campbell-Bannerman) made it clear that the Liberal Government would not accept amendments passed in the House of Lords to water down the Education Bill. Lord Hugh Cecil, from the other end of the political spectrum, argued that the position of Liberal ministers was weaker than it seemed.[23] The Bishops themselves were divided. Edmund Knox, the Bishop of Manchester, sought to rally both ecclesiastical and public opinion against the legislation, taking part in public demonstrations against the Bill.[24] The Archbishop plaintively wrote to the King's Private Secretary in May 1906 that 'the educational controversialists on both sides bombard me'.[25]

Davidson's patient attempts to broker agreement between two irreconcilable positions failed, although in the event the Liberal Government's proposals to reform the status of Church schools came to nothing, victim of political opposition and delaying tactics in the House of Lords. The issue nevertheless signalled how easily the Church of England could find itself at odds with a Government that had been elected with a large majority ('a perilous situation' the Archbishop called it).[26] Davidson's hopes of securing a compromise reflected his failure to grasp the depth of feelings on both sides. The Archbishop could not broker agreement between politicians precisely because the popular passions raised by the Education Bill meant that political leaders were constrained by the opinions of their supporters. The next few years were to show how easy it was for the Church of England to become caught up in partisan conflicts that went to the very heart of the character of the British Constitution itself.

The Archbishop and the constitutional crisis of 1909–11

In April 1909, Lloyd George as Chancellor of the Exchequer delivered his 'People's Budget', designed to address the challenge of poverty by introducing a series of measures to be paid for by higher taxation of the better off.[27] Lloyd George's Budget subsequently became the focus of a constitutional crisis when the House of Lords refused to pass the resulting Finance Bill. Asquith, who was by now Prime Minister, called a General Election in early 1910, which resulted in the return of a minority Liberal Government. The Finance Bill was passed in April by the House of Lords, but the Asquith Government was already preparing a new Parliament Bill, designed to constrain the power of the House of Lords to reject future finance bills (as well as limiting the Second Chamber's ability to delay other legislation). The Government made it clear that it would, if necessary, create hundreds of new peers to ensure that the Bill passed through the Lords. The death of Edward VII in May 1910 also complicated the crisis since his successor, George V, was considerably less adroit in political affairs.

After a second General Election at the end of 1910, the crisis was at least partially resolved in 1911, when a new Parliament Act was passed enshrining the constitutional supremacy of the House of Commons.

The stand-off between the House of Commons and the House of Lords was in many ways a conflict between the forces of tradition and change. Support for radical social policies was strong amongst some Anglican clergy, reflecting a genuine if somewhat moralistic commitment to improving popular welfare, and meetings like the 1908 Pan-Anglican Congress in London were often the setting for lively debate on such subjects as the moral virtues of socialism.[28] The Christian Social Union, first established in 1889, provided an important forum for clergy such as William Temple and Henry Scott Holland to develop their ideas about a new social gospel that had traditionally been more associated with the various Nonconformist churches.[29] Randall Davidson was well aware that major political and constitutional change could undermine the Church of England's national position, yet he also recognised the danger it faced by being closely associated in the public imagination with the interests of certain elite groups. For two years, he devoted immense energy to brokering agreement between Liberal and Unionist ministers in the hope of persuading them to place national harmony above political division. It was a valiant effort, but the process once again showed that the Archbishop did not always understand that deep-seated tensions could not be resolved simply by promoting consensus among those at the top of the political pyramid.

The Liberal Government formed by Asquith early in 1910, following the first General Election of that year, relied on Labour and Irish Nationalist MPs for a majority. The Prime Minister therefore faced pressure to pursue policies that he might otherwise not have adopted. It was partly for this reason that the Government started work on a new Parliament Bill to reduce the power of the House of Lords (the Lords had already defeated educational reform, as well as opposing Lloyd George's Budget, and was likely to veto the Disestablishment of the Welsh Church and any moves towards Irish Home Rule). Davidson took a cautious line from the moment the crisis began to erupt in 1909, warning the Unionist peer Lord Lansdowne that the Upper House should be wary of rejecting the Finance Bill, since it would provide 'the extreme men' with an excuse to call for radical constitutional change.[30] The Archbishop also noted that while he was intensely concerned about constitutional issues, he did not worry so much about 'the evil character of the Budget', reflecting his determination not to be seen as an unashamed supporter of those who opposed paying higher taxes to fund social welfare. When Lord Halifax wrote to him early in 1910, defending the constitutional *status quo*, Davidson replied that some flexibility might be necessary to secure a compromise that would preserve the best of the current system:

> I am by no means certain that these principles [hereditary, spiritual] will commend themselves to the people at large, and it may quite possibly be a wise policy on our part to consent to some arrangement which shall

introduce new elements into the Second Chamber if by so doing we can in the main preserve the historic character upon which you rightly lay so much stress.[31]

The constitutional situation became more fraught as the question arose of whether the King should agree to create new peers to pass the proposed Parliament Bill if asked to do so by Asquith (a request that would inevitably bring the monarchy firmly within the ambit of partisan politics). Davidson went to great lengths to give advice to the Palace about how best to deal with this fraught situation. Although he was by his own admission never 'on terms of special intimacy' with Edward,[32] and had on more than one occasion spoken to the King about his 'personal conduct', the Archbishop was determined to protect the institution of monarchy from damage.[33] The task was not an easy one. In a meeting with Balfour and Lord Knollys (Edward VII's Private Secretary), that took place in the spring of 1910, the Archbishop noted the difficulty faced by the monarch in 'avoiding the Scylla of appearing to side with the Unionist Party, and not falling into the Charybdis of appearing to dance to the Liberal pipe'.[34] In an interview a few days later, with the owner of the *Spectator*, Davidson noted that compromise between the Unionists and Liberals would only come about if their leaders 'over-ride their respective extremists'.[35] He failed to recognise that political leaders could not simply ignore the opinion of their supporters.

The accession of George V to the throne in May 1910 did not make Davidson's attempts to promote compromise any easier (he found the new monarch both naive and remarkably indiscreet when discussing political questions).[36] By the start of 1911, the crisis was as acute as ever, and Davidson was warned by one leading Liberal Minister that 'we must face the fact we are entering a revolutionary period'.[37] The Archbishop himself was still urging on all sides the need for 'caution and patience' as they worked for a national consensus. He advised senior figures at the Palace that the King should at least consider creating new peers if the House of Lords continued to block the Parliament Act, although he also warned that George should not make any definite commitment to that effect, unaware that the monarch had already made such a pledge to Asquith before the December General Election.[38] Davidson's long experience of royal politics meant that he felt a special responsibility to protect the monarchy from being damaged by the dispute. As the crisis reached its denouement, in the summer of 1911, the Archbishop also became increasingly concerned that the position of the Church of England could itself be undermined by the crisis.

The votes of the Bishops in the House of Lords were likely to prove influential in determining the fate of the Parliament Act. Senior Unionist and Liberal peers repeatedly approached the Archbishop asking how the Bishops would vote. Davidson was himself inclined to abstain. His voluminous correspondence with other Bishops suggested that many planned to do the same.[39] The Archbishop was, however, concerned that if the Bishops failed to support the

Bill, then Liberal backbenchers would once again raise the whole question of Disestablishment. Davidson knew that the Parliament Act would eventually be passed, given the promise Asquith had extracted from the King to create hundreds of new peers, and after a good deal of agonising he eventually decided to support the measure. So too did most of the Bishops. In his speech to the House of Lords, Davidson caused something of a stir when announcing his intention, saying (not altogether correctly) that his views had been changed 'by the course of the debate', and that with 'a grave sense of public duty' he would support the Government's Bill.[40] The decision by most Bishops to follow his lead meant that 'diehard' peers were unable to prevent its passage.

The politics of the crisis meant that it was virtually impossible for the Bishops to remain neutral. Davidson was deeply unhappy about the constitutional changes introduced by the Parliament Act, which sharply constrained the power of the House of Lords, but he was shrewd enough to realise that the Government could claim an electoral mandate for the reforms. In the weeks that followed, his in-tray was filled with countless letters condemning him for voting in support of a Government that wanted to disestablish the Welsh Church and (argued his critics) probably the English Church as well. The Bishops were attacked for 'servile sychophancy' worthy only of 'contempt'.[41] Davidson typically replied that, by supporting the Parliament Act, the Bishops had moderated hostility towards the Established Church and preserved at least some residue of power and prestige for the House of Lords. His belief that compromise was necessary to preserve both the authority of the Church and the unity of the nation was, for the Archbishop, a matter of principle as well as prudence. Davidson knew the Church of England would weaken its authority if it tried to stand out against the tide of social and political change symbolised by the assault on the powers of the Lords. Nor, it should be added, did he believe that it could be right for the Church to do so.

Two years later, in September 1913, Davidson wrote a long memorandum reflecting on how the political crisis of 1909–11 had been rooted in deep changes in the character of British politics and society. He noted that the rise of 'vehement democratic views' and 'Lloyd Georgism' were facts of political life rather than theories: 'The political cries which arouse a public meeting are quite different from the political cries which aroused the Radicals in our fathers' days. They give voice to what people are really thinking'. He went on to suggest that members of the older generation had to avoid seeing such changes simply as 'pernicious and evil-tempered'. It was instead necessary to mould 'into better and safer shapes the tendencies which, whatever shape they assume, will certainly persist and hold their own'.[42] Davidson's words captured his own internal sense of schism. The Archbishop's emotions were rooted in a Victorian world of social privilege and political hierarchy. His intellect recognised that Edwardian Britain was experiencing changes that touched on virtually every aspect of contemporary life. Davidson's behaviour during the crisis of 1909–11 was prompted by a desire to search for compromises that preserved at least some semblance of tradition as the old world collided with the new.

The Archbishop and the Home Rule crisis

The passing of the Parliament Act into law did not bring an end to the tensions that dominated political life in Britain before 1914. In April 1912, Asquith introduced a new Bill to provide Home Rule for Ireland, a subject that had periodically convulsed British politics for half a century.[43] The prospect of Home Rule was deeply unpopular both in Ulster and among Unionists in Great Britain, but the passage of the Parliament Act the previous year meant there was little prospect of the Bill being defeated at Westminster, since the House of Lords had lost its power of indefinite veto. It quickly became apparent over the next year or so that the introduction of Home Rule might lead to civil war in Ireland, prompting extensive discussions in London about ways to resolve the crisis, including the possibility of excluding Ulster from the new measure.

Davidson was particularly concerned about the impact the crisis might have on the position of the monarch. In early 1914, the Archbishop had a long interview with the King, who was 'more vehement and upset than I have ever seen him',[44] anxious that he might be blamed by posterity as the monarch who allowed Britain to slide into civil war. A few days later, Davidson met Arthur Balfour to discuss the crisis. Over the next few weeks, a number of prominent Unionists issued veiled threats that if Home Rule were introduced without the issue being submitted to the electorate, they would be ready to take steps to prevent the Government using force to impose its will in Ulster. By the start of March, it looked as though a conflict might also develop between the Government and the army, should officers and their men refuse to act against the Ulster Volunteers. The Curragh Mutiny that took place later in March dramatically highlighted the potential danger of the situation.[45] In the weeks that followed, renewed efforts were made to reach a compromise in London, giving Davidson the opportunity to play his familiar role of intermediary.

In a meeting with the Prime Minister, in March 1914, which followed one Davidson had with the Unionist leader Andrew Bonar Law, the Archbishop offered his 'service at a moment of crisis'. He added that because he represented 'the man in the street' he could play the role of 'a non-partisan intermediary' (a rather optimistic claim – but one that reflected Davidson's sense of his role as the representative of the nation).[46] Asquith described with considerable frankness the dilemmas facing his Government, and sketched out possible solutions to the Ulster crisis, after which he gave Davidson permission to report their conversation to Bonar Law. Bonar Law, for his part, gave tentative approval to the Prime Minister's idea that the six counties might for the moment be excluded from Home Rule pending a future referendum. A couple of days later, Davidson had further separate meetings with both men. The Archbishop does seem on this occasion to have played a significant role by acting as an honest broker. He was determined to assist both Party leaders in finding a way to step back from the abyss, in order to prevent the Home Rule crisis from leading to civil war in Ireland and massive political strife across the rest of the country.

Davidson continued to involve himself in efforts to resolve the Irish Home Rule crisis during the weeks that followed. He had further meetings with Bonar Law and Asquith, along with other leading political figures including the Unionist peer Lord Lansdowne and the Liberal Cabinet minister John Morley, and spoke at some length on the crisis in the House of Lords in early July. He also continued to liaise regularly with the Palace. Davidson was, though, unable to change the fundamental dynamic of the Home Rule crisis. He was adept at facilitating communication across Party lines, but communication and goodwill alone could not resolve the deep-seated divisions over the Irish question, which led to the collapse of the Conference held in July 1914 to seek solutions to the crisis. Davidson's *modus operandi* as ever rested on the assumption that there existed a national interest which transcended narrow sectional interest, with the result that political leaders could, if they had sufficient goodwill, resolve even the most complex and divisive problems. Some challenges were, though, simply too divisive to be dealt with in this way. Members of the British political elite struggled to identify solutions to the major problems facing Britain in the years before 1914 precisely because the issues at stake were so stark and so divisive. It has even been suggested – though it should be said rather tendentiously – that the British government went to war in 1914 in part because of a desire to mask the domestic crisis beneath an outburst of patriotism.[47]

The challenge of Welsh Disestablishment

Davidson sought to act both in the Parliamentary crisis of 1909–11 and the Home Rule crisis of 1912–14 as a national figure detached from the passions and interests of the political fray. The questions raised by the introduction of a Bill to disestablish the Welsh Church, early in 1912, by contrast pitted the Church of England against the Liberal Government in a way more reminiscent of the earlier controversy over the control of Church schools.[48] The threat posed by the prospect of Welsh Disestablishment was made more intense by a widespread (and not necessarily groundless) fear that it might prove to be a step on the road to Disestablishment in England as well. The passage of the 1911 Parliament Act meant that there was little prospect of the House of Lords preventing the Bill from becoming law. The Archbishop therefore had to identify ways of defeating the Bill, or at least ameliorating some of its clauses, without making his actions seem like the defence of narrow sectional interest.

The Royal Commission that reported in 1910 on the position of the Established Church in Wales heard much evidence about popular resentment over its status, given that a majority of the Welsh population were Nonconformist. Davidson nevertheless reflected the views of most senior clergy in arguing that the four Welsh dioceses were an organic part of the Church of England. In a speech to 8,000 people in Caernarvon, in April 1912, he told the audience that Disestablishment would weaken the Church and make it harder to carry out its work.[49] A week later, the Upper House of Canterbury Convocation called for 'strenuous opposition' to attempts to remove the Welsh provinces (the Archbishop himself noted he would do 'everything that is in me' to lead opposition – though cautious as ever he warned the time might not yet be ripe).[50] Numerous meetings were held up and down the country throughout 1912 and 1913 complaining about the prospect of Disestablishment. In November 1913, Davidson gave an uncharacteristically powerful speech at the Albert Hall, telling the audience that the Bill was 'a mischief which would affect the whole life the people'.[51] The Archbishop was fearful that Disestablishment might prove to be the first act in a process that would lead to the declining 'power and influence of religion in national life'.[52]

One of the main problems posed by the Bill, at least in the eyes of its opponents, was the proposal to remove all endowments dating from before the seventeenth century. Just as the Education Bill of 1906 was attacked by many Unionists for seeming to expropriate Church property, so plans to remove the endowments of the Welsh Church were widely condemned as little more than a confiscation of its assets. The Archbishop warned an audience in Croydon that many supporters of Disendowment made little secret 'that the terms imposed upon the Church in Wales are chosen with the thought in the background of what ought ultimately happen [. . .] in England'.[53] He also repeated an argument that he had made since the 1880s – namely, that the Church's endowments were needed for it to maintain a presence in every community. The Liberal Government nevertheless pushed ahead with the Bill, despite furious opposition in the House of Commons. It duly received the Royal Assent in September 1914, but only came into effect five years later, following the end of the First World War. The failure of the Church of England to prevent the Disestablishment of the Welsh Church showed how difficult it was for its leaders to prevent measures with which they disagreed, particularly following the passing of the 1911 Parliament Act. Neither Davidson nor any other leading Anglican could identify an effective strategy to defeat the Bill.

Archbishop Davidson and international politics

Questions of international politics loomed large for some of the main Nonconformist churches in the 20 years before 1914, filling the pages of papers like the *Methodist Recorder* and the *British Weekly*, as well featuring in countless sermons and debates.[54] The plight of the Armenian Christians in the Ottoman Empire aroused enormous concern. So too did the arms race between the main European powers. Nonconformists continued to provide – as they always had – the main impetus behind the organisations that made up the peace movement in Britain.[55] Members of the Church of England, both clerical and lay, were seldom so heavily involved in such developments (although Edward Hicks, appointed Bishop of Lincoln in 1910, was involved in the Church of England Peace League, whose small membership was committed to 'combating the war spirit as contrary to the spirit of Christianity').[56] Nor did the Church suffer the kinds of division encountered by some of the Nonconformist denominations over the Boer War (although some prominent Anglicans, including

Charles Gore, opposed the conflict).[57] Davidson was wary of making public pronouncements on the rights and wrongs of international politics. When he wrote to political leaders on such questions, he typically emphasised that he was not a 'diplomatist', and had no 'special information' on the subject at hand.[58] He also generally rebuffed efforts to ask him to put his name to petitions about foreign affairs, on the grounds that such utterances tended to be 'twisted into a political declaration'.[59] The Archbishop was nevertheless interested in foreign affairs, and well aware that issues of 'religion' could seldom be separated completely from questions of international politics, even as he sought to avoid placing himself in a position that might create public controversy.

Davidson was from an early age interested in the Christian East (he had travelled widely in the Levant as a young man). When Russia erupted in revolution, in 1905, the Archbishop sent a letter to the Metropolitan of St Petersburg expressing his sympathy at the violence. He also wrote to the Chief Rabbi in Britain recording his horror at the pogroms that had taken place across the western provinces of the Tsarist Empire (the two letters taken together constituted something of a paradox given the deep anti-Semitism in the Russian Orthodox Church). Such correspondence was, however, inspired by a desire to express concern rather than commit the Church of England to a definite position on such issues. More typical was his cautious response in 1908 to a letter from the Archbishop of Belgrade, who had asked for support in the campaign against the Austrian annexation of Bosnia-Herzegovina, in which Davidson noted,

> The Bishops of the Church of England abstain carefully from intervention in the [. . .] difficult political questions which press at present upon the people of Eastern Europe, feeling that their knowledge of the problems is not sufficient to justify them in expressing opinions upon the subject.[60]

Davidson also politely batted away many requests to give his name to appeals to aid victims of political violence, or even natural catastrophes, asking his secretary to respond to one such request with a note that there was much 'misapprehension [. . .] in Eastern Europe and in Western Asia regarding the powers of the Archbishop in such matters'.[61] He also refrained from commenting on more immediate matters of war and peace, writing to the Wesleyan J. Scott Lidgett in 1909 that he was reluctant to make a joint statement expressing belief in the importance of a 'peace-loving spirit', since such a statement might be seen as some form of definite political opinion on issues like military expenditure or policy towards Germany. The Archbishop had, though, previously been ready to give his support to a visit by a group of German Protestant and Catholic Churchmen to Britain, even praising the Kaiser in the souvenir volume for his 'eloquent expressions' in favour of peace.[62] Davidson also gave his (slightly muted) support to a return visit to Germany by an ecumenical group of Anglicans, Catholics, and Nonconformists. The Archbishop's private correspondence shows that whilst he was ready to discuss international affairs in the years before

1914, he remained cautious about saying anything that might inadvertently involve himself in political disputes.

Davidson was more willing to express his firm support for international arbitration as a means of combating war. At The Hague Conferences of 1899 and 1907, leading governments signed a series of conventions designed to introduce innovative mechanisms to resolve conflict and establish new ways of regulating the conduct of warfare in the event that it could not be avoided. A few weeks before the second Hague Conference, Davidson made a long speech at Convocation in support of a motion that

> it is the duty of every Christian man, by earnest prayer and by the use of such influence as he possesses, to strengthen and consolidate the growing sentiment in favour of international amity and peace, to promote a higher ideal of international intercourse, and to further prevent the efforts of Governments and statesmen in the direction of preventing the horrors and calamities of war by the systematic and recognised adoption of arbitration when international difficulties arise.[63]

The Archbishop lamented the fact that the most prominent figures active in promoting arbitration did not seem to have any connection with any Church. He also – and not entirely fairly – claimed that the subject was seldom discussed at length by Christians around the world. Davidson's speech was as ever well informed and politically nuanced. He suggested, doubtless with a nod to the 'Dreadnought' lobby and the National Service League, that supporting arbitration should not mean losing sight of the importance of Home Defence. The Archbishop did not, though, engage in much depth with the fundamental causes of international conflict. Although he did not share the progressive view of writers who argued that war could in time be abolished, once Governments realised how futile it was as a means of furthering national interest,[64] Davidson's outlook meant that he was naturally inclined to the view that reasonable political leaders of all countries could come to agreement if they were suitably motivated. The concept that war might be part of the human condition, rooted in the animal nature of humanity or the perennial competition for resources, was largely alien to him.

The Archbishop was on occasion more forthcoming on international issues, particularly those relating to imperial questions that had a directly 'moral' character. His pronouncements created few problems when they dealt with such matters as developments in the Congo Free State, a kind of private colony of the Belgian King Leopold, where huge numbers of Africans died as a result of exploitation on a scale unusual even at a time when harsh imperial rule was widespread across Africa and Asia (the horrors formed the background of Joseph Conrad's *Heart of Darkness*). The subject became a source of huge controversy in Britain, and in May 1907 Davidson told the Upper House of Canterbury Convocation that although he was normally reluctant for such a body to express its views on foreign affairs, in the case of the Congo there was an 'imperative duty' to do so.[65] His interventions on imperial questions caused more controversy when they dealt with conditions in Britain's own colonies. The Archbishop was, like many other Church leaders, concerned about the import of Chinese labour into South Africa in the early 1900s to work under appalling conditions in the Transvaal mines. Although Davidson was careful to make it clear in his pronouncements that he was talking about the moral rather than the political aspect of the subject, his words still attracted sharp criticism. The Archbishop was well aware that imperial issues were politically divisive, and he was cautious about taking too definite a line, particularly after the 1906 General Election returned many Liberal MPs who were critical of British imperial rule across the globe. Davidson had already in 1904 warned the Church against becoming too involved in preparations for a proposed Empire Day, fearing that it would create controversy, and re-enforce the negative views of the Church's critics.[66]

Davidson was nevertheless aware that the success of the Church of England's missionary activities was closely bound up with British imperial power. He maintained a detailed correspondence with Henry Montgomery, who in 1901 became Secretary of the Society for the Propagation of the Gospel and was author of a number of books and articles outlining how colonial Governments could play an important role in fostering the work of Christian mission.[67] Montgomery believed that a focus on mission could energise the Church of England and help to overcome some of its internal divisions in pursuit of a common goal.[68] Davidson's interest in mission work was instead closely bound up with his wish to build closer relations between the various Anglican churches around the world (a subject discussed in the following chapter). Davidson's attitude towards the imperial project during this period was indeed characteristic of many members of the British Establishment. He believed that the Empire provided opportunities for Christian mission that formed part of the 'white man's burden'. He told Convocation in May 1907 that, whilst Britain once brought 'woe' to the 'dark continent of Africa', it was now a source of 'beneficence', adding that imperial rule should be used to improve the lives of the indigenous population.[69] Davidson shared few of the ethical or economic concerns about the Empire sometimes heard on the radical wing of British politics, but nor was he a 'gung-ho' imperialist in the style of Rudyard Kipling or Lord Milner, who were convinced that the Empire could provide a source of renewal of Britain's moral fibre. Imperial matters sometimes raised moral questions for the Archbishop, but like most of his generation he seldom agonised at length about issues of racial equality or economic exploitation. He believed that the spread of Christianity, when combined with benign Anglo-Saxon rule, provided local populations with the benefits of 'civilisation'.

The Archbishop and social and economic questions

The 'Edwardian Crisis' was not simply a conflict over the constitutional distribution of power. It also reflected anxieties about changes taking place in the social and cultural fabric of Britain. The growth of the Suffragette Movement signalled growing questioning of the traditional status of women both at home and in the public sphere. In a similar way, the creation of the Labour Representation Committee in 1900 symbolised determination to obtain greater political representation for the working class *and* a more diffuse challenge to conventional notions of deference and hierarchy. Such developments did not necessarily pose a challenge to the churches in general or the Church of England in particular. They did, though, question many of the assumptions and values of what might loosely be called 'Christian Britain'.[70] Randall Davidson was well aware that these challenges could not simply be denied or defeated. During his first ten years at Canterbury, the Archbishop tried to accommodate both himself and his Church to the forces of change, whilst at the same time seeking to frame a response that recognised their complex and uncertain character.

Davidson struggled when trying to frame his response to the rise of the Suffragette Movement (a subject on which he chose not to speak in the Lords given its controversial character). The issue preoccupied a good number of Church members. The Church League for Women's Suffrage, set up in 1909, soon had more than 100 branches. Yet many other voices criticising female suffrage were also raised within the Church of England. The Archbishop was inundated in the years before 1914 with letters asking him to set down his views one way or another. In 1907, he cautiously told one correspondent that he was 'in favour of the extension of the Suffrage to women, provided some clearer and more consistent scheme can be devised than I have yet seen in print'. He nevertheless refused to sign any declaration to that effect. He also criticised those who believed that it was right to break the law to bring attention to the cause, condemning 'a line of conduct which is absolutely fatal to the fundamental principles of ordered progress and constitutional line of action'.[71] The Archbishop's personal papers show that he followed the whole suffrage question carefully, even whilst refusing to take sides publicly, fearing that such a move might damage the authority of the Church of England by setting it at odds with an important section of public opinion. He also avoided saying much on such questions as the force-feeding of women on hunger strike. Davidson characteristically declined requests to chair public debates on the suffrage question on the grounds that

> I have kept outside this controversy altogether: not because I am uninterested in it or unsympathetic with the aim of the wise-minded among those who are moving for legislation, but because I already have far too many things on hand.[72]

The limited extent of his private sympathy for the suffragettes can perhaps be measured his remark to one (female) correspondent that 'the enthusiasm of good women is apt to lack the kind of balanced judgement which is specially called for in dealing with large political questions'.[73]

The Archbishop's correspondence with the writer and women's campaigner Ethel Smyth, a distant relative who sometimes stayed with him at Lambeth

Palace, revealed his distinct lack of comfort over the whole suffrage issue. Davidson sharply attacked attempts by some suffrage campaigners to disrupt Church services, in an effort to attract attention for their cause, and dismissed the views of those like Smyth who criticised the Church for neglecting 'the greatest moral revolution that has ever happened'.[74] He did maintain a cautious correspondence with Emmeline Pankhurst, when she asked to see him whilst on hunger strike, making clear that he was happy to talk about private spiritual issues but not about any 'public questions'. The Archbishop naturally faced sharp criticism in some quarters for his conservatism, not least when he gave the police permission to arrest one suffragette who refused to leave Lambeth Palace, perhaps unsurprisingly given his distaste for anything that smacked of direct action. A close reading of Davidson's letters suggest that his equivocation on the whole suffrage question was not merely about the rights and wrongs of law-breaking and other forms of drastic public action. He was instinctively hesitant in the face of an unsettling challenge to the orthodoxies of the social and political class to which he belonged. Davidson was, as so often, torn between his desire to respond to the changing demands of the age and his fear of committing himself or his Church to a position that was bound to prove controversial.

Davidson's ambivalence about female suffrage may also have reflected a more diffuse anxiety about the changing place of women in Edwardian Britain. If so, then he was not alone. There were many examples of Edwardian literature that promoted a kind of 'anti-feminism' in which notions of female emancipation were condemned as a form of moral anarchism.[75] Callum Brown has shown how religious literature throughout the nineteenth century typically constructed an ideal of femininity, in which modesty and piety were combined with a ready acceptance of the private sphere of home and hearth as the natural place for a woman.[76] Nor, despite the fact that women formed a majority of most Church of England congregations, were they usually involved in any significant way beyond the work of parish sick visiting and similar charitable work. It is worth noting that Davidson himself was not opposed to efforts to increase the role of women in the life of the Church. He criticised the decision in 1903 to exclude women from voting to select delegates to the first Church Representative Council. And, in the years that followed, he was sympathetic to attempts to involve women more in Church affairs.[77] It will indeed be seen in a later chapter that his stance later brought him into sharp conflict with some leading Anglo-Catholics.

It would be difficult, and perhaps impertinent, to delve into Davidson's private life in an effort to get a more nuanced sense of his views on these issues. His wife Edith, so far as can be judged, seems throughout her husband's long career to have effortlessly played the role of Bishop's (and Archbishop's) wife according to the conventions of the age.[78] Her older sister Lucy did, though, repeatedly fail to abide by contemporary notions of femininity, both in her abrasive manner, and in the intimate relationship she developed in later life with the widow of Archbishop Benson.[79] The scant evidence indicates that Davidson's own tolerance extended even to such an unorthodox relationship, albeit one conducted discreetly, suggesting perhaps both a natural tolerance and a willingness to accept notions of the feminine that were far from common in Edwardian society. When Bishop of Rochester he had also been an enthusiastic supporter of reviving a Deaconess order as a means of promoting 'practical [...] efficiency in poor parishes', although a moment's pause suggests that such words did little more than delineate a distinctive female sphere, characterised by the conventional notion that women's work should focus on improving the situation of the needy. Davidson's views on 'The Woman Question' were, as so often, informed by his instinctive caution on the one hand and, on the other, a recognition of the wisdom found in the maxim that *tempora mutantur, nos et mutamur in illis*.

Davidson was well aware that the development of the labour movement created a powerful challenge to the social and political *status quo*. The Archbishop was instinctively hesitant in the face of a new form of politics designed to advance the welfare and power of the working class. In June 1905, he was asked by the Rev. F. L. Donaldson to receive a delegation of unemployed men, who planned to march to London from Leicester, in order to highlight their plight (they optimistically hoped to be received by the King). Davidson refused, excusing himself by saying that although he sympathised with the plight of the unemployed, he lacked the time to study the whole question. The marchers were widely described in the press as 'pilgrims', reflecting Donaldson's desire to present the scourge of unemployment as a moral issue, and on return home they were greeted by a crowd of 30,000.[80] The letters between Davidson and Donaldson were published, resulting in a good deal of adverse comment on the Archbishop's views.[81] The Labour leader Keir Hardie was particularly scathing:

> The Archbishop [...] said he had to devote seventeen hours a day to his work and had no time left to form opinions on how to solve the unemployment question. The religion which demands 17 hours a day for organisation and leaves no time for a single thought about starving and despairing men, women and children has no message for this age.[82]

Davidson defended himself in his private correspondence,[83] criticising the march for seeking to bring 'pressure to bear upon the public mind', which he thought would do little to advance the cause of the marchers. Nor were Keir Hardie's strictures altogether justified. Davidson strongly defended the Bishops of Southwark and Stepney for speaking out in favour the Unemployed Workmen Bill, which would have provided financial assistance to those without work, telling Hensley Henson (then a Canon at Westminster) that Churchmen had the right to express their views as individuals 'whose position gave [them] means of knowledge'. The Archbishop's concern about unemployment was genuine. But so too was his dislike of any form of demonstration that hinted at a challenge to social and political convention. Davidson was, as always, uncomfortable with a politics that flowed outside the borders of Westminster and London's Club Land. He was not inclined to address the question of whether some form of direct action – strikes, marches – could alone bring about some form of real social and economic change.

The Archbishop was again cautious when serious labour unrest broke out in 1912. In a speech to Convocation, he took his usual line of warning against ignorant comment by those with no specialist knowledge, since the Government alone had the 'high expert knowledge' needed to deal with the situation. He also told his fellow Bishops that Church leaders had over the previous 20 years seen their authority on such issues decline to the point where 'it hardly exists today' (a point that his own regular behind-the-scene interventions into political questions rather seemed to disprove). Davidson was careful when speaking in the House of Lords to avoid such controversial issues as the 1909 Taff Vale judgement (which prevented trade unions from collecting a levy from their members to fund the Labour Party). He was more forthcoming on general questions of poverty. The Archbishop had, whilst Bishop of Rochester, been much affected by the appalling living conditions suffered by many who lived in his diocese. When at Canterbury he routinely gave his support to a range of initiatives designed to help children escape poverty.[84] He also supported clergy who established friendly societies to promote thrift and relieve poverty among their parishioners.[85] The Archbishop even supported attempts to shame landlords of sub-standard properties in an effort to raise the standards of housing in Britain's big cities.[86]

Davidson carefully followed the activities of the Royal Commission on the Poor Laws, which sat between 1905 and 1909, and issued two separate reports once it became clear that its members could not agree on a set of recommendations. The Majority Report assumed that poverty was typically the result of a failure of individual responsibility, or simple bad luck, made worse by various shortcomings in the system of poor relief. The Minority Report, whose authors included the socialists George Lansbury and Beatrice Webb, focused by contrast on the 'structural' character of poverty.[87] When the reports were published, the Archbishop made a long speech in the House of Lords, setting down his views on the problem of poverty. He focused on the Majority Report, and although he ended his speech with a rousing statement that, 'I at least have tried to do my part by calling attention to the need of action in a matter vitally affecting the credit and the well-being of a Christian country', he did little more than summarise the key bureaucratic recommendations made by the reports.[88] He certainly made no attempt to interrogate more fundamentally the causes of poverty.

The Archbishop had long respected the work done by many Anglican clergy, typically from the Anglo-Catholic wing of the Church, to minister to the poor of London and other major cities. Although no radical, he greatly admired Brooke Foss Westcott, his Harrow housemaster and later Bishop of Durham, who co-founded the Christian Social Union (CSU), and became an influential figure in promoting concern about poverty within the Anglican Church (Davidson's wife Edith was a member of the CSU).[89] He did not, though, share the views of Anglicans such as Charles Gore – successively Bishop of Worcester,

Birmingham, and Oxford – who criticised the prevailing economic system for creating huge disparities of wealth. Although the thinking of most members of the CSU owed more to William Morris than Karl Marx, and was often marked by a striking paternalism which assumed that the conditions of the poor could only be improved by their social betters, there was a widespread sense (in Alan Wilkinson's words) that 'economic relations could and should be moralised and brought under political control'.[90] Davidson by contrast saw poverty as a moral challenge that demanded a response as an act of Christian virtue. The Christian socialism of individuals like Gore and Henry Scott Holland, or Walter Frere and his fellow members of the Community of the Resurrection, was alien to the Archbishop.[91] He believed that Christian charity and a more effective system of poor relief could together mitigate the worse of the inequities.

Archbishop Davidson was more comfortable when dealing with social issues that came within the traditional moral purview of the Church. In May 1908, he told Convocation that a 'National Church' had 'a peculiar responsibility' to comment on the 'great moral questions' of the day.[92] The question of Sunday Observance had concerned Davidson since his time as Bishop of Rochester, when he called for Sunday opening of museums and galleries, in order to provide 'respectable' opportunities for improving leisure. By 1905, though, he was deeply concerned about the erosion of 'the treasure and heritage of the day of rest'.[93] In the House of Lords, he spoke in support of a motion enforcing Sunday closing laws, fretting 'that Sunday relaxation [. . .] which has been so long a marked characteristic of English life [is] being seriously imperilled'.[94] Two years later, he joined with other Church leaders in stressing 'the importance of this matter to the well-being of the nation'.[95] In 1908, the Archbishop once again spoke in the Lords in support of action to enforce Sunday closing[96] – a move he said was popular both with the medical establishment and the Labour movement. Davidson usually articulated his defence of the traditional English Sunday in terms of its practical benefit for the working class rather than scriptural authority. He saw both the opportunities for rest and the traditional rituals of Church attendance and family dinner as central to the Christian character of Britain.[97] The British Sunday was not of course a purely Anglican affair. Indeed the emphasis on the Sabbath was even stronger in many Nonconformist churches. The Archbishop was nevertheless convinced that Sunday Observance promoted the social and moral welfare of the whole population and should therefore be championed by the National Church.

The question of Sunday Observance was often bound up with licensing laws (there was a perennial fear both within the churches and beyond that the working classes would use their leisure not for self-improvement but for drinking). The Temperance Movement was closely associated with Nonconformity and its political representatives in the Liberal Party. The interests of the brewers were strongly associated with the Unionists. The 1904 Licensing Bill, introduced by Balfour's Unionist Government, in effect reduced the numbers of pubs but provided generous compensation to licensees who lost their trade. Davidson was strongly committed to 'licensing reformation' as part of a campaign against 'devilry and wrong'. He supported the proposals in the Licensing Bill, including the payment of compensation, but believed that such payments should only last for a fixed period of time.[98] The Archbishop therefore spoke in favour of an amendment in the House of Lords, which stipulated that compensation for a lost licence would end after 14 years.[99] The proposal was rejected by the Balfour Government. Five years later, Davidson supported the Asquith Government's Licensing Bill, which was in turn opposed by the Unionist Opposition on the grounds that the changes it introduced were damaging to the interests of the major brewers. The Archbishop was quite happy, even as head of a Church sometimes derisively referred to as 'the Conservative Party at Prayer', to support measures opposed by most leading Unionists. Although the Anglican Conscience was less distinctive than its Nonconformist counterpart, and certainly far from universally endorsed by all members of the Church of England, it was not altogether absent when social issues were under review.

One of the most controversial social issues faced by Davidson during his first ten years at Canterbury concerned changes to the laws relating to marriage. In 1907, the House of Commons passed legislation permitting a man to marry the sister of his deceased wife, an act previously prohibited both by statute and Canon Law. The issue was the subject of numerous letters in *The Times*, including one from Hugh Cecil bitterly complaining that Parliament was trespassing on the authority of the Church.[100] Other letter writers protested that the new law made women second-class citizens, since it did not touch on the issue of a woman being able to marry a deceased husband's brother.[101] Davidson made a powerful speech in the House of Lords, arguing against the removal of a prohibition on a moral injunction rooted both in scripture and 'Christian experience'. He also suggested,

> It is a matter of common notoriety that the greater number of those who voted for this Bill in the Commons will tell you that they do not really care much about it, but that, on the whole, as the Bill is only permissive, and does not affect many people it is just as well that the permission should be given.[102]

The Archbishop was by instinct critical of such Liberalism in social policy even if it was, as he rightly noted, largely symbolic.

Davidson also opposed the reform of divorce law proposed by the Royal Commission that reported in 1912. The Archbishop was wary of changes to the legal framework regulating social institutions, in part because they seemed to encroach on the moral authority of the Church. He was even more perturbed by the potential threat to the traditional fabric of British society. Davidson was nevertheless ready to temper his opinions and acknowledge the reality of changing social *mores*. The Archbishop had indeed supported the idea of a Royal Commission to review marriage laws within a few weeks of his appointment to Canterbury. Davidson understood that the Church could influence the climate of social regulation, both directly and indirectly, but would be doomed to impotence if it strayed too far from both public and legislative opinion.

Conclusion

Davidson was in a ruminative mood at Easter 1913, dictating a lengthy memorandum looking back over his first ten years as Archbishop. He noted ruefully how much of the 'important work' he had carried out throughout his life had been 'done out of sight, and rather as a quiet helper to other people's effectiveness' – something which he believed had hidden the extent of his influence from many people. Davidson took pride in the way he had advised both Edward VII and George V on sensitive constitutional and political questions. He also believed that his friendships with leading politicians had given him an opportunity to ensure that the Church of England continued to have an influence on important national issues. Davidson was convinced that

> the man who holds the Archbishop's position should have this kind of natural and friendly access to the men to whom is given the responsibility for the nation's affairs. It places not the Archbishop only, but the Church, in quite different relation to public life in its religious and secular aspects. I do not mean to imply that I have used these continuous opportunities with wisdom or effectiveness, but it cannot fail to have done a great deal for [the] bridging of difficulties.[103]

There was perhaps something rather wistful about Davidson's words. He seems to have regretted the lack of public awareness of his role both in the Church of England and British political life, yet he was convinced that his influence was at its strongest when it was most hidden.

Davidson's assessment of his influence has sometimes been taken at face value by scholars,[104] doubtless re-enforced by the voluminous correspondence with leading members of the British Establishment that fills his private papers. The Archbishop's part in managing the tensions that erupted in the Church of England during the years before 1914 will be explored in the next chapter. More relevant here is an assessment of Davidson's success in protecting his Church's influence in public life during the Edwardian era. His experience as a 'courtier-priest' during the reign of Queen Victoria, combined with his extensive work 'behind the scenes' on various questions of Church politics and administration, was not a natural training ground for the skills needed to deal with a more open political environment. Davidson was, though, shrewd enough to realise the pitfalls facing the Church if it simply allied itself with Unionist-Conservative MPs and peers who sought to defend the *status quo* following the election of a new Liberal Government in 1906. The Archbishop understood that the political turmoil and constitutional wrangling that took place in the years before the First World War were symptomatic of bigger changes in British society. In taking this view, Davidson sometimes alienated both senior clergy and Unionist politicians, but he was adroit in understanding that the Church of England needed to change if it was to keep its place in the modern world.

It is nevertheless hard to identify important public questions on which Davidson had a definite or at least measurable impact. The Education Bill proposed by the Liberal Government in 1906 failed because it could not be passed through the House of Lords, rather than through any decisive action by Davidson or the Anglican hierarchy, who were indeed more inclined to compromise than many of the 'diehard' peers.[105] The Archbishop was unable to use his political connections to prevent Welsh Disestablishment. Davidson was certainly confided in by numerous senior politicians on topics of national importance, and he was occasionally used as a kind of unofficial diplomat, charged with facilitating communication between the leaders of the main political parties. It is nevertheless striking how seldom Davidson appears in the memoirs of political leaders when they subsequently recalled at leisure the turbulent politics of the Edwardian Age. As Archbishop of Canterbury, Davidson was treated with great respect by members of the political class. They trusted him and were ready to confide in him as a prominent figure in the British Establishment. But there is little evidence that they saw him as a pivotal figure in the great political dramas of the age.

Notes

1. For a useful overview of the complex identity of 'Christian Britain' before the First World War, see Callum Brown, *Religion and Society in Twentieth-Century Britain* (London: Pearson, 2006), pp. 40–87.
2. For a classic treatment of changing patterns of Church in Britain, see Robert Currie et al, *Churches and Churchgoers: Patterns of Church Growth in the British Isles Since 1700* (Oxford: Clarendon Press, 1977).
3. On the regional dimension of Christian Britain, see Keith Robbins, *England, Ireland, Scotland, Wales: The Christian Church, 1900–2000* (Oxford: Oxford University Press, 2008), *passim*.
4. For two classic discussions of different aspects of the Edwardian Crisis see George Dangerfield, *The Strange Death of Liberal England* (London: Constable, 1936); Samuel Hynes, *The Edwardian Turn of Mind* (Princeton, NJ: Princeton University Press, 1968). For a nuanced critique of the idea of an Edwardian Crisis, see David Powell, *The Edwardian Crisis, 1901–1914* (Basingstoke: Macmillan, 1996); Donald Read, 'Crisis or Golden Age?', in Donald Read (ed), *Edwardian England* (New Brunswick: Rutgers University Press, 1982), pp. 13–20.
5. *Times*, 5 August 1903, Letter by Davidson.
6. *Times*, 15 Dec 1903, Letter by Davidson.
7. *Daily News*, 2 November 1905.
8. *Cambrian News*, 10 November 1905.
9. For a useful discussion of Liberalism and the Liberal Government before 1914, see George Lurcy Bernstein, *Liberalism and Liberal Politics in Edwardian England* (Boston: Allen and Unwin, 1986).
10. *Church Times*, 26 January 1906.
11. For a valuable discussion putting the divisions over education in a broader context, see Machin, *Politics and the Churches*, pp. 248–305.
12. For a dated but lively biography of Asquith (and one that records in some detail his interactions with Davidson), see Roy Jenkins, *Asquith* (London: Collins), 1964). Haldane, perhaps curiously, made no mention of the Archbishop in his own memoirs. See Richard Burdon Haldane, *An Autobiography* (London: Hodder and Stoughton, 1929).

56   *The Edwardian Crisis*

13 D.P. 12, fos. 317–24, Davidson Memorandum, 28 September 1913 (quotation fos. 317–18). For a longer exert from this Memorandum, see Documents Section 1.
14 Lockhart, *Halifax*, p. 157.
15 *Times*, 5 February 1906 (Letter by Davidson).
16 D.P. 309, fo. 33, Davidson to Bishop of Southwark, 5 March 1906; fos. 34–35, Davidson to Ogle, 9 March 1906.
17 D.P. 309, fos. 108–11, Davidson Memorandum, 25 March 1906.
18 D.P. 309, fos. 114–20, Davidson Memorandum, 6 March 1906 (quotations fos. 116–17).
19 *Times*, 11 April 1906 (Letter by Davidson).
20 D.P. 309, fos. 187–88, Davidson to Knollys, 13 April 1906 (quotation fo. 187).
21 D.P. 309, fos. 253–57, Davidson to Edward VII, 23 April 1906 (quotation fo. 257).
22 D.P. 309, fo. 266, Davidson to Bishop of Manchester, 24 April 1906.
23 D.P. 310, fos. 20–32, Cecil to Davidson, 6 May 1906 (including Memorandum).
24 Edmund Arbuthnott Knox, *Reminiscences of an Octogenarian, 1874–1934* (London: Hutchinson, 1935), p. 241 ff.
25 D.P. 310, fo. 36, Davidson to Knollys, 7 May 1906.
26 British Library Western Manuscripts, Campbell-Bannerman Papers, Ad. Mss. 41222, fo. 190 (Davidson to Loreburn, 27 October 1906).
27 For a subtle treatment of the politics surrounding the People's Budget, see Bruce K. Murray, *The People's Budget 1909/10: Lloyd George and Liberal Politics* (Oxford: Oxford University Press, 1980).
28 For a useful if not entirely balanced discussion of this issue, see Norman, *Church and Society in England*, pp. 221–78.
29 On the CSU, see Wilkinson, *Christian Socialism*, p. 42 ff. For a discussion of the theological background to the development of Christian Socialism, see Link-Wieczorek, 'Mediating Anglicanism'. Also see Norman, *Church and Society*, p. 180 ff.
30 D.P. 12, fos. 115–16, Davidson Memorandum 'As to Interview with Lansdowne', 26 October 1909.
31 D.P. 437, fos. 41–2, Davidson to Halifax, 4 March 1910 (quotation fo. 41).
32 D.P. 12, fos. 304–16, Davidson Memorandum, Easter 1913 (quotation fo. 310). For a valuable scholarly edition of this document, along with other useful material about Davidson, see Barber (ed), 'Davidson: A Partial Retrospective'.
33 On Davidson's role in fostering changes in the character of the monarchy, see William M. Kuhn, *Democratic Royalism: The Transformation of the British Monarchy, 1861–1914* (London: Palgrave Macmillan, 1996), pp. 82–111.
34 D.P. 12, fos. 134–41, 'Memorandum of a Conference at Lambeth', 27 April 1910 (quotation fo. 136).
35 D.P. 12, fos. 144–48, Davidson Memorandum, 2 May 1910 (quotation fo. 148).
36 D.P. 12, fos. 342–50, Davidson Memorandum, 16 February 1913.
37 D.P. 12, fos. 161–3, Undated Davidson Memorandum, c. November 1910 (quotation fo. 161).
38 D.P. 12, fos. 165–72, Davidson Memorandum prepared for Bigge, 11 January 1911.
39 See, for example, D.P. 437, fos. 183–4, Bishop of Wakefield to Davidson, 27 July 1911; fo. 207, Davidson to Bishop of Winchester, 29 July 1911).
40 *Parliamentary Debates (Lords)*, 11 August 1911, col. 1059.
41 D.P. 437, fos. 283–4, M.C. Green to Davidson, n.d. (quotations fos. 283, 284).
42 D.P. 12, fos. 317–24, Davidson Memorandum, 28 September 1913 (quotations fos. 318, 319).
43 Among the huge literature on Irish Home Rule see, for a nuanced and rather controversial interpretation, Alan O'Day, *Irish Home Rule: 1867–1921* (Manchester: Manchester University Press, 1998).
44 D.P. 12, fos. 359–65, Davidson Memorandum, 22 January 1914 (quotation fo. 361).
45 On the role of the army in the crisis, see Ian Beckett, *The Army and the Curragh Incident* (London: Bodley Head for Army Records Society, 1986).

46 For Davidson's account of these critical days, see D.P. 12, fos. 393–422, Various Davidson memoranda, 22–4 March 1914.
47 Arno Mayer, 'Domestic Causes of the First World War', in Leonard Krieger and Fritz Stern (eds), *The Responsibility of Power* (New York: Garden City, 1967), pp. 286–93.
48 On the crisis over Welsh Disestablishment, see Machin, *Politics and the Churches*, pp. 305–10. For a fuller discussion, see P.M.H. Bell, *Disestablishment in Ireland and Wales* (London: SPCK, 1969).
49 *Western Daily Press*, 23 April 1911.
50 *Chronicle of Convocation: Convocation of Canterbury (Upper House)*, 30 April 1912.
51 *Times*, 21 November 1913.
52 Davidson, *Character and Call of the Church of England*, quoted in Norman, *Church and Society in England*, p. 277.
53 *Yorkshire Post and Leeds Intelligencer*, 14 November 1913.
54 D. W. Bebbington, *The Nonconformist Conscience* (London: Allen and Unwin, 1982), pp. 106–26; Hughes, *Conscience and Conflict*, pp. 17–45.
55 Among the large literature on the peace movement, including material on the contribution of the Nonconformist churches, see Martin Ceadel, *Semi-Detached Idealists: The British Peace Movement and International Relations, 1854–1945* (Oxford: Oxford University Press, 2000); *Paul Laity, The British Peace Movement, 1870–1914* (Cambridge: Cambridge University Press, 2001).
56 G.R. Evans, *Edward Hicks: Pacifist Bishop at War* (Oxford: Lion Books, 2014), p. 124.
57 G.L. Prestige, *The Life of Charles Gore: A Great Englishman* (London: William Heinemann, 1935), pp. 224–27.
58 Bell, *Davidson*, Vol. 1, p. 481.
59 Bell, *Davidson*, Vol. 1, p. 591.
60 Bell, *Davidson*, Vol. 1, p. 589.
61 Bell, *Davidson*, Vol. 1, p. 587.
62 Alan Wilkinson, *The Church of England and the First World War* (London: SPCK, 1978), p. 22.
63 *Chronicle of Convocation: Convocation of Canterbury (Upper House)*, 30 April 1907.
64 For the classic statement of this position, see Norman Angell, *The Great Illusion: A Study of the Relation in Nations of Military Power to their Economic and Social Advantage* (London: William Heinemann, 1910).
65 *Chronicle of Convocation: Convocation of Canterbury (Upper House)*, 2 May 1907.
66 Steven S. Maughan, *Mighty England do Good* (Cedar Rapids: Eerdmans, 2014), p. 425. For a useful discussion of the close links between mission and Empire during this period, see Andrew Porter, *Religion versus Empire: British Protestant Missionaries and Overseas Expansion, 1700–1914* (Manchester: Manchester University Press, 2004), pp. 282–315.
67 H.H. Montgomery, *The Relation of the Civil Government to Christian Missions* (London: SPG, 1910).
68 On this topic, see Maughan, *Mighty England*, pp. 395–431.
69 *Chronicle of Convocation: Convocation of Canterbury (Upper House)*, 2 May 1907.
70 For a somewhat different view of religious sentiment in the inter-war years, see Callum Brown, *The Death of Christian Britain* (London: Routledge, 2001), *passim*.
71 D.P. 515, fo. 3, Davidson to Miss Gardner, 1 July 1907.
72 D.P. 515, fos. 60–2, Davidson to Chapman, 19 October 1910 (quotation fo. 60).
73 D.P. 515, fo. 47, Davidson to Miss Thompson, 25 October 1909.
74 Bell, *Davidson*, Vol. 1, p. 664.
75 See, for example, Mrs Humphry Ward, *Daphne, or Marriage a La Mode* (London: Forgotten Books, 2013, original 1909).
76 Brown, *Death of Christian Britain*, pp. 58–87.
77 Brian Heeney, 'The Beginnings of Church Feminism: Women and the Councils of the Church of England, 1897–1919', *Journal of Ecclesiastical History*, 33, 1 (1982), pp. 89–109.

78 On Edith Davidson, see M.C.S.M. (Mary Mills), *Edith Davidson of Lambeth* (London: John Murray, 1938).
79 On Lucy Tait and her relationship with the Benson and Davidson families, see Bolt, *As Good as God, as Clever as the Devil*.
80 *Bedfordshire Times and Independent*, 23 June 1905.
81 *Times*, 13 June 1905.
82 Quoted in Wilkinson, *Church of England*, p. 132.
83 Norman, *Church and Society*, p. 257.
84 See, for example, *Times*, 4 May 1907 (letter by G.H.S. Walpole).
85 *Times*, 3 April 1908 (Letter by Davidson).
86 *Parliamentary Debates (Lords)*, 14 September 1909, cols. 1165–68; Norman, *Church and Society*, p. 223.
87 Beatrice Webb, *Break Up the Poor Law and Abolish the Workhouse (Being the Minority Report of the Poor Law Commission)* (London: Fabian Society, 1909).
88 For Davidson's full speech, see *Parliamentary Debates (Lords)*, 15 September 1909, cols. 1195–2017.
89 On Westcott, see Westcott, *Life and Letters of Westcott*. Also see Edwards, *Leaders of the Church of England*, pp. 218–31.
90 Alan Wilkinson, *Christian Socialism*, p. 69. It should be noted that some authors have seen Morris himself as a more radical socialist than often realised. See E.P. Thompson, *William Morris: Romantic to Revolutionary* (New York: Pantheon Books, 1997).
91 On Frere see Benjamin Gordon-Taylor and Nicholas Stebbing CR (eds), *Walter Frere: Scholar, Monk, Bishop* (Norwich: Canterbury Press, 2011). On the Community of the Resurrection, see Alan Wilkinson, *The Community of the Resurrection: A Centenary History* (London: SCM, 1992).
92 *Chronicle of Convocation: Convocation of Canterbury (Upper House)*, 1 May 1908.
93 *Times*, 21 October, 1905 (Letter by Davidson).
94 For Davidson's full speech, see *Parliamentary Debates (Lords)*, 14 March 1905, cols. 1340–48.
95 *Times*, 5 January 1907.
96 *Parliamentary Debates (Lords)*, 17 March 1908, cols. 332–35.
97 On the role of Sunday lunch in the traditional British Sunday at this time, see Brown, *Religion and Society in Twentieth-Century Britain*, pp. 52–4.
98 *Times*, 27 April 1904.
99 For Davidson's speech see *Parliamentary Debates (Lords)*, 1 August 1904, cols. 187–96.
100 *Times*, 22 August 1907 (Letter by Cecil)
101 *Times*, 23 August 1907 (Letter by 'Equal Justice').
102 For the Archbishop's full speech, see *Parliamentary Debates (*Lords), 20 August 1907, cols. 359–66.
103 D.P. 12, fos. 304–16, Davidson Memorandum, January 1917 (quotation fo. 314).
104 Derek W. Blakely, 'The Archbishop of Canterbury, the Episcopal Bench, and the Passing of the 1911 Parliament Act', *Parliamentary History,* 27, 1 (2008), pp. 141–54.
105 On the aristocratic 'diehards', and their place in the wider society, see Gregory D. Phillips, *The Diehards: Aristocratic Society and Politics in Edwardian England* (Cambridge, MA: Harvard University Press, 1979).

3 Archbishop Davidson and the boundaries of Anglicanism (1903–14)

Randall Davidson probably had a better knowledge of the Church of England than anyone else alive when he became Archbishop of Canterbury in 1903. His time at Lambeth Palace as a young Chaplain during the 1870s had given him an understanding of the internal workings of the Church, whilst his six years as Dean of Windsor provided an excellent insight into the relationship between the ecclesiastical and political establishments. As Bishop of Rochester, and then Winchester, he gained experience of the day-to-day challenges of running a diocese. Although Davidson expressed concern about his own 'inadequacies', following news of his appointment as Archbishop, few of his predecessors were as well prepared for the post. Nor, perhaps, were many as aware of its challenges.

The Church of England had, since the rise of the Oxford Movement in the 1840s, faced perennial tension between its 'High' and 'Low' wings (although such labels often concealed as much as they revealed). As an Established Church, issues of ritual and doctrine often spilled over into the public domain, as politicians and lay people sought to assert their views on ecclesiastical issues. The violent riots that took place in the middle of the nineteenth century, directed against the 'hellish' use of altar candles and choirboy surplices, were not repeated during the years leading up to 1900. The question of Ritualism nevertheless continued to create division, leading to many strident protests during the archiepiscopate of Frederick Temple, a stark reminder that the fissures within the Church of England had far from vanished.[1] The rise of a new critical theology that sought to develop Christian teaching in response to advances in science and literary scholarship – usually and not always helpfully subsumed under the term 'Modernism' – was also by the early twentieth century creating tensions within the Church. Disagreement increasingly flared up over such issues as the nature of miracles and the meaning of creedal statements concerning the Resurrection and the Virgin Birth. New divisions emerged and old ones remained unresolved, making the fissures within the Church more complex than ever, as Evangelicals and Anglo-Catholics alike looked with concern at what they considered an abandonment of the fundamental doctrines of the Christian faith.

The first part of this chapter examines Davidson's attempts to manage these tensions within the Church of England in the years before 1914, before going on to review his efforts to build closer ties amongst the provinces of the Anglican Communion. The second part then explores how he sought to develop relations with the various Nonconformist churches, not out of any definite ecumenical spirit, but rather in the hope of promoting a sense of 'good neighbourliness' at a time of sharp divisions over such questions as the funding of Church schools. The most far-reaching efforts to build such links took place in the missionary sphere, where denominational divisions were more fluid, their significance muted in the face of the shared challenge of propagating the gospel under difficult and sometimes dangerous conditions. The celebrated Kikuyu controversy, which erupted shortly before the outbreak of the First World War, nevertheless showed how ecumenical developments far from home could have a disruptive resonance within the Church of England. Davidson was throughout his first decade at Canterbury forced to call on his considerable reserves of tact and patience when seeking to manage the tension amongst Anglicans who held seemingly irreconcilable positions on a whole host of issues.

Ritualism and the question of ecclesiastical discipline

Davidson's long career meant that he was intimately aware of the potential for the Ritual question to create unrest both in the Church of England and beyond. He had been Chaplain to Archbishop Tait during the years following the introduction of the 1874 Public Worship Regulation Act, which was introduced to calm the furore created in parishes up and down the country over the supposed excesses of Ritualism.[2] His subsequent role in advising Archbishop Benson over the prosecution of the Bishop of Lincoln, in 1888–9, had given Davidson still more insight into the political and judicial problems inherent in establishing orthodoxy in matters of liturgy and ceremony. So too had the furore surrounding the case of Father Dolling, which he had been forced to confront soon after his appointment as Bishop of Winchester. Davidson freely acknowledged that the Anglo-Catholic wing of the Church of England contained some of the most energetic clergy, including many who were instrumental in extending the Church's influence into the poorest areas of Britain's biggest cities. Although he had little sympathy for the ritual of High Church services, or with such 'Catholic' practices as the Perpetual Reservation of the Sacrament, he was well aware (as he subsequently wrote) that

> no man with his eyes open can have any doubt that English religion finds natural expression nowadays in a more dramatic, aesthetic, symbolic form than was habitual to a generation ago [...] For old-fashioned Bishops and Deans to decry or gird against the love of ornate services is, in my view, both stupid and mischievous.[3]

Yet Davidson also knew that such practices were looked on with abhorrence by those who considered the Church of England to be a Protestant Church that had turned its back on these things at the time of the Reformation.

The Archbishop was confronted with the Ritual question within weeks of arriving at Lambeth Palace. In March 1903, a 100-strong delegation visited him to complain about the extent of 'novel practices' in many Anglican churches, arguing that they threatened the 'dignified services which have been a source of comfort to Church people for many generations'. Members of the delegation also made the familiar argument that such practices were not authorised by the Book of Common Prayer. Davidson responded by suggesting that there had been a 'marked modification' [i.e. *reduction*] in such practices compared with a few years previously. He also condemned the 'inflammatory character' of much of the recent literature that had been published condemning 'Ritualism' (Davidson doubtless had in mind the writings of W. E. Bowen).[4] The Archbishop was determined to refute the suggestion that the Bishops were remiss in not enforcing ecclesiastical discipline (a Bill was already before Parliament designed to weaken their ability to prevent prosecutions through the ecclesiastical courts). Davidson also defended the clergy against the charge that they were beginning to form a separate 'caste'. The Archbishop did, however, acknowledge that there was a handful of clergy who openly defied Episcopal authority and were 'reckless of the true Church of England spirit'. To the applause of the delegation, he promised that, in such cases, 'I desire and intend that we should now act, and act sternly'.[5] Davidson's address to his visitors represented a masterly attempt to defend a spirit of tolerance, whilst trying to reassure those worried that the Church of England was being hijacked by a particular faction determined to make changes to Church services unwanted by their congregations.

Not all lay pressure was directed towards reining in the 'excesses' of Anglo-Catholic clergy in parishes across England.[6] When Davidson's appointment as Archbishop was announced, he received a characteristically lengthy missive from Lord Halifax, president of English Church Union (ECU), who had over the previous 25 years established himself as the leading lay Anglo-Catholic in the Church of England. Although Davidson had served as Chaplain to Archbishop Tait, who was bitterly criticised by the ECU over the 1874 Public Worship Regulation Act, Halifax regarded the new Archbishop with surprising warmth. He told Davidson that despite the differences in their views, 'I can say with absolute truth that in view of our present circumstances [...] I am unfeignedly glad that you are to succeed to the Primacy' (Halifax told another leading Anglo-Catholic layman, Athelstan Riley, that they should do everything they could to 'make it easy' for Davidson).[7] He then went on to list the problems facing the Archbishop, most obviously the fact that 'that within the Church of England there are practically two religions'. Halifax urged Davidson to pursue a policy of tolerance, so 'that nothing is done by the rulers of the Church to make the recovery of Catholic doctrine and practices more difficult'.[8] The Archbishop's response was diplomatic, noting that he was always keen to hear from Halifax on Church issues, whilst carefully avoiding any commitment to a particular course of action.[9] Davidson was hopeful that he would in the years ahead be able to promote a kind of *via media*, based on a spirit of toleration, that would prevent conflict between Halifax's 'two religions' from exploding into unmanageable conflict.

Davidson was no Erastian,[10] and although he acknowledged that Parliament had both the legislative right and the moral authority to involve itself in Church affairs, throughout his time at Canterbury he sought to maintain the delicate balance between the autonomy of the Church and the rights of Parliament. The Archbishop's political skills were put to the test in 1904, when anger among some Unionist MPs over the Ritual question threatened to create a crisis in Church-State relations. In February, Davidson told Francis Paget, Bishop of Oxford, that there was 'going to be trouble on the Ritual question'. The prospect of a Parliamentary Select Committee calling on the Bishops to give evidence about ritualistic practices was a particular source of anxiety for the Archbishop, who knew that lay interference in the life of the Church would meet with intense resentment among 'the advanced men'. Davidson was also convinced that he was going to face personal attack for not taking the lead in imposing discipline on Anglo-Catholic clergy. Nor were his fears soothed by an interview with Balfour, who noted that Parliament had the right to find out 'what is happening in a Church established by law'.[11] Davidson pursued his usual tactics in the days that followed, consulting widely with a number of Bishops and politicians. As a result of his soundings, he decided to push for a Royal Commission rather than a Select Committee, in the hope that its members would be less likely to pursue their own agendas in pushing for firmer action against Ritualism. Balfour agreed to the establishment of a Royal Commission, although the decision was not universally welcomed in the House of Commons, where a number of MPs demanded that the Government 'introduce legislation for the better enforcement of discipline in the Church of England'.[12] The Prime Minister responded by urging MPs to wait for the report of the Commission before demanding further action.

Davidson was adroit in pushing for a Royal Commission rather than a Select Committee (though Lord Halifax still considered it 'a gross piece of impertinence' and a challenge to the Church of England's spiritual autonomy).[13] The nature of the Commission, with its focus on the careful collection of large amounts of evidence, was less likely to lead to the kind of sharp exchanges that would have taken place in a committee of MPs. Davidson himself sat on the Commission, which heard from dozens of witnesses, before producing its report in 1906. The evidence was exhaustive, and included numerous reports from parishes around England, describing in detail various practices at odds with the 1874 Public Worship Regulation Act. The Commission was chaired by the Unionist politician Michael Hicks Beach, and included a mixture of laymen and clergy, roughly divided between 'Low', 'Broad', and 'High'. Many of the witnesses were members of the Evangelical Church Association, which had for years taken a lead in condemning Ritualism. One witness representing the Association described how he had attended services where the priest wore 'biretta, chasuble, alb, stole, maniple, girdle and amice'.[14] He complained, too, of the burning of incense and the use of candles 'when not required for the purpose of giving light'. Other witnesses from the Church Association complained of services where the Sacrament was reserved and incense burned. The

Commission also considered responses from some of the clergy criticised by witnesses, who typically pointed out that their practices were of long-standing, and authorised by their local Bishop. A number were indignant at having to respond to charges made by some 'anonymous character' who 'might or might not be a parishioner'.[15] Although Davidson served as one of the Commissioners, he was also called as a witness, giving extensive evidence about the historical background of the Ritual question and his understanding of the challenges it raised.

Davidson's evidence was extraordinarily detailed and reflected his preference for measured statement over crude assertion. At the heart of his discussion of the background to the 'present strife' was a claim that there had never been 'complete uniformity' in the liturgical practice of the English Church.[16] Davidson criticised the use of the word 'Ritualism' as 'popular rather than accurate' and, in a masterly attempt at balanced equivocation, suggested that the 'rule of uniformity in public worship' should always be 'interpreted by reasonable men who [recognised] the varying needs with which they need to deal'.[17] He also rejected the argument that the Bishops only acted to suppress Ritualism when the clamour of public opinion left them with no choice. Davidson's evidence was designed to subject an emotionally charged issue to a more dispassionate discourse. He ended his second day of evidence by noting optimistically, 'how hopeful in my judgement is the situation now created by the readiness of people of all sorts to fall back upon principles rather than deal with superficial details of a polemical kind'.[18]

The Archbishop gave further evidence a few days later, drawing on his own experience when serving as Bishop, especially at Winchester, where he had been involved in the conflict with Father Dolling. Davidson once again told the Commissioners that he had never regarded such issues as 'the Eastward Position' or the singing of the anthem 'Lamb of God' during the Eucharist as being matters of 'grave importance', and lamented how certain practices had become associated in the minds of many with particular doctrinal positions or allegiance to a certain faction in the Church. He warned once again of the danger of assuming *any* particular practice was sanctioned by history, noting instead that there had always been a degree of diversity in all forms of divine service.[19] Davidson also reiterated his argument that the Bishops had not taken the issue of discipline lightly, but instead acted in a way that was true to the traditions of the Church of England, which had always accepted considerable latitude in doctrine and practice among its clergy. The final report of the Commission broadly echoed the Archbishop's view that the 'extraordinary revival of spiritual life and activity' associated with the Anglo-Catholic wing of the Church required a degree of 'self-adjustment' to incorporate a range of practices. It also called for 'reasonable elasticity' in the reform of legislation pertaining to the prosecution of clergy who refused to refrain from ritual practices deemed contrary to good order.[20]

The Royal Commission was from Davidson's perspective something of a triumph. A Parliamentary Select Committee would almost certainly have taken a much more adversarial stance, and demanded that the Bishops act to impose greater uniformity upon the clergy. The report of the Royal Commission by contrast managed to remove much of the heat out of the debate, providing latitude for a range of practices to flourish within the Church of England. It echoed Davidson's own instinctive commitment to soothing rather than exacerbating divisions. Although a Liberal Government had taken office by the time the Commission's Report was published in June 1906, the response in Parliament was comparatively muted. Nonconformist Liberal MPs were more worried than their Unionist counterparts about the privileged position of the Church of England in national life rather than the conduct of its internal affairs. Hostility to the principle of Establishment meant that many of them were sceptical about politicians intruding into the religious sphere, preferring to focus on ways of reducing the influence of the Church of England in areas such as education. When tension developed in the Church of England towards the end of 1906 over the use of *The English Hymnal*, which seemed to approve teachings about the invocation of the Blessed Virgin inconsistent with traditional Anglican formularies, the issue had surprisingly little political resonance. Davidson's stout defence of toleration, combined with political changes that shifted attention away from the internal affairs of the Church of England, and towards questions about its role in the life of the nation, meant that much of the sting was drawn from the vexed issue of Ritualism. The controversy that erupted in the 1920s over the Malines Conversations and the adoption of a new Prayer Book nevertheless showed – as will be seen in a later chapter – that anxiety about 'Catholic' practices in the Church of England remained a fraught subject for many years to come.

The challenge of 'Modernism'

Just as the word 'Ritualism' was used in Victorian and Edwardian England to describe a wide variety of practices deemed by some to be inconsistent with the Protestant heritage of the Church of England, so the term 'Modernism' was often employed as a vague description of developments in theology and Bible criticism that seemed to break with traditional beliefs and teachings. The influence of European theologians such as Harnack and Schweitzer on some more cerebral members of the clergy was immense. Nevertheless, as Michael Ramsey pointed out many years ago, the Anglican 'Modernists' included figures as diverse as the Christian Platonist W. R. Inge and the historian and philosopher Hastings Rashdall.[21] Although the formation in 1898 of the Churchmen's Union for the Advancement of Religious Thought might seem to have signalled the emergence of a coherent group of thinkers, there was in reality huge diversity among its members. If there was any connecting theme among the Anglican 'Modernists', it was simply a readiness to re-examine traditional dogmas in the light of new scientific and literary knowledge.[22]

The intellectual character of these debates meant that they never attracted so much public attention as the array of practices typically subsumed under the label of Ritualism. Congregations could see with their own eyes any changes to the pattern of Church services. They were less interested in what could seem obscure intellectual debates about the nature of Christian belief. Randall Davidson was no theologian. The emotions that many individuals invested in the controversies that erupted over the Modernist challenge were largely alien to him. He saw them above all as a potential challenge to the unity of the Church of England. The Archbishop therefore devoted himself to the difficult task of maintaining a balance between competing views, acknowledging the rights of free intellectual inquiry, whilst seeking to keep intact the broad if elusive doctrinal foundations of Anglican belief.

The central figure in the debates over doctrinal orthodoxy was Charles Gore, awkward in personality, yet without doubt one of the most able Anglican theologians of the twentieth century.[23] Gore was appointed Bishop of Worcester in 1902, before going on to serve as Bishop of Birmingham and then Oxford. For some, he was an almost saintly figure, uncompromising in defence of his principles, which included a Christian socialism grounded in his belief that common participation in the Eucharist was incompatible with the social and economic divisions characteristic of modern capitalist society. Others took a less charitable view of Gore. Hensley Henson described him as a natural 'Party leader' who 'had the singular and dangerous power of investing practical policies with the mysterious glamour of moral crusades'.[24] Although Henson was himself no sluggard in attracting criticism from members of the Church hierarchy, there was no shortage of Bishops who shared his opinion of Gore (Gore for his part took a bleak view of his fellow members of the Episcopal bench). Gore had been the leading figure behind the *Lux Mundi* collection of essays, published in 1889, which sought to reconcile traditional Christian teaching with recent advances in scholarship. And yet, despite his earlier efforts to engage with intellectual and scientific change, Gore subsequently became one of the most determined proponents of creedal orthodoxy. In a series of books and essays, such as his Bampton lectures of 1903, Gore set down at length his understanding of how Christ could be both 'supernatural yet natural'.[25] He maintained his belief in the historical truth of the Virgin Birth and miracles. In doing so, he became perhaps the leading opponent of Modernism within his Church. In the words of Henson, 'Gore deliberately set out to make the Church of England a sect', which excluded all those who did not accept a particular interpretation of doctrine.[26]

Davidson and Gore developed a warm but troubled relationship from the moment the former went to Canterbury in 1903. Gore, for all the subtlety of his theology, sought the kind of clarity in matters of doctrine that Davidson believed would create division – division that the Archbishop believed was best avoided through tolerating a range of practices and beliefs. Even before moving to Canterbury, Davidson kept up a detailed correspondence with Gore, gently warning him against seeking definite answers to such vexed questions as the duty of obedience owed by a priest to his Bishop when disagreeing with him on doctrine. Within a few weeks of arriving at Lambeth, Davidson received letters from Gore asking for reassurance that no Bishop would be allowed to ordain a priest 'who did not believe in the Articles of the Creed, particularly the Virgin Birth'. The Archbishop replied that any doctrinal pronouncement by the Bishops on such questions should be carefully discussed in detail in Convocation, since any declaration 'means virtually an addition to our formularies'.[27] Davidson was concerned, as he wrote many years later, that any attempt to lay down firm rulings on matters of doctrine might create 'something of the nature of a schism wherein the Church would [lose] from her active and fully recognised ministry some of the men whom we can least afford to spare'.[28] He was right. Back in 1903, the Archbishop received a long letter from Henson, then Vicar of St Margaret's Westminster, deploring the prospect of 'any doctrinal pronouncement from the Episcopal Bench' that would limit the freedom of the clergy to develop their own understanding of the nature of Christian belief.[29]

Davidson's reluctance to peer too deeply into the beliefs of his clergy was shown by his readiness to ordain William Temple (the son of Frederick Temple and himself a future Archbishop of Canterbury). Temple had as a child assumed that he was destined for ordination, but whilst teaching philosophy at Oxford he developed doubts as to whether any 'men of intellect *can* take orders', even though he was equally convinced that there was a pressing need for 'attack from within the Church on the existing conceptions of religion'.[30] His concerns were prompted in part by the Church's lack of energy in dealing with social problems (Temple shared a version of Gore's Christian socialism – even if he did not share the older man's views on doctrinal orthodoxy). Temple was unsure whether he could be ordained, given that he did not accept in full the affirmations set down in the creeds. In 1906, he nevertheless approached the Bishop of Oxford, Francis Paget, writing that he was 'very tentatively' ready 'to accept the doctrine of the Virgin Birth, and, with rather more confidence, that of the Bodily Resurrection of our Lord'. Paget was unwilling to ordain as priest one who 'stands on such uncertain, precarious, unsteady ground'.[31] There the matter rested for two years. In 1908, though, Randall Davidson took the decision to ordain Temple. He told Paget that Temple had reassured him that his faith was 'a far more genuine and absorbing thing than it was two years ago'. Whilst Temple still acknowledged a degree of 'perplexity' about the Virgin Birth and the Resurrection, he now took a position which Davidson believed was not 'a dangerous one'. The Archbishop acknowledged that Temple did not express himself with 'the distinctness [at least as to detail] which has been usual in Orthodox theology'. He nevertheless went on to add, 'I can see no reason why he shd. not now be ordained'.[32]

Davidson's willingness to ordain Temple reflected his acceptance that a genuine Christian (and Anglican) faith could sustain a good deal of doctrinal ambiguity. Such a position informed the Archbishop's response when dealing with the Modernist question in the years immediately before the outbreak of war in 1914. The catalyst for the most turbulent period was the publication of a number of works – including Henson's *The Creed in the Pulpit* (1912), J. M. Thompson's *Miracles in the New Testament* (1912), and the selection of essays edited by Canon B. H. Streeter under the title *Foundations* (1913) – although the underlying issues had been building up over many years. The nature of the Modernist 'challenge' was as ever very diffuse, but the challenge to Orthodox belief was unquestionable. Streeter noted in his introduction to *Foundations* that he and his fellow authors 'fully recognise the obligations of loyalty to the traditions of the Church to which we belong', but tellingly added that 'we are young men, and our responsibility is of a different kind. It is the responsibility of making experiments'.[33]

Gore was predictably incensed by the expression of advanced views on such questions as the historical truth of miracles, and took the lead in demanding that the Bishops respond to the challenge. Personal tensions may also have played their part (Gore and Henson had clashed a few years earlier, when Henson preached at a Nonconformist service in Birmingham, where Gore was Bishop, against the wishes of the local Anglican priest).[34] Gore demanded that the Bishops issue a declaration on clerical orthodoxy setting down the permissible boundaries of belief. His efforts were not always welcome, even to those who shared his views about the role of the Church in modern society. Henry Scott Holland, who co-founded the Christian Social Union in 1889, warned Gore that 'the method of repressive authority' should only be used 'when all other methods and resources have failed'.[35] Some of his fellow Bishops complained in private about Gore's 'copious [. . .] allocutions' at meetings.[36] The issue of doctrinal orthodoxy continued to torment Gore, made worse when his old friend William Sanday announced that he too had lost his belief in miracles, at least as conventionally understood (Sanday was Lady Margaret Professor of Divinity at Oxford). The Bishop of Oxford considered resignation, and had a lengthy meeting with Davidson, who worked hard to discourage him from leaving his post. Davidson was motivated by his high personal regard for Gore, both as a scholar and a priest, as well as a fear that the departure of such a well-known figure would give the impression that 'the Anglican position' had become untenable.

Gore remained in his post, but the whole issue rumbled on, and by February 1914, it was Davidson who was considering resignation. The dispute had by now become very public, and *The Times* carried a number of letters condemning Gore's position, on the grounds that it would do violence to the conscience of clergy who could not subscribe to a literal belief in every word of the creeds.[37] Davidson was feeling the stress of seeking to reconcile the competing views within the Church of England. When the Bishop of London proposed a draft declaration to be considered by the Upper House of Canterbury Convocation, Davidson wrote to him warning against the danger of any move that might 'render intolerable the position of quite a large group of our best and most thoughtful clergy'.[38] He also hinted that he might resign should the draft declaration be put to Convocation. Gore for his part continued to question whether men who did not believe in the Resurrection or the Virgin Birth should be allowed to take services in which they claimed that such things were true. A compromise was eventually reached, taking the form of a Resolution that referred rather elliptically to the need to maintain the 'Catholic Faith in the Holy Trinity and the Incarnation as contained in the Apostles' and Nicene Creeds', but without spelling out in greater detail the exact nature of what such words meant.[39] The outbreak of the First World War a few weeks later helped to divert attention from what could, at a moment of national crisis, appear to be minor doctrinal matters of limited significance in the greater scheme of things.

The disagreement between Gore and Davidson was at its heart a difference about whether the Church of England should be a 'gathered' or a National Church. The former once told a fellow Bishop that the

> one real function of the Church is to draw lines [. . .] if it is at all true to its traditions and apostolic precedents, it must always appear as a body knowing it has an essential programme to preserve.[40]

Davidson's search for compromise on doctrinal issues was by contrast rooted in his inclusive understanding of Anglicanism. In *The Character and Call of the Church of England* (1912), the Archbishop wrote that the Church was defined by its

> emphasis upon the historic continuity of [our] corporate and organic life. We stand accordingly for a sacramental, governmental, ministerial and even ritual system which, with adaptation to local requirements, has come down to us from Apostolic days. We stand for the unfettered study of Holy Scripture and for its circulation in the vernacular tongue whatever it be. We stand for the liberty of private judgement in the interpretation of Holy Scripture and in matters of faith, combined, as regards our own members, with the definiteness of such actual *credenda* as are set forth in our Formularies. We stand for the right of National Churches to a wide elasticity and variety in system, in ritual and in worship, combined with a general loyalty to the principles and usages which have come down to us from the past, and especially from the first six centuries.[41]

Davidson echoed these words in his address to the Upper House of Canterbury Convocation, in April 1914, when he emphasised the importance of every individual using their reason to interrogate the scriptures and doctrines of the Church as they saw fit. And even if this took an individual

> far from the beaten path [. . .] do not imagine therefore that God has deserted you [. . .] come and be nourished by the Sacrament of His love if you can honestly take it and hold yourself in any real sense a Christian.

The coherence of Davidson's views was not rooted in a particular view of scripture or doctrine. Nor were the different elements necessarily held together in a logical whole. Their coherence instead rested in balancing the claims of reason and experience in a way that acknowledged how permanent truths were remade through the complexity of history.[42] The Archbishop's commitment to holding together the different strands within the Church of England was rooted in his conviction that Anglicanism was, by its history and culture, fluid and broad-minded both in doctrine and outlook.

Davidson and the worldwide Anglican Church: the 1904 visit to North America

Davidson was closely involved in the three Lambeth Conferences that took place in the last quarter of the nineteenth century. He had as a young man participated in the preparations for the 1878 Conference (as Chaplain to Archbishop Tait), before taking a much bigger role in organising its successor ten years later, helping to set the agenda and decide who should speak on particular issues. His involvement was still greater at the 1897 Conference, where he served as Episcopal Secretary. The Lambeth Conferences represented for Davidson something more than an opportunity to use his formidable administrative skills. He was deeply interested in the development of the worldwide Anglican Communion, both in the British Empire and beyond, for he was convinced that Anglicanism possessed an identity in its own right as a distinct branch of the Christian Church. When preparing for the 1897 Conference, he had a long exchange with the Bishop of Albany about the correct relationship between the Church of England and the overseas provinces (Albany was opposed to anything that might 'establish any authoritative relation' between the American Church and the See of Canterbury). Davidson replied that he was firmly opposed to any attempt to turn Canterbury into a sort of Patriarchate, although he did believe that greater leadership and advice was needed by some of the smaller Anglican churches. He also raised the possibility of establishing some kind of 'central tribunal of reference' to deal with doctrinal issues across the Anglican Communion.[43]

The issue was discussed at length at the 1897 Lambeth Conference by a Committee set up to 'consider and report upon the subject of the organisation of the Anglican Communion'. Its report followed Davidson in recommending the establishment of a 'tribunal' to review any questions submitted 'by the Bishops of the Church of England, or by Colonial and Missionary Churches'.[44] In the event, the Conference agreed only to set up 'a consultative body', partly because of concern among the American Bishops of any move that might seem 'to clothe the Conference with even the semblance of authority'.[45] Maintaining the balance between the centripetal and centrifugal forces within Anglicanism was as ever a delicate matter. Davidson himself found the 1897 Conference a slightly dispiriting affair, in part because Frederick Temple behaved with his accustomed brusqueness and lack of tact, but his own interest in the development of Anglicanism across the world subsequently became a major theme of his own archiepiscopate.

It was not by chance that Davidson decided to make a long visit to the USA and Canada in the year after he became Archbishop, for he recognised that the

Anglican Church in North America was becoming increasingly influential in the worldwide Anglican Communion, given the wealth and importance of the region. He was first invited to the USA in the summer of 1903, to attend the General Convention of the Episcopal Church, and was eventually persuaded to make the trip by William Lawrence, Bishop of Massachusetts, who visited London in June 1904. Davidson and his wife sailed to New York two months later, before taking a train to Quebec,[46] where the Archbishop preached in the Anglican cathedral.[47] Three days later, he gave an address in Montreal, where he reflected on the growing closeness of the relationship between Lambeth Palace and the other Anglican churches. He went on to argue that there was a need for 'something in the nature of a central pivot – a pivot which takes the tangible shape as a man, an Archbishop', in order to provide a focus for communication and the development of a 'common life'.[48] Davidson made it clear that he was talking 'of a pivot, not a pope', but such a statement reflected his conviction that the Archbishop of Canterbury had a central role to play in the Anglican Communion, even though he had no formal jurisdiction over the various provinces. He was astute enough to recognise that even the most cautious statement could raise concerns, given the unease at the 1897 Lambeth Conference over the proposal for a 'tribunal of reference', but he was convinced of the need to promote closer relations between the various Anglican provinces.

In a speech in Toronto, four days after his address in Montreal, Davidson reflected on how relations between the Canadian and English churches formed part of the warp and woof of Empire. It was seen in the previous chapter that the Archbishop shared the imperial instincts characteristic of many Britons of his background, and he believed that Anglicanism helped to supplement the 'loyal and fraternal friendship' between Britain and the Canadian provinces. He also drew parallels between the British and Roman empires, with the implication that Canadians and Britons shared a single citizenship, even though separated by three thousand miles of water. In another speech in Toronto, Davidson referred to Britain's 'great Empire', and suggested that its work was a kind of 'sacred trust'.[49] The role played by the various British churches in the development of the British Empire, most particularly through mission work in the non-white colonies, was enormous. The 'white man's burden' often formed part of the ideological justification for colonialism. In Canada, though, Davidson was more concerned with emphasising how Anglicanism formed part of the historical nexus binding together the Anglo-Saxon people. Such views were hardly exceptional. The idea that the white Dominions were in some sense part of a 'Greater Britain', which formed an integral part of the international order, was a commonplace of the time articulated by politicians like Joseph Chamberlain and writers such as Kipling.[50]

Davidson's visit to Canada was generally well received in the country's press, which covered his trip across the country in considerable detail, although coverage in the French language press was predictably less effusive. The Archbishop was wise enough to avoid even the mild imperial rhetoric he had used in Canada when he crossed the border into Maine. He spent two weeks on

Mount Desert Island, giving a number of talks and sermons, as well as attending numerous garden parties and dinners. The Archbishop's rhetoric when talking to American audiences in the weeks that followed emphasised the sense of common identity between 'English-speaking men and women' rather than shared imperial sentiment.[51] He also, when talking to Anglican audiences, spoke of 'the storied past which belongs to us both'.[52] In New York he described his amazement at the pace of life in the city and his fears that modern life might squeeze out any spiritual sense (as a lifelong lover of the countryside, and country sports, urban life was for Davidson always in some sense a part of a modern world with which he was never entirely at ease).

The Archbishop was careful to emphasise when talking to meetings of Episcopalians that he was in the United States 'to learn rather than to speak'.[53] Davidson was well aware that many Bishops in the American Church were sensitive to the suggestion that the Archbishop of Canterbury had any form of jurisdiction over them. His tactful approach was rewarded by the warm reception he received across the Eastern Seaboard, not least when he attended the General Convention of the Episcopal Church in Boston, where his informal manner won him considerable plaudits.[54] He was nevertheless still anxious to emphasise the shared heritage of the English and American churches and, more generally, to stress the affinities between the different branches of the 'English-speaking race', with its common commitment to 'liberty and freedom under wise guidance and control'.[55] The imperial rhetoric visible in some of Davidson's Canadian addresses was replaced by an Anglo-Saxon rhetoric when he travelled south of the 49th parallel.

Davidson's trip to North America was motivated in part by genuine curiosity. He made extensive notes on all that he saw and heard. He met many leading scholars and politicians (and was entertained at the White House by President Theodore Roosevelt).[56] His visit was nevertheless prompted, above all, by his wish to build closer links between the various Anglican provinces. Even before coming to Canterbury, Davidson had maintained a voluminous correspondence with many Bishops abroad. His role at successive Lambeth Conferences allowed him to witness at first-hand the complex process of trying to develop an Anglican identity – on matters ranging from doctrine to foreign missions – without having the machinery or the formal juridical hierarchy to impose order where none was to be found. Davidson was quite genuine when telling his audience in Quebec that the Archbishop of Canterbury should be a pivot rather than a pope. He spent a good deal of his archiepiscopate trying to play such a role, without trespassing on the freedom of the various Anglican churches to make their own decisions.

The Pan-Anglican Congress and the 1908 Lambeth Conference

The 1908 Lambeth Conference, which brought more than 200 Anglican Bishops to London, was preceded by the first Pan-Anglican Congress. The Congress was in part the brainchild of H. H. Montgomery, Secretary of the Society for the Propagation of the Gospel in Foreign Parts, and a former Bishop of Tasmania. Several thousand representatives arrived in London from around the world, along with thousands more from Britain, whilst 17,000 attended discussions and debates in a series of venues across the capital. The Congress received extensive coverage in the national press, and produced a voluminous set of documentation on subjects ranging from matters of doctrine through to economics ('covered the whole range of life as it touches members of our Churches' in the words of one of those attending).[57] The Congress in a sense represented 'an effort at self-realisation on the part of the whole Anglican Communion',[58] that is an ambitious attempt to seek an Anglican identity through discussion and debate rather than through definition by an ecclesiastical hierarchy. The strong lay representation was indeed one of the most striking aspects of the Congress. Davidson's correspondence files show that he followed preparations for the meeting even though he had little official involvement. The Archbishop also attended a number of the discussion sessions and services held as part of the Congress, describing the proceedings at one meeting as 'a week without parallel in our history'.[59]

Although there was a high level of Episcopal involvement in the Pan-Anglican Congress, made possible because so many Anglican Bishops were in London to attend the Lambeth Conference, Davidson seems at times to have been a little uneasy with the ethos and culture of the meetings. He did not contribute much to the discussions he attended. This may in part simply have been a question of time and energy, given the need to prepare for the forthcoming Lambeth Conference. But it may be, too, that he was temperamentally ill suited to appreciate the slightly chaotic ambience that signalled the coming together of the Anglican Communion in its search for 'self-realisation'. Davidson was certainly adept at informality, but it was the informality of the late supper at Lambeth Palace, rather than the more free-form ethos of the Congress. The latter formed part of the changing world that Davidson recognised as inevitable and perhaps desirable – changes that would in Henry Scott Holland's words 'blow away our stuffiness'[60] – but they were not something with which the Archbishop was instinctively comfortable. Nor was he comfortable with the unashamedly radical tone which informed many of the discussions at the Congress about social and economic issues.

Davidson was by contrast far more in his element at the 1908 Lambeth Conference. Henry Montgomery, who was invited by Davidson to attend even though he was no longer a Bishop, recalled how

> the programme [was] drawn up by the Archbishop of Canterbury by tacit consent. There are no rules for it. All depends upon tact. No Patriarchate of Canterbury is acknowledged. Cantuar is simply the Head of the Church in its old home [. . .] Any attempt to dominate other Churches *officially* by the Primate of all England would wreck the Conference [. . .] Archbishop Davidson was so trusted for fairness and impartiality that he won through

miraculously. He used to get up and say, 'We could spend a day over this one resolution. We have six others which must also be passed to-day. Will you trust me? As soon as we rise I will guarantee that I and three or four others (naming them) will do the best we can and report tomorrow morning.' Next morning his verdict was always accepted.[61]

Montgomery was right in suggesting that Davidson sought to manage the Conference through informal influence rather than by asserting an authority he could not formally claim. The delicate question of the organisation of the Anglican Communion was examined by one of the committees set up to review important items of business. In its report, the Committee on Organisation within the Anglican Communion argued that the expansion of the Church around the world meant there was a need for a reconstructed Consultative Committee to provide 'information and advice'. The Committee also cautiously noted that any development of a binding tribunal of reference would 'need to be accepted by all parts of the Communion' (it noted, too, the juridical difficulties that would be faced by such a Tribunal). The members also firmly declared that they were convinced that 'no supremacy of the See of Canterbury over Primatial or Metropolitan Sees outside England is either practicable or desirable' (although they also noted 'the universal recognition in the Anglican Communion of the ancient precedence of [. . .] Canterbury').[62] Davidson himself was happy with such a position. He was quite genuine in believing that the Archbishop should be a 'pivot', and was temperamentally inclined to seek agreement through the gentle exertion of his naturally restrained personality, rather than by any more formal assertion of precedence. The fluid character of international Anglicanism meant that agreement – and even fruitful discussion – always had to be mediated rather than imposed.

The 1908 Lambeth Conference considered numerous issues ranging from 'The Supply and Training of Clergy' through to 'Religious Education in Schools'. One committee examined the impact of recent scientific and philosophical developments on Christian faith, arguing that recent Idealist thought provided a mechanism for countering the materialism of a particular kind of science, and suggesting that much scientific inquiry was itself becoming less infused by an uncritical naturalism. The Committee's report also noted how 'Art' could provide access to truths that could not be captured by a simple empiricism ('beauty depends on mind as much as matter').[63] Another Committee examined the moral foundations of democracy and what would now be called the market economy. The Committee that produced a report on 'The Subject of Foreign Missions' encouraged, among other things, efforts to adapt Christian ritual to local traditions so that the Church did not come to the people 'in a foreign dress'. There was also great emphasis in the report on fostering the self-government of local churches in the various colonies.[64] The Committee on Foreign Missions did indeed avoid the more 'traditional' rhetoric of the white man's burden, still often visible in contemporary writings, including to a degree those of H. H. Montgomery himself.[65] It also considered the vexed problem of relationships between Anglican missionaries in the field and those of other churches – an issue soon to explode over developments at Kikuyu (see the following discussion) – urging cooperation, but also emphasising the right of Christians to be looked after by a minister or clergyman of their own denomination.

Davidson was a constant presence at the Conference, seeking to smooth over disagreements and find consensus wherever possible. The studied informality of proceedings – the Bishops were provided with a smoking room and regularly asked to tea or dinner with the Archbishop and his wife – helped to secure consensus on potentially vexed topics. Of particular interest to Davidson, given his long-standing interest in the Eastern churches, was the report on 'The Subject of Reunion and Intercommunion'.[66] The report noted the growth of friendly relations with the Eastern churches over the previous 20 years,[67] and expressed hope for better relations with the Roman Catholic Church in years to come, although it deplored recent regulations laid down by Rome that a mixed faith marriage could only be recognised if performed by a Catholic priest. The report also discussed the development of relations with the various Protestant churches both in Britain and Europe. There was perhaps something rather formulaic about the Conference Resolution that 'care should be taken to do what will advance the reunion of the whole of Christendom'.[68] The growth of interest in the subject over the previous two decades was nevertheless quite genuine. In the years before 1914, Davidson's own 'ecumenical outlook' – the phrase perhaps hints at something more definite than is warranted – was rooted in his instinctive tolerance on issues of doctrine and ecclesiology. There were nevertheless occasions when he revealed the deeper instinct towards Christian unity that was to become a marked feature of the final decade of his archiepiscopate.

Davidson and the Nonconformist churches at home and abroad

Since Davidson worked early in his career at the heart of the Anglican establishment, both when acting as chaplain to Archbishop Tait and whilst serving as Dean of Windsor, it was not until he became Bishop of Rochester that he began to develop a first-hand understanding of the role played by Nonconformist churches in the cities and towns of Britain (although when still at Windsor he had attended services led by a number of leading Nonconformist preachers). The Diocese of Rochester included large swathes of south London, and Davidson quickly developed a friendly relationship with the leading Wesleyan J. Scott Lidgett, who had recently established the Bermondsey Settlement.[69] Soon after arriving at Rochester, the new Bishop also wrote to the Congregationalist minister J. Guiness Rogers, assuring him of his wish 'to co-operate in all possible ways with fellow-workers outside the Communion of the Church of England'.[70] And, as noted in the last chapter, he attended the funeral of the prominent Baptist C. H. Spurgeon, pronouncing the blessing, an action that caused considerable consternation in some High Church circles.[71]

Although the ecumenical significance of such acts should not be exaggerated, Davidson was by the time he arrived at Canterbury in 1903 committed to working more closely with the Nonconformist churches, even as he sought to defend the influence of the Church of England in areas such as education. It was no easy matter to reconcile these two positions.

The crisis that followed the 1902 Education Act inevitably created tension between the Church of England and the main Nonconformist churches. The Archbishop took much of the flak in the furore over the Act, as well as during the attempts by the new Liberal Government to introduce a replacement following the 1906 election. He nevertheless worked hard to overcome the division between Anglicans and Nonconformists. Davidson tried to maintain good personal relations with Nonconformist leaders, writing to Clifford to congratulate him on the fiftieth anniversary of his pastorate in west London, as well as co-operating with the leaders of other denominations on such questions as Sunday Observance. The Archbishop's relationship with Lidgett was particularly warm, even when marked by disagreement. During the political crisis over the status of the House of Lords, Davidson wrote with remarkable frankness to Lidgett, complaining that Lloyd George was using religion as a way of mobilising support for political change ('this spirit of sheer unmitigated scornful *hatred* [. . .] seems to me to be in the most literal sense the work of the Devil'). Lidgett for his part replied stressing how Nonconformists were intensely 'tenacious of the privileges of the House of Commons', although he added that he would whenever possible work with the Established Church in order to 'seek compensation in wider agreements'.[72] Davidson's appeal to Lidgett reflected his perennial commitment to using his behind-the-scenes contacts to help resolve political and religious conflict. The Archbishop hoped to reduce the bitterness of divisions over the constitutional crisis by preventing it from becoming too caught up in the passions of both religious and political partisanship.

In his letter to Lidgett, Davidson referred to the forthcoming 'great Edinburgh Missionary Conference', which among other things was designed to promote cooperation between Protestant churches at home and abroad on mission questions. The detailed preparations for the Conference were coordinated by J. H. Oldham, a sometime missionary, who was subsequently to become a central figure in the international missionary movement.[73] Also heavily involved in the preparations for Edinburgh was the American Methodist layman J. R. Mott, who later played a major role in the YMCA, winning the Nobel Peace Prize in 1946 for his work. The two men led a deputation to Davidson in the summer of 1909, asking him to address the opening meeting of the Conference. The request posed a significant problem for the Archbishop, who was personally inclined to accept the invitation, but recognised that the prospect of growing cooperation among the various churches would raise anxiety among Anglicans determined to preserve the distinct organisational and doctrinal boundaries of their Communion. It was already widely recognised that denominational boundaries tended to be less rigidly observed in the mission 'field' than at home, reflecting local conditions, as well as a widespread sense among non-Catholic missionaries that their most important task was to evangelise rather than obsess too deeply about questions of doctrine and liturgy. Davidson was concerned that his presence at the Conference might suggest that his 'whole Church was committed'. The Archbishop understood that building relations with other churches could, paradoxically, cause new divisions within the Church of England at a time when the memories of the anger raised by the Ritual question were still strong (ironically some Anglicans who urged greater activity in the mission field did so precisely because they thought it could help create greater unity within the Church of England).[74]

Davidson's papers show that he remained uneasy about what role to play right down to the opening of the Conference. The issue received a good deal of coverage in the press during the spring of 1910, after the invitation to speak was leaked, whilst anxiety continued to be expressed in some quarters that the Conference would deal with issues of 'faith and order' as well as mission. In March, he was still telling Oldham that he would not attend proceedings at Edinburgh, though he was willing to write a letter expressing his support.[75] In the middle of April, he told Cosmo Lang, now Archbishop of York, that he was tempted to go given 'the magnitude of the occasion'.[76] On the same day, he told Oldham that he would address the opening session, adding that he understood he was expected 'to say something on the opening subject which is so large that what is said about it might really consist of general words on the significance and key-note of the Conference'.[77] These words seem striking given Davidson's words when he finally spoke at the Edinburgh Conference in June. Much of his speech was predictable, emphasising that 'the place of missions in the life of the Church must be the central place and none other', sentiments that broadly echoed the words of previous speakers. It was, however, his concluding sentences that created something of a sensation in the hall. The Archbishop told the audience that 'it may be that [...] there be some standing here tonight who shall not taste of death till they see the Kingdom of God come with power'.[78] His words, with their echo of Matthew 16:28, seemed to imply that greater cooperation in the missionary sphere could transform inter-Church relations and bring about a fundamental change in the spiritual condition of humanity.

One of those present at the Edinburgh Conference later wrote that

> it seemed almost as if the speaker himself stood before his own word as one taken by surprise. For one supreme moment, it seemed, God had stood forth nakedly revealed, and had spoken in Him who first spoke those words and now lives in the Divine glory.[79]

The same author rightly noted that Davidson was not known for dramatic pronouncements or flowery rhetoric. The Archbishop was certainly not one to be carried away by the occasion. The moment passed, leaving the audience somewhat perplexed, and the Conference continued over the coming days to find ways of building relations between missionaries based on 'a deep and real unity of aim and purpose'. It may be that Davidson was not fully aware of the dramatic nature of his words (although the clear Biblical resonance makes that seem unlikely). His words may instead have reflected his sense both of the importance of evangelism and the consequences that missionary work could have on relations between the churches. Davidson's address was striking precisely because it was so out of character. In reality, of course, missionary zeal could never alone overcome division between churches. It was this harsh truth that became clear a few years later, when the Archbishop had to deal with the Kikuyu crisis, which erupted when developments in Africa raised controversial questions about the relationship between Anglican missionaries and those from other major denominations. Davidson's words in Edinburgh nevertheless provide a rare clue that, beyond the Archbishop's perennial caution and focus on practical questions, lay a deeper if seldom expressed sense of the transformative power of the gospel.

The basic story of the Kikuyu crisis of 1913–14 can be briefly told. In the summer of 1913, W. G. Peel and J. J. Willis, Bishops of (respectively) Mombasa and Uganda, attended an inter-denominational Communion Service in the Church of Scotland's Kikuyu parish (an area that forms part of modern-day Kenya). The service took place following a conference to discuss ways of promoting closer cooperation between the different missionary organisations in East Africa. Although the proposals allowed for each missionary society joining the proposed Federation to maintain its autonomy, they also permitted church members to take Communion at the services of other denominations when they were temporarily resident outside their own area. The planned Federation would also allow ministers and clergy to preach in one another's churches (there was talk, too, of the need for a common form of service to be used on occasions when members of different churches came together).

These proposals were deeply opposed by the Anglo-Catholic Bishop of Zanzibar, Frank Weston, who announced that if the details of what took place at Kikuyu were confirmed, then his own diocese would end Communion with the dioceses of Uganda and Mombassa. Weston was, in the words of one man who knew him, a veritable 'saint', devoid of racial prejudice, and committed to the spiritual and material welfare of those he lived among. And, like many such people, he was also 'difficult to manage and perhaps sometimes hard to endure'.[80] Weston was certainly not a man willing to compromise on what he saw as matters of principle. In September 1913, he took his complaint to the Archbishop of Canterbury, denouncing the action of Peel and Willis as heretical and schismatic, and demanding that Davidson call together a jury of Bishops to hear the case. He also wrote a pamphlet publicly setting down his criticisms of the Kikuyu proposals as incompatible with the traditions and character of Anglicanism.[81]

The Kikuyu case came to prominence at a time when the whole question of 'Modernism' was creating division within the Church of England, with the result that, what at first seemed like a distant issue in a remote part of Empire, rapidly became a *cause célèbre*. Weston was something of a protégé of Gore, as well as a sharp critic of Streeter's *Foundations*,[82] and he was convinced that any form of intercommunion with non-Episcopal churches was incompatible with Anglican tradition and ecclesiology ('on earth the local Bishop is our link with the Catholic Church'). The Kikuyu controversy was also discussed at length in the secular press, particularly among 'letters to the editor', evidence perhaps of how the affairs of the Established Church continued to play a major part in the life of the nation. The prominent Anglo-Catholic Athelstan Riley, who had previously been closely involved in moves to build closer links between the Church of England and the Roman Catholic and Orthodox churches, argued in a letter to *The Times* that many like himself could not surrender the 'fundamental tenet [. . .] that Episcopacy is necessary to a Church'.[83] Others responded by pointing out that the Church of England had for a long time not forbidden Communion to Nonconformists – and had indeed for a time in the seventeenth century actually supported tough penalties on those who abstained.[84]

Many of the issues raised by the meeting at Kikuyu were not new. There had already been a number of cases back in Britain of Anglican clergy preaching in Nonconformist places of worship. The Lambeth Conference of 1908 had, at least rhetorically, emphasised the need to work for Christian unity. So too had the 1910 Edinburgh World Missionary Conference. Indeed, the Upper House of Canterbury Convocation had discussed in 1911 the Bishop of Hereford's invitation to Christians of different denominations to a shared Communion Service (a decision that Davidson gently deprecated, sympathising with the impulse, but fretting that it might crack the 'thin ice' trodden by those who desired better relations between the churches).[85] The Kikuyu controversy certainly represented a defeat for those, like Henry Montgomery, who hoped that the development of Anglicanism in the Empire might provide a foundation for overcoming the old antagonism between Evangelicals and Anglo-Catholics.[86] The real source of the controversy rested, however, on a much deeper uncertainty about how Anglicanism should define itself in relation both to its own traditions and the other main churches.

Davidson was as ever 'anxious to have the facts' before deciding how to proceed.[87] The distances involved and the poor communications in Africa meant, as he wrote to Weston in early October 1913, that 'the action of the two Bishops [might not be] what you suppose it to have been'.[88] Charles Gore at Oxford also tried to ease Weston's concerns, perhaps rather surprisingly, and pointed out that there was no legal basis for having the issue discussed by a jury of provincial Bishops since the missionary dioceses came directly under the authority of Canterbury.[89] The Archbishop himself eventually asked Weston to return to London for discussions, although he was beaten there by Willis, who met with Davidson and persuaded him that the scheme for some kind of Federation scheme was in itself reasonable (although the two men disagreed on whether it could ever be right to invite members of non-Episcopal churches to an Anglican Communion Service). Gore by this time was becoming increasingly concerned that the Kikuyu principles would, if accepted, weaken the Church of England (he noted in November 1913 that Weston was 'quite right' in protesting against 'indiscriminate Communion').[90] Davidson was not personally much exercised by developments at Kikuyu but, as he told one correspondent, there were bigger issues at stake which he could not ignore:

> Our thoughts cannot be limited to the Mission Field. We are face to face with intense difficulties on the whole subject of Re-union and the indirect result of action taken in a particular Diocese may be considerable for good or ill.[91]

When Davidson and Weston met in London, in February 1914, the Archbishop found the Bishop of Zanzibar curiously inconsistent in his views, although 'delightfully loyal [. . .] and frank'. The Archbishop made it clear, though, that he would not allow any 'trial' of Peel and Willis for heresy, but would instead refer the case to the Consultative Committee originally set up at the 1897 Lambeth Conference. Weston predictably deprecated such a move, given that the scope and authority of the Consultative Committee remained largely untested. Davidson was for his part irritated at Weston's continued public pronouncements, wishing that he would instead spend his time 'quietly thinking over everything' (he told the Bishop of Rochester that he wished it was possible to put a 'padlock on the tongue' of those who insisted on talking and writing about Kikuyu).[92] He also arranged a meeting between Weston and Willis in a half-successful attempt to resolve the worst of the tension. The Archbishop was unhappy about the coverage of the whole affair in the secular and religious press, fearing that it highlighted division within the Church of England at a time when it needed to assert its unity as the Established Church.[93] He was also worn down by the numerous letters and memoranda he received on the issue, including one from Hugh Cecil, who argued that the Kikuyu proposals were the product of a Modernism 'utterly destructive' to the Church (Lord Halifax was by contrast unusually quiescent about the whole issue).[94] Davidson replied mildly that he thought the proposals might be evidence that the Nonconformist denominations were becoming more 'Churchy'.[95] He also recognised – as so often before – that any attempt to set down binding decisions on questions of doctrine would serve to make divisions worse. The Consultative Committee finally met at the least auspicious time possible, the end of July 1914, just as Europe was sliding into war. The conflict at least ensured that public debate over Kikuyu faded rapidly in the face of more pressing problems.

It was not until the spring of 1915 that Davidson found the time to publish a more considered statement. In his short book *Kikuyu*, the Archbishop noted that such important questions required a 'quietness of thought' that had been lost among the clamour of the 'controversialists'.[96] He carefully reviewed the development of the whole affair, describing how the Consultative Committee had worked through a huge pile of evidence, as well as noting some of the legal problems raised by the fact that missionary Bishops like Weston and Willis worked in areas where there was no formal Anglican province. At the heart of Davidson's judgement was the search for a balance between encouraging inter-denominational cooperation in the mission field and maintaining Anglican identity and teachings. He suggested that many of the *desiderata* explored by those who met in Kikuyu could be secured by cooperation rather than federation, whilst still holding out the prospect of 'ultimate union in a Native African Church'.[97] Davidson also sought to remove much of the 'sting' from the Kikuyu controversy by noting that the two Anglican Bishops involved in the original Communion Service had no intention of paving the way for some grander scheme of intercommunion ('a spontaneous act of devotion to their Lord').[98] He concluded with a gentle warning against 'such services as the closing service at Kikuyu' (an approach that echoed his restrained rebuke to the Bishop of Hereford in Convocation four years earlier).[99] Davidson's short book reflected his commitment to an Anglican faith that sought to avoid defining itself in precise doctrinal terms. The public response to its publication was muted at a time when the slaughter on the Western Front put into perspective the issues raised by the desire of two Anglican Bishops, in a distant part of East Africa, to work more closely with their fellow Christians.

There is – as hinted at earlier – a danger in speaking too definitely of Davidson's 'ecumenical outlook' in the years before 1914. This was partly a matter of ecclesiastical politics. The Archbishop knew perfectly well that those who sought closer relations with the Orthodox and Roman Catholic churches, like Lord Halifax and Athelstan Riley, came from the Anglo-Catholic wing of the Church of England: their activities were prompted in large part by a desire to assert the Catholicity of Anglicanism. In a similar way, those like Hensley Henson, who were more committed to developing closer links with the main Nonconformist churches, were typically determined to emphasise how the Church of England was a Protestant Church that owed its origins to the Reformation. Davidson's commitment to building better relations with other churches, both at home and abroad, was perfectly genuine. He was instinctively sceptical about the way in which intricate questions of doctrine were used by some Anglicans as a means of setting themselves apart from other Christian denominations. It was only with First World War, though, that Davidson's ecumenism moved beyond a general commitment to building better relations with non-Anglican churches towards a more definite desire to look beyond the divisions of the past.

Conclusion

There is perhaps a danger when focusing on such controversial issues as the Kikuyu controversy, or the Parliamentary crisis of 1909–11, in forgetting how much of Davidson's time was spent on more routine issues.[100] His voluminous correspondence files show that the Archbishop attempted to maintain a detailed knowledge both of developments in the 'grass-roots' of his Church as well as the country as a whole. In the years before 1914, he was less inclined to delegate much of this routine work than he was in the later part of his archiepiscopate (although a good deal of the routine work in the Canterbury diocese was carried out by the suffragan Bishops of Dover and Croydon). Davidson was temperamentally ill equipped to understand the strong passions expressed on religious and political questions by laymen like Hugh Cecil and Lord Halifax or clergymen such as Frank Weston and Charles Gore. And yet he was able to appreciate both the depth of their convictions and the foundations of their views. His search for compromise on issues of controversy – the pursuit of a *via media* – was not simply a matter of convenience. Nor was it just an acknowledgement of the fact that the Church of England by its very nature included people of widely differing opinions on matters both secular and sacred. Davidson's pragmatism was also rooted in a deeper sense that controversialist positions often reflected a failure to take a rounded view of a topic. He sought compromise on the assumption that sensible people of good will would, if they thought long and hard, realise that the differences between them were often illusory.

Davidson's personality played an important part in allowing him to mediate on sensitive questions concerning both politics and religion. It was not simply that his own instinctive tolerance enabled him to build close relations with individuals holding views that were very different from his own. He was also effective at winning the trust of those he met. The memoir literature is full of accounts by clergy and lay people alike recalling with fondness the informal atmosphere of a private dinner or afternoon meeting at Lambeth Palace. The Archbishop was seldom described as saintly by those who met him. Nor was he praised for his learning or charisma (one Canadian newspaper described him in 1904 as 'not an imposing-looking man, and his appearance is neither decorative nor impressive').[101] His lack of pomposity and self-regard nevertheless meant that he was adept at using the authority of his office in a way that allowed him to respond to the challenges facing his Church and his country in the years before 1914. There were certainly times when, to quote one of his early biographers, his belief in 'the power of negotiation' was weakened by his failure to find in others the 'sweet reasonableness which he himself possesses'.[102] And, perhaps more importantly, the challenge of reconciling the forces of change with the traditions of the past was often simply too great to be achieved through the process of discussion. Archbishop Davidson's personal disposition nevertheless meant that he was remarkably adept during his first ten years at Canterbury in managing the divisions within the Church of England, as well as maintaining its authority at a time when it faced considerable threats to its position in national life. The outbreak of war in 1914, and the cataclysm that followed, was to pose new challenges both for the Archbishop himself and the Church he led.

Notes

1 For a useful discussion to the background of these tensions, see the discussions in Bentley, *Ritualism and Politics in Victorian Britain*; Hinchliff, *Archbishop Temple*. Also see, Martin Wellings, *Evangelicals Embattled: Responses of Evangelicals to Ritualism. Darwinism and Theological Liberalism, 1890–1930* (Cumbria: Paternoster Press, 2003).
2 For Davidson's unconvincing defence of Tait's handling of the ritual question, see Davidson and Benham, *Life of Archibald Tait*, Vol. 2, pp. 186–266.

3 D.P. 12, fos. 317–24, Davidson Memorandum, 28 September 1913 (quotation fos. 320–21).
4 W.E. Bowen, *Contemporary Ritualism: A Volume of Evidence* (London: Spottiswoode, 1902).
5 *Times*, 12 March 1903.
6 For a valuable account of developments in several parishes influenced by the Anglo-Catholic movement, see Michael Yelton, *Outposts of the Faith: Anglo-Catholicism in Some Rural Parishes* (Norwich: Canterbury Press, 2009).
7 Lockhart, *Halifax*, p. 140.
8 D.P. 5, Letter 16, Halifax to Davidson, 20 January 1903.
9 D.P. 5, Letter 17, Davidson to Halifax, 31 January 1903.
10 For a somewhat different view, see Adrian Hastings, *A History of English Christianity, 1920–1985* (London: Fount, 1986), p. 60.
11 Bell, *Davidson*, Vol. 1, p. 454 ff.
12 *Parliamentary Debates (Commons)*, 16 March 1904, col. 1263, Question by David Maciver.
13 Lockhart, *Halifax*, p. 143.
14 *Minutes of Evidence Taken Before the Royal Commission on Ecclesiastical Discipline*, Vol. 1, 5410, Evidence by W.H. Bond (4 April 1904).
15 *Minutes of Evidence*, Vol. 1, 7089, Letter by Rev E.G.L. Mowbray (Edmonton), 9 April 1904.
16 *Minutes of Evidence*, Vol. 2, 12849, Evidence by Davidson, 2 February 1905.
17 *Minutes of Evidence*, Vol. 2, 12850, Evidence by Davidson, 2 February 1905.
18 *Minutes of Evidence*, Vol. 2, 12962, Evidence by Davidson, 3 February 1905.
19 *Minutes of Evidence*, Vol. 2, 13222, Evidence by Davidson, 10 February 1905.
20 *Report of the Royal Commission on Ecclesiastical Discipline*, Cd 3040 (1906), p. 76.
21 Ramsey, *An Era in Anglican Theology*, p. 66.
22 For a useful broad discussion see Alan M.G. Stephenson, *Rise and Decline of English Modernism: The Hulsean Lectures, 1979–80* (London: SPCK, 1984).
23 On Gore's theology, see James Carpenter, *Gore: A Study in Liberal Catholic Thought* (London: Faith Press, 1960); for an accessible collection of Gore's writings, see Peter Waddell, *Charles Gore: Radical Anglican* (Norwich: Canterbury Press, 2014). See, too, Link-Wieczorek, 'Mediating Anglicanism'.
24 Hensley Henson, *Retrospect of an Unimportant Life* (London: Oxford University Press, 1942–50), 3 vols. Vol. 1, p.156.
25 T.C. Fry (ed.), *Why We Christians Believe in Christ: Bishop Gore's Lectures Shortened for Popular Use* (London: John Murray, 1904).
26 Quoted in Waddell, *Charles Gore*, p. xxxiii.
27 Bell, *Davidson*, Vol. 1, pp. 396–7.
28 D.P. 12, fos. 327–40, Davidson Memorandum, January 1917 (quotation fo. 329). A scholarly edition of memorandum can also be found in Barber (ed), 'Partial Retrospective', pp. 428–38.
29 Henson, *Retrospect*, Vol. 1, p. 74.
30 Iremonger, *William Temple: Archbishop of Canterbury* (London: Oxford University Press, 1948), p. 98.
31 Iremonger, *Temple*, 109. See, too, Kent, *William Temple*, pp. 13–14.
32 Iremonger, *Temple*, pp. 115–7.
33 B.H. Streeter (ed), *Foundations: A Statement of Christian Belief in Terms of Modern Thought* (London: Macmillan), p. x.
34 Henson, *Retrospect*, Vol. 1, pp. 92–6; Prestige, *Gore*, pp. 305–7.
35 Prestige, *Gore*, p. 348.
36 Bell, *Davidson*, Vol. 1, p. 673.
37 See, for example, *Times*, 5 February 1914 (Letter by Rashdall); 20 April 1914 (Letter by Sanday).
38 Bell, *Davidson*, Vol. 1, p. 676.
39 *Chronicle of Convocation: Convocation of Canterbury (Upper House)*, 29 April 1914.

40 Prestige, *Gore*, pp. 244–5.
41 Davidson, *Character and Call of Church of England*, p. 46. For a longer exert, see Documents Section 1.
42 *Chronicle of Convocation: Convocation of Canterbury (Upper House)*, 30 April 1914.
43 Bell, *Davidson*, Vol. 1, pp. 300–2.
44 *The Six Lambeth Conferences, 1867–1920* (London: SPCK, 1929), 1908 Conference, pp. 212–4.
45 Alan M.G. Stephenson, *Anglicanism and the Lambeth Conferences* (London: SPCK, 1978), pp. 104–5.
46 *New York Times*, 28 August 1904.
47 For Davidson's major sermons and addresses during his North America trip, see Randall Davidson, *The Christian Opportunity* (London: Macmillan, 1904).
48 Davidson, *Christian Opportunity*, p. 46. For a fuller version of Davidson's talk, see Documents Section 1.
49 Davidson, *Christian Opportunity*, p. 85.
50 For a discussion on this theme, see Duncan Bell, *The Idea of Greater Britain: Empire and the Future of World Order, 1860–1900* (Princeton, NJ: Princeton University Press, 2007).
51 Davidson, *Christian Opportunity*, p. 107
52 Davidson, *Christian Opportunity*, p. 127
53 Davidson, *Christian Opportunity*, p. 165.
54 For descriptions of the reception of the Archbishop in the USA see, for example, *Evening Star*, 26 September 1904; *New York Times*, 28 September 1904; *Brooklyn Daily Eagle*, 6 October 1904.
55 Davidson, *Christian Opportunity*, p. 184.
56 *The Inter-Ocean*, 25 September 1904.
57 W.E. Gibraltar, 'The Pan-Anglican Congress', *The Irish Church Quarterly*, 1, 4 (1908), pp. 274–90. For a characteristically highly coloured view of the Congress, see Henry Scott Holland, *A Bundle of Memories* (London: Wells, Gardner, Darnton, 1915), pp. 231–41.
58 Gibraltar, 'Pan-Anglican Congress', p. 274.
59 *Aberdeen Journal*, 25 June 1908.
60 Scott Holland, *Bundle of Memories*, p. 236.
61 M.M., *Bishop Montgomery: A Memoir* (London: SPG, 1933), p. 77.
62 *Six Lambeth Conferences*, 1908 Conference, pp. 417–8.
63 For a copy of the report, see *Six Lambeth Conferences*, 1908 Conference, pp. 338–47.
64 For a copy of the report, see *Six Lambeth Conferences*, 1908 Conference, pp. 372–82.
65 See H.H. Montgomery, *Christian Missions in the Far East* (London: SPCK, 1905); H.H. Montgomery, *Service Abroad* (London: Longmans, Green & Co, 1910).
66 For a copy of the report, see *Six Lambeth Conferences*, 1908 Conference, pp. 420–39.
67 For a summary of these developments see Geffert, *Eastern Orthodox and Anglicans*, pp. 9–29; Michael Hughes, 'The English Slavophile: W.J. Birkbeck and Russia', *Slavonic and East European Review*, 82, 3 (2004), pp. 680–706. Also see the chapters by George Florovsky and Nicolas Zernov in Ruth Rouse and Stephen Neil, *A History of the Ecumenical Movement, 1517–1948* (London: SPCK, 1967); Nicolas Zernov, *Orthodox Encounter: The Christian East and the Ecumenical Movement* (London: James Clarke and Co, 1961), pp. 132–56.
68 *Six Lambeth* Conferences, 1908 Conference, p. 331 (Resolution 58).
69 On Lidgett, see Alan Turberfield, *John Scott Lidgett: Archbishop of Methodism?* (Peterborough: Epworth Press, 2003).
70 Bell, *Davidson*, Vol. 1, p. 213.
71 *Pall Mall Gazette*, 11 Feb 1892.
72 Bell, *Davidson*, Vol. 1, pp. 599–602.
73 On Oldham, see Keith Clements, *Faith on the Frontier: A Life of J.H. Oldham* (London: Bloomsbury, 1999).
74 Maughan, *Mighty England*, p. 412 ff.
75 D.P. 269, fo. 55, Davidson to Oldham, 8 March 1910.

84 *The boundaries of Anglicanism*

76 D.P. 269, fo.66, Davidson to Lang, 18 April 1910.
77 D.P. 269, fos. 67–9, Davidson to Oldham, 18 April 1910 (quotation fo. 67).
78 *Times*, 15 June 1910. The paper did not quote the more dramatic of Davidson's words, perhaps raising the prospect that for some present they did not seem as startling as they did to others. Also see Clements, *Oldham*, pp. 90–2; Brian Stanley, *The World Missionary Conference: Edinburgh 1910* (Grand Rapids: MI: Eerdmans 2009), pp. 1–3
79 W.H.T. Gairdner, *Edinburgh 1910: An Account and Analysis of the Edinburgh Missionary Conference* (Edinburgh: Oliphant, Anderson and Ferrier, 1910), p. 44.
80 Dark, *Davidson*, p. 135. For a biography of Weston, see H. Maynard Smith, *Frank, Bishop of Zanzibar: Life of Frank Weston, D. D., 1871–1924* (London: SPCK, 1926).
81 Frank Weston, *The Case Against Kikuyu: A Study in Vital Principles* (London: Longmans, 1914).
82 Prestige, *Gore*, p. 358.
83 *Times*, 3 January 1914 (Letter by Riley).
84 *Times*, 24 December 1913 (Letter by H.A. Wilson).
85 *Chronicle of Convocation: Convocation of Canterbury (Upper House)*, 4 May 1911. See, too, D.P. 261, fos. 60–4, Davidson to Percival, 15 May 1911.
86 Maughan, *Mighty England*, pp. 436–7.
87 D.P. 226, fo. 15, Davidson to Bardsley, 26 September 1913.
88 Bell, *Davidson*, Vol. 1, p. 695
89 Prestige, *Gore*, p. 359.
90 D.P. 226, fos. 22–3, Gore to Bishop of Winchester, 1 November 1913 (quotation fo. 22).
91 D.P. 226, fos. 86–9, Davidson to Bishop Tugwell, 25 November 1913 (quotation fo. 86). For a fuller version of this letter see Documents section 6.
92 D.P. 226, fo. 186, Davidson to Bishop of Rochester, 23 December 1913.
93 See, for example, *Church Times*, 2 and 9 January 1914 (various letters). *The Times* published sixteen letters on the subject between January and March 1914, along with two long editorials on 9 January and 10 February.
94 D.P. 227, fos. 226–38, Hugh Cecil Memorandum on 'The Kikuyu Question', 30 April 1914; Lockhart, *Halifax*, pp. 233–4.
95 D.P. 227, fos. 239–40, Davidson to Cecil, 23 April 1914 (quotation fo. 239).
96 Randal Davidson, *Kikuyu* (London: Macmillan, 1915), pp. 1–2.
97 Davidson, *Kikuyu*, p. 23.
98 Davidson, *Kikuyu*, p. 33.
99 Davidson, *Kikuyu*, p. 36.
100 For a useful account of Davidson's working day, see Harold Spender, 'The Primate of All England: An Impression', *Pall Mall Magazine*, 41, 182 (1908), pp. 647–62 (for a longer extract from this article see Documents Section 2); Charles T. Bateman, 'An Archbishop's Busy Life', *Quiver*, 47, 12 (1912), pp. 1,096–1,104.
101 *Ottawa Journal*, 29 August 1904.
102 Dark, *Davidson*, p. vii.

4 Archbishop Davidson and the First World War (1914–1918)

On 23 July 1914, the Chancellor of the Exchequer David Lloyd George told the House of Commons that relations with Germany were 'much better than they were a few years ago'. Despite the murder of Archbishop Franz Ferdinand in Sarajevo, three weeks before, there was still widespread confidence in Britain that conflict could be avoided. And yet just 12 days later, the Government of Herbert Asquith declared war, the last piece in a jigsaw that saw a minor crisis in the Balkans erupt into a continental conflagration.[1] Archbishop Davidson was, like so many, taken by surprise at the speed with which the crisis engulfed Europe. Davidson noted in a sermon just two days before Britain entered the war that, 'This thing which is now astir in Europe is not the work of God but of the devil'.[2] Yet he still refused to sign any of the numerous memorials that were being circulated demanding that Britain stay out of the conflict, partly to avoid being drawn into political controversy, but also because he was still hopeful that the Government would be able to keep the country at peace.

The Archbishop, like most of his compatriots, could never have imagined the scale and character of the war that raged over the following four years. The slaughter on the Western Front combined the culture of medieval brutality with the power of modern technology. The mobilisation of the Home Front to support 'total war' created changes that fundamentally affected the social and political character of British society. The First World War also transformed the pattern of global politics, as three empires collapsed, and a fourth, Germany, was subjected to the crippling demands of the Versailles Peace Treaty. Although it may be too simplistic to see the conflict of 1914–18 as a deep rupture in the character of Britain's development, it both accelerated and provoked change in areas ranging from culture to politics, as well as transforming the world beyond Britain's shores.

The outbreak of the First World War posed enormous challenges to the Church of England. The Church needed to respond to the needs of the millions of men who found themselves in khaki.[3] Clergy back home had to minister to bereaved families. The Church also had to respond to the complex moral issues raised by the war. Should it rally to the national cause and proclaim the duty of young men to enlist? Should it endorse the use of modern weapons of war even if they caused casualties among innocent civilians? Or should the

Church instead seek to offer some kind of alternative perspective that rejected the demonisation of the enemy and instead urge the combatant nations to work towards peace?

The Church of England has often had a bad press for its role in the First World War.[4] Much has been made of the rhetoric of men like Arthur Winnington-Ingram, Bishop of London, who used his sermons to defend the war against Germany as a 'crusade'.[5] It is certainly true that Anglican voices were not prominent among those who opposed the war. Nor were Anglicans heavily represented amongst the men who refused to fight following the introduction of conscription in 1916. The Church of England was not, though, simply the uncritical handmaiden of a Government determined to mobilise the country for war.[6] Randall Davidson was unambiguously committed to the principle that Britain was fighting for a just cause in its struggle with Germany and its allies, but he was concerned too about the impact of the hatred whipped up by both sides on the behaviour of troops on the battlefield. The Archbishop also repeatedly fretted about how the conflict was fuelling a division between Christian nations that could prove impossible to assuage once the slaughter was over. The war forced Davidson to deal with issues that would have seemed almost unimaginable to his predecessors. He did so with a characteristic mixture of industry and caution.

The Archbishop and the Government in wartime

It was seen in previous chapters how Davidson took pride in his close relationship with members of the British political elite, believing that it gave him an opportunity to assert discreetly the influence of the Church of England in the corridors of power. A few months before the end of the war, in August 1918, the Archbishop recalled that he had throughout the conflict continued to talk regularly with leading politicians and civil servants both about events on the battlefield and developments closer to home. He even believed that he might have gained 'a wider knowledge than many with whom I converse, even though they be officials with access to Government information'.[7]

Davidson's memory of the previous few years was unduly optimistic. The Archbishop had, in fact, found it difficult to obtain the kind of access to senior political figures that he took for granted in the years before 1914. It is true that he was on good personal terms with Asquith, who served as Prime Minister until the end of 1916, and the two men did meet on occasion to discuss issues ranging from the use of poison gas through to the status of the clergy under the Military Service Act of 1916. And, a few months after the outbreak of hostilities, Davidson was still happy to record that he was able to have 'interviews of real importance almost every week with the leading Government folk'.[8] Yet by the summer of 1915, the Archbishop was becoming concerned about

> my present inability to know the actual facts about public affairs [...] I did not find Asquith either very responsive or very illuminating, and men like

Balfour [...] have their hands full ... [and] I did not feel justified in seeking for full statements on the situation.[9]

It was for this reason that he approached Lord Curzon, the recently appointed Lord Privy Seal, in the hope of obtaining information about the views of the Cabinet on important wartime questions.[10] The Archbishop also continued to meet regularly with Lord Stamfordham (the King's Private Secretary who – as plain Arthur Bigge – had worked closely with the Archbishop for many years).[11] Both men were forthcoming, but the files at Lambeth Palace suggest that Davidson had fewer meetings with politicians than before the outbreak of war. It seems unlikely that ministers were snubbing the Archbishop, although his plain speaking on questions ranging from propaganda to the use of gas certainly caused irritation. The pressure of business simply meant political leaders did not have as much time for the kind of informal meetings that had taken place in Government offices and Private Clubs during the years before 1914.[12] The First World War helped change both the culture and administration of British politics.

Davidson was anxious when Lloyd George replaced Asquith at the end of 1916, fearing the new Prime Minister both for his radicalism and his quizzical attitude towards the Church of England. During the political crisis that led to Lloyd George replacing Asquith, the Archbishop made it clear in a private note that he did not think the Welshman could deal with the big issues of the war.[13] In later memoranda he wrote that he 'profoundly' distrusted Lloyd George since 'he is certainly not straight in the ordinary and simple sense'.[14] Davidson thought the Prime Minister 'a stimulating arouser of people', words which were not intended as praise from a man who was never comfortable with the rise of mass politics, even if he accepted its inevitability. The Archbishop also disliked having to deal with Lloyd George over matters of ecclesiastical appointments. It is not clear what Lloyd George thought of Davidson (he made no mention of him in his voluminous *War Memoirs*). The differences between the two men both in temperament and outlook meant that the relationship between them was always likely to prove uneasy.

Although Davidson regularly met Stamfordham, he continued to have a somewhat uneasy relationship with the monarch. George V was, as has often been pointed out, in some ways more 'Victorian' than Queen Victoria herself, emotionally restrained and disturbed by threats to the traditional social hierarchy.[15] Such attributes were hardly likely to perturb the Archbishop, but he did continually fret that the King was not sufficiently visible to his people, which Davidson feared might create a gulf between them at a time of growing popular radicalism. The 1917 February Revolution in Russia, which overthrew the Tsar, fuelled concern in some quarters that the Royal Family in Britain might one day suffer a similar fate (it was one of the reasons why the Tsar and his family were refused permission to come to Britain). In May 1918, Davidson contrived to have a meeting alone with the King and Queen, when he told George of 'things which I heard people saying freely, and which they probably would not say to him, or to one of his immediate staff'. He suggested that the monarch was isolating himself from 'some of the very people whom he ought to know best'. The Archbishop advised George to make a greater effort to meet with newspaper editors and senior business people. He added that the King should also appear more in public, driving through the streets in an open carriage, and awarding honours before a large audience rather than in the privacy of the throne room. George reluctantly agreed, urged on by the Queen, whilst the Archbishop noted afterwards that he had only got his message across by talking determinedly and refusing to be interrupted by the monarch.[16] Davidson was probably optimistic in thinking that his words were responsible for the monarch's increasing public appearances in the months that followed (in fairness to the King, he had never been as invisible as Davidson seemed to imagine). The curious episode nevertheless showed once again that the Archbishop was not simply a smooth-tongued 'courtier-priest'. He was ready to talk frankly to George V, just as he had taken Edward VII to task for reports about his private life and, before that, warned Queen Victoria for associating herself too readily with the memory of John Brown. Davidson recognised that the monarchy needed on occasion to re-invent itself in order to maintain its influence and place in British life.[17]

Davidson and the ethical challenge of war

The ethical challenge posed by the use of military force had prompted considerable discussion among some churches in Great Britain throughout the nineteenth century. The Peace Society formed in London in 1815, which committed itself to unconditional pacifism, attracted most of its supporters from the Nonconformist churches (above all the Quakers).[18] Many more Nonconformists were convinced that there were few occasions when it could be right for a Government to use force, even if they were not willing to commit themselves to the view that there were *never* any circumstances under which it could be justified. Questions of war and peace were far less discussed in the Church of England. Few of its members questioned the authority of Article 37 of the 39 articles, which declared that it was lawful to bear arms when commanded by the authorised civil power. Anglican critics of the South African War of 1899–1902, like Bishop Percival of Hereford and Canon Hicks of Manchester, were widely condemned for their stance. The Church of England Peace League, which was not formed until 1910, only attracted a tiny membership. Far more typical were the kind of 'pacificist' views expressed by the Bishops at the 1908 Lambeth Conference,[19] who passed a Resolution praising the agreements reached at the Hague Conferences of 1899 and 1907, by which Governments committed themselves to settling their differences 'by peaceful methods'.[20] Such sentiments broadly echoed Randall Davidson's views on international conflict. The Archbishop supported efforts to promote international agreement, but he was never convinced that conflict could be eliminated altogether, believing instead that governments sometimes needed to use armed force to counter the triumph of wrongdoing.

The widespread jingoism that followed the declaration of war was quickly increased still further when reports circulated in Britain detailing atrocities by the German troops who had invaded Belgium. Newspapers like the *Daily Mail* described events in towns like Louvain, which suffered enormous destruction and loss of life, as a 'holocaust' of destruction.[21] Local newspapers carried numerous stories of how German soldiers were under orders 'to set fire to villages and [. . .] kill the inhabitants', many of whom were burnt alive, after having their arms and legs cut off'.[22] The Bryce Report on German Atrocities, which reported in May 1915, added credence to many of these earlier reports, containing numerous descriptions of how Belgian and French citizens had been scalped and women raped. Responses to these reports among Church of England clergy varied considerably. The reaction of the Bishop of London, speaking towards the end of 1915, was predictable in its uncompromising bellicosity:

> Everyone that loves freedom and honour [. . .] are banded in a great crusade – we cannot deny it – to kill Germans; to kill them, not for the sake of killing, but to save the world; to kill the good as well as the bad, to kill the young as well as the old, to kill those who have shown kindness to our wounded as well as those fiends who crucified the Canadian sergeant, who superintended the Armenian massacres, who sank the *Lusitania*, and who turned the machine-guns on the civilians of Aerschott and Louvain – and to kill them lest the civilisation of the world itself be killed.[23]

Such rhetoric was extreme. Some senior soldiers, like Lord Kitchener, were actually wary of seeing the pulpit used to support recruitment efforts. Many clergy did nevertheless encourage enlistment. Randall Davidson himself called on families not to 'hold back' their loved ones from the battlefield. Charles Gore rightly pointed out that most leading clergy came from a broadly similar social background to senior army officers and politicians.[24] It was therefore hardly surprising that most of them shared the prevailing view that right was on the side of Britain.

Although most leading Anglican clergy believed the war was justified, few of them made explicit use of the language of Just War when talking about the conflict, instead employing a rhetoric that was not strikingly different from the language used by politicians and newspaper editors. Some of the distinctions associated with the Just War tradition did, though, tacitly inform Davidson's thinking. The Archbishop's support for the war was unambiguous: he had no doubt that Britain was fighting not just for the material interests of the British Empire, but also for the principles of international law and, more generally, the triumph of civilisation. He was, in other words, convinced that the British declaration of war was in accord with the dictates of *jus ad bellum*, since it was responding to aggression by another State, and acting in accord with its own treaty commitments. In a sermon he gave a year after the start of the war, the Archbishop noted that Britain was fighting with 'a clear conscience' against 'the dominance of force and force alone'.[25] A few months later, when preaching at

Canterbury, Davidson told the congregation that there should be no 'flagging in our high and stern resolve that the cause which we believe in our hearts to be that of righteousness and honour and truth'.[26] The Archbishop was nevertheless from the start of the war intensely wary of engaging in any rhetoric which seemed to identify the British cause 'with the Divine Will to such an extent as to claim that God is simply on our side'.[27] He was not, in other words, ready to treat the conflict as a Holy War. Davidson was conscious that, at some point in the future, the combatant nations would have to negotiate peace and start rebuilding Europe. He was perturbed by the use of a language that might so blacken the reputation of Germany as to make it impossible to rebuild relations with a country widely respected by many Anglican clergy for its contributions to theology and culture.[28]

Whilst Davidson never doubted the fundamental justice of Britain's position, he fretted a great deal more about *jus in bello*, that is the question of deciding which means of warfare were permissible. The issue became most pressing over the question of reprisals. He repeatedly fretted that the jingoistic public mood and the desire for victory might lead to a downward spiral of brutality on the battlefield. The nature of trench warfare, which became the hallmark of the Western Front, meant that machine guns and heavy artillery could now be used to destroy thousands of lives a day. More troubling still, for Davidson, was the deployment of poisonous gas on the battlefield and the use of aerial bombing to hit civilian targets. The Archbishop worked hard to raise these questions throughout the war, frequently earning a good deal of criticism for his efforts, both in the press and (more mutedly) from those in Government.

In May 1915, Davidson wrote to Asquith on 'a matter which is causing me great concern' – namely, the reports circulating that the British Government was considering whether to authorise the use of gas in response to its use by German forces

> The infamous conduct of the German military authorities in deliberately organising this mode of warfare and the fact that it has been put into effective operation in defiance of every principle of international ethics have aroused a burning sense of indignation among all reasonable men. I am no soldier, but as a Christian citizen I try to understand the situation as it exists, and I confess that I am profoundly disquieted by the indications that our army may be bidden to meet the new situation by itself adopting these inhuman tactics.[29]

He went on to argue that the judgement of history would take little notice of who first used such 'vile weapons'. It was not simply the horrors of chemical warfare that worried the Archbishop. He was equally concerned by the emphasis on retaliation. In another letter to the Prime Minister, which reflected on the rumours of German atrocities in Belgium and elsewhere, he warned against the danger of Britain being 'induced or driven to a course which would lower us towards the level of those whom we denounce'.[30] The British Government was unmoved by such appeals. In 1915, commanders in France were given permission to use gas as a weapon on the battlefield.

Davidson doggedly continued to warn against reprisals. In February 1916, he spoke at length in a Convocation debate which passed a motion condemning 'the killing and wounding of non-combatants', arguing that the Church should point out that the war raised 'ethical as well as military considerations'. The Archbishop also warned that retaliation would only provoke further reprisals, leading to a level of brutality more associated with medieval times, rather than a conflict 'between Christian nations today'.[31] Such sentiments were not always welcomed. Davidson received numerous letters attacking his views, including one satirical missive which described how Germany would welcome the intervention of those 'two old women, the Archbishops of Canterbury and York' (Archbishop Lang had also warned against reprisals).[32] The following year, Davidson spoke in the House of Lords on reprisals, defending the 'international code of elementary honour with regard to the helpless, the defenceless and the sick', which he argued had held fast over many centuries.[33] The Archbishop's words were inspired by his concern about possible British reprisals for the zeppelin raids that took place against London and other towns up the east coast of England (in October 1915, he had told the Mayor of Croydon, following a recent attack on the borough, that despite the destruction 'I disbelieve in retaliation of any kind').[34] In an exchange of letters with the novelist Sir Thomas Hall Caine, Davidson argued that while civilians might sometimes become the unavoidable casualties of war, they should never be targeted directly (Hall Caine took a contrary view).[35] Nor was the Archbishop alone in making such a case. Many leading clergy in the Church of England – including even the Bishop of London – warned that targeting civilians in revenge for loss of life in Britain was morally unacceptable.

Davidson was especially perturbed by the demonisation of both Germany and Germans. The Archbishop took a leading role early in the war in organising a response by Church leaders in Britain to the 'Appeal to Evangelical Churches Abroad', issued by a number of leading German theologians, which had attacked the 'web of conspiracy against Germany'. The reply orchestrated by Davidson criticised the Appeal for its failure to acknowledge 'the plain facts of this grave hour in European history'. The appeal did nevertheless note, 'We unite whole-heartedly with our German brethren in deploring the disastrous consequences of the War'.[36] In the years that followed, Davidson eagerly interrogated visitors from neutral countries, such as the American John Mott, seeking details about opinion among leading German theologians including Adolf Harnack and Julius Richter.[37] He also warned against whipping up storms of national hatred that could prove difficult to calm down. There was a risk in pursuing such a strategy. The Archbishop of York attracted widespread public opprobrium when he suggested at one public meeting that the Kaiser had not lightly embarked on the war.[38] Both Archbishops – like many ministers from all denominations – still looked on Germany not just as a Christian nation but also as the homeland of some of the world's leading theologians and pastors. It was for this reason that they repeatedly tried to draw a distinction between the militarism of the regime and the sentiments of ordinary Germans. Such sentiments seldom received a warm hearing at a time when thousands of Britons were dying on the battlefields of Europe.

The challenge of conscription

The introduction of conscription at the start of 1916 raised difficult ethical problems, since compulsory military service meant that those who opposed the war, whether on grounds of faith or politics, could no longer simply choose not to enlist. Most men who refused to fight on the grounds of their faith belonged to one of the smaller churches, most often the Quakers or Christadelphians, although a significant number of Methodists and Baptists also became conscientious objectors (COs).[39] The challenges faced by some of these men before the tribunals set up to hear pleas for exemption is well known.[40] Most of those willing to take some form of alternative service – perhaps in the Army Medical Corps or in vital work on the Home Front – were given exemption from combatant service (although they often faced ostracism by friends and neighbours). The situation was worse for 'absolutists' who refused any work that could help the war effort. Several thousand COs were sent to prison (where some died as a result of harsh treatment and neglect). A number committed suicide. Although attitudes towards COs varied within Nonconformity – the Wesleyans in particular were unsympathetic – there was significant support for the right of individuals to obey their conscience rather than the law.[41] Such a tradition was far weaker within the Church of England. There were comparatively few Anglicans amongst the absolutist COs. The treatment of COs was nevertheless a sufficiently controversial public question for Davidson to take a detailed interest in the subject.

The Archbishop was deluged in the first weeks of 1916 with requests for support by individuals who refused to fight. He was also regularly contacted by such organisations as the No-Conscription Fellowship. Davidson was careful to avoid committing himself, repeatedly noting that he could not become involved in individual cases, although he made no secret of the fact that he found it difficult to understand the position of the COs. The Archbishop nevertheless told his secretary to write to one correspondent, who had asked whether being a conscientious objector was compatible with membership of the Church of England, that

> while [the Archbishop] cannot himself regard as reasonable or consistent with Christian common-sense the position of those who claim for themselves and their property the protection of a civilised order to society while still repudiating its corresponding claim upon their service, he ha[s] learned by experience that membership of a religious community is not found to be incompatible with even the extreme vagaries of individual opinion.[42]

In another letter, Davidson's secretary noted that the Archbishop found the position of those who refused even to help the wounded in war – for example, as medical orderlies – as 'not only impossible to defend but difficult to understand',[43] but he still rejected demands that COs should be refused Communion.

Davidson tried to avoid public comment, but as time passed he became more concerned about the situation faced by COs sent to prison for refusing to fight. Although the 'conchies' never received much public support, many of their cases were raised in Parliament, where some MPs expressed concern about reports of force-feeding and harsh beatings. The Archbishop was by the end of 1916 sending private letters to officials arguing that it was pointless to send 'these hopelessly unreasonable people' to military camps (a policy he thought 'as irrational as it is cruel').[44] The following year he wrote to Lord Milner about the case of the Quaker CO Stephen Hobhouse, along with others who 'are really as conscientious as he is', suggesting that there was no point in applying military law to such men. Davidson acknowledged that although he had 'no brief' for the men in question, 'a little arbitrarily exercised common-sense will solve a problem insoluble by either law or logic'.[45] The issue was for the Archbishop one of both ethics and practicalities. While he was not impressed by the claims of conscience expressed by men who refused to fight, he did believe they should be honoured, and that the COs should be entitled to the protection set down in the Military Service Act.

The status of the clergy as potential combatants posed a problem for the Church of England – and, indeed, the other main churches – throughout the war. Thousands of Anglican clergy volunteered as chaplains during the first few weeks of the war (many more than the armed forces actually needed). More problematic was the situation of clergy who wished to leave their parishes in order to fight. In September 1914, Davidson wrote to the Bishops advising them that their clergy should not abandon their ministry (although he was, perhaps a little contradictorily, ready to see them enlist in the Royal Army Medical Corps). By the end of 1915, as the introduction of conscription approached, the Archbishop was happy to recommend that candidates for ordination should enlist, but he still resisted pressures to encourage the recruitment of those already ordained. Davidson defended conscription in the House of Lords early in 1916 ('a vigorous endeavour to meet a situation which is extremely difficult'),[46] but continued to support exemption of the clergy, a position that earned him some criticism in the months that followed. It was partly for this reason that, in 1917, many Anglican clergy voluntarily undertook a form of National Service, typically by taking the place of those who had left for the Front (many also joined local defence forces). During the military crisis caused by the German advance in the spring of 1918, a new Military Service Bill proposed to end the exemption for ministers of religion, a change which Davidson accepted, telling Lloyd George that Anglican clergy recognised the need to respond to 'the call of the nation'. The point became moot when the Government decided not to proceed, fearing the possible reaction in Ireland to conscription of Roman Catholic priests, but the episode allowed the Archbishop to tell the House of Lords that the Anglican clergy had shown themselves ready to serve their country.

The Archbishop and the war at the Front

One of the most striking aspects of the First World War in Europe was the contrast between the experiences of the men (and occasionally women) at the Front with their compatriots at home. An officer could be in the trenches one day and attend a dance at a grand hotel in London the following evening. Although discussion of the war filled the newspapers, it was impossible for civilians to comprehend the full horrors of a type of warfare unprecedented in human history. Soldiers who went home on leave often found it hard to relate to their families, whose lives had gone on uninterrupted in their absence, leading one soldier to write how

> a man's first meeting with his wife after being taken for a soldier is one of strange pathos [...] Something of his personality has been shorn away from him, something of that which made him lovable to her.[47]

Perhaps strangely, many of those who served at the Front did not share the hatred of the Germans that was so prevalent back in Britain. The celebrated, if much mythologised, Christmas truce of 1914 shows how the demonisation of the enemy could be less common among those who fought when compared with those who viewed the war from a distance. Although the guns of the Western Front were from time to time heard in Kent, whilst zeppelins occasionally appeared over the towns and cities of eastern England, the psychological boundary between the Home Front and the Military Front remained stark throughout the war.

The Church of England moved quickly to find ways of ministering effectively to the millions of men who volunteered (or were later conscripted) to fight. The careers of Anglican chaplains like 'Woodbine Willie' (G. S. Kennedy) and Philip 'Tubby' Clayton have become part of the mythology of the First World War, celebrated examples of men who sought to minister through practical service, rather than by preaching an arid gospel remote from the experience of ordinary soldiers. Recent research has shown how hard it is to generalise about the role of chaplains (both Anglican and non-Anglican).[48] The organisation of chaplaincy was chaotic during the early months of the war, in large part due to shortcomings at the War Office, and Davidson corresponded regularly about the problems both with senior officials and the Chaplain-General (Bishop J. Taylor Smith). The Archbishop welcomed the appointment of Bishop L. H. Gwynne in 1915 as Deputy Chaplain-General, who subsequently helped to shape the organisation of chaplaincy in the field, a task made easier by his success in winning the support of the military authorities. The supply of chaplains nevertheless remained a perennial problem. Davidson acknowledged that some dioceses were poor at organising the recruitment of chaplains. It was partly for this reason that, at the end of 1917, Lambeth Palace itself became an important 'clearing house' in maintaining lists of men willing to serve in the field. The problems associated with the expansion of military chaplaincy were not, though, simply administrative. There was also a persistent misunderstanding by those at home of the conditions facing chaplains when serving at the Front.

This problem was vividly illustrated by Lord Halifax, early in the war, when he demanded that all soldiers should have the opportunity to attend Sunday Communion and have access to Confession. Such words showed little comprehension of the chaotic nature of modern warfare. The most effective chaplains were typically those who won the trust of the troops by offering practical help rather than giving sermons on the finer points of Christian doctrine. The experience of chaplaincy work was, indeed, one of the factors that helped to shape the development of the ecumenical instinct during the war, as chaplains from the various denominations were required to minister to those of all faiths. They also quickly learnt that the religion of soldiers was – to the extent it existed at all – typically a matter of the heart rather than the head. In a 1917 collection of essays, *The Church in the Furnace*, one author warned padres against the danger of using their sermons to focus 'on matters of no particular importance' to troops.[49] Many chaplains who wrote about their experiences noted how questions of doctrine faded when confronted with the need to respond to a tide of human misery and fear.[50] For those back home in Britain, the challenge of chaplaincy was all too easily seen as a matter of administration. The situation looked very different from the perspective of the trenches.

Davidson met from time to time with those who had experience of the sharp end of war, and his letters show that he worked hard to understand the nature of the battlefield. It was nevertheless hard for him – as it was for all those in positions of authority in Britain – to grasp the full impact of the conflict on those condemned to fight. It was partly for this reason that, in May 1916, the Archbishop spent a week visiting troops near the front line in France and Belgium. Davidson kept a detailed diary describing his experiences, including visits to towns like Poperinge, where the Anglican chaplains Neville Talbot and 'Tubby' Clayton had established their pioneering mission at Talbot House.[51] He was shocked by the scenes of 'indescribable' devastation he witnessed at nearby Ypres, where the medieval cloth hall had been razed to the ground, and British troops were living in dugouts and cellars since all the houses had been destroyed.[52] The Archbishop met a number of senior commanders, including General Haig, as well as talking informally with some of the 'tommies'. He also had the unwelcome experience of seeing and hearing artillery shells explode whilst travelling close to the trenches on the Vimy Ridge section of the Front. Army commanders sometimes resented the presence of visiting dignitaries at the Front. Davidson's low-key approach meant that he was viewed with more sympathy by the top brass (though William Temple later heard that some officers believed the visitor was too old to grasp the full import of what he saw). The Archbishop was, inevitably, spared the experience of the more brutal aspects of the battlefield. Perhaps as a result, he was still inclined to view the troops through the romantic lens of the Home Front, writing in his diary of the men's 'quiet simplicity' and the 'unconscious dignity' of the chaplains who had 'grown' in moral stature since taking up their posts.

War, morality, and social change

When back in London, Davidson continued to fret about the moral welfare of British troops both at home and abroad, a subject that had preoccupied him from the start of the war. His files show that he corresponded regularly with the Home Office and the War Office on matters ranging from alcohol to venereal disease (subjects which also aroused the periodic concern of Convocation). Davidson raised the issue of venereal disease in the House of Lords, in a debate in April 1918, acknowledging that the rise in the number of cases was almost inevitable given the exigencies of war.[53] The Archbishop was nevertheless sharply critical of the existence in France and Belgium of 'licensed house(s) of so-called inspected women',[54] suggesting that such semi-official brothels did little to prevent disease, whilst appearing to give a kind of official *imprimatur* to immorality. He went on to demand that the British authorities take a lead in putting an end to such institutions – a call that was predictably ignored by those responsible for the situation on the ground.

The Archbishop was equally perturbed about the effect of the war on the morals of the civilian population. Although the military impact of the conflict on the Home Front was limited, the social impact was enormous, not least as large numbers of women moved into munitions production or agriculture. Davidson was anxious from the start of hostilities about the rise in drinking among women whose husbands had joined the army, telling Kitchener in October 1914 that, 'It sounds horrid to say it, but the fact is that the women dependents of the soldiers are getting more money than they can wisely handle'.[55] He also fretted at the practice of civilians pressing drinks on soldiers bound for the Front. Early in 1915, he joined with the Archbishop of York and other church leaders in calling on Britons to follow George V by giving up drink for the duration of the war (some other leading Anglicans – including Gore and Henson – looked askance at such puritanism).[56] Davidson also fretted about the moral complexities of deciding whether unmarried mothers should receive financial support when their 'husbands' joined up – leading Lloyd George's mistress Frances Stephenson to note waspishly in her diary that the Archbishop did not want their children to starve, but nor did he wish them to be seen as 'deserving of relief'.[57] The question of Sunday Observance also once again raised its head, particularly in relation to agricultural labour, although on this occasion the Archbishop was ready to take a permissive attitude at a time when ensuring a reliable food supply was a national priority.[58] Davidson was no bigot. Nor was he an unthinking traditionalist. But the Archbishop was as so often uncomfortable about developments which he saw as inevitable yet undesirable.

The impact of the First World War on women's lives has been endlessly debated by historians, not least in terms of whether changes to their role in both the public and domestic spheres were a consequence of the conflict, or simply represented an acceleration of developments that had been underway for many years. The need to mobilise female labour certainly increased the economic opportunities available to younger women in particular. It was seen in a previous chapter that Archbishop Davidson was ambivalent on the question of female suffrage, offering muted support to the principle, but distancing himself from definite efforts to bring about reform. Such views were not uncommon. In the summer of 1916, Asquith told Davidson that, although he was a lifelong opponent of female suffrage, he had no doubt it had become inevitable, although he still fretted about 'the future of women's industrial work'.[59] The Prime Minister's words reflected the Archbishop's own long-standing attitude to many of the social and cultural manifestations of the modern world: that change had to be accommodated if not welcomed with enthusiasm.

The Archbishop was nevertheless unusually terse when responding to complaints that the National Mission of Repentance and Hope, launched by the Church of England in 1916, was creating pressure for women to play a greater role in the Church. Davidson wrote to the leading Anglo-Catholic layman Athelstan Riley, pointing out how rural parishes relied heavily on female parishioners to carry out vital parochial work of various kinds. Riley was not convinced by such arguments, warning that the Archbishops seemed to be losing control of a movement they had themselves set in motion, citing the 'intolerable' pressure to allow women speakers in Church. Riley was even more incensed that radical Anglicans like Maude Royden were raising the possibility of women priests.[60] He warned Davidson in unusually trenchant terms that 'the clergy and laity' would act to prevent such developments if the Archbishops proved 'powerless' to control the demands for change created by the National Mission.[61]

The tensions revealed in the correspondence between Davidson and Riley reflected divisions both about the National Mission in particular and the role of the Church of England in national life more generally. The Archbishop was cautious when proposals for such a mission were first raised, worrying that the Church lacked the capacity to undertake such an ambitious development during a time of hostilities, although he was in time willing to recommend the project to the Bishops.[62] The origins of the National Mission were to be found in a sense that the horrors of war both could and should be used as a catalyst to encourage deeper reflection on Christian faith. The 'Call' issued by Davidson in September 1916 explicitly argued that victory against Germany would be of no value:

> If it is our earthly enemies only who are defeated [...] Among us at home the forces of sin and ignorance are mighty [...] Through the National Mission of Repentance and Hope we in Christ's name call upon every English man and woman to strike a blow at Christ's enemies.[63]

Whilst such language did not necessarily assert a definite link between Christianity and social reform, some critics of the Council of the National Mission believed that it was too inclined to lose focus on spiritual issues in favour of what Athelstan Riley called 'a mass of more or less irrelevant matter' (Riley himself sat on the National Council).

Although some leading Churchmen were sceptical about proposals for the National Mission,[64] many clergy who supported 'Christian socialism' were convinced that spiritual renewal and social reform were intimately bound together. Henry Scott Holland believed that if the combatant countries had been more deeply imbued with Christian values – rather than the 'curse of materialism' – then war could have been avoided. William Temple, who was one of those asked by Davidson to consider how a National Mission might work, defended it against critics who thought repentance 'a miserable kind of thing'.[65] The ambitious nature of the Mission inevitably meant that the committees set up by its Council had to engage with far-reaching questions about the nature of the Church of England and its place in national life. One of Riley's criticisms of the Council of the National Mission was, indeed, that its Committee on Relations with Other Movements placed too much emphasis on working with trade unions, leading to 'the usual platitudes on social questions'. Another leading Anglo-Catholic layman, Hugh Cecil, also expressed deep unease about the direction taken by the National Mission. Hensley Henson characteristically stood aloof, noting in his diary that 'a dervish-like fervour cannot be maintained, and is not really illuminating or helpful'.[66] The very nature of the National Mission, with its high ideals of turning Britain back towards the Christian faith, too often simply highlighted the divisions and uncertainties that already dogged the Church of England.

Davidson's caution about the National Mission was justified. Even its staunchest proponents acknowledged that the Mission's influence never really extended beyond those already in the pews. The Archbishop was not by temperament or inclination a supporter of such grandiose efforts to transform national life. Although George Bell paints a positive picture of Davidson's involvement in the Mission, pointing out that he made great efforts to enthuse the clergy in his own diocese, the Archbishop cut a somewhat peripheral figure in the nationwide flood of activities and discussion. He was nevertheless conscious of the social challenges posed by the war (challenges which Temple later described as 'the great social cleavages and industrial strifes [that show] something is fundamentally wrong in our national life').[67] Davidson had been concerned about the growth of labour unrest in the years before 1914, and was shrewd enough to recognise that the rallying call of patriotism could not delay indefinitely a crisis in industrial relations. The Archbishop was no 'enthusiast', in any sense of the word, but he was alert to a *zeitgeist* which assumed that the post-war world was likely to be very different from the one that existed before the conflict.

Archbishop Davidson and wartime doctrinal controversies

The outbreak of the war in 1914 did not end the doctrinal controversies that had caused division within the Church of England during the pre-war years.

The Reservation of the Sacrament continued to provoke particular tension, in large part because the exigencies of war led to ever more diverging practices in different dioceses, something which predictably angered Charles Gore who (as always) favoured ecclesiastical uniformity. Archbishop Davidson was by contrast convinced that such questions were of secondary importance in wartime 'when our thoughts and prayers are concentrated on other things'.[68] The question nevertheless continued to preoccupy many Anglicans, and formed the subject of lengthy debate in Convocation early in 1917, when Davidson criticised a Memorial signed by 1,000 clergy warning against restricting access to the Reserved Sacrament. The Archbishop ruefully noted that the divisions largely reflected a split between his own generation and a new generation of 'younger men'. Some Bishops believed that Davidson failed to provide a strong lead. The Archbishop himself hoped to contain the problem precisely by avoiding action that would make the situation more rancorous.[69]

Davidson also had to respond to tensions caused by the vexed question of 'Prayers for the Dead', a subject that became more pressing as the casualty lists mounted. Much has been written about the rise of esoteric forms of belief during the First World War.[70] The growing interest in Spiritualism, in particular, was prompted by a desire of many of the bereaved to contact their loved ones, a phenomenon that was sometimes found even among those with impeccable scientific credentials.[71] Davidson had earlier in his archiepiscopate made it clear that he was opposed to including Prayers for the Dead in Church services, but within a few weeks of the start of the war he accepted there should be 'a place for a gentler recognition of the instinctive, the natural, the loyal craving of the bereaved'. His sentiments were widely shared, but the issue was still capable of creating controversy, particularly among those on the Evangelical wing of the Church of England. When prayers for the departed were included in new Forms of Prayer, issued for the third anniversary of the outbreak of the war in August 1917, Bishop Chavasse of Liverpool wrote to Davidson protesting that the move had created a good deal of distress in his diocese. Chavasse's protest doubtless reflected the views of some Anglicans in Liverpool, a city where the sectarian divide had deep roots, but there is little evidence that Prayers for the Dead really caused much widespread public concern. Davidson recognised that the Church of England had to respond to the exigencies of war if it were to command popular sympathy and maintain its authority as the National Church.[72]

The debates about 'Modernism', which had so preoccupied the Church of England before 1914, also continued to raise passions during the war years, erupting in controversy in 1917, when the retirement of Bishop Percival of Hereford created the first Episcopal vacancy since Lloyd George's arrival in Downing Street.[73] The Prime Minister had little experience or understanding of such questions, leading Davidson to note privately how 'it [was] a curious experience handling these matters with a man who has so little knowledge either of the conditions of Church life, the nature of different regions ecclesiastically, or the men who might be appointed to them'.[74] The Archbishop warned Lloyd George against appointing Hensley Henson to Hereford, particularly given the recent appointment of the leading Modernist Hastings Rashdall as Dean of Carlisle, pointing out that such a move would provoke controversy. The Prime Minister paid attention, agreeing that the post should be offered to other candidates, but when they declined Lloyd George once again pressed Henson's cause as a man who 'has never yet failed to devote himself eagerly to whatever work lay before him'.[75] Davidson recognised that the appointment of the author of *The Creed in the Pulpit* to a Bishopric would create fierce opposition, and in the final weeks of 1917 he worked hard to change Lloyd George's mind. When the task proved impossible, the Archbishop devoted his energy to preventing the controversy from creating new divisions in the Church.

Charles Gore predictably took the lead in opposing Henson's appointment to a Bishopric, on the grounds that 'Dr Henson falls outside the limits of tolerable conformity'.[76] Davidson met with Gore to discuss the crisis, noting in a private memorandum that the Bishop of Oxford was opposed to the appointment of a man who believed that Christ had 'rotted in a tomb'. The Archbishop's notes show that he was greatly irritated by Henson's behaviour during a visit to Lambeth Palace, writing with unusual acerbity that his guest was 'pleasant and friendly, but disappointed me with his self-satisfaction, and his rather venomous denunciation of those who were opposing his appointment'.[77] The furore that surrounded news of Henson's nomination was considerable. The *Church Times* reacted with anger. *The Times* published a letter from Lord Halifax fulminating against the appointment (although it also included other letters welcoming the news).[78] One Conservative newspaper carried letters suggesting that Lloyd George was using the appointment to weaken the Established Church.[79] Many Bishops told Davidson they would not take part in Henson's consecration. The Archbishop found the situation increasing stressful and even considered whether he might need to resign. Lloyd George had not been looking for a fight with the Church of England hierarchy in nominating Henson, but the Prime Minister's decision to support such a controversial candidate threatened to create a rupture between Church and State, as well as foment division within the Church itself.

Davidson continued to find Henson hard to deal with, describing him as 'cocksure' and 'strangely sensitive to criticism', even as he proclaimed his indifference to the complaints by Gore about his refusal to accept Church teachings on miracles and the Virgin Birth. When the two men met to discuss the situation further, early in 1918, Henson told the Archbishop that he believed in the Virgin Birth and the Resurrection, but 'with regard to the details he adopts a position of what he calls Christian Agnosticism, considering it to be true to state historical facts in a different way at different epochs'. Davidson pointed out that such statements seemed to contradict what Henson had said in his published writings, later noting

> he must, I think, have seen that I did not regard his answer as very satisfactory. He went on to press the point that it had somehow fallen to him to be the champion of the principle that wide toleration of Modernism is now the duty of the honest man within the Church.

The Archbishop also noted that he found his guest 'opinionated, self-confident and not by any means profound. But he was frank, and to me personally most friendly, and, if the word is a right one, loyal'.[80] Henson noted in his diary, rather optimistically, that he thought 'we were, in the matter of personal belief, substantially agreed'.[81]

The public controversy became still louder following the publication of Gore's protest in *The Times* (though Davidson also received letters from senior clergy supporting Henson, including one from W. R. Inge, who warned against any 'postponement of the consecration').[82] Halifax noted in the middle of January that the Archbishop was 'evidently in great anxiety and trouble'.[83] Davidson nevertheless persisted in seeking a resolution to the crisis, meeting Henson on a number of occasions, and the two men eventually agreed on the wording of a memorandum setting down the latter's views. On 16 January 1918, the Archbishop wrote to Gore noting that he was now satisfied that Henson 'regards the Incarnation of the Son of God as the central fact in human history'.[84] The Bishop of Oxford duly withdrew his protest against Henson's consecration, which took place without (in Henson's words) any 'Fanatick [. . .] crying out some protest or insult'.[85] Although Henson's appointment to Hereford continued to attract criticism, Davidson had weathered the storm, and turned his attention to giving advice about how the new Bishop could best put the controversy behind him. There was perhaps a degree of dissimulation and self-deceit on both sides. Henson was sufficiently ambiguous about his position to convince the Archbishop that his views were in accord with Anglican teaching. The Archbishop was sufficiently flexible to believe him.

Church and State in wartime

The relationship between Church and State became a general source of debate within the Church of England during the final years of the war. A growing number of Anglo-Catholics like Gore increasingly chafed against State control, whilst others (including the Archbishop) continued to see Establishment as vital for preserving the Church of England's influence and status. Nor was it only on the Anglo-Catholic wing that there was growing concern about the need to assert the autonomy of the Church. In 1916, a report was issued by the Archbishops' Committee on Church and State, set up three years earlier, which sought to identify new ways of reconciling the 'spiritual independence of the Church' and 'the national recognition of religion'.[86] Davidson broadly welcomed the report in Convocation, but expressed reservations about some of its detailed recommendations,[87] not least because he thought it unwise to devote too much attention to such issues at a time of national crisis.

It was against this background that William Temple took the lead in forming the Life and Liberty Movement within the Church of England, designed in the words of one historian 'to deal with the twin threats of state encroachment and working class alienation'.[88] Life and Liberty typically attracted those who thought that the Bishops lacked the vision to provide effective leadership to the Church of England, at a time of great social and political change, with the result that Establishment in its current form was failing to provide an effective means for promoting Christian influence in national life.[89] Although the leading figures in the movement initially avoided direct criticism of Church leaders, the emphasis on the need for greater action, when combined with a quizzical view of the effectiveness of the National Mission, together highlighted the commitment of (some) younger clergy and lay people to promoting fresh ways of dealing with 'the new world [that] is already being born'.[90]

Davidson's response to the creation of Life and Liberty symbolised his increasing difficulty in engaging with the changes in outlook that were taking place amongst some members of the Church of England. He seems, at least in part, to have shared the views of Hensley Henson, who scathingly told the Archbishop that the opening meeting had been dominated by 'upper middle class people, who form the congregation of West-end churches' (and were by implication profoundly unrepresentative of the Church of England as a whole).[91] When Davidson met Temple and other members of the Life and Liberty Council, in the summer of 1917, he made it clear that he thought no constitutional changes should be considered until the Representative Church Council had been given an opportunity to comment on the report of the Archbishops' Committee on Church and State. He also noted that he doubted the wisdom of raising such matters until the war was over. One member of the Council wrote many years later that he and his colleagues believed that Davidson was deeply reluctant to push for reform.[92] He was almost certainly right. Even when the Representative Church Council finally met, towards the end of 1917, its members were given little effective opportunity to vote on whether action should be taken to obtain a greater measure of Church self-government.

William Temple viewed Davidson with genuine warmth, not least because of the Archbishop's support during his struggle for ordination many years earlier, but he was deeply frustrated by the lack of progress. His biographer (and fellow Life and Liberty Council member) F. A. Iremonger probably reflected Temple's views when he later wrote that Davidson found such a 'forward' movement as Life and Liberty 'freakish [...] he had reached the time of life when adjustment to new ways is always difficult and unpleasant'.[93] A public statement published by Life and Liberty in December 1917, which criticised the Church of England leadership for failing to give a clear lead in spiritual and organisational matters, must have wounded Davidson (it included references to 'obstructionists').[94] Nor was the statement entirely fair. The Life and Liberty movement was itself something of a 'mixed bag of enthusiasts, socialists, feminists and pacifists', whose members seemed united more by a common discontent with the *status quo*, rather than by agreement on any set of positive objectives.[95] Davidson did mildly point out to Temple in a private letter that he was on friendly terms 'with the men prominent in our public life on whose aid we should have to rely' [in promoting greater Church self-government], adding that he was convinced his policy of avoiding 'hustle and push in matters ecclesiastical' during the war years was the right one.[96] A few weeks later, he wrote again to Temple noting a little sadly that whilst the younger generation should not look at the world 'through the eyes of an old man like myself [. . .] None the less I do believe that old men do have a contribution to make to the solution of new problems'.[97] Davidson's caution may have been prompted by his wariness about supporting any action that could weaken the Church of England's status as the National Church. He was, however, also right in acknowledging that he found it difficult to understand the passions that inspired a younger generation of clergy and lay people.

The search for peace and the development of relations between the churches

Randall Davidson's belief in the justice of Britain's cause in the conflict with the central powers did not prevent him from taking a sustained interest the search for peace. He seems to have been well informed about the background to the publication of Lord Lansdowne's controversial letter to *The Daily Telegraph*, in November 1917, which called for a negotiated peace with Germany in order to prevent the destruction of civilisation. Although there is no evidence that Davidson directly supported the proposals, in a memorandum written some months later he made it clear that he thought there should be 'a discussion as to whether peace terms are available'. He also noted his 'growing suspicion' that the Government

> has got no coherent plan [to secure peace], or even the outline of a large policy [. . .] unhappily the strangely assorted group of men who now govern us are most of them quite unable to handle subjects so vast, and so intricate, and so dependent on a real grasp of public affairs.[98]

Davidson supported proposals to establish some kind of League of Nations after the war, although not necessarily with the exuberant optimism expressed by some others in the Church of England. He spoke warmly at Convocation in February 1918 in support of a Resolution welcoming the idea of a new international organisation to 'promote the brotherhood of man'.[99] The prospect of a League of Nations caused some division within the British political and diplomatic establishments, prompted by concern that such an organisation might weaken Britain's freedom to defend its imperial interests. The Archbishop was nevertheless responsive to those, like Lord Robert Cecil at the Foreign Office, for whom the virtues of establishing such an organisation was an article of faith. Davidson's letter to *The Times* in September 1918, arguing that the Church's commitment to the principle of the League of Nations was no mere lip-adherence, was prompted at least in part by Cecil's intervention.[100] A private note written by the Archbishop a few days later nevertheless showed that he still had doubts about how effective a new League of Nations would be in practice, writing that although the Church was committed to the principle of collective security, 'I am painfully conscious of its somewhat general and even vague character'.[101]

The principle that the churches should play an active role in promoting peace was widely expressed during the war. It was seen earlier that Davidson refused to endorse the 'Appeal to Evangelical Christians Abroad', which was circulated by German theologians in 1914, dismissing it for failing to acknowledge German responsibility for the conflict. The Archbishop did, however, write to Archbishop Nathan Söderblom of Uppsala in Sweden, noting that he would strongly support any moves towards 'a righteous and enduring peace' (that is one which acknowledged the fundamental justice of the cause being fought for by Britain and its allies). More than three years later, early in 1918, Söderblom wrote to Davidson asking the Church of England to send representatives to a conference in Stockholm, intended to encourage debate between the churches from both sides of the conflict on a range of diplomatic and social issues. Davidson was wary of committing his Church to participation in a conference that might do little more than produce platitudes about the benefits of peace. He was also convinced that the Church of England should not take part in a meeting without clear permission from Government ministers.[102] The Archbishop received contradictory answers from the politicians, and the invitation was quietly declined, although in a meeting with Asquith a few days later Davidson showed that he was still greatly exercised by the failure of the churches to play a bigger role in resolving international conflict.

The appointment of George Bell as Davidson's Chaplain in 1914 proved to be a significant moment in the evolution of Davidson's archiepiscopate. Davidson was already 65 when the war broke out, and his prodigious workrate was taking an increasing toll on his fragile health, making greater delegation of work almost inevitable. Although the Archbishop never 'left everything' in [Bell's] hands, as has been claimed,[103] he quickly established an excellent relationship with his new Chaplain. Bell for his part had been interested in ecumenical questions since his time at Wells Theological College. Within a few weeks of his appointment, he helped to organise a Conference of Christian Ministers and Laymen – including many prominent representatives of the Nonconformist churches – to consider the impact of the war on Britain (Bell ruefully noted many years later than it 'revealed a good deal of difference, implicit or explicit, on the rightfulness of war').[104] The following year, Bell edited a collection of essays by leading Anglicans on *The War and the Kingdom of God*, which all supported the war, but emphasised that 'there is a greater cause than the cause of the patriot [and] a devotion higher to country or home'.[105] Bell had a strong interest in social and economic reform – he had initially hesitated in accepting Davidson's offer to become Chaplain because he was not sure the Archbishop shared his concerns – and he was convinced that the churches needed to work together to achieve progress. And, like many others, Bell was appalled by the way in which the churches across Europe had, following the outbreak of the war, acted as agents of division by aligning themselves uncritically with the cause of the nation rather than the ideal of peace. The death of two of his brothers on the battlefield only strengthened his convictions.

Bell was predictably closely involved in one of the more curious ecumenical wartime initiatives. Many Serbian Orthodox priests, including the leading theologian Fr Nikolai Velimirović, fled to Britain after their country was invaded by Austrian forces (Velimirović had excellent relations with a number of religious figures in Britain and America, and was deeply committed to promoting ecumenical understanding).[106] Velimirović proposed that the Church of England should help to organise theological training for young Serbian seminarists, an idea to which Davidson reacted with caution, not least because he was unable to secure the definite approval of the Archbishop of Belgrade (who was in exile on Corfu). George Bell played an important intermediary role in arranging a meeting between Velimirović and Davidson, which eventually led to the establishment of a training scheme under the supervision of Canon William Carnegie of St Margaret's Westminster, who himself had long developed a strong interest in the Eastern churches.[107] Some 60 Serbian students were eventually trained at Cuddesdon and Oxford.

Bell was also involved in efforts to improve relations between the Church of England and the main Nonconformist churches during the war. Church leaders came together to issue appeals and proclamations on issues ranging from temperance through to National Days of Prayer.[108] There was also greater cooperation at local level on such issues as ministering to the millions of soldiers who passed through military camp in Britain, before being sent to France, whilst many chaplains at the Front were profoundly influenced by their experiences of working with ministers from other denominations. The Bishop of Lincoln, Edward Hicks, recorded in his diary that in 1915 a number of Wesleyan ministers even raised the possibility of Reunion with the Church of England (Davidson invited the Bishop to sit on a committee to discuss the issue).[109] When F. Scott Lidgett wrote an article in the *Contemporary Review* the following year, proposing the establishment of a new Council of Churches to facilitate cooperation across the denominations, the Archbishop invited him to Lambeth to discuss the subject in detail ('our interview was most satisfactory in all ways').[110] The recognition of the need to address social and economic problems also increasingly cut across denominational boundaries. Many of the great post-war ecumenical meetings, such as the Conference on Christian Politics, Economics and Citizenship that met in Birmingham in 1924, had their roots in the shared experience of wartime. The determination to prevent another war also encouraged hundreds of local congregations to become corporate members of the League of Nations Union and, in time, fostered the inter-war peace movement (which itself became a setting for ecumenical debate in the 1930s).[111]

Although Davidson welcomed such developments, he remained intensely aware that the relationship between the Church of England and the other main churches could easily become a divisive issue for some Anglicans. He had repeatedly warned before the war that pushing too hard on the ecumenical question could hamper progress. The Archbishop echoed these sentiments in the summer of 1918, when meeting a group of Anglican clergy and lay people who wanted to build relations with local Nonconformist congregations. The deputation argued that promoting such measures as the exchange of pulpits – which would have allowed Nonconformist ministers to preach at Church of England services – was necessary to begin the long process of Christian Reunion. Davidson warned that such proposals would be difficult to regulate.[112] The Archbishop became a little less cautious in the months following the Armistice, in November 1918, when a number of initiatives took place to foster better relations between the churches. But even then, as will be seen in the following chapter, Davidson sought to forestall any definite developments until full discussion could take place at the Lambeth Conference of 1920.

The First World War did not destroy a stable pre-war *ancient régime* – which was itself something of an illusion – but the conflict undoubtedly accelerated change in areas ranging from the role of women through to the functions of the State. The mechanised slaughter of the Western Front served as brutal metaphor for a multifaceted modernity, which ripped through the established social and cultural landscape, and raised important questions about the future ordering of British society. The most pressing questions that the war raised for the Church of England were practical ones relating to such issues as the provision of chaplains. Important, too, was the need to situate the conflict within a religious vocabulary that was capable of engaging with a secular language about the righteousness of the national cause. Randall Davidson's familiar skills of diplomacy and consensus building in some ways served him well during the years 1914–18. He also showed real courage in warning against demonising the enemy at a time when public opinion wanted to hear about the brutality of the 'Hun'. The Archbishop's opinion was, though, less sought after than it had once been by Government ministers. Senior political figures were often too busy to see him. They were also perhaps less inclined to confide in him than had once been the case. The change should not be exaggerated, but Davidson did become a somewhat more peripheral figure beyond his own Church than had once been the case.

The Archbishop understood that he also faced the risk of falling out of touch with the aspirations of some within the Church of England itself. Although he commanded a good deal of respect and affection, he recognised that there was a perception in some quarters that he lacked the energy and imagination to engage with the concerns of a younger generation of clergy. Davidson himself sometimes seemed to agree. He certainly found his duties increasingly onerous. A few weeks before the Armistice, he wrote a long letter to Edward Talbot, Bishop of Winchester, describing his punishing schedule, and the challenge it posed in keeping 'a reasonable proportion between the great things [. . .] and the small things'.[113] He also echoed the opinion that had once been expressed by Archbishop Benson, many years before, that it seemed impossible to find any effective way of delegating much of the work. In the event, though, Davidson continued to serve as Archbishop of Canterbury for another decade, guiding the Church of England through a changing post-war world in which it faced issues that were less dramatic, but in some ways just as demanding, as the challenges of 1914–18.

Notes

1. For two excellent recent accounts of the origins and outbreak of the war, which base their analysis on the most recent scholarship, see Christopher M. Clark, *The Sleepwalkers: How Europe went to War in 1914* (London: Penguin Books, 2013); Thomas Otte, *July Crisis: The World's Descent into War* (Cambridge: Cambridge University Press, 2014).
2. Randall Davidson, *Quit You Like Men* (London: SPCK, 1915), p. 7.
3. Among the large literature on Anglican chaplains see, for example, Edward Madigan, *Faith Under Fire: Anglican Chaplains and the Great War* (London: Palgrave Macmillan, 2011); Michael Snape and Edward Madigan (eds), *The Clergy in Khaki: New Perspectives on British Army Chaplaincy in the First World War* (Farnham: Ashgate, 2013).
4. Amongst the large literature on the Church of England in the First World War, see Albert Marrin, *The Last Crusade: The Church of England in the First World War* (Durham, NC: Duke University Press, 1974); Robbins, *England, Ireland, Scotland, Wales*, pp. 96–151.
5. Among Winnington-Ingram's writings on the subject, see his *The Church in a Time of War* (London: Wells, Gardner, Darnton, 1915). For a helpful but dated biography, see S.C. Carpenter, *Winnington-Ingram: The Biography of Arthur Foley Winnington-Ingram, Bishop of London 1901–1939* (London: Hodder and Stoughton, 1949). For a recent nuanced discussion, see Stuart Bell, 'Malign or Maligned: Arthur Winnington-Ingram, Bishop of London, in the First World War', *Journal for the History of Modern Theology / Zeitschrift für Neuere Theologiegeschichte*, 20, 1 (2014), pp. 117–33. For a useful discussion of the reaction of leading British theologians to the war, particularly in the light of the dominant Germanophilia of a few years earlier, see Charles E. Bailey, 'The British Protestant Theologians in the First World War: Germanophobia Unleashed', *The Harvard Theological Review*, 77, 2 (1984), pp. 382–95.
6. On this topic, see Marrin, *Last Crusade*, pp. 143–76.
7. D.P. 13, fos. 315–23, Davidson Memorandum on 'Fourth Anniversary of the Beginning of the War', 4 August 1914 (quotation fos. 315–16).
8. D.P. 13, fos. 14–27, Davidson Memorandum, 13 December 1914 (quotation fo. 14).
9. D.P. 13, fos. 31–35, Undated Davidson Memorandum, c. 23 August 1915 (quotation fo. 31).
10. For memoranda describing Davidson's long talks with Curzon on the war see, for example, D.P. 13, fos. 31–6, c. 23 August 1915; fo. 36, 5 October 1915; fos. 37–42, 18 November 1915.
11. Stamfordham also wrote regularly to the Archbishop about war issues and political questions more generally. See, for example, D.P. 6, Letter 11, Stamfordham to Davidson, 17 August 1916; Letter 27, Stamfordham to Davidson, 18 August 1918.
12. For a valuable insight into the changing face of Government during the war, from the perspective of a superbly placed observer, see the relevant pages of the first volume of Stephen Roskill, *Hankey: Man of Secrets* (London: Collins, 1970–74), 3 vols.
13. D.P. 13, fos. 77–85, Davidson Memorandum, 24 December 1916.
14. D.P. 13, fos. 192–201, Davidson Memorandum, 9 December 1917 (quotation fo. 196).
15. For a lively study of George V, see David Canadine, *George V: The Unexpected King* (London: Allen Lane, 2014).
16. D.P. 13, fos. 311–14, Davidson Memorandum, 12 May 1918 (quotation fo. 312).
17. Kuhn, *Democratic Royalism*, pp. 82–111.
18. Among the large literature on the peace movement, see Ceadel, *Semi-detached Idealists*; Laity, *The British Peace Movement*. Laity, *The British Peace Movement*.
19. For the distinction between 'pacifism' and 'pacificism', see Martin Ceadel, *Pacifism in Britain, 1914–1945: The Defining of a Faith* (Oxford: Oxford University Press, 1980), pp. 1–8.
20. *Six Lambeth* Conferences, 1908 Conference, p. 329 (Resolution 52).
21. *Daily Mail*, 31 August 1914.
22. *Western Daily Press*, 21 August 1914; *Evening Dispatch*, 29 September 1914. For a valuable discussion of the extent to which these atrocities were real, rather than the creation of

propaganda, see John N. Horne and Alan Kramer, *German Atrocities, 1914: A History of Denial* (New Haven, NJ: Yale University Press, 2001).
23   For a recent discussion of the sermon, which seeks to challenge some traditional interpretations, see Bell, 'Malign or Maligned'.
24   Wilkinson, *Church of England*, p. 5. For a useful discussion on the social backgrounds of the Episcopacy in the period 1860–1960, see D.H.J. Morgan, 'The Social and Educational Background of Bishops – Continuities and Changes', *British Journal of Sociology*, 20, 3 (1969), pp. 295–310.
25   Randall Davidson, *The Testing of a Nation* (London: Macmillan, 1919), Sermon given in St Paul's on 4 August 1915.
26   D.P. 538, fos. 85–110, Sermon preached at Canterbury Cathedral, 26 October 1915 (quotation fo. 87).
27   Bell, *Davidson*, .Vol. 2, p. 736.
28   For a useful discussion of the various perspectives on Germany and Germans amongst Anglicans, see Marrin, *Last Crusade*, pp. 82–118.
29   D.P. 366, fos. 192–94, Davidson to Asquith, 7 May 1915 (quotation fo. 192). For a longer version of this letter see Documents Section 5.
30   D.P. 366, fos. 198–200, Davidson to Asquith, 15 May 1915 (quotation fo. 199).
31   *Chronicle of Convocation: Convocation of Canterbury (Upper House)*, 17 February 1916.
32   Bell, *Davidson*, Vol. 2, p. 778.
33   *Parliamentary Debates (Lords)*, 2 May 1917, col. 1015.
34   D.P. 194, fo. 195, Davidson to Mayor of Croydon, 22 October 1915.
35   D.P. 366, fos. 266–7, Davidson to Hall Caine, 17 April 1917.
36   *Times*, 30 September 1914.
37   D.P. 13, fos. 14–27, Davidson Memorandum, 13 December 1914.
38   J.G. Lockhart, *Cosmo Gordon Lang* (London: Hodder and Stoughton, 1949), pp. 248–51.
39   For a useful if dated discussion of the Conscientious Objector issue, see John Rae, *Conscience and Politics* (London: Oxford University Press, 1970). For a more recent and sophisticated discussion, see Lois Bibbings, *Telling Tales About Men: Conceptions of Conscientious Objectors to Military Service During the First World War* (Manchester: Manchester University Press, 2009). On conscientious objectors in the Methodist Church, see Hughes, *Conscience and Conflict*, pp. 57–70.
40   John Boulton, *Objection Overruled* (London: MacGibbon and Key, 1967).
41   For the most elegant contemporary argument on these lines, see A.S. Peake, *Prisoners of Hope: The Problem of the Conscientious Objector* (London: George Allen and Unwin, 1918). The articles had previously appeared in the *Primitive Methodist Leader*.
42   D.P. 348, fo. 39, Letter by Davidson's secretary to Collier, 23 April 1916.
43   D.P. 348, fo. 40, Letter by Davidson's secretary to W.O. Bishop, 27 April 1916.
44   Bell, *Davidson*, Vol. 2, p. 820.
45   Bell, *Davidson*, Vol. 2, p. 821.
46   *Parliamentary Debates (Lords)*, 25 January 1916, col. 1016.
47   Stephen Graham, *A Private in the Guards* (London: Heinemann, 1928), pp. 64–5.
48   See, for example, Madigan, *Faith Under Fire*; Snape and Madigan, *Clergy in Khaki*.
49   F.B. Macnutt (ed), *The Church in the* Furnace (London: Macmillan, 1917), p. 74.
50   For an account by perhaps the best-known Anglican chaplain detailing his efforts to focus on practical service, see P.B. Clayton, *Tales of Talbot House* (London: Chatto and Windus, 1919). See, too, G.A. Studdert-Kennedy [aka Woodbine Willy], *The Hardest Part* (London: Hodder and Stoughton, 1918), pp. xi–xvii.
51   On the formation of Talbot House, see P.B. Clayton, *Plain Tales from Flanders* (London: Longmans, 1929); Clayton, *Tales*.
52   For a valuable discussion of Davidson's visit to the Front, along with his diary, see Michael Snape, 'Archbishop Davidson's visit to the Western Front, May 1916', in Melanie Barber, Stephen Taylor with Gabriel Sewell (eds), *From the Reformation to the Permissive Society: A Miscellany in Celebration of the 400th Anniversary of Lambeth Palace Library* (Woodbridge: Boydell Press for the Church of England Record Society, 2010), pp. 455–520.

53 The issue had, though, concerned the Bishops from early in the war. See Lambeth Palace Archives, BM 6, Meeting of Bishops, 28–9 January 1915.
54 *Parliamentary Debates (Lords)*, col. 669.
55 D.P. 374, fos. 42–4, Davidson to Kitchener, 23 October 1914 (quotation fo. 42). Also see D.P. 13, fos. 14–27, Davidson Memorandum, 13 December 1914.
56 Wilkinson, *Church of England*, p. 103.
57 Quoted in Wilkinson, *Church of England*, p. 105. See, too, Lambeth Palace Archives, BM 6, Meeting of Bishops, 20–1 October 1914.
58 *Times*, 28 April 1917 (Letters by Davidson and Horton).
59 D.P. 13, fos. 51–5, Davidson Memorandum on Interview with Prime Minister, 26 May 1916 (quotation fo. 54).
60 On Royden, see Sheila Fletcher, *Maude Royden: A Life* (Oxford: Basil Blackwell, 1989).
61 D.P. 195, fos 273–77, Riley to Davidson, 14 July 1916; fo. 307, Davidson to Riley, 22 July 1916; fos 309–10, Riley to Davidson, 25 July 1916.
62 Iremonger, *Temple*, pp. 206–7.
63 *Times*, 14 September 1916.
64 Henson in particular regarded the Mission as 'a grave practical blunder for the time was inopportune'. Evelyn Foley Braley (ed), *Letters of Herbert Hensley Henson* (London: SPCK, 1951), p. 14.
65 Iremonger, *Temple*, p. 211.
66 Henson, *Retrospect*, Vol. 1, p. 179.
67 Wilkinson, *Church of England*, p. 72.
68 Bell, *Davidson*, Vol. 2, p. 809.
69 *Chronicle of Convocation: Convocation of Canterbury (Upper House)*, 9 February 1917.
70 For an illuminating discussion see Jay Winter, *Sites of Mourning, Sites of Memory* (Cambridge: CUP, 1995, pp. 54–79.
71 See for example the book by the physicist Oliver Lodge, *Raymond, or Life and Death* (New York: George Doran, 1916).
72 Bell, *Davidson*, Vol. 2, pp. 829–30.
73 For a useful discussion, see Owen Chadwick, *Hensley Henson: A Study in the Friction Between Church and State* (Oxford: Clarendon, 1983), pp. 128–57.
74 D.P. 13, fos. 184–86, Davidson Memorandum, 5 August 1917.
75 Bell, *Davidson*, Vol. 2, p. 853.
76 Prestige, *Gore*, p. 395.
77 D.P. 13, fos. 226–32, Davidson Memorandum, 25 December 1917 (quotations fos. 229–30). For a longer extract from this Memorandum see Documents Section 1.
78 *The Times*, 20 December 1917 (Letter by Halifax); 22 December 1917 (Letter by William Sanday and others).
79 *Morning Post*, 17 December 1917 (Letter by Lord Woolmer).
80 D.P. 13, fos. 233–7, Davidson Memorandum, 8 January 1918 (quotations *passim*).
81 Henson, *Retrospect*, Vol. 1, p. 238.
82 W.R. Inge, *Diary of a Dean: St Paul's 1911–1934* (London: Hutchinson, 1934), p. 44.
83 Lockhart, *Halifax*, p. 251.
84 Bell, *Davidson*, Vol. 2, p. 876.
85 *Letters of Henson*, p. 16.
86 *The Archbishops' Committee on Church and State: A Report With Appendices* (London: SPCK, 1916).
87 *Chronicle of Convocation: Convocation of Canterbury (Upper House)*, 4 July 1917.
88 Matthew Grimley, *Citizenship, Community and the Church of England* (Oxford: Clarendon Press, 2004), p. 18.
89 For an account of the meeting which led to the formation of Life and Liberty, see *Times*, 16 July 1917. On Temple's role in Life and Liberty, see John Kent, *William Temple: Church, State and Society in Britain, 1880–1950* (Cambridge: Cambridge University Press), pp. 73–94. See, too, Norman, *Church and Society in England*, pp. 275–6; Kenneth A. Thompson, *Bureaucracy and Church Reform: The Organizational Response of the Church of England to Social Change 1800–1965* (Oxford: Clarendon Press, 1970), pp. 156–75.

90 *Times*, 20 June 1917 (Letter by Temple *et al*).
91 Henson, *Retrospect*, Vol. 1, p. 207.
92 Iremonger, *Temple*, pp. 235–6.
93 Iremonger, *Temple*, p. 243.
94 Iremonger, *Temple*, pp. 244–46; Kent, *Temple*, pp. 90–1.
95 Stuart Mews, quoted in Grimley, *Citizenship, Community and the Church of England*, p. 18.
96 Iremonger, *Temple*, p. 248
97 Iremonger, *Temple*, p. 251.
98 D.P. 13, fos. 315–23, Davidson Memorandum on the 'Fourth Anniversary since the Beginning of the War', 4 August 1918.
99 *Chronicle of Convocation: Convocation of Canterbury (Upper House)*, 7 February 1918.
100 *Times*, 30 September 1918 (Letter by Davidson).
101 Bell, *Davidson*, Vol. 2, p. 912.
102 D.P. 366, fo. 24, Davidson to Cecil, 11 February 1918; fos. 25–7, Davidson to Söderblom, 12 February 1918; fo. 50, Balfour to Davidson, 30 March 1918.
103 W. Lowther Clark, quoted in Ronald C.D. Ronald Jasper, *George Bell, Bishop of Chichester* (Oxford: Oxford University Press, 1967), p. 22.
104 Bell, *Davidson*, Vol. 2, p. 744. See, too, Jasper, *Bell*, pp. 23–4.
105 G.K.A. Bell (ed), *The War and the Kingdom of God* (London: Longmans, 1915), p. 5.
106 On Velimirović's time in London, see, for example, Hughes, *Beyond Holy Russia*, pp. 110-11. For a brief biography of Velimirović in English, see Florida State University (Strozier Library, Special Collections), Stephen Graham Papers, Box 581, 23A, 'Nikolai Velimirović in London'.
107 On Carnegie's role in fostering dialogue between Anglicans and Orthodox during the first year of the war, see Stephen Graham, *Part of the Wonderful Scene* (London: Collins, 1964), pp. 102–4.
108 For some useful information on Days of Prayer during this period, see Philip Williamson, 'National Days of Prayer: The Churches, the State and Public Worship in Britain 1899–1957', *English Historical Review*, 128 (2013), pp. 323–66.
109 Evans, *Hicks*, pp. 3–4.
110 D.P. 261, fo. 92, Davidson Memorandum on 'Interview with Scott Lidgett at Lambeth', 9 January 1917.
111 Donald Birn, *The League of Nations Union, 1918–1945* (Oxford: Clarendon Press, 1981), pp. 133–35.
112 D.P. 261, fos. 138–49, Material relating to a visit to Lambeth Palace by a delegation seeking to promote local inter-church dialogue (quotation fo. 144).
113 D.P. 13, fos. 324–8, Davidson to Bishop of Winchester, 15 September 1918 (quotation fo. 324). For a longer extract from this letter, see Documents Section 2.

5 Archbishop Davidson and the development of the Ecumenical Movement (1918–1928)

Randall Davidson's health was as poor as every during his final decade at Canterbury. He nevertheless still worked tirelessly throughout the last decade of his archiepiscopate, although his holidays became longer and, judging from his correspondence, more important to him as a source of physical and mental well-being. Archbishop Lang began to play a larger role in important Church issues than before, taking the lead on such matters as relations with the Nonconformist churches. Davidson also delegated a good deal of work to George Bell, who drafted much of the Archbishop's correspondence, as well as playing a significant role in the discussions with other churches that took place throughout the 1920s.[1] Indeed, when Bell left Lambeth Palace in 1924 to become Dean of Canterbury, Davidson noted that 'there are some considerable departments of our central doings which have really been chiefly in his hands and he knows more about them than I do'. Amongst the 'doings' he noted were Bell's dealings with the Foreign Office and Colonial Office, along with his deep knowledge of Eastern Christianity, and the intricacies of politics in the Near East. Although the Archbishop believed that 'nothing has passed without my knowledge', at least in the most important areas of business, his growing detachment influenced the way in which he reacted to developments.[2]

The social, political, and cultural landscape of inter-war Britain was very different from the Edwardian period. Literary works like T. S. Eliot's *The Wasteland* (1922) echoed the sense of desolation and anomie of the post-war world.[3] The election of a minority Labour Government in 1924 reflected important, if uncertain, shifts in political power. The General Strike of 1926 showed the potential for long-standing social and economic divisions to explode into industrial unrest. Middle-class families found it harder to afford servants. The flapper became as potent a symbol of female emancipation as the right to vote. Russia was controlled by the Bolsheviks, who threatened to spread their revolutionary creed around the world, sweeping away the old social and economic order. The seeds of many of these changes were sown long before the outbreak of the First World War, but the feeling that times were changing was palpable, fuelled by a sense that something as traumatic as the Great War could not leave the world unaltered. Davidson continued to believe that the Church of England needed to adapt in order to retain its position in national life. There was certainly no shortage of controversial and difficult subjects for the Archbishop to deal with during the decade following the Armistice, ranging from Prayer Book revision to the Church of England's relationship with Parliament, but he was confident that he still had much to contribute. On more than one occasion, he gently pointed out that the elderly sometimes had experience that gave them a more accurate perspective on life than the young.

Davidson remained staunchly committed to maintaining the Church of England as a broad Church throughout his last decade at Canterbury. In the years before 1914, the uncertain boundaries of Anglican 'orthodoxy' had usually been interrogated by debates over questions of Ritualism and Modernism. In the years after 1918, questions of doctrinal orthodoxy continued to loom large, but issues of Ritualism were for a time supplanted by disagreement over policy towards other churches, a subject which nevertheless raised similar questions about the nature of Anglican identity. It was seen in the last chapter that the First World War gave an important impetus to ecumenism, fuelled by anxiety about the way in which the passions of nationalism had so easily eclipsed the bonds of faith (Davidson himself noted that 'the war has done much to break down middle walls of partition, and to open people's eyes to one another's fields and flowers and fruits').[4] The 'Appeal to All Christian People', issued by the Lambeth Conference of 1920, signalled a desire among the Anglican hierarchy to search for new forms of Christian unity that would still allow the various churches to 'retain much that has long been distinctive in their methods of worship and service'.[5] The years that followed were marked by numerous attempts to develop closer relations between the Church of England and other churches both at home and abroad.

Many of these discussions seem, decades later, to have been surrounded by a patina of unreality. Davidson's approach to ecumenical questions was governed, at least in part, by their potential impact on the unity of the Church of England. He never shared the grandiose hopes of those who believed in moving quickly to sweep away the denominational boundaries that had for so long disfigured the universal Church. The Archbishop instead sought to foster what might be termed a kind of Christian good neighbourliness. This is not to say that he was blind to what Lord Halifax called, at one point in the Malines Conversations, 'the glory of the vision' of a reunified Church.[6] Davidson did not, though, believe that the vision could be made actual in the near future. The Archbishop was too pragmatic to believe in the possibility of a single leap out of the constraints of history. His ecumenism consisted above all in promoting a 'wholesome attitude' towards other churches, fostering agreement on issues of importance, whilst accepting that the politics of Church Reunion set definite boundaries to what could be achieved.

The 1920 Lambeth Conference and the 'Appeal to All Christian People'

Davidson did not look forward to the 1920 Lambeth Conference, fretting a few weeks before it started that the prospect was causing him 'infinite anxiety', in large part because he thought the whole question of creedal orthodoxy was going to be raised once again.[7] Charles Gore even believed that the Church of England might be heading for a formal split. Davidson also knew that the question of relations with other churches was likely to prove divisive. The potential for controversy was made clear when a conference between leading figures from the Church of England and various Nonconformist churches took place at Mansfield College Oxford, early in 1920, and published a series of resolutions calling for greater interchange of pulpits and a relaxation of rules relating to admission to Communion.[8] The ECU promptly responded by suggesting that such proposals made 'for unreality instead of true unity, and violat[ed] all Catholic order'.[9] Other clergy argued that the Mansfield resolutions would, if adopted, 'destroy our hope of reunion with the Orthodox Churches of the East, or with the Roman Catholic Church'.[10] Davidson repeatedly suggested that such issues should be referred to the Lambeth Conference, perhaps hoping that the assembled Bishops would be able to frame some kind of agreement capable of commanding a wide degree of assent. When the Conference finally met, it addressed numerous questions, ranging from international relations to 'the position of women in the Councils and ministrations of the Church', but its most far-reaching move was to issue the Appeal calling on all Christians to work for 'a visible unity of the whole Church'.

It is, perhaps, a surprise that the Bishops ever agreed on the format of the Appeal and the associated resolutions, which included a revised version of the Lambeth Quadrilateral, approved by the 1888 Conference, that set down the principles which should inform any move towards Reunion with other churches. The Appeal softened the fourth point of the Quadrilateral, though, which had stated that 'the historic Episcopate, locally adapted in the methods of its administration' should form the basis of any reunited Church. It instead acknowledged that other ministries could be 'manifestly blessed and owned by the Holy Spirit' – a clear attempt to reach out to the non-Episcopal churches – whilst still suggesting that history and experience indicated the value of Episcopacy. The assembled Bishops at Lambeth almost unanimously approved both the 'Appeal' and the associated report produced by the Committee on Reunion and Intercommunion. It is striking in hindsight that men as different as Hensley Henson and Frank Weston could agree on such a potentially divisive issue. And, it seems, the extent of support for the Appeal even took participants at the 1920 Lambeth Conference by surprise.

Cosmo Lang, who chaired the Committee on Reunion and Intercommunion, shared Davidson's forebodings about the Lambeth Conference in general and the work of his Committee in particular. He believed that it would be difficult to secure consensus among 'a crowd of Bishops representing every possible point of view' – and certainly any agreement that went beyond 'mere platitudes'.[11] The early sessions of the Committee seemed to confirm his fears. Much time was spent hearing evidence, but there were also wrangles among members on such questions as the validity of Presbyterian orders, as well as divisions over a proposed scheme for uniting a number of different churches into a single South Indian Church. Henson noted in his diary that he was treated with 'rudeness' by one of the Scottish Bishops (it is possible that some Bishops might have thought they were treated rudely by the acerbic Henson).[12] He also thought the Bishop of Zanzibar (Frank Weston) might threaten schism if he did not get his way.

It is hard to know, given such unpromising early signs, why the mood of the Committee changed halfway through the Conference. Lang was so struck by the sudden turnaround that he believed it must be the result of divine inspiration. A more prosaic view suggests that the Archbishop of York was himself instrumental in advancing discussions, by suggesting that the Committee produce a general appeal for Christian unity, rather than focus on more thorny practical questions about inter-denominational relations. George Bell also played a key role, not least by suggesting to Davidson that a small group of the younger Bishops should meet to prepare the Appeal (Bell himself acted as secretary to the group). Disagreements still continued, even after a draft was sent to the full Conference. Henson moved a number of amendments. Some Anglo-Catholic members criticised any watering down of the commitment to Episcopal governance as a necessary condition of Reunion. Frank Weston nevertheless proved unusually cooperative, despite his recalcitrance a few years earlier over Kikuyu, refusing to support the small group of Anglo-Catholic Bishops who were unhappy with the final document. The Appeal was eventually approved by the full Conference – an event marked by 'the singing of the Doxology [. . .] with much fervour'.[13]

Randall Davidson was present at some of the discussions of the Committee on Reunion, although he was not a particularly active participant (in part due to his perennial ill health). Many of those who attended the 1920 Lambeth Conference paid tribute to the Archbishop for creating an atmosphere designed to foster understanding and agreement.[14] The Archbishop of Armagh told Bell that Davidson was 'a wonderfully wise old man' (Bell agreed, noting that Davidson's readiness to allow each Bishop to have his say helped to diffuse tension, even though it made the full sessions of the Conference quite lengthy).[15] Henry Montgomery, the former Secretary of the Society for the Propagation of the Gospel, also believed that the Archbishop's manifest sense of 'fairness' helped to promote agreement on many issues.[16] Davidson noted in his private reflections that he had made considerable efforts to ensure that all the committees were provided with the detailed documentary evidence needed to inform their deliberations. His decision reflected both his own *modus operandi* and a hope that such an approach would foster agreement (the Archbishop was as ever inclined to the view that reasonable people could agree about even the most controversial subjects if they studied them with enough care). Davidson's perennial skill at reconciling opponents formed part of the organisational warp and woof within which the Lambeth Appeal was drafted and approved. The presentation to the Archbishop and his wife of an ebony crozier at the close of the Conference reflected genuine warmth of feeling among the Bishops, whilst a motion praising Davidson for 'the unfailing ability and strength and courtesy with which he has fulfilled the duties of President of the Conference' was met with 'profound applause'.[17]

Despite the positive response to the Appeal, the final text still contained its share of the 'mere platitudes' that had concerned the Archbishop of York before the Conference started. The real difficulties were effectively postponed until the time came to translate general declarations of goodwill into practical proposals. The 1920 Conference passed off without the divisions that Davidson had feared. He believed that the Appeal was 'far more generous, far less controversial, and in a true sense much more spiritual than any corresponding document which has been issued by any gathering of importance'. The Archbishop had, however, long been sceptical of grand rhetoric. The notion of the prophetic voice was in many ways alien to him. Davidson noted shortly after the Conference that there would soon be demands for action from those who 'think having said all this we ought to go straight ahead'.[18] In the spring of 1921, he noted in a private memorandum that

> we cannot get Reunion by a short cut [. . .] It will take years to get our principles rightly understood and assimilated and any attempt to press hurriedly forward is bound to defeat itself. But it is very difficult to persuade eager men and women, whose interest in these subjects is recent and crude, that we must go step by step, and steadily avoid even the appearance of hurry. This delay is always distasteful to the enthusiasts, and especially the young enthusiast, and I have to fulfil the unpleasant role of curbing the sort of buoyant and sanguine expectations that the work can be accomplished forthwith [. . .] so sound are its principles, so Christian its aim'.[19]

The Church of England and the Eastern churches

Davidson had been interested in Eastern Christianity since he was a young man, but he never shared the hopes of those who believed that it might be possible to achieve some form of Reunion (or at least rapprochement) between the Eastern Orthodox churches and the Anglican Communion, a prospect that had strong appeal to some on the Anglo-Catholic wing of the Church of England after *Apostolicae Curae* (1896) destroyed any prospect of a closer relationship with Rome. He did, however, establish the Eastern Churches Committee in 1919 to monitor the situation of Christians in Eastern Europe and the Near East. The Committee included a number of individuals, like Sir Samuel Hoare, who were active in diplomacy and politics. The collapse of the Tsarist and Ottoman Empires in 1917–18 created a crisis for the Eastern churches. Many Russian Orthodox clergy fled to the West. Those who remained often faced persecution and death at the hands of the Bolshevik regime. The collapse of the Ottoman Empire, and the subsequent creation of a Turkish State, created huge uncertainty both for the Greek population in the west of Asia Minor and the Armenian minority in the eastern districts (many of whom had died as a result of persecution during the war). The future of the Ecumenical Patriarchate in Constantinople was also brought into question by the creation of the new Turkey.

The 1920 Lambeth Conference expressed its 'heartfelt sympathy' with the plight of many Christians in the former Ottoman lands, along with its 'deep sympathy' for a Russian Church that was already facing 'terrible persecution'.[20] It also passed resolutions thanking the Ecumenical Patriarch for expressing a wish to confer with the Anglican churches (a delegation from the Greek Church attended the Lambeth Conference, including some sessions of the Committee on Reunion and Intercommunion, although its members were perplexed to see how Anglicans 'differ from each other in faith' whilst claiming 'to constitute one undivided whole').[21] Davidson's attention over the next few years was directed primarily towards helping members of the Eastern churches facing persecution, not least through discussions with the Foreign Office, rather than with more specific questions about the future relationship between Anglicanism and Eastern Christianity. There were, though, many Anglicans who believed that, in the wake of the Lambeth Appeal, the time had come to work towards a fuller relationship between the Church of England and the Eastern churches in general and the Eastern Orthodox churches in particular.

It was difficult for members of the Church of England hierarchy to work with the various Eastern churches. The Eastern Orthodox Church alone was divided into a number of Patriarchates (the authority of the Ecumenical Patriarch at Constantinople was strictly limited – a feature favourably contrasted by some Orthodox theologians with Papal authority in the Roman Catholic Church). The Russian Church in emigration was deeply fragmented. So too was the Orthodox Church in Russia itself (particularly after 1922 with the emergence of an officially sponsored 'Living Church'). The plight of Orthodox clergy who remained in Russia received extensive coverage in the British press – reports that formed part of a broader narrative about the threat posed to civilised values by Soviet communism.[22] Davidson received numerous reports describing the murder of Russian priests, as well as the effects of the famine ravaging the country, and he worked hard to persuade the British Government to support relief efforts.[23] When Patriarch Tikhon was arrested in 1922, Davidson raised his case in the House of Lords, and took the lead in organising a letter of protest by Church leaders to the Soviet Government (the predictable response from Moscow was that Tikhon had worked 'hand in hand' with the last Tsar rather than helping the poor). In July, the Soviet Deputy Foreign Minister wrote to George Bell, rejecting Davidson's proposal to send representatives to Russia to see the situation at first-hand, adding that the proposal was typical of senior clerics bound together by self-interest and class solidarity.[24] The following year, the Archbishop again joined with other Church leaders to protest about the 'savage persecution' taking place in Russia against 'all forms of religious belief. Davidson's protests were not motivated by any sense that the Church of England had a particular affinity with the Russian Orthodox Church. They instead reflected his strong feeling of responsibility for helping fellow Christians who were suffering brutal persecution.

There were many within the Church of England who took a more far-reaching view of the potential for building relations with the Eastern churches. Canon J. A. Douglas, who served on the Eastern Churches Committee, founded the journal the *Christian East* in 1921, which published numerous articles and reports on Eastern Christianity and its relationship to the Western churches. The journal was published under the auspices of the Anglican and Eastern Churches Association, an organisation dating back to 1864, whose members were committed to working for Reunion with the Eastern Orthodox churches.[25] The potential for discussions about Reunion to cause division within the Church of England was shown clearly by the developments that took place in 1921–22. In 1921, at the request of Davidson, Arthur Headlam (then Regius Professor of Divinity at Oxford) drafted on behalf of the Eastern Churches Committee a statement on the *Terms of Intercommunion Suggested between the Church of England and the Churches in Communion with Her and the Eastern Orthodox Church*.[26] The document was carefully written to exclude anything that might complicate relations with the Nonconformist churches. It was as a result somewhat vacuous when dealing with such questions as the *filioque* and the number of sacraments, contenting itself with the suggestion that differences between the churches were as much a matter of historical contingency as doctrinal significance.

The same was not true of a Declaration of Faith issued the following year by members of the ECU, including Douglas and Gore, addressed to the Ecumenical Patriarch in Constantinople. The signatories declared that there were seven sacraments. The declaration also included a firm commitment to the doctrine of Real Presence as well as a statement that 'honour should be given to the holy and ever-virgin Mother of God and the Saints departed'.[27] The Declaration of Faith was published in the *Church Times*, and quickly met with a barrage of criticism, not least from Headlam, who pointed out that it should be seen as a 'sectional document'. More vehement was the response of the Chairman of the Church Association, who fretted that the Church of England was abandoning many of the doctrines and practices set down during the Reformation. The development of closer relations with the Eastern churches was not as sensitive to the Protestant wing of the Church of England as dialogue with the Roman Catholic Church. Many books had, though, been published in English over the previous 50 years condemning the corruption of Eastern Christianity in general and the Russian Orthodox Church in particular.[28] Members of the ECU, for their part, continued to favour building closer relations with the Eastern Orthodox churches in order to cement Anglicanism within a universal Church untainted by Protestantism.

Davidson recognised that the situation of all the Eastern churches was bound up with the international upheavals that followed the end of the war. The fate of the Ecumenical Patriarch, in particular, was governed in large part by the future of Constantinople. The city was occupied by allied forces at the end of 1918, but over the next few years bitter fighting took place between Greeks and Turks across the western fringes of Asia Minor, whilst Constantinople itself was eventually placed under Turkish rule. Davidson found himself in an invidious position in 1922, when the two candidates for the post of Patriarch came to London to lobby for his support, and the Archbishop predictably declined to take sides (the rivalry between the two candidates was itself closely bound up with Greek political divisions). Davidson was impressed by the candidate who eventually proved successful, Meletios Metaxakis, who was closely aligned with the radical Greek politician Eleuthérios Venizelos.[29] He was shrewd enough to recognise that Meletios was 'a vigorous politician', keen to mobilise international support both for his own position and for the Patriarchate more generally, though he mixed 'policy and principle' in a way that Davidson found disconcerting.[30] It was for this reason that the Archbishop responded cautiously to a letter from Meletios, in July 1922, offering recognition of Anglican orders. Although Meletios's action was prompted by a genuine ecumenical instinct, he was also shrewd enough to realise that British support could be invaluable at a time when the Turkish Government was threatening to expel the Patriarchate from Constantinople. Politics also played a part in the decision of the Jerusalem Patriarch Damianos to offer qualified recognition of Anglican orders in 1923, since he hoped to win the financial and political support of the British authorities in Palestine. The Roman Catholic press in Britain was not unfair in suggesting that 'the exigencies of the Jerusalem Patriarchate [. . .] dictated a policy calculated to secure support and protection from the Anglicans and the British Imperial rulers of Palestine'.[31] The process of building Christian unity could never be divorced from questions of political calculation.

Davidson frequently met with Foreign Secretary Lord Curzon to discuss the situation of the Ecumenical Patriarchate in the run up to the 1922-3 Lausanne Conference (which provided a formal end to the hostilities that had raged in south-east Europe during the First World War). The Archbishop consistently argued that the Patriarchate should remain in Constantinople. He also asked Curzon to use his position to help the Armenians, many of whom remained under Turkish rule, as well as calling on the Foreign Secretary to do what he could to protect members of the Nestorian Assyrian Church.[32] The Archbishop remained sceptical, though, about the potential for radically improving relations between the Church of England and the Eastern churches. His doubts were broadly shared by Charles Gore, who chaired the Eastern Churches Committee, and himself undertook a long tour of south-east Europe in 1923 in order to increase his knowledge.[33] Gore's long-standing emphasis on the need to set down the doctrinal boundaries of Anglicanism meant that he was unable to share the hopes of those enthusiasts who believed that centuries of division could somehow be swept away in a headlong rush for greater understanding and even Reunion. For all the temperamental and intellectual differences between Gore and Davidson, both men understood that it was impossible to escape from the constraints of history. Their interest in Eastern Christianity did not blind them to the enormous differences between the Christian traditions of East and West.

The visit of numerous dignitaries from the Eastern Orthodox Church to London in 1925, to celebrate the sixteen-hundredth anniversary of the Council of Nicaea, provided a brief new flurry of ecumenical enthusiasm. In a sermon preached at Westminster Abbey, attended by (among others) the Orthodox Patriarchs of Alexandria and Jerusalem, Davidson told the congregation that the original Council should be admired for seeking to represent 'the voice and conscience of the whole Christian Church'.[34] The lasting impact of such assemblies was, though, once again nugatory (although the Nikaean Club, formed with Davidson's support in 1925, survives to this day with a mission 'to further relations with non-Anglican Christian churches'). Nor was Davidson particularly surprised or disappointed. In a separate speech, attended by many of the distinguished visitors, he once again made clear that Reunion in all its forms would necessarily be a long-term process.[35] Davidson had in any case for some time only taken a limited personal interest in the details of relations with the various Eastern churches, despite his long-standing interest in the subject (the Lambeth Palace files suggest that George Bell dealt with much of the correspondence on his own initiative). The Archbishop was certainly ready to devote energy to easing the plight of Christians caught up in the turmoil that swept through the Eastern and South-Eastern Europe in the wake of the First World War. He was much less convinced about the wisdom of building closer ties with an array of churches that were fragmented and vulnerable to the vicissitudes of international politics.

The Malines conversations and relations with the Roman Catholic Church

Although relations with the Eastern churches created unease among some in the Church of England, it was a far less controversial question than the relationship with Rome. The Report on Reunion approved by the 1920 Lambeth Conference noted that the Church of England would always be ready 'to discuss conditions of reunion' with the Roman Catholic Church,[36] but also acknowledged the difficulties that would be involved in such a process. Davidson was as well aware of the obstacles as anyone. The Archbishop was therefore perturbed when, in the summer of 1921, Lord Halifax informed him that he would shortly meet with Cardinal Mercier, Archbishop of Malines (Mechelen) in Belgium.[37] Halifax was to be accompanied by the Abbé Fernand Portal, who had been closely involved in the previous round of conversations between Anglicans and Roman Catholics in the mid-1890s, which ended with the publication of *Apostolicae Curae* by Leo XIII. Davidson consulted with Archbishop Lang before writing a cautious letter of introduction to Mercier, noting that Halifax was not 'an ambassador or formal representative of the Church of England', with the result that anything he said was simply 'personal opinion'.[38] His caution was merited. When visiting Mercier in the autumn of 1921, Halifax proposed a conference between Anglicans and Roman Catholics, a suggestion that seems to have taken the Cardinal by surprise, although he quickly agreed to future talks. Halifax was typically both ingenuous and calculating. He had been sincerely inspired by the ideals set down in the 'Appeal to all Christian

People' – but he was also shrewd enough to recognise that many of the Bishops who assembled at Lambeth had assumed the most likely advances would be in relations with Protestant churches both in Britain and in Europe. Any form of 'conference' between representatives of the Anglican and Roman Catholic Churches was bound to prove controversial.[39]

The first of the Malines Conversations took place in December 1921, when Halifax returned to Belgium accompanied by Walter Frere from Mirfield and Armitage Robinson (Dean of Wells and a friend of Davidson).[40] The participants agreed to meet again – the initial focus was on preliminary attempts to sketch out areas of agreement and disagreement on theological questions – although in the event their meeting was delayed for more than a year. Davidson was still extremely nervous about giving any official *imprimatur* to Halifax's activities (he was unwilling to make any kind of private statement of support unless the Pope was ready to act in a similar vein). Archbishop Lang, who knew Halifax well, was equally cautious. In 1922, Halifax published a book *A Call to Reunion Arising out of Discussions with Cardinal Mercier*,[41] although it attracted surprisingly little interest, doubtless because it was viewed as little more than a fresh expression of its author's well-known position. The two Archbishops' fears were certainly roused when they saw the statements drawn up by the participants in the second round of conversations that took place early in 1923.

The memoranda drawn up at Malines blithely suggested that the focus of future discussions should be on administrative rather than doctrinal questions (a distinction that was in practice unreal). They also affirmed that the Papacy should be seen 'as the centre and head on earth of the Catholic Church'. Davidson knew that such ideas would be deeply controversial for many Anglicans. The Archbishop had already told a meeting of Bishops a few weeks earlier about the Conversations, making a number of them 'rather uncomfortable'. Hensley Henson, who was by now Bishop of Durham, pointed out that the delegates were hardly representative of the wider Church'.[42] Davidson himself wrote in one of his private notes that,

> This is a big matter which may mark the beginning of a movement which will loom large in Church history, but I do not myself attribute to it in my heart the importance which is attributed to it by Halifax and his friends, or, on the other hand, by the Bishop of Durham who was the one Bishop at our meeting on the 25th to criticise unfavourably what had been done.[43]

Davidson could not share the hopes and fears felt by many at the prospect of closer relations with Rome – but he did understand the potential divisions that could be caused by any significant moves in that direction.

The following months proved to be a difficult time for Davidson. On reading the statements produced at Malines, Davidson quickly wrote to Halifax noting with characteristic understatement that 'I think the difficulties loom larger to me than they do to you'.[44] The Archbishop had already written to Robinson expressing his concerns, most notably about the question of Papal supremacy, which he regarded as a critical doctrinal and administrative question.[45] He wrote to Mercier a few days later, expressing a similar view, adding that the principle of Papal authority 'is not one to which the adherence of the Church of England could be obtained'.[46] Mercier replied with a long letter responding to Davidson's concerns, and wrote privately to Halifax expressing anxiety about the caution of both Davidson and Lang, which he feared might prevent progress.[47] Halifax for his part regretted the lack of 'enthusiasm' shown by the two men, but was ready to take on board Davidson's concerns, which the Archbishop repeated to Mercier in another letter in May 1923 ('the underlying questions of a fundamental character remain quite unsolved').[48] Davidson also worked closely with Lang during these critical months (the two Archbishops prepared a joint memorandum in April 1923 making clear their view that there was little value discussing administrative questions as a means of seeking to resolve deep doctrinal divisions).[49] George Bell continued to play a significant background role, not least in holding informal talks with a number of leading English Catholics, who were generally sceptical about the chances of fundamentally changing the relationship between the Anglican and Roman Catholic churches. Although Halifax's talks at Malines became the best known and most controversial of the dialogues that took place between representatives of the Church of England and the Church of Rome during the first half of the 1920s, there was a web of other informal discussions within Britain itself, even if they never acquired the prominence later accorded to the Malines Conversations.

Davidson's concerns were amplified by his anxiety over the increasing divisions within the Church of England. The revision of the Prayer Book – which was to explode so dramatically a few years later – was already creating friction between the Evangelical and Anglo-Catholic wings of the Church. Such tensions were not eased when, in July 1923, the second Anglo-Catholic Conference sent a telegram to the Pope using what one critic described as 'almost obsequious language'.[50] Davidson was anxious that the full details of the Malines Conversations should not become public. In July 1923, he even made a night-time dash to Kings Cross Station, in order to intercept Gore, who was on his way to Northumberland, to urge him to use his influence to ensure that Halifax did not say or do anything that was likely to cause controversy.[51] The Archbishop was in a difficult position. Davidson was too aware of what was taking place to be able to maintain indefinitely the fiction that the Malines Conversations were nothing more than a private exchange of views. Yet he also knew that if he tried to exercise greater control over proceedings, then it might give an even clearer *imprimatur* to the activities of Halifax.

In the autumn of 1923, Davidson wrote a formal memorandum setting down what had happened over the previous 18 months. He also suggested that the delegation to any third round of conversations should include Charles Gore who, despite his strong Anglo-Catholicism, had long been sceptical about the possibility of Reunion with Rome, and was passionately committed to the defence of the distinctive identity of Anglicanism. Beresford Kidd, the Church historian and Warden of Keble College Oxford, was also proposed as a delegate. Davidson presided over a meeting at Lambeth Palace in early October 1923, ahead of the third round of conversations,[52] in which he told those going to Belgium that the statements agreed at Malines in March would do 'untold mischief' if they were to become public. Yet he also firmly declined to set an agenda for the talks, insisting that the delegates should use their own judgement, a move that was presumably designed to maintain the fiction that the Malines Conversations were entirely unofficial. The Archbishop was in an invidious position, seeking to constrain the scope of the talks, whilst insisting that he was not involved in the process.

The conversations that took place at Malines in November 1923 were less dramatic in scope than the previous set of talks, although they continued to focus on the Biblical foundations for Papal authority, exploring in particular the distinction between spiritual and temporal authority. Gore predictably objected to any attempt to establish a strong basis for Papal authority, at least as anything more than a purely spiritual phenomenon, leading to some sharp exchanges with Mercier (Halifax later noted that he found Gore's presence very distracting since it disrupted the harmonious tone that had prevailed in previous discussions).[53] Both delegations once again came up with summaries of the proceedings. Davidson himself decided to make public the Malines Conversations, in December 1923, when he mentioned them in a public letter to the Metropolitans of the Anglican Communion. He circulated a draft of his letter to a number of those involved in the talks, making some changes in response, although he considered his final choice of wording 'reticent'.[54] Most of the letter focused on relations with the various Protestant churches in Britain and beyond, along with the discussions that had taken place with representatives from the various Eastern Orthodox churches, but the final section reviewed the talks at Malines.

Davidson stressed that the Conversations were not 'negotiations' and that the delegates were not 'representatives' of 'the Church as a whole'. He did, however, note that further talks were likely. The subsequent furore was predictable. In the middle of January 1924, a 'Great Service for Protestants' was held in south London to protest against any moves towards closer relations with Rome. Similar events were held up and down the country. The Conservative Minister William Joynson-Hicks wrote to Davidson pointing out that men like Halifax and Gore were hardly representative of the Church of England. He also criticised the Archbishop for offering 'official or quasi-official authorization' (a charge that was not altogether unfounded). Joynson-Hicks also suggested that the Malines Conversations fell outside the terms of the Lambeth 'Appeal', which had noted the readiness of the Church of England to *respond* to any approaches from Rome, rather than take the initiative.[55] Davidson replied with unusual asperity that Joynson-Hicks took too 'petty a view' of the road to Christian unity.[56] The Archbishop nevertheless faced many other sources of criticism. Henson wrote a long letter to *The Times* describing revelations of the Conversations as 'surprising and even startling' (an odd claim given that he had been told of the talks almost a year before).[57] He also noted that he had expressed his reservations privately to Davidson. The Archbishop had for many months worried about a hostile response to news of the Conversations at Malines. He was not disappointed. Although further rounds of discussions took place, they eventually fizzled out, in part because of the deaths of Portal and Mercier in 1926, but still more because the public reaction in England showed that the grand ambitions of the participants were never going to be fulfilled within their own lifetimes.

Davidson's normally deft management of controversial issues seemed to desert him when dealing with the Malines talks, even though he devoted a great deal of time and energy to the topic. The Archbishop was torn between treating the Conversations as a purely private affair whilst also wanting to make clear to the participants his own views. In August 1923, he noted in a private memorandum that he realised he might be best-advised 'to let the matter severely alone', but was unwilling to do so, since he did not want to turn a 'deaf ear' to 'the tentative enquiry [. . .] which reaches us from the Roman side'.[58] He was convinced that the Lambeth Appeal made it impossible *not* to give some informal blessing to the activities of Halifax. In the various letters he wrote in the days after his Letter to the Anglican Metropolitans became public, he acknowledge that whilst the talks had done nothing to promote Reunion, they had helped to create a more 'wholesome atmosphere'.[59] The Archbishop told the Moderator of the Free Churches that, despite the short-term outcry, the Conversations should be seen as evidence of 'goodwill' among Christians.[60] He told the Bishop of Ely more ruefully that 'there seems to be a curious idea afloat that I am expectantly arranging early union with the Vatican. Personally I do not believe my grandsons (if I had any) would live to see it'.[61] When talking to Convocation, in February 1924, he repeated his suggestion that stopping the Conversations would have been to turn away from the spirit of the Lambeth Appeal. Davidson added that such inaction would have been 'contrary to every principle which I have entertained in religious matters'.[62] The Archbishop was speaking honestly. He was deeply committed to an ecumenism that promoted what a later generation would term dialogue between the churches. At the same time, though, he was sceptical about the possibility of transforming relations with the Roman Catholic Church. His position was made extraordinarily difficult when he found himself squeezed between those like Halifax, committed to the 'glory' of Reunion with Rome, and others who viewed any discussions with the Catholic hierarchy as a betrayal of the Protestant character of Anglicanism. The search for Christian unity had the paradoxical effect of threatening the unity of the Church of England itself.

The Church of England and the Nonconformist churches

The development of closer ties with the Nonconformist churches at home – let alone any moves towards Reunion – was in some ways as difficult a process as building relations between the Church of England and the Eastern and Roman Catholic churches. The history of humanity provides graphic evidence that geographical and cultural propinquity can fuel division as much as good neighbourliness. The reports issued by the 1920 Lambeth Conference made a distinction between the challenges involved in seeking Reunion with Episcopal and non-Episcopal churches. The Appeal nevertheless explicitly acknowledged that ministries could be 'blessed and owned by the Holy Spirit' even in the absence of Episcopal ordination.

There was still division among the Bishops assembled at Lambeth about whether Nonconformist ministers should be allowed to preach in Anglican churches. There was also disagreement about whether Nonconformist ministers would need to be ordained by a Bishop before their ministry could be recognised in a new united Church. Even so, the Report of the Sub-Committee on Reunion with the non-Episcopal churches, appended to the Lambeth Appeal, set down some proposals about how the process might develop.[63] The immediate response from the Free Churches was positive. The President of the Wesleyan Conference proclaimed that 'we feel that we are living in a new world'.[64] The leading Baptist John Clifford welcomed the 'spirit of unity' expressed in the Appeal.[65] The Free Church Council commended the 'important' Appeal for its 'brotherly and eirenical spirit', although its members also noted that there were elements which did not command their 'assent', and committed themselves to a more detailed consideration of the question.[66] Davidson himself noted with satisfaction early in 1921 that the Nonconformist churches had 'paid something more than lip service or courteous compliment to our Appeal'.[67] A few weeks later, the Free Church Council published a detailed report identifying the areas that would need to form the basis of detailed discussion with the Church of England if the process of Reunion was to go ahead, including acceptance of the validity of non-Episcopal ordination and a commitment to maintaining spiritual freedom.[68]

Davidson was well aware that even the most tentative discussions of possible Reunion with the various Nonconformist churches would, as always, lead to division within the Church of England. The response of the Primitive Methodist Church, which welcomed the Appeal from 'this historic and honoured Church of the Protestant Reformation',[69] was unlikely to be welcomed by the likes of Lord Halifax or Walter Frere. In December 1920, Davidson nevertheless invited a number of prominent Nonconformists to a meeting at Lambeth Palace to discuss the Appeal. The Archbishop began by reviewing developments over the previous few months, gently pointing out that some people had been 'a little too enthusiastic at first', and suggested that the Appeal should be seen as dealing with principles rather than as a clear guide to action. Archbishop Lang then provided a more detailed discussion of the issues, arguing that the Appeal was designed to secure more than mere spiritual unity, though he too acknowledged the difficulties that lay ahead. The subsequent discussion was generally good-natured, although the Presbyterian Minister Carnegie Simpson sharply criticised the two Archbishops for not thinking through the practical problems involved in any serious attempt at Reunion. Davidson allowed Lang to take the lead in the discussion, but when pressed by Simpson he noted that he himself believed that the Nonconformist churches formed part of the Catholic Church, but added with characteristic caution he could not 'bind' 250 other Bishops.[70]

The meeting in December identified the issues that were to dominate discussions between members of the Church of England and the Nonconformist churches over the next few years. These more formal talks began towards the end of 1921, when a meeting took place at Lambeth Palace chaired by Davidson (recovering, as so often, from illness), at which he once again noted that the Appeal was 'a vision – not a proposed or defined plan'.[71] Archbishop Lang then took the chair, as he did at all the meetings over the next three years. A measure of agreement was secured on some issues. An interim report produced in the spring of 1922, just a few months after the first meeting, suggested that a new united Church should accept Episcopal governance whilst preserving the 'elements of presbyteral and congregational order' found in 'large sections of Christendom'. Such a formulation predictably created considerable confusion when it was published.[72] Davidson continued to attend many of the meetings, trying to use his influence to promote agreement, although his private notes showed that he doubted whether the talks would achieve much progress in the short term. He nevertheless wanted them to continue.

> In my own mind I greatly doubt whether these friendly utterances will really eventuate at any early date in positive action of the sort to strike the public. I keep on repeating that we should go slow, and I am sure that this is right, but the going slow may probably mean that years may pass before we do things which are likely to arrest the attention of the man in the street. None the less, the conferences are *abundantly worth while, for they break down the barriers which are severing us from one another, and at the least they prepare the way for larger unity in the future* [italics added].[73]

Davidson's closest confidante amongst the Nonconformists was J. Scott Lidgett, former President of the Wesleyan Conference, who was by the early 1920s also active in local politics in London. Lidgett regularly advised Davidson about attitudes within the Free Churches.[74] He was also instrumental in inviting Davidson to address the 1923 Wesleyan Conference, an occasion which the Archbishop used perhaps rather pointedly to talk about Christian unity rather than Reunion, although he spoke warmly of the need 'of drawing together and standing together'.[75] Despite the expressions of goodwill that continued to inform the talks between representatives from the Church of England and the Nonconformist churches, the question of whether Nonconformist ministers would need to be re-ordained by a Bishop before having their ministry recognised in a new united Church proved intractable. Nor were the talks helped when news of the Malines Conversations became public at the end of 1923. The leading Wesleyan layman Sir Robert Perks, who was generally well-disposed towards Anglicanism, wrote in a letter to *The Times* that there were few Methodists 'who would desire any form of union whatever with the Church of England if such union involved or paved the way for union with the Church of Rome'.[76] The immediate crisis passed, but Davidson's instinctive sense that too rapid a search for Reunion with the various Nonconformist churches might create division and even Christian *disunity* proved to be well grounded.

The failure of the post-war talks to make significant progress towards building a closer union between Anglicanism and Nonconformity revealed the depth of the divisions that remained. Davidson played a smaller role in the process than he did when seeking to mould developments at Malines, leaving much of the detailed work to Cosmo Lang. George Bell also played a significant role in the discussions with the Nonconformist churches, and was responsible for much of the correspondence with the leading figures. Davidson continued to take an interest in relations with the Nonconformist churches, but his letters and memoranda show that he was sceptical about the potential for anything approaching full Reunion. His attitude was perhaps best summed up in an address he made to the General Assembly of the Church of Scotland, in 1921, at which he argued that the Lambeth Appeal should be understood as 'an idea or vision, rather than a plan'.[77]

Davidson was not closely involved in preparations for the long-awaited Conference on Faith and Order, which took place in Lausanne in 1927, in part because the burgeoning Prayer Book controversy demanded most of his time and energy. Nor was he closely involved in other inter-church initiatives such as the Conference on Christian Politics, Economics and Citizenship, held at Birmingham in 1924, or the 1925 Stockholm Conference on Life and Work. The departure of George Bell from Lambeth in 1924, to become Dean of Canterbury, probably helps to explain Davidson's cautious response to such initiatives. It was not that the Archbishop was hostile to such developments – far from it – and he was genuinely hopeful that greater contact between the churches could foster closer relationships that might in time develop into something more far reaching. But Davidson's ecumenical vision was a pragmatic one, which recognised obstacles as well as opportunities, and without Bell's energy the Archbishop was increasingly ready to see the Lambeth Appeal as an ideal rather than a commitment. There was wisdom as well as caution in Davidson's view that the growth of an ecumenical spirit would necessarily be a slow process that could not take place free from the constraints of the past. Almost 100 years later, in Britain at least, relations between the main churches have improved immeasurably. They nevertheless remain distinct. The obstacles to Reunion appear to be as strong as ever. But the spirit of ecumenical understanding, which Davidson helped to foster in the years after 1918, represents something of profound value when compared with the sectarian divisions of an earlier age.

Notes

1 For a valuable account of Bell's involvement in various ecumenical initiatives before his appointment as Bishop of Chichester, see Charlotte Methuen, 'Fulfilling Christ's Own Wish That We Should Be One': The Early Ecumenical Career of George Bell as Chaplain to the Archbishop of Canterbury and Dean of Canterbury', *Kirchliche Zeitgeschichte*, 21, 2 (2008), pp. 222–45. For Bell's reaction in 1914 to being invited to become Chaplain, along with a brief overview of his role, see Peter Raina, *Bishop Bell: The Greatest Churchman: A Portrait in Letters* (Peterborough: Churches Together in Britain and Ireland, 2006), pp. 21–5.

2 D.P. 14, fos. 334–55, Davidson Memorandum, 17 February 1924 (quotations fos. 347, 351).
3 Among the vast literature on Britain between the wars which focuses on the sense of crisis see, for example, Richard Overy, *The Morbid Age: Britain and the Crisis of Civilization, 1919–1939* (London: Penguin, 2010). For rather different and highly readable accounts of the inter-war years, see Roy Hattersley, *Borrowed Time: The Story of Britain Between the Wars* (London: Abacus, 2007); D.J. Taylor, *Bright Young People: Rise and Fall of a Generation* (London: Vintage, 2008).
4 D.P. 14, fos. 8–12, Davidson Memorandum, 14 March 1920 (quotation fo. 11). In the post-war years, Davidson's personal notes often took the form of diary notes rather than the more formal memoranda which he favoured during the first part of his time at Canterbury. For the sake of consistency, these semi-formal diary notes are still referred to here as memoranda.
5 For the text of the Appeal, see *Six Lambeth Conferences*, 1920 Conference, pp. 133–39.
6 D.P. 462, fos. 238–40, Halifax to Davidson, 29 December 1923.
7 D.P. 14, fos. 24–31, Davidson Memorandum, 16 May 1920 (quotation fo. 24).
8 *Documents Bearing on the Problem of Christian Unity and Fellowship, 1916–1920* (London: SPCK, 1920), pp. 81–6.
9 D.P. 261, fo. 334 (Resolution by English Church Union).
10 D.P. 261, fos. 342–3.
11 Lockhart, *Lang*, p. 267.
12 Henson, *Retrospect*, Vol. 2, p. 9.
13 Henson, *Retrospect*, Vol. 2, p. 16.
14 For a valuable scholarly account of the origins of the Appeal to All Christian People, see Charlotte Methuen (ed), 'Lambeth 1920: The Appeal to All Christian People: An Account by G.K.A. Bell and the Redactions of the Appeal', in Barber, Taylor and Sewell eds), *From the Reformation to the Permissive Society*, pp. 521–64.
15 Methuen, *Lambeth 1920*, p. 535.
16 M.M., *Bishop Montgomery*, p. 77. For a fuller extract from this document, see Documents Section 2.
17 D.P. 6, Paper 53, Extract from Proceedings on the Last Day of the Lambeth Conference.
18 D.P. 14, fos. 40–60, Davidson Memorandum, 15 August 1920 (quotations fos. 51, 56).
19 D.P. 14, fos. 61–84, Davidson Memorandum, 6/13 February 1921 (quotation fo. 69).
20 *Six Lambeth Conferences*, 1920 Conference, p. 32 (Resolutions 17, 20).
21 Geffert, *Eastern Orthodox and Anglican*, p. 79.
22 See, for example, the reports in *Times*, 27 May 1922; 9 June 1922; *Manchester Guardian*, 2 May 1923; 29 May 1923.
23 Charles M. Edmondson and R. Barry Levis, 'Archbishop Randall Davidson, Russian Famine Relief, and the Fate of the Orthodox Clergy, 1917–1923', *Journal of Church and State*, 40, 3 (1998), pp. 619–37.
24 Bell, *Davidson*, Vol. 2, pp. 1,074–75.
25 For a brief history of the Society, see A.T.J. Salter, 'An Outline History of the Anglican & Eastern Churches Association', www.aeca.org.uk/articles/AECA_Outline_History.pdf. See, too, Hughes, 'English Slavophile'.
26 G.K.A. Bell, *Documents on Christian Unity, 1920–1924* (Oxford: Oxford University Press, 1924), pp. 77–89.
27 Bell, *Documents on Christian Unity, 1920–1924*, pp. 90–2.
28 See, for example, R.S. Latimer, *Russia under Three Tsars: Liberty of Conscience in Russia, 1856–1909* (London: Morgan and Scott, 1909).
29 D.P. 14, fos. 125–9, Davidson Memorandum, 21 January 1922.
30 Geffert, *Eastern Orthodox and Anglicans*, p. 88.
31 Geffert, *Eastern Orthodox and Anglicans*, p. 96.
32 D.P. 14, fos. 183–91, Davidson Memorandum, 27 October 1922.
33 Prestige, *Gore*, pp. 468–78.

34 Davidson sermon on 'The Council of Nicaea', published in *Occasions* (London: Mowbray, 1925), pp. 102–3.
35 Geffert, *Eastern Orthodox and Anglicans*, p. 100.
36 *Six Lambeth Conferences*, 1920 Conference, p. 144.
37 For Mercier's interest in Reunion, which predated the Lambeth Appeal, see John A. Dick, *The Malines Conversations Revisited* (Leuven: Leuven University Press, 1989), pp. 66–8. For a short review of all the Malines Conversations, see Bernard and Margaret Pawley, *Rome and Canterbury through Four Centuries* (London: Mowbray, 1974), pp. 281–97.
38 Bell, *Davidson*, Vol. 2, p. 1,255.
39 For a detailed account of the conversations, see Dick, *Malines Conversations*.
40 For a first-hand account, see Walter Frere, *Recollections of Malines* (London: Centenary Press, 1935).
41 Viscount Halifax, *A Call to Reunion* (London: Mowbray, 1922).
42 Henson, *Retrospect*, Vol. 2, p. 139. See, too, Lambeth Palace, BM 7, fo. 306 (Bishops Meeting 25–6 January 1923).
43 D.P. 14, fos. 202–6, Davidson Memorandum, 4 February 1923 (quotation fo. 203).
44 D.P. 461, fos. 120–21, Davidson to Halifax, 20 March 1921 (quotation fo. 120).
45 D.P. 461, fos. 109–15, Davidson to Dean of Wells, 19 March 1923.
46 D.P. 461, fos. 132–34, Davidson to Mercier, 24 March 1923 (quotation fo. 133).
47 D.P. 461, fos. 150–57, Mercier to Davidson, April 1923; fos. 208–9, Mercier to Halifax, 24 April 1923.
48 D.P. 461, fos. 229–34, Davidson to Mercier, 15 May 1923 (quotation fo. 232).
49 D.P. 461, fos. 178–79, Memorandum by the Archbishops of Canterbury and York, 18 April 1923.
50 *Times*, 1 August 1923 (Letter by J.E.C. Weldon).
51 D.P. 461, fos. 254–57, Davidson to Gore, 7 July 1923.
52 D.P. 462, fos. 12–22, 'Conferences at Malines: Preliminary Conversations at Lambeth Palace, 2 October 1923'.
53 Prestige, *Gore*, p. 483.
54 D.P. 462, fo. 146, Davidson to Robinson, 10 December 1923.
55 D.P. 462, fos. 354–58, Joynson-Hicks to Davidson, 24 January 1924 (quotation fo. 354).
56 D.P. 462, fos. 360–62, Davidson to Joynson-Hicks, 16 January 1924 (quotation fo. 360).
57 *Times*, 28 December 1923 (Letter by Henson).
58 Bell, *Davidson*, Vol. 2, p. 1,278.
59 D.P. 462, fo. 236, Davidson to Bury, 29 December 1923.
60 D.P. 462, fo. 248, Davidson to Moderator of the Free Churches (Milligan), 31 December 1923.
61 D.P. 462, fo. 246, Davidson to Bishop of Ely, 31 December 1923.
62 *Chronicle of Convocation: Convocation of Canterbury (Upper House)*, 6 February 1924.
63 *Six Lambeth Conferences*, 1920 Conference, pp. 142–43.
64 *Yorkshire Post and Leeds Intelligencer*, 21 August 1920.
65 *Hartlepool Mail*, 14 August 1920.
66 Bell, *Documents on Christian Unity, 1920–1924*, pp. 118–20.
67 D.P. 14, fos. 61–84, Davidson Memorandum, 6–13 February 1921 (quotation fo. 68).
68 Bell, *Documents on Church Unity, 1920–1924*, pp. 118–41.
69 D.P. 261, fos. 368–70, Armstrong to Davidson including a Note on Lambeth Conference (quotation fo. 369).
70 D.P. 262, fos. 9–16, 'Appeal to All Christian People: Informal Conference at Lambeth, December 8, 1920'.
71 D.P. 262, fos. 268–70, Davidson notes for his address to the conference with Free Church leaders held at Lambeth Palace, 30 November 1921 (quotation fo. 269).
72 For a copy of the report, see Bell, *Documents on Christian Unity, 1920–1924*, pp. 143–51.
73 D.P. 14, fos. 130–42, Davidson Memorandum, 18 June 1922 (quotation fos. 130–31).

74 D.P. 262, fos. 112–14, Davidson Memorandum on 'Long Interview [. . .] with Dr Scott Lidgett', 16 June 1921.
75 *Times*, 23 July 1923.
76 *Times*, 29 December 1923 (Letter by Perks).
77 Randall Davidson, *Lambeth and Edinburgh: An Address to the General Assembly of the Church of Scotland* (London: SPCK, 1921), p. 11.

6 Archbishop Davidson and the challenge of social and economic reform (1918–1928)

The previous chapters have shown how Randall Davidson believed he could best develop the Church of England's influence in public life by discreet but sustained engagement with leading political figures. To put it somewhat glibly, he was convinced that the Established Church's influence depended on its leading figures forming an active part of the Establishment. The changed conditions of the post-war world inevitably raised questions about the role of the Church of England in public life. The Church's position in some ways became stronger after the First World War. The decline of Nonconformity and the eclipse of the Liberal Party reduced demands for Disestablishment, whilst Nonconformist congregations were particularly vulnerable to social and economic changes that undermined the tight-knit communities which had for so long sustained them. Nor was Britain rapidly becoming a secular society, despite the jeremiads routinely heard from leaders of all the main denominations, who often conflated social change with religious decline.[1] Many of the traditional practices of Christian Britain remained at least partly intact throughout the inter-war years.[2] There were nevertheless important social and political changes taking place to which the Church of England needed to adapt. The appointment of the first Labour Government in 1924 – albeit that it only remained in office for nine months – reflected both the extension of the franchise and a concomitant shift in the boundaries of the political nation. Recurrent upsurges in industrial unrest, most obviously during the 1926 General Strike, were at least in part a consequence of widespread resentment about the traditional distribution of wealth and power. The growing popularity of radio and cinema symbolised significant changes in popular culture. Archbishop Davidson had to spend the last ten years of his time at Canterbury steering his Church through a landscape that was both familiar and strange. And he had to do so at a time of growing frailty and old age.

The creation of the Christian Social Union in 1889 reflected a growing sense amongst many Anglican clergy and lay people about the need for a social gospel that directly addressed the injustice and poverty of industrial Britain.[3] The establishment of urban Settlements, largely staffed by young men from the universities, was testimony to a widespread desire to take the teachings of the Bible from the pulpit into the community. The outlook of many Anglicans who shaped the Church of England's response to social and economic questions after 1918 – ranging from William Temple to R. H. Tawney – was forged during these critical years before the First World War.[4] The 1920s witnessed significant reflection among many leading Anglicans about how the Church of England could shape the life of the nation. Writers ranging from Gore and Temple to Tawney and Ernest Barker wrote extensively about the vexed relationships between Individual and Community and Church and State. Some, like Gore, had already moved towards the view that Disestablishment was necessary to guarantee the Church of England freedom from State control. Other Christian socialists like Tawney grappled with the problem of deciding how the State could use its authority to transform social and economic relations. Temple wrote at length on the need to promote greater economic justice, whilst acknowledging that the labour movement could itself easily descend into materialism and selfishness, unless tempered by a powerful awareness of the spiritual foundations of social life. Deliberations about the right relationship between the Church and the State – and the relationship of both to the National Community – spawned a rich dialogue that has not always received enough recognition from historians of political thought.[5]

Randall Davidson was largely oblivious to the subtleties of these intellectual debates. He understood the importance of the questions which underpinned them, but showed little inclination to consider them in a systematic manner, reflecting his penchant for the particular and concrete rather than the theoretical and abstract. The Archbishop continued to argue that the Church of England had both the right and the duty to express its views on social issues such as marriage and divorce. He also remained committed to the principle that the Church should when possible foster agreement on important issues of public policy. It might indeed be possible to tease out a hidden political philosophy (or perhaps political theology) in Davidson's words and actions, resting on the principle that Church, State, and Society each had their own identity, even as they intersected with one another in ways that could prove beneficial or harmful.[6] Davidson certainly believed that his Church had a duty to articulate a Christian view on issues of social policy. He was, though, wary of those who argued that the Church of England should take the lead in calling for social and economic reform. The Archbishop was, as so often, a pragmatist, responding to circumstances as they developed, rather than seeking to lead a national debate on important matters of policy. His position set him apart from a new generation of Anglicans who believed that the Church should respond more vigorously to the challenge of a changing world.

Industrial unrest and the General Strike of 1926

The First World War raised popular expectations that peace should pave the way for greater prosperity and justice. Lloyd George's rhetorical commitment to build 'a land fit for heroes' echoed a pervasive sense that the slaughter on the Western Front was in some way bound up with the bankruptcy of the existing social and economic order. Such hopes soon faded – across continental Europe as well as in Britain itself – and 1919 saw revolutionary upheaval and major industrial unrest throughout the continent.[7] The changing mood within the Church was articulated in the 1918 'Report of the Archbishops' Commission on Industry' (itself a product of the National Mission launched two years earlier). The Commission included men like Tawney and George Lansbury – who subsequently became leader of the Labour Party – and its report was striking for sharply condemning the historical 'subservience of the Church to the possessing, employing and governing classes'.[8] Davidson's introduction to the report was perhaps a little cool (he described it as 'not an official document' but rather the views of 'specially qualified men and women'). The general direction of thinking among many prominent figures within the Church of England was nonetheless clear. The Committee on Industrial Problems, set up at the Lambeth Conference of 1920, was more circumspect in its language than the Report of the Commission on Industry. It too, though, demanded the establishment of closer relations with the labour movement, and called on the Anglican Communion to move beyond 'pious aspirations' when considering social and economic questions.[9] The idea that the Church of England should take a critical position towards the *status quo* was hardly new, but it did gain greater traction in the years after 1920, albeit in the face of protests of senior clergy like Henson, Inge, and Headlam (the latter vigorously condemned the notion that 'State socialism is an integral part of Christian teaching').[10] The move within the Church towards a more critical idiom on questions of social and economic justice was not vociferously opposed by Archbishop Davidson. But nor was he in the vanguard of such a movement either.

Davidson was more exercised when deciding how to respond to specific incidences of labour unrest. The challenges involved were starkly demonstrated by the 1921 Coal Strike, in which the Archbishop offered his services to broker a compromise between the two sides, an echo of his perennial belief that conflict could often be resolved given sufficient flexibility and goodwill. The potential for division within the Church became clear during the debates that took place at Convocation in April. The Bishop of Lichfield moved a Resolution noting that the points at issue in the coal dispute were as much 'moral' as 'economic'. The Resolution attracted significant support, but also considerable criticism, not least from the Bishop of Exeter, who complained that the Upper House of Convocation was being asked to endorse socialism as a political theory. The radical tone of the speeches also infuriated some Conservative politicians, including William Bridgeman, who subsequently wrote to Davidson complaining that many speakers had been 'ill informed' and offered 'a sentimental view rather than an economic one'. Davidson's own speech struck a decidedly moderate tone (characteristically he noted that he had neither the expertise nor experience to pronounce on the issue – words that may have been a veiled rebuke to some other speakers). The Archbishop did, however, shrewdly note that the social and economic tensions facing Britain arose in part from disillusionment, since many had thought that 'the War was going to lead us into sunnier conditions and greater freedom, and we are disappointed'. He also pointed out that the principle of emphasising the moral character of economic questions was itself uncontroversial: the key question was the nature of the critique and the remedies proposed. Davidson skilfully skirted around important questions of nationalisation and – as so often – proved himself adept at building a consensus behind a position that was itself so vague as to lack definite meaning.[11]

It is striking that Davidson chose to have little involvement in the inter-denominational Conference on Christian Politics Economics and Citizenship that took place in Birmingham in 1924 under the chairmanship of William Temple (there may have been strategy in his decision to holiday in Italy during the weeks it met).[12] Temple himself made no secret that he thought the labour movement 'essentially an effort to organize society on the basis of freedom and fellowship. As such it has a right to claim the sympathy of the Church'.[13] The debates at the Conference, and the reports produced by its committees, broadly reflected Temple's view that the Church had a duty to support social and economic reform (or 'Christianize the corporate life of mankind in all its activities' to use the phrase that prefaced all the COPEC reports).[14] Davidson warned Temple in advance of COPEC that he thought the Conference's objectives were so broad that the outcomes would necessarily prove platitudinous.[15] The Archbishop also recognised that if discussion about 'Christianizing' social and economic relations ever moved beyond the platitudinous, then it was likely to create enormous controversy, potentially creating divisions both within the Church of England and between the Church and State. Davidson was anxious – though he did not overtly acknowledge it – about attempts by a group of younger clergy to commit the Church of England to a radical social policy. He may even have considered resignation in 1923, on the grounds that he was (in one scholar's words) 'out of sympathy with the fashion for social theology'.[16] The Archbishop was convinced that the influence of the Church of England would always depend on its ability to maintain a detached 'national' position. His critics were perturbed by the inherent conservatism of such a view. Even Mervyn Haigh, who replaced Bell as senior Chaplain in 1924, and later became an admirer of Davidson, thought during his early months at Lambeth that the Archbishop lacked the 'kind of appeal which fires the imagination and quickens the pulses of the young'.[17]

The General Strike of 1926 created serious challenges both for Davidson and the Church of England.[18] The heated political rhetoric either condemned the Strike as an attack on private property and public order or presented it as a struggle for greater social and economic justice. Davidson was initially trenchant in condemning the Strike. In a speech to the House of Lords on 5 May, shortly after the Strike began, he described it as 'so intolerable that every effort is needed, is justifiably called for and ought to be supported, which the Government may make to bring that condition of things as speedily as possible to an end'. He claimed, without much evidence, to have a good understanding of the concerns of 'the poorer classes'. Davidson also suggested, with still less evidence, that there was a general spirit of 'good-humouredness' among the parties to the Strike. He concluded, 'The Government have everyone behind them in what they are doing'.[19] The Archbishop changed his views over the next two days. On 7 May, he agreed the wording of a statement on the Strike with a number of senior Bishops and leading Nonconformists, including the Wesleyan J. Scott Lidgett and the Congregationalist R. F. Horton, to be broadcast by the Archbishop himself the following day. The 'Appeal from the Churches' called on both sides to 'simultaneously and concurrently' take action to end the Strike (in effect demanding that the unions agree to return to work and the employers withdraw notices of dismissal). Davidson immediately went to the Houses of Parliament, to rally support for the Appeal, but quickly found out that the Prime Minister did not approve of the phrase 'simultaneously and concurrently' (Baldwin was under great pressure from 'diehard' ministers like Churchill and Joynson-Hicks to defeat the Strike). And then, later the same day, Davidson received news from John Reith, Director of the BBC, that the Corporation would not broadcast the Appeal.[20]

Reith denied that pressure had been put on the BBC to refuse to broadcast the Appeal (a disingenuous claim, given that some members of the Cabinet wanted to exercise direct control over the organisation during the crisis). Davidson was unusually trenchant in his protest, asking rhetorically, 'if the Churches desire to put something forth their grave utterances must be subject to the approval of its wording by the Broadcasting Committee'. Reith visited the Archbishop in person later on 8 May, telling Davidson that, if the BBC had broadcast the Appeal, it would have 'weakened' Baldwin's hands in dealing with his more intransigent colleagues (the official *British Gazette*, published by the Government during the Strike, also refused to publish the Appeal).[21] As news of the affair became known, the Archbishop found himself at the centre of a political storm, not least because many Government MPs condemned Church leaders for interfering in a dispute that was supposedly none of their business. Davidson and other senior Church figures were, by contrast, lauded by supporters of the Strike. The Archbishop used a broadcast sermon at St Martin-in-the-Fields, on 9 May, to seek to ease the crisis. He argued that obedience to 'law and order' was a Christian duty, whilst acknowledging the importance of raising living standards, concluding with a 'grave' call on his listeners to do all they could to promote industrial peace.[22]

Davidson met Baldwin two days later, when he urged the Prime Minister to understand that the churches were not seeking to take an 'antagonistic' position towards the Government, although he did express concern about the 'truculent and fighting attitude' of some ministers.[23] The Strike itself was called off by the unions shortly afterwards, ending the immediate crisis, but the events of the previous few days had created lasting tension. In a private letter to the Bishop of Oxford, written two weeks later, Davidson made it clear that he thought union leaders should have made more effort to restrain their members, but the Archbishop was under no illusion that some Cabinet ministers were furious with him for not taking the Government's side more forcefully.[24] From within the Church, Henson of Durham inveighed against a 'criminal strike', and wrote in his diary that Davidson and other senior Bishops had put themselves in a 'very humiliating' position.[25] In June he told the Archbishop that recent events showed that many Anglican clergy were too inclined 'to substitute for religious teaching, a declaratory, sentimental socialism'.[26] The Appeal issued by Church leaders on 7 May had been even-handed in calling on both sides to end the Strike, but such a policy did not appeal to many leading Conservative politicians, who believed that only defeat for the unions could restore order and prevent future labour unrest. Resentment over the behaviour of the Bishops may indeed have helped to fuel the tension that led the following year to Parliament's rejection of the revised Prayer Book.

The Archbishop – not for the first time – paid a price for seeking to promote consensus. In a memorandum written towards the end of May, he described how, after the BBC refused to publish the Appeal from the churches, Lambeth Palace received numerous letters and phone calls of both anger and praise.[27] Davidson actually began to take a rather harder line during the summer of 1926, when he responded sceptically to attempts by a number of senior figures from across the churches to end unrest in the coalfields (the miners themselves did not return to work with the end of the General Strike). The Archbishop made it plain in his correspondence that he was afraid the Church of England would become too closely identified with defending the miners at a possible political cost to its own interests. He also repeated his conviction that Baldwin, in particular, had behaved with 'perfectly good faith' throughout the crisis.[28] It was not a position calculated to appeal to those, like Temple, who believed that the Church should play a pivotal role in extending Christian values to every element of national life.

Archbishop Davidson and the politicians

It was seen a previous chapter that Davidson sometimes found it difficult to meet regularly with members of Britain's political establishment during the First World War, since the sheer pressure of business made ministers less accessible than in peace-time. He was at least partly successful in re-establishing relations with leading politicians following the end of hostilities. The Archbishop was confident that he regained the influence he enjoyed – or believed he had enjoyed – in the years before 1914. Davidson's diaries and notes show that he had numerous formal and informal meetings with ministers throughout the 1920s. He also continued to attend many of the dinners and receptions at which political gossip flowed freely. The Archbishop was nevertheless increasingly seen by some politicians as a largely 'ceremonial' figure, whose views could no longer necessarily be treated as the representative voice of the Church of England, nor (still less) the nation itself. And, whilst Britain remained in some fundamental sense a Christian country, the decline in Nonconformity did not automatically increase the authority of the Church of England, at a time when Victorian and Edwardian values were mutating into something more 'modern'. It is striking that Stanley Baldwin, who was himself the author of a slew of books and articles about England and Englishness, showed little interest in specific questions of Church governance and doctrine. The Church of England did not play a great role in many of his nostalgic panegyrics about the character of his country (the Prime Minister himself was not from an Anglican background).[29] Nor do the private papers of other leading political figures from this period provide much convincing evidence of Davidson's influence on important political questions. The Archbishop was still widely consulted on many important matters of state. It is less clear whether such consultation translated into influence.

The Conservative Party dominated British political life in the ten years after 1918, with the brief exception of the first Labour Government, which held office in 1924. Lloyd George headed a coalition government from 1918 to 1922, and although Davidson continued to regard the 'Welsh wizard' somewhat quizzically, their relationship was reasonably cordial if not close. The Archbishop was by contrast more positive about Baldwin, although he was sometimes frustrated by the Prime Minister's reluctance to give a firm lead on important political questions, particularly those relating to the relationship between Church and State. Davidson was much less enamoured of Winston Churchill, who occupied a number of important political posts during the 1920s, believing that he was both intemperate and intolerant. The same was true of William Joynson-Hicks, who served as Home Secretary from 1924–1929, and became one of the leading figures in defeating the revised Prayer Book. The Archbishop was – despite such reservations – generally impressed by the calibre of ministers who served in Baldwin's Cabinets. He wrote early in 1925 that he believed the new Cabinet was made up of 'a group of men whose standard of religious principle, honourable conduct, and what I may call "gentlemanliness" in politics is higher than any which I have known during 40 years share in public life'.[30]

It would nevertheless be wrong to see the Church of England in the 1920s as the Conservative Party at prayer. The focus of some leading Anglicans on questions of social and economic justice perturbed many leading Tory politicians. So too did the influence of Anglo-Catholic clergy within the Church, which some Conservative MPs criticised for alienating congregations whose members were wary of anything that smacked of Ritualism. Davidson himself recognised that the Church of England had to adapt to the forces of social and political change if it was to maintain its claim to be the National Church. It was seen in a previous chapter that the Archbishop understood the significance of the 'new' Liberalism that emerged early in the twentieth century, recognising it as a reflection of a significant strand of public opinion, even as he looked askance at many of the reforms demanded by its most vocal advocates. He responded in a similar fashion to the rise of the Labour Party in the 1920s, acknowledging that it represented the interests of a significant part of the new electorate that had expanded sharply following the franchise reform of 1918. When Ramsay MacDonald became Prime Minister at the start of 1924, Davidson did not share the elation of clergy like William Temple, but nor did he echo the views of those who believed that 'the party of revolution approach their hands to the helm of the state [...] with the design of destroying the very bases of civilized life'.[31]

Davidson's private memoranda show that he was fascinated by the political machinations that surrounded the rise and fall of the first MacDonald Government. In the middle of December 1923, he had a long talk with Margot Asquith about the looming political crisis, which followed a General Election at which the Conservatives failed to win enough seats to form a majority Government. Later the same day, he had a meeting with his old friend Lord Stamfordham, George V's Private Secretary, who was canvassing opinion about the most appropriate course of action. Davidson also met Baldwin, who told the Archbishop that 'nothing would please me better than to have your advice at a very difficult juncture', and urged him to 'give him any counsel that might occur to me'.[32] Davidson had already formed a positive judgement about MacDonald. After meeting the Labour leader a few weeks earlier at a dinner party, the Archbishop noted that he found his dining companion 'extraordinarily interesting'.[33] He was similarly impressed by MacDonald's performance in Parliament once he became Prime Minister, praising him in a letter to Edward Talbot, the former Bishop of Winchester, for taking 'a rather drastic line with his more exuberant followers'. The Archbishop believed that the appointment of the first Labour Government represented a 'whole new start in public life and government', and told Talbot that the scale of the political changes forced 'everybody who is worth their salt to look afresh on the really large things that matter [...] things have been forcing me personally into a new standpoint of observation and vision'. The Archbishop was not able to conceal altogether, though, his amusement at the thought of working class ministers like Stephen Walsh and J. H. Thomas giving instructions to 'aristocratic' field marshalls and Colonial Office officials.[34]

MacDonald had moved politically to the right during the early 1920s and, in the eyes of his more radical followers, was already too inclined to value the good opinion of the social and political establishment. The publication of the forged Zinov'ev Letter in the autumn of 1924, which purported to provide instructions to the British Communist Party by Moscow, renewed popular fears about the influence of left-wing radicals (a phenomenon which brought about a huge increase in the number of Conservative MPs returned at the October General Election). Davidson tacitly welcomed the return of a Conservative Government in large part because he was on good terms with many ministers, and could 'talk to them privately with perfect freedom about public affairs'.[35] Although he had known some ministers in the Labour Government, most notably Parmoor and Haldane, the return of a slew of familiar faces meant that he could again look forward to the kind of informal exchanges he held so dear. The Archbishop recognised that the appointment of Labour to office in 1924 represented the culmination of deep-seated social and political changes. Yet whilst he was ready to acknowledge the inevitability of such a development, he remained emotionally wedded to a more traditional politics, which took place primarily within the confines of a narrow political establishment. Davidson always remained ill at ease with the rituals and language of mass politics.

Archbishop Davidson and the challenge of cultural and social change

A good deal of ink has been spilt by scholars discussing whether the First World War marked a fundamental rupture in the development of European culture. The roots of Modernism – as seen in the poetry of T. S. Eliot or the paintings of Picasso – can without doubt be traced back to changes in the dominant artistic sensibility that emerged during the final quarter of the nineteenth century. Randall Davidson was not greatly interested in such matters. His taste in fiction – whenever he had the time to indulge it – was decidedly 'middle-brow'. Nor does he seem to have had much interest in music or art. The Archbishop was for many years a trustee of the British Museum, but his main interest in this role was the provision of suitably improving leisure opportunities for the people of London, rather than a passionate concern for the development of the Museum's collections. Davidson was alert to the rise of both cinema and broadcasting during the 1920s, recognising the potential of such media to shape popular culture for good or ill, as well as provide new opportunities for the Church to communicate with a wider audience than those who attended Sunday worship. The development of radio particularly intrigued him.[36] Following an approach by John Reith of the BBC about the possibility of transmitting religious services, Davidson himself made his first broadcast at the end of 1923.[37] The Archbishop used his New Year's Message to reflect on the shadows that were still being cast on British society by the First World War, more than five years after the end of hostilities ('We must translate the poetry and glamour of the exciting war years into the prose of common days'). He went on to reflect on the challenge of turning humdrum lives 'behind the shop counter' or at 'the dull office desks' into 'gold'. His words were worthy, though less striking than those of a Church of Scotland minister, who broadcast a message the same night calling for an end to the class struggle. Davidson's broadcasts, like his sermons, were thoughtful and well-argued if perhaps a little dull.

Despite his fitful interest in cultural matters, the Archbishop recognised that they could raise important questions of public morality and taste.[38] George Bell noted in his biography that Davidson had little interest in the theatre (at least beyond a limited taste for Shakespeare). Even so, at a time when the Lord Chamberlain still exercised power of censorship over what could be performed on the London stage, the Archbishop's opinion was inevitably sought from time to time on the rights and wrongs of particular plays. His comments on E. T. Thurston's unremarkable *Judas Iscariot* were limited to an expression of relief that the text was far more 'proper and reverent' than anything George Bernard Shaw might have written on the subject. The Archbishop was more concerned by John Masefield's play *The Trial of Jesus*, not on the grounds that it was blasphemous, but rather because it broke the convention that the figure of Christ should not be represented on stage. Davidson thought well of Masefield, who was appointed Poet Laureate a few years later, but he told the Lord Chamberlain that there would be little protest if his office refused to license the play (it was not performed publicly until 1932).[39] It is from a modern perspective difficult to credit the rationale of such a decision, not least at a time when novelists like D. H. Lawrence and John Cowper Powys were publishing novels far more calculated to offend public *mores*, but there was no equivalent of the Lord Chamberlain's Office holding sway over fiction. The great tide of artistic and literary experimentation seemed to flow around the Archbishop without evoking much reaction beyond an occasional quizzical comment about the lack of restraint shown by many modern artists and writers.

Davidson was by contrast more exercised by questions which came squarely within what he considered the proper moral purview of the Church of England. The Archbishop took a prominent role in opposing the 1920 Matrimonial Causes Bill, based on the recommendations of the earlier Royal Commission, which broadened the grounds on which a marriage could be dissolved (to include desertion and cruelty as well as adultery). There is little doubt that the proposals accorded with that most elusive phenomenon – the 'spirit of the age' – both in seeking to improve the options available to women and more generally by acknowledging the possibility that marriages might fail. Davidson's speech in the House of Lords criticising the Bill was poorly received – *The Times* suggested that 'neither of the Primates has come well out of the debate' – and even sympathetic peers suggested that the Church was obsessed with the physical rather than the spiritual dimension of marriage.[40] The press did contain letters of support for the Archbishops, but far more from critics, and in April *The Times* itself published an editorial supporting the Bill.[41]

Davidson was intensely exercised by the issues of Church-State relations thrown up by the Matrimonial Causes Bill. He argued with some vigour in the House of Lords that the prohibition on divorce could be traced back 'to the Founder of our faith'. He also proposed a new clause forbidding the remarriage in Church of any person whose former spouse was still living. Davidson told the Lords that the Church of England could not be expected to give up its own traditional teaching in response to a decision by Parliament. And, in a statement reflecting the depth of his feelings, he noted,

> I yield to none in my sense of the value to the nation of the Establishment, for which I care with my whole heart; but there are higher considerations even than that, if you do force us into the position of loyalty to the one thing or of loyalty to the other thing. I cannot believe that your Lordships, when the facts are fully before you, desire to place us Bishops as well the clergy – perhaps more than the clergy – in that intolerable position. Most seriously do I protest against it, and tell you that from this protest I cannot conscientiously depart.[42]

Davidson's protests counted for little, and the Bill was passed by the Lords, evidence perhaps of the extent to which the Archbishop was out of touch with public opinion (although it is perhaps worth noting that the *elected* House of Commons later rejected the Bill). His words certainly illustrated the continued potential for fissures in the relationship between Church and State despite the recent passage of the Enabling Bill (a subject returned to in more detail in the following chapter). Davidson was also out of step with many members of his own Church. The debates which took place at COPEC several years later on the subject of marriage and divorce showed that many Anglicans and non-Anglicans alike took a very different view from the Primate.

Although it would be wrong to suggest that there was a wholesale change in attitudes on marriage and divorce during the inter-war years, there were subtle shifts, and attitudes that had once been unquestioned were increasingly seen as old-fashioned. Even so, Davidson found it easier to bring questions about marriage within the purview of a moral gaze rather than the kind of social and economic questions discussed earlier. Such a position in turn reflected his deeply held, but largely unstated, view that issues of morality were above all about personal behaviour. Difficult questions of labour relations, for example, were for Davidson most easily solved when businessmen and workers sought agreement based on the assumption that they had a duty to behave in a way that was not motivated by simple material self-interest. It was a language that might have been accommodated within the rhetoric of nineteenth-century One Nation Conservatism or, perhaps, progressive Whig Liberalism. It appeared more archaic in the 1920s, when (paradoxically) both individualism and collectivism were becoming ever more powerful principles in British society.

The issue of education proved far less controversial in the 1920s than was the case before 1914. The change was in part due to the decline in both Nonconformity and political Liberalism, although it may also have reflected the development of an ecumenical ethos across the churches, which made some of the earlier vitriol seem both outmoded and unjustifiable. The Education Act passed in 1918 did not address many of the issues which had inspired so much debate a decade earlier: the nature of the religious education to be offered to children; the maintenance of a denominational presence in schools that were state-funded, and so on.[43] The Education Secretary H.A.L. Fisher was therefore keen to re-establish discussion on these matters, a view shared by Archbishop Davidson, who authorised Church of England participation in a Conference to consider some of the outstanding issues. The discussions led to consensus on a set of broad principles, including the provision of better teacher-training and agreement that religious instruction could have some denominational form, although in the event it proved impossible to develop these proposals into definite legislative form. Some of the opposition came from within Nonconformist circles. But Davidson also faced a setback in 1923 at a meeting of the National Society for Promoting Religious Education, when delegates approved a motion calling on Church of England leaders to abandon a 'policy of negotiation for the surrender of Church schools'. It was a development that showed how old denominational tensions had not altogether faded as a result of total war and comradeship on the battlefield. It was also, and perhaps tellingly, something of a snub to the Archbishop himself.

International politics in the post-war years

The creation of the League of Nations attracted wide support across the British churches.[44] The League proved to be a perennially troubled institution in the years that followed, uncertain in role and flawed in structure, not least because politicians from the various member countries could seldom agree on how it should operate in practice.[45] Although its formal powers were limited, it acquired a kind of totemic status amongst a war-weary public, a focus for hopes that it might prove possible to build a new international order based on consultation and law. Randall Davidson was 74 when he accepted an invitation in 1922 to visit the League's Headquarters in Geneva and preach a sermon at St Peter's Cathedral ahead of the opening of the Third Assembly. Following his arrival in Switzerland, the Archbishop attended meetings at the International Labour Office and the League's Council. He also spoke with politicians from a number of countries (including both Balfour and Robert Cecil who were also in Geneva). Davidson used his sermon to argue with some passion that the core values which underpinned the League's Covenant were consistent with the principles of a 'Christian Faith [that] lies at the core of the progressive history of mankind', adding that in supporting the League 'we are simply applying the Christian faith to international life'. He described the League as 'a living pulsing body', capable of responding to the development of human society, adding that it represented a determined effort by humanity to take control of its destiny whilst still looking for divine guidance. The Archbishop concluded with a vigorous call for the League to become 'chief on earth among those powers ordained of God', and demanded that Governments 'bring common resolve and effort to bear upon securing what is true and just'. Davidson was seldom an enthralling speaker, but he was confident that his words made an impression on the invited congregation.[46]

The decision to invite the Archbishop to Geneva was seen by some Anglicans as evidence 'of the unique position of the Church of England in the eyes, not only of Christendom, but of the civilized world'.[47] Davidson's words certainly attracted attention around the globe. The *Ottawa Journal* spoke of a 'remarkable peace sermon'.[48] The *New York Times* reported the sermon at length – admittedly somewhat belatedly – under the title 'Archbishop Hails League as Holy'.[49] The Melbourne newspaper *The Age* described how Davidson had argued that the League of Nations could bring about the end of 'militarism'.[50] Such worldwide coverage – at least in the Anglophone world – was a reminder that the Archbishop of Canterbury was still seen as a figure of great international importance. It was for this reason – as was seen in the previous chapter – that Davidson continued to receive so many approaches from across the world about both secular and religious matters. His unusually forceful words in Geneva were not, though, evidence that the Archbishop really expected a millennial transformation in the character of international politics. In the months and years following his Geneva sermon, Davidson retreated to his more habitual caution, refusing to express support for any public initiative that might involve controversy, including requests to sign statements calling on Governments never to go to war. This was not simply, as the Archbishop told the veteran anti-war campaigner Arthur Ponsonby, that he had 'never been able to support the principles which Tolstoy inculcated' [that is of non-resistance].[51] It also reflected his shrewd recognition that grand rhetoric about the need to transform international politics could not easily be translated into workable programmes of action. His readiness to espouse publicly the value of peace, and the role of the League of Nations in securing it, did not mean that Davidson was blind to the complexities facing those charged with managing international diplomatic relations.

Davidson also continued from time to time to raise the question of the role and purpose of the British Empire. In a talk given at Wembley in May 1924, to celebrate Empire Day, he described the Empire as a 'pulsing, throbbing reality' and 'much more than a nation'. And, whilst the Archbishop did not go so far as to suggest that the Empire was divinely inspired, he did tell his audience that 'we recognize from Whom and under Whom we [...] live and move and have our being'. Davidson described the building of Empire as 'a solemn trust' that rested on bringing education and knowledge to the population of India and Africa.[52] The following year, he preached a sermon in east London on Australia Day, in which he made a parallel between the Church and the Empire, both made up of different parts, each of which had 'its own work to do, the unity for that reason being all the more solid'. He went on to shower praise on Australians for making use of the rich natural resources of their country in order to build a modern society.[53]

Davidson's language was in keeping with the times in which he lived. He did briefly note the emergence of Indian nationalism in his Empire Day talk, doing little more than raise the prospect that such developments might be 'wise or foolish', but he was in general content to restrict himself to the language of organic unity and mutual benefit. Nor did he argue as strongly as he once had that the Anglican Communion was the Communion of Empire. His paean of praise for the Empire reflected an unspoken assumption about its value and beneficence, not perhaps as an instrument of God's will, but certainly as an institution that rested on consensus and goodwill rather than conflict and exploitation. Davidson was nevertheless acute enough to realise how racial tensions were capable of leading to problems in the colonies. He gave his vigorous support to Anglican clergy in Africa who opposed civilian authorities and employers who sought to conscript local workers for little or no pay. The Archbishop was nevertheless still careful to note, as ever, that such problems were best resolved by a mixture of compromise and goodwill.[54]

The Archbishop was circumspect both in public and private about commenting on international politics in more specific terms. He was ready to applaud the importance of peace and cooperation, but far less willing to pronounce on the rights and wrongs of particular conflicts. It was seen in Chapter 5 that he took a strong position towards the Soviet Government, protesting about the treatment of the Orthodox clergy, as well as offering support for a large-scale programme of famine relief. Such interventions were rare. Davidson's occasional pronouncements on developments in the Near East were typically made in response to the situation of the local Christian population. The behaviour of major powers like France and Germany seldom attracted his comment. Nor does the Archbishop seem to have been particularly interested even in the negotiation of major international agreements such as the 1925 Locarno Pact. Davidson had always been averse to speaking in public on subjects about which he was not well informed. He was also nervous of intruding on subjects that were likely to prove politically controversial. The inevitable result was that the Archbishop's pronouncements on international politics after 1918 tended towards the platitudinous. It was perhaps unavoidable. As a number of his successors at Canterbury have discovered, an Archbishop who becomes too involved in political questions runs the risk of being accused of meddling in things beyond their competence.

There was one area of (semi-) international politics where Davidson did risk controversy: the Irish question. The Archbishop told Lloyd George in May 1920 that although he had 'no special knowledge' of Irish matters, the Government should make more effort to tease out the real views of Catholic priests and Bishops, in order to show publically that members of the Catholic hierarchy were not so unequivocally in favour of the independence movement as widely believed. Davidson presumably thought that such a course of action would weaken the vigour of the nationalist cause by weakening its religious *imprimatur*. He was, though, by no means ready to give unconditional support to those seeking to preserve British rule in Ireland. In the autumn of 1920, he made a speech in the House of Lords condemning reports of atrocities committed by the Black and Tans, a move which led some to condemn Davidson for not taking a harder line towards the atrocities carried out by Sinn Fein.[55] And then, in February 1921, he made a thoughtful speech in which he argued that nationalist atrocities could never be cited as a way of justifying 'wrongdoing' by those tasked with keeping order.[56] The Archbishop welcomed the agreement between British and Irish negotiators, at the end of 1921, with the predictable result that his in-tray was filled with correspondence condemning him for abandoning 'the loyal and faithful people of Southern Ireland who have stood by the Empire'.[57] He also faced sharp condemnation in papers such as *The Morning Post* for welcoming a peace settlement that many believed had been won by force and intimidation. Davidson could never have hoped to find a *via media* capable of winning the support of both sides in the Irish crisis. His natural instinct to espouse the value of compromise was hardly likely to prevail in the context of a struggle characterised by enmity and intolerance. But Davidson did remain true to his values, and was ready to accept some of the sharpest criticism of his career, refusing to respond to the pressure of those who believed that the Anglican Primate should unambiguously defend the cause of Great(er) Britain.

Archbishop Davidson's approach to social and economic questions during the 1920s was, as it always had been, both cautious and conservative. A younger generation of clergy like William Temple and Dick Sheppard were increasingly committed to developing a new political theology – focused on restructuring relationships between Church, State, and Society – in an effort to promote greater social justice. Davidson, by contrast, continued to espouse a more conventional outlook that broadly accepted the legitimacy of the social and economic *status quo*. Such a position in part reflected his recognition that the Church of England would find itself the focus of political controversy if it began to challenge existing patterns of privilege and power. It also reflected his longstanding view that social ills such as poverty and poor housing were not systemic problems that required fundamental reform, but rather discrete issues that needed to be dealt with on an *ad hoc* basis. The Archbishop was comparatively sanguine about the rise of the Labour Party precisely because he understood – unlike many other members of the social and political establishment – that its demands for reform were essentially modest. He certainly did not accept the idea that there was an irreconcilable conflict between the interests of capital and labour.

Davidson remained confident during the last decade of his archiepiscopate that he had both the right and duty to discuss affairs of State with the political leaders of all parties. He also believed that the Church of England was bound to comment on those issues – such as marriage and divorce – which came firmly within the purview of a traditional moral vocabulary. Although there is little doubt that some younger clergy and lay people were frustrated by Davidson's reluctance to engage with demands for more radical social and economic change, he continued to command widespread respect within the Church. Nor, it must be said, is there much compelling evidence that large numbers of ordinary 'pew' Anglicans shared the more radical views expressed by men like Temple: if anything the reverse was true. The Church of England had traditionally formed part of an Establishment that, although sometimes fragmented, shared a fundamental sense of identity and interest. The growing political influence of the Nonconformist churches in the 50 years before 1914 had certainly begun to raise important questions about the role of the Church of England in the life of the nation. The social and cultural changes of the 1920s probably accelerated the process still further. It was not that the number of Anglicans in Britain fell away (it did not). Nor is it that members of the Church of England attended fewer services than before (they did not). The process was instead more complex and less tangible: a subtle downgrading in the public imagination of the Church's role in national life. Yet the phenomenon should not be exaggerated. As the next chapter will show, questions about ritual and doctrine were still capable of arousing passionate public debate and political division throughout the 1920s. Davidson faced the delicate task of ensuring that the influence which the Church of England derived from its status as an Established Church was not paid for by surrendering its right to determine important questions of doctrine and liturgy.

Notes

1 Among the many works on the vexed questions of the decline of the Church of England, along with the growing secularisation of Great Britain, see Brown, *Death of Christian*

Britain; Robert Currie et al, *Churches and Churchgoers*; Alan D. Gilbert, *The Making of Post-Christian Britain: A History of the Secularisation of Modern Society* (London: Longmans, 1980); S.J.D. Green, *The Passing of Protestant England: Secularisation and Social Change c. 1920–1960* (Cambridge: Cambridge University Press, 2011), esp. pp. 3–94; Hastings, *History of English Christianity, passim.*

2 For a valuable discussion of this issue, acknowledging the complex development of Christian observance in Britain between the wars, see Brown, *Religion and Society in Twentieth-Century Britain*, pp. 116–76.

3 Norman, *Church and Society in England*, p. 229; Wilkinson, *Christian Socialism*, pp. 42–75.

4 For a recent account of Tawney's life and thought, see Lawrence Goldman, *The Life of R.H. Tawney: Socialism and History* (London: Bloomsbury, 2013). On Temple, see Iremonger, *Temple*; Kent, *Temple*. Also see Edmonds, *Leaders of the Church of England*, pp. 314–49.

5 For a striking exception, though, see Grimley, *Citizenship, Community and the Church of England*.

6 For some useful comments on the nature of Davidson's 'religion' by the man who served as his Chaplain from 1924 until 1928, see F. Russell Barry, *Mervyn Haigh* (London: SPCK, 1964), pp. 98–9.

7 On 1919 as a year of social and political challenge across Europe, see Margaret Macmillan, *Peacemakers: Six Months That Changed the World* (London: John Murray, 2003); Anthony Read, *The World on Fire: 1919 and the Battle with Bolshevism* (London: Pimlico, 2009).

8 *Christianity and Industrial Problems* (London: SPCK, 1918), p. ix.

9 For the Report, see *Six Lambeth Conferences: 1920 Conference*, pp. 59–77.

10 G.I.T. Machin, *Churches and Social Issues in Twentieth-Century Britain* (Oxford: Clarendon Press, 1998), pp. 15–16.

11 Bell, *Davidson*, Vol. 2, pp. 1,046–47; *Chronicle of Convocation: Convocation of Canterbury (Upper House)*, April 27–8 1921.

12 Machin, *Churches and Social Issues*, p. 32.

13 Iremonger, *Temple*, p. 333.

14 Grimley, *Citizenship, Community and the Church of England*, p. 40. On COPEC see Norman, *Church and Society*, 279–313.

15 Kent, *Temple*, p. 123. For a more detailed review of the discussions between Temple and Davidson over COPEC, see Norman, *Church and Society*, pp. 288–90.

16 Kent, *Temple*, p. 120.

17 Barry, *Haigh*, pp. 81–2.

18 For a useful summary of the churches' response to the General Strike, see Machin, *Churches and Social Issues*, pp. 35–40. For useful accounts taken from the perspectives of two key Government ministers, see Keith Middlemas and John Barnes, *Baldwin: A Biography* (London: Weidenfeld and Nicolson, 1969), pp. 418–43; Martin Gilbert, *Winston S. Churchill* (London: Heinemann, 1966–88), Vol. 5, pp. 146–74.

19 *Parliamentary Debates (Lords)*, 5 May 1926, cols. 49–50.

20 On the role of the BBC in the General Strike, see Asa Briggs, *The Birth of Broadcasting* (London: Oxford University Press, 1961), pp. 360–83.

21 D.P. 15, fo. 68, Undated Davidson Memorandum. See, too, Briggs, *Birth of Broadcasting*, pp. 378–80.

22 *Times*, 10 May 1926.

23 D.P. 15, fo. 65, Davidson Memorandum on 'Interview [. . .] at Downing Street with Mr Baldwin', 11 May 1926.

24 D.P. 6, Letter 107, Davidson to Bishop of Oxford, 25 May 1926.

25 Henson, *Retrospect*, Vol. 2, ps.119, 124. For a discussion of Henson's role during the strike, see Chadwick, *Henson*, 158–81

26 Bell, *Davidson*, Vol. 2, p. 1,316.

27 Davidson Papers 15, fos. 70–95, Davidson Memorandum, 23 May 1926. For a sample of these letters, see D.P. 6, Paper 108.

28 Kent, *Temple*, p. 142.
29 In his famous speech 'What England Means to Me', given in May 1924, Baldwin made no mention of the Church instead focusing on 'the tinkle of hammer on anvil in the country smithy, the corncrake on a dewy morning, the sound of the scythe against the whetstone, and the sight of a plough team coming over the brow of a hill'. Baldwin's thoroughly non-denominational views on religion found some expression in his *On England* (London: Philip Allan, 1926), pp. 195–212. For a fascinating discussion of Baldwin focusing on the genesis and character of his ideas, see Philip Williamson, *Stanley Baldwin: Conservative Leadership and National Values* (Cambridge: Cambridge University Press, 1999).
30 D.P. 15, fos. 2–10, Davidson Memorandum, 11 January 1925 (quotation fo. 2).
31 *English Review*, January 1924, pp. 3–4.
32 D.P. 14, fos. 260–6, Davidson Memorandum, 12 December 1923 (quotations fos. 264, 266).
33 D.P. 14, fos. 240–58, Davidson Memorandum, 18 November 1923 (quotation fo. 255).
34 D.P. 14, fos. 288–92, Davidson to Talbot, 27 January 1924 (quotations *passim*).
35 D.P. 15, fos. 2–10, Davidson Memorandum, 11 January 1925 (quotation fo. 3).
36 Robbins, *England, Ireland, Scotland, Wales*, pp. 158–59.
37 *Times*, 1 January 1924.
38 For a valuable discussion, see Peter Webster, 'The Archbishop of Canterbury, the Lord Chamberlain and the Censorship of the Theatre, 1909–49', *Studies in Church History*, 48 (2012), pp. 437–48.
39 Bell, *Davidson*, Vol. 2, pp. 1,213–15; Kimball King (ed), *Western Drama Through the Ages*, 2 vols. (London: Greenwood Press), Vol. 2, p. 318.
40 *Times*, 25 March 1920.
41 *Times*, 16 April 1920 (Letter by T.A. Lacey); 17 April 1920 (Editorial).
42 *Parliamentary Debates (Lords)*, 11 May 1920, col. 249.
43 On the 1918 Education Act, see G.E. Sherrington, 'The 1918 Education Act: Origins, Aims and Development', *British Journal of Educational Studies*, 24, 1 (1976), pp. 66–85.
44 Birn, *League of Nations* Union, pp. 133–35.
45 For the classic critique of Idealism in international relations, and its affect on the interwar global system, see E. H. Carr, *The Twenty Years Crisis* (London: Macmillan, 1939).
46 Davidson, *Occasions*, pp. 1–22, Sermon on the League of Nations.
47 *Times*, 4 September 1922 (Letter by J.E.C. Welldon).
48 *Ottawa Journal*, 8 September 1922.
49 *New York Times*, 24 September 1922.
50 *The Age*, 5 September 1922.
51 Bell, *Davidson*, Vol. 2, p. 1,210.
52 Davidson, *Occasions*, pp. 62–5, 'Address on Empire Day'.
53 Randall Davidson, 'Australia Day' (Sermon preached at St Dunstan's-in-the-East on Australia Day, 26 January 1925).
54 Bell, *Davidson*, Vol. 2, pp. 1,233–34.
55 *Parliamentary Debates (Lords)*, 2 November 1920, col. 143. For a note by an old friend on Davidson's bravery in broaching the question, see Bell Papers 224, fos. 321–22, J.C. Gordon to Bell, 27 February 1932.
56 For the full speech, see *Parliamentary Debates (Lords)*, 22 February 1921, cols. 79–91
57 Bell, *Davidson*, Vol. 2, p. 1,063.

7 Archbishop Davidson, Church, and State (1918–1928)

It was seen in Chapter 5 how the ecumenical initiatives which blossomed after the end of the First World War sometimes actually heightened divisions *within* the Church of England. Randall Davidson's caution about pursuing any far-reaching moves towards closer relations with other churches was, indeed, rooted in his understanding that the comprehensive character of the Anglican Communion made it vulnerable to internal fissures. Much of his ecclesiastical career had been devoted to preserving the balance between competing elements within the Church of England. Such a thankless task was by its nature unending. As Davidson noted on more than one occasion, his efforts to search for consensus usually went unnoticed, above all when he was successful in smoothing over the differences between those who were in fundamental disagreement. The furore that erupted once news of the Malines Conversations became public, at the end of 1923, nevertheless showed there were limits to the extent to which such disagreements could be contained.

The British politician Enoch Powell once observed that, 'All political lives, unless they are cut off in midstream at a happy juncture, end in failure, because that is the nature of politics and of human affairs'. The maxim could, at first glance, be applied to Davidson, given that his resignation in the summer of 1928 followed close on the heels of Parliament's second rejection of the revised Prayer Book. The Archbishop failed to assuage the concern of some in positions of political power that the Church of England was abandoning its Protestant heritage. And yet it would be unfair to hold Davidson solely or even primarily responsible for the debacle. If he was culpable, it was because, as so often during his long career, he failed to grasp the raw emotional power that fuelled those who held strong opinions about the character of the Church of England. The religious enthusiasms of the Victorian era were not simply echoes of 'dead themes', as A.J.P. Taylor once claimed,[1] and remained potent above all because they touched on matters that went beyond simple questions of religion.

John Maiden has pointed out that the passions which fuelled the Prayer Book crisis of 1927–28 were so powerful precisely because they were not concerned merely with such questions as changes to the rubrics of the Communion Service.[2] They were instead about more fundamental questions of national identity. For many people, both within and beyond the Church of England, the country's post-Reformation Protestant heritage was central to what it meant to be British (or perhaps English) – a central pivot of national identity.[3] Britain was a less secular place during the inter-war years than sometimes imagined,[4] and the character of the Church of England was necessarily bound up with the identity of the wider society. Any tendencies within the National Church that might be seen (rightly or wrongly) as 'Roman' – Reservation, Confession, and the like – could easily be rejected for undermining the prevailing narrative of national identity. It is this, more than anything else, which explains why issues relating to the internal life of the Church of England had the capacity to evoke such powerful emotions. Britain's Protestant heritage had in some ways been eroded by the growth of religious toleration over the previous two centuries,[5] but it continued to exercise a hold on the imagination of a significant part of the population. As an Established Church, forming part of the delicate web of institutions that helped define the character of the British Constitution, questions of doctrine and practice were bound to resonate far beyond the boundaries of the Church of England itself.[6]

The status of the Church of England as an Established Church, which Randall Davidson had defended staunchly throughout his long ecclesiastical career, continued to provoke controversy during the 1920s. Political pressure for Disestablishment from the Nonconformist denominations – and above all Nonconformist MPs in Parliament – was far *less* after 1918 than it had been before the war (due both to the decline of the Liberal Party and the removal of a long-running bone of contention with the final Disestablishment of the Church in Wales). There was, however, growing scepticism about the value of Establishment *within* the Church of England. A small number of clergy and lay people thought that the time had come to break the link with the State once and for all. And many more believed that it was time to consider how the Church of England could remain an Established Church whilst enjoying greater autonomy from Parliamentary control (a theme that can be traced back to the creation Life and Liberty in the closing years of the war).

Matthew Grimley has shown how the Church of England's relationship with the State had by the 1920s become an important focus of interest for a number of Anglican thinkers, both lay and clerical, ranging from William Temple and Hensley Henson to the Anglo-Catholic priest J. N. Figgis and the philosopher Ernest Barker. Some, like Figgis, believed that the Church of England would benefit from Disestablishment, becoming instead a 'gathered Church', committed to witness by means of its own purity and example (a view largely shared by Charles Gore in his old age). Others, like Temple, believed that the Church of England should make greater efforts to assert its spiritual autonomy whilst using its Established status to play a central role in shaping the moral identity of both nation and State. Such intellectual subtleties did not find a ready audience amongst the many MPs who were determined to assert Parliament's right to legislate on Church affairs – sentiments that received ample public expression during the debates over the Enabling Bill in 1919 and (particularly) the new Prayer Book in 1927–28. A significant number of Parliamentarians interpreted any demands for greater independence for the Church of England as a strategy to gain the freedom needed to make doctrinal reforms of a decidedly Anglo-Catholic character.

Archbishop Davidson continued to value Establishment in the years after 1918, both as a central feature of the British Constitution and as a vital means of giving the Church influence in public life. He still thought of the Church of England as *the* National Church, its status deriving both from formal Establishment *and* from its long history stretching back to the time of Augustine. It was perhaps this unspoken assumption which sometimes made Davidson seem remote from the passions that informed debates about the Church's status during the 1920s. He had little real understanding of the intellectual concerns of Anglicans – ranging from Temple to Gore – who fretted about the right relationship between Church and State. Davidson was no Erastian in the sense of believing that Parliament had the right to dictate all aspects of the Church of England's doctrine and liturgy: he was convinced that the Church had a distinctive identity which included elements of both Episcopal and Lay governance. The Archbishop did, however, accept the right of Parliament to legislate on certain aspects of Church life. When the question of Church-State relations was raised during the 1920s, he tried to deal with it as he always dealt with such matters, seeking agreement by means of personal diplomacy and appeals for compromise. The strategy that had served him so well for so long proved less successful than before. The Archbishop was still held in high regard by almost all those he dealt with during the final decade of his archiepiscopate. Advancing age nevertheless meant that he sometimes struggled to rise to the new challenges that faced the Church of England in maintaining both its status and its influence.

Randall Davidson and the Enabling Bill

It was seen in Chapter 4 that the relationship between Church and State became an issue of some controversy during the final years of the First World War. Davidson was – with reservations – ready to accept that the National Mission launched in 1916 represented an appropriate way of harnessing the emotional intensity of war to the promotion of spiritual renewal. The growth of the Life and Liberty Movement was, by contrast, fuelled by a sense in some quarters that the Church should be involved in pushing for more far-reaching changes. Davidson had dragged his feet following the publication in 1916 of the report by the Archbishops' Commission on Church and State, chaired by Lord Selborne, arguing that politicians had no time to deal with issues of Church governance during a time of total war. He was also wary of encouraging debate about questions that could raise difficult questions about the nature and significance of Establishment.

A few weeks before the end of the war, Davidson had a meeting with a delegation from Life and Liberty and the Church Self-Government Council, at which demands were made for the Archbishop to give a 'definite lead' to the Church.⁷ The Archbishop predictably remained equivocal, warning against a policy of 'spasm or scream'.⁸ Shortly afterwards, though, he endorsed the report issued by a committee of the Representative Church Council (RCC), which outlined ways of putting into effect the proposals previously made by the Archbishops' Commission. The report suggested the establishment of a new National Assembly of the Church of England (to replace the RCC). It also proposed that the franchise qualification for voters to the new Assembly should be Baptism rather than Confirmation (in effect broadening the number of those deemed to belong to the National Church). The proposals attracted considerable attention in both the national and local press – a reminder of how such issues were still widely seen as being of general importance rather than a minor matter of ecclesiastical governance.⁹ At the heart of the report was the notion that the Church of England should take greater responsibility for its own governance, effectively reducing Parliamentary oversight, a position that was bound to prove provocative for those who took a more Erastian view of Church-State relations.

Davidson was anxious in the days leading up to the debate that took place in the full meeting of the RCC in February 1919. The Archbishop feared that the proposals were likely to be criticised by some on the Anglo-Catholic wing of the Church who wanted greater independence from the State. He also knew that others like Hensley Henson would, by contrast, oppose the scheme on the grounds that it might weaken the principle of Establishment. Davidson made a long speech at the RCC, in which he carefully tried to rebuff the claim that loosening Parliamentary control represented a weakening of the traditional foundations of Church of England governance. He nevertheless also warned that the mere 'waving of a wand' could not alone provide the Church with the kind of independence that would allow it to pursue its spiritual mission more effectively.¹⁰ Above all, though, the Archbishop used his speech to present the proposals for greater independence as a practical measure designed to allow the Church to manage its affairs more effectively (he wanted, as he noted in a private memorandum, to avoid 'fine-drawn theories').¹¹ Davidson's speech was, of course, somewhat disingenuous: the question of the governance of the Church of England was in large part a question about its character.

Although the proposals were adopted by a large majority of the RCC, the reaction during the following weeks showed how the issue remained sensitive both amongst senior clerics and in the country at large. The reaction of Henson was both predictable and typical. He wrote a series of letters to *The Times* criticising the measures approved by the RCC, warning at the end of March that the proposals would lead to authority being vested in 'the hands of a small section' of metropolitan clerics who were unrepresentative of the Church of England as a whole.¹² William Temple, for his part, weighed into the debate with a strong denial that Life and Liberty wanted Disestablishment.¹³ *The Times* carried numerous letters both opposing and supporting Henson's claim that reducing the role of Parliament in the governance of the Church of England would destroy its Protestant heritage (the leading Primitive Methodist minister Arthur Guttery fretted that the changes would make possible 'a secret conspiracy against our faith and traditions').[14]

Davidson once again found himself having to deal with a recalcitrant Charles Gore. Gore wrote to the Archbishop in March 1919, resigning as Bishop of Oxford in order to spend the rest of his life in 'serious study', although he noted that the decision of the RCC to opt for an electoral franchise based on Baptism rather than Confirmation was also a factor. The move was, he wrote, symbolic of a readiness to sacrifice 'principle to the desire for larger numbers on our rolls, and that largely for the sake of maintaining the "national" position of the Church' (he was probably right)![15] Gore had for decades sought to push the Church of England towards more definite doctrinal positions, to be enforced by the Bishops, and his views echoed a growing readiness amongst Anglo-Catholics to place spiritual autonomy above Establishment. It was a view at odds with those who, like William Temple, believed that Establishment was needed to promote spiritual principles throughout the body politic. Gore's departure from Oxford attracted surprisingly little coverage in the secular press. *The Times* noted a little gnomically that those who knew him best would not be 'altogether surprised at his decision'.[16] And, whilst it printed the exchange of letters between Gore and Davidson under the heading 'The Crisis in the Church',[17] its comments reflected a well-founded sense that the question of the franchise for electing members of the new Church Assembly was the occasion rather than the cause for the Bishop of Oxford's resignation. Davidson himself was left to ponder the danger of Gore falling 'into the hands of friends who press him forward on unwise paths'.[18]

The principles agreed by the RCC prompted extensive debate at Convocation in May 1919. Henson noted (not unreasonably) that the move for greater self-government was led by 'a strangely ill-assorted association of clergymen'. Some Anglo-Catholics hoped it would lead to 'spiritual independence' and the suppression of 'heresy'. A number of Evangelicals thought it would ensure greater obedience among the clergy to the rubrics of the Prayer Book. Davidson diplomatically thanked Henson for his public-spirited comments. He also noted that he would himself never support any move that could undermine the National Church.[19] The Archbishop was well aware that the real challenge would come in getting Parliamentary support for the Enabling Bill which would be needed to provide legislative authority for the proposed changes. The passionate debate in the newspapers suggested that it would not be an easy task. If the legislation was to be piloted through both Houses of Parliament, it was likely to need the kind of deft political skills on which Davidson had long prided himself.

It is perhaps surprising – not least given the later controversy over the new Prayer Book – that the Enabling Bill received legislative approval. The Enabling Bill, which eventually passed into law as The Church of England Assembly (Powers) Act, gave the proposed new National Church Assembly the right to pass primary legislation on matters relating to Church governance (in effect delegating the right from Parliament). The Bill also allowed for the two Houses of Parliament to maintain a Legislative Committee that would review proposals by the National Assembly and report accordingly. On 3 June 1919, Davidson spoke for an hour in the House of Lords calling for the Enabling Bill to be given a second reading, a speech in which he once again worked hard to remove some of the polemical sting that surrounded the whole issue. He emphasised how the growth in population over the previous hundred years, along with the expanding legislative programme faced by Parliament, meant that new procedures were needed to ensure more effective Church governance. The Archbishop also placed particular emphasis on the fact that the proposed changes did not fundamentally change the relationship between Church and State nor touch on 'deeper spiritual things':

> We can go on as we are, but can go on only lamely and hampered and crippled in our work. I apologise for using a figure which I have used more than once, but it seems to me exactly to represent the position. We are like a man called upon to do some important work and who has got a broken finger. He is not going to give up the work, but he will not be able to do it so completely or so perfectly as if he had not a broken finger'.[20]

Davidson's soothing words were not sufficient to ease the concerns expressed by many critics of the Enabling Bill. *The Times* opposed the Bill on the grounds that it would change the character of the traditional relationship between State and Church. Organisations like the National Free Church Council also expressed opposition (not least because the legislation seemed to give the Church of England greater autonomy whilst allowing it to maintain its privileged position in national life). It is therefore not surprising that the Archbishop was amazed at how 'smooth' the process was of securing legislative approval for the Bill. In his biography of Davidson, George Bell praises his subject for piloting through such a potentially controversial piece of legislation. If true, this would suggest that the Archbishop retained the deft political touch he had shown earlier in his archiepiscopate. The actual course of events was, though, rather more complex than Bell acknowledges. In the first place, other leading Church figures like William Temple played a significant part in shaping public opinion. And, perhaps more importantly, members of the Lloyd George Government were for their own reasons willing to see the Enabling Bill passed into law.[21]

Political opposition to the Bill was initially strong. Lord Haldane as Lord Chancellor opposed it on the grounds that it changed the country's constitutional settlement. When the Cabinet considered the Bill at the end of June, it was condemned by Lord Birkenhead as 'thoroughly bad'. Herbert Fisher, who chaired the Cabinet's Home Affairs Committee, thought that the proposed legislation gave too much to the Church of England whilst asking it to give up little in return. In the weeks that followed, Davidson engaged in his usual round of diligent lobbying, talking to leading peers including Grey and Selborne. He also worked closely with his long-term confidante, the ecclesiastical lawyer Sir Lewis Dibdin, who in turn spoke with numerous MPs and journalists.

Considerable effort was made to mobilise support in the Commons, whilst a number of amendments in both Houses made the legislation more palatable to some of its critics. Davidson himself met a number of leading Free Churchmen, including Scott Lidgett, in an effort to broker support.

The campaign certainly played a role in securing the passage of the Enabling Bill into law. Members of the Government were, however, preoccupied at the time by a serious outbreak of industrial unrest. They were reluctant to use up too much political capital opposing the legislation. Ministers also recognised that they were likely to need the support of Davidson and other leading Anglicans on issues ranging from education through to the implementation of the legislation creating the Church in Wales. In any case, the decline in the number of Liberal Nonconformist MPs meant that the status of the Church of England was a less sensitive political issue than was once the case. Davidson certainly played his part in the political manoeuvres that saw the Enabling Bill become law – but he probably overestimated his part in the process when he wrote in a private note that his 'leadership' had been the pivotal factor in securing its approval. The Archbishop's failure to secure approval for the revised Prayer Book, a few years later, showed how even ecclesiastical diplomacy could not be effective when the political omens were not propitious.

The Commission on Doctrine

It will be seen later that the House of Commons' decision to reject the new Prayer Book at the end of 1927 was rooted in suspicion that it was introducing doctrinal changes of a Catholic character. Nor were such concerns absent in the debates about the Enabling Bill. A number of MPs who looked sceptically at the legislation during its passage into law sought reassurance that Parliament would still have the authority to approve any changes to the Prayer Book. There were also concerns within the Church itself. The Bishop of Manchester, Edmund Knox, later described how he believed that one of the aims of the Bill was 'to go a long way towards a counter-Reformation by means of a new Prayer Book'.[22]

The pattern of doctrinal division within the Church of England in the wake of the First World War was extremely complex. The long-standing split between Evangelicals and Anglo-Catholics continued. So too did the more recent tension between Modernists and Traditionalists. Cutting across these fault-lines was a distinction between those who thought that the Church should play a role in promoting social justice and others who believed that it should focus on 'religious' questions. Davidson's lack of a theological cast of mind helped him to reconcile in his own mind outlooks and beliefs that seemed at odds to those of a more systematic outlook or less generous spirit. It also meant that he appeared at times to advocate a doctrinal fuzziness that feared systematic inquiry as a potential source of division rather than enlightenment.

Many of these tensions came to the fore in the months leading up to the creation in 1922 of an Archbishops' Commission on Christian Doctrine (which only finally reported in 1938). The main architect of the process was Bishop Hubert Burge of Oxford. Burge played a central role in a series of informal discussions, primarily between university theologians, that led to a proposal for a Doctrinal Commission to determine 'For What Does the Church of England Stand'. Such a process could not by its nature be confined to theological and doctrinal matters, for if agreement was reached then it raised the question of how such beliefs should be enforced. Davidson initially blanched at the suggestion of creating a Commission, fearing it might lead to division and bitterness, albeit that Bishop Burge and his colleagues hoped it would promote agreement and harmony.

Davidson predictably couched his concerns obliquely. He questioned whether a group of individuals could ever command sufficient trust across the Church of England for their pronouncements to be accepted. He instead suggested to Burge that it would be more sensible for those interested in such a course to work along the lines of the individuals involved in the *Lux Mundi* symposium 40 years before.[23] Not unreasonably, Burge replied that *Lux Mundi* had been written by contributors of a broadly similar outlook, and pointed out that the proposed Commission was designed to search for common ground amongst those who were most definitely not of a common mind. The issue had become more sensitive following the Conference on Christ and the Creeds held at Cambridge, in August 1921, the proceedings of which were published in *The Modern Churchman* a few weeks later. E. W. Barnes (later Bishop Barnes of Birmingham) wrote about the reception of Divine Grace in the unconscious. Hastings Rashdall considered whether divinity had been attributed to Christ rather than claimed by him. The introduction to the journal acknowledged that some of the articles were controversial, but rejected the charge that contributors were denying the divinity of Christ, insisting that they were instead searching for a fresh perspective on the relationship between Christ's divine and human attributes.[24] The Conference was widely reported in the secular press,[25] and news of the proceedings inevitably aroused controversy, which was not assuaged by suggestions that the views put forward by participants were less controversial than widely assumed.

A number of Bishops were approached by the ECU demanding that it issue a declaration stating that many of the ideas put forward at the Cambridge Conference were 'entirely subversive of the Christian Faith'. When the Bishop of Gloucester presented the petition to Convocation, Davidson made an uncharacteristically incautious remark, commenting that some people were reacting to the Conference as though, 'there was a great phalanx of heresiachs set in battle against the doctrine of the Church Catholic [...] In my belief the whole of that is greatly exaggerated'.[26] Such a trenchant statement offended some leading figures in the Church, most notably Charles Gore, who had previously criticised participants in the Cambridge Conference for indulging in an 'excessive emphasis on the immanence of God' that tended towards Unitarianism.[27] Hastings Rashdall had reacted angrily to such claims, but Gore persisted in his criticism of 'the higher pantheism', which (he argued) asserted that God and man were of one substance. It was inevitable that the erstwhile Bishop of Oxford was appalled by Davidson's somewhat glib dismissal of the concerns expressed by the ECU ('this sort of chaff, or apparently light-hearted disparagement of the gravity of the situation tends to drive us wild').[28] Not for the first time, the Archbishop had failed to take into full account the emotional fervour that issues of doctrine aroused in some of his fellow-Anglicans. He responded soothingly to Gore, with his perennial suggestion that 'we meet the difficulty best by meeting the thing calmly'.

The issue was again discussed in Convocation in May 1922. Davidson defended his words at the February Convocation, arguing once again that the questions raised by the Cambridge Conference had taken on 'an exaggerated form', adding that the participants had simply discussed ideas 'which are stirring men's minds to-day'. He also pointed out that ideas put forward in the past by men like Wilberforce and Maurice had at the time caused great controversy. He acknowledged that the so-called 'advanced guard' often went 'far beyond what it can ultimately defend'. The Archbishop also repeated the point that he had made during debates about Modernism before the First World War: that members of the clergy had an intellectual and moral duty to pursue their inquiries, even if it led them to question existing doctrinal orthodoxy, but that they should consider resignation if they found themselves unable to reconcile their ideas with their position in the Church. In other words, Davidson acknowledged the right (and indeed duty) of free inquiry – but he did not necessarily accept that an individual should be permitted to articulate their ideas from a position of influence. The speech was unusually trenchant for Davidson. He was clear both in defending the principle of free thought, and in acknowledging that there were boundaries to the elasticity of the doctrine propounded by the Church of England. What he did not do, of course, was set down where the boundary lay between permitted debate and the expression of ideas that could not be reconciled with Anglican orthodoxy.[29]

Davidson had started to change his mind about the wisdom of establishing a Commission on Doctrine even before the February 1922 meeting of Convocation. A few weeks earlier, he had received a long letter from nearly 30 clerics and scholars, once again led by Burge, calling for a Commission to 'endeavour to find a basis of doctrinal agreement' on issues that had for years created division within the Church of England. The signatories suggested that, in the absence of such agreement, tensions would grow worse and make the task of governing the Church still harder in the years ahead.[30] Although Davidson was by now ready to concede the principle of a Commission, he was uncertain who should be appointed to it, and tellingly questioned the suggestion that 'comparatively young men' under 45 should form a substantial part of the membership (he had, ever since his sharp exchange with Temple a few years earlier, been inclined to emphasise the value of wisdom and age in matters ecclesiastical).

The Archbishop also questioned the criteria to be used when ensuring that the Commission reflected different viewpoints within the Church. The Bishop of Oxford responded to some of these points, acknowledging the scale of the task facing members of the Commission, not least because they would need to find ways of overcoming long-standing disagreements on important points of principle. Burge also suggested – not entirely coherently – that Commission members should commit themselves to respecting the principle of liberty of conscience whilst resolving 'grave doctrinal differences'. By the end of 1922, Davidson was finally ready to authorise the establishment of the Commission (Burge himself was appointed Chair). It was a characteristic response from the Archbishop, which was designed to respond to a difficult issue through compromise: he realised that, despite his reservations, opposing a Commission was likely to put him at odds with a significant number of prominent Anglicans drawn from a younger generation of clergy. Davidson was also probably astute enough to realise that it would be a long time before the Church of England had to deal with the fallout from the Commission's recommendations. It did not report until eight years after his death.[31]

Davidson and the Prayer Book crisis of 1927–28

Although questions of doctrine exercised many members of the clergy, they seldom had such powerful resonance for most Anglican lay people, except when they had a palpable impact on the character of Church services. It was partly for this reason that the new Prayer Book placed before Parliament at the end of 1927 proved so controversial. The proposed reforms of certain rubrics, along with (comparatively minor) changes to the Communion Service, were bound to prove controversial for those who thought of the 1662 Prayer Book in the same way they thought of the King James Bible: as something permanent, possessing a sacred form hallowed by time. A number of changes were of real significance, most notably allowing Reservation of the Sacrament for administration to the sick, something that was always likely to be seen by some as a slippery slope towards allowing Permanent Reservation (and Adoration) of the Sacrament. Hensley Henson wrote in his memoirs that the revised Prayer Book 'was finally rejected in deference to an organized outburst of Protestant feeling in the nation'.[32] There was a good deal of truth in his words. The irony was that the 20-year process which led up to the production of a revised Prayer Book began in response to demands, so loud in the early years of Davidson's archiepiscopate, for the restoration of clerical discipline in the face of perceived challenges by Anglo-Catholic clergy.

It was seen in Chapter 3 how the Royal Commission on Ecclesiastical Discipline, which reported in 1906, was set up in response to popular disquiet about the introduction of such 'illegal practices' as Reservation and the use of incense. The Commission's conclusion that 'the law of public worship in the Church of England is too narrow for the religious life of the present generation' led to its recommendation for a 'revision of the law' designed to secure clerical obedience. The Commissioners hoped, in other words, that by expanding the limits of practices deemed permissible it would be possible for the Bishops to enforce the new boundaries more effectively. It was the kind of practical response that fitted well with Davidson's instinctive sense that tolerance was necessary to reduce friction within the Church.

The Ritualism question died down following the publication of the Commission's Report, eclipsed by the growing tension over the role of the Church of England in education, along with the various political crises that erupted in the years before 1914. The Church's drift towards tolerating 'Catholic' rituals and practices nevertheless continued to raise concern in some quarters. It was seen previously that both Reservation and Prayers for the Dead became matters of intense debate during the First World War, fostered by the huge loss of life, and a concomitant yearning for practices that gave some kind of consolation to the living. Convocation discussed these questions at length during the war years, as part of the debate on the reform of Prayer Book rubrics, a process that flowed ineluctably towards broader discussion about the need for a revised Prayer Book that went beyond mere tinkering with existing formularies. A new draft Book was published early in 1923, which prompted alternative proposals from various parts of the Church, including two from Anglo-Catholic groups suggesting more far-reaching changes. The furore that erupted once news of the Malines Conversations became public at the end of 1923 showed how dislike of 'Catholicism' in both its Roman and Anglo-Catholic forms remained a potent force in Britain. One of the reasons Archbishop Davidson was so cautious about the Malines Conversations was, indeed, that he realised they could raise passions that would complicate the revision of the Prayer Book. Davidson himself had no great desire to see the introduction of a new Prayer Book, but he knew that many Anglo-Catholic clergy wanted change, and hoped that the introduction of a revised Book would help to ensure order within the Church.

The draft of the new Prayer Book introduced to the Church Assembly in the summer of 1923 included provision for Reservation of the Sacrament (for administration to the sick) as well as a modified Communion rite. The proposals met with broad approval in the Assembly, although in the weeks that followed Evangelical groups published numerous petitions protesting against the changes. The religious press was full of letters and articles discussing the proposals. The subject also filled the columns of *The Times*, evidence yet again of the extent to which concern about such issues spilled out far beyond the Church.[33] When the final task of revision began in the autumn of 1925, Davidson noted that he had received more than 500 memorials on the subject, mostly opposing any change to the Communion Service. The main work of producing the definitive version of the new Prayer Book was carried on by the Bishops' meeting in private at Lambeth Palace – the final Book was widely referred to as the Bishops' Book – a procedure that the Archbishop hoped would soothe away disagreements in an atmosphere of informality and goodwill. A number of Bishops were opposed to any change (most notably the Bishops of Norwich, Worcester, and Birmingham). Davidson was generally sanguine about the extent to which tensions were kept in check ('uncannily harmonious' he thought), but he also noted with some acerbity that there were times when

Barnes of Birmingham could be 'odd' whilst Frere of Truro occasionally 'lost his temper'.[34]

The Archbishop's involvement in detailed discussion of the new Prayer Book was limited. Davidson was convinced that the most important issues should be discussed privately, since public debate would complicate the process of building agreement, although in retrospect such an approach may simply have stoked the fears of those worried about a possible threat to the Protestant character of the Church of England. In early 1926, he set down his views in a lengthy memorandum:

> I have found it very difficult to know what speaking generally ought to be my own line in regard to proposals for changing the Communion Office. On the one hand my own instinct would have been for leaving that Office alone and adhering to what has satisfied the English people for more than three centuries. And I am convinced that such is the view of the overwhelming majority of English Churchmen throughout the country. The average MP or County Councillor, or local Squire, or man of business, says emphatically "leave it alone". Ought it to be one's policy to fall in with that wish or give leadership in that direction and practically refuse what the ecclesiastically minded folk want in the way of change or reform or reversion to older usage? The answer is not easy. These people who have given their thoughts to the structure of a service which to many of them means more than anything else on earth, have been working for years at trying to bring about the sort of changes which they think could make our Office more Catholic without imparing its really English character.[35]

Davidson's ambivalence was understandable – and certainly shows he was aware that the new Prayer Book would be seen in some quarters as a betrayal of the Church of England's Protestant heritage. He nevertheless worked hard to defend the new Book once the Bishops had agreed on its final form and passed it on to Convocation for discussion.

When Davidson spoke to Convocation in February 1927, he carefully traced the genesis of the new Book, noting that, 'I wish to say emphatically that in my deliberate judgement nothing that we have suggested makes any change in the doctrinal position of the Church of England'.[36] He also stressed that congregations could continue to use the existing Prayer Book if they wished. Davidson took a similar line at a joint meeting of the Convocations of York and Canterbury a few weeks later:

> We desire now in the twentieth century to give the people of England a Book of Common Prayer enriched and adapted to the needs of contemporary life with its new conditions and sympathies, its new aspirations and endeavours. But emphatically it must be a Book which retains the priceless treasure of the old Book which is our heritage: a Book, in short, which does not break with the habits and forms of worship endeared to

generations. And the Book must continue to bear, beyond all doubt, the distinctive character which marks the Church of England Catholic and Reformed.[37]

The logic of the Archbishop's approach was clear. He wanted to steer a course between those who wanted change and those who did not. The publication of numerous pamphlets and letters to the press over the next few months showed that such a hope was likely to prove forlorn (the Church Assembly itself approved the final version of the revised Prayer Book in July 1927).[38] The failure of Baldwin's Government to find Parliamentary time to consider the new Book also caused problems since it meant that the fractious public debate dragged on for months. An ominous foretaste of the political challenges ahead can be seen in an exchange of letters between Davidson and Home Secretary William Joynson-Hicks in the spring of 1927 (the two men had exchanged sharp words over the Malines Conversations three years earlier). 'Jix' wanted to know how the Church would ensure that the clergy observed the rubrics in the new Prayer Book (not least given that there was no shortage of Anglo-Catholic voices arguing that Reservation should not be limited to the provision of the Sacrament to the sick). The Archbishop's response was weak, consisting of little more than platitudes designed to reassure the Home Secretary that Anglican clergy would abide by the new Prayer Book. Jix responded tersely, noting that Evangelicals were reluctantly prepared to accept change on questions such as vestments and even Reservation, but wanted reassurance that the Bishops would act to prevent any further movement towards 'Catholic' practices and doctrines. Davidson had previously written to *The Times* promising that the Bishops would act to impose discipline,[39] but the Home Secretary was probably right in questioning their readiness to do so, given the experience of the previous few decades.

A veritable deluge of pamphlets appeared in 1927 expressing sharply competing views on the new Prayer Book. The newspapers were also full of discussion. *The Times* published more than 250 letters on the subject. Edward Knox, the former Bishop of Manchester, warned that the new Book would produce 'chaos' (some years later, he somewhat unfairly criticised Davidson and Lang for being ready to put the Prayer Book 'in the melting pot', valuing it only for its 'Pre-Reformation traditions [. . .] rather than for its Protestantism').[40] Many Nonconformists argued that the Church of England, as the Established Church, had a duty to remain true to its Protestant heritage. Joynson-Hicks made public his concern that the Bishops would not enforce ecclesiastical discipline.[41] Other correspondents by contrast argued that the Church should unite behind the new Book in order to end 'party strife'.[42] Davidson himself was deluged by letters from individuals and organisations demanding that he offer leadership in a particular direction. The Federation of Catholic Priests (an Anglican group) wrote to the Archbishop saying that its members would not obey any ban on Perpetual Reservation.[43] The decidedly Protestant Northern Council of the Committee for the Maintenance of Truth and Faith told Davidson that public opinion was strongly against the new Book.[44] As the months passed, attention focused increasingly on how Parliament was likely to respond when asked to approve the new Prayer Book (or the Deposited Book to give it its formal title).

Once the Church Assembly approved the new Prayer Book, in July 1927, its opponents recognised that they would have to turn to Parliament to prevent its formal adoption.[45] The files in the Lambeth Palace archives show that senior figures in the Church of England devoted considerable time to discussing the Prayer Book with MPs and peers (they also unusually gave a number of interviews to the press). Davidson himself met with senior figures in the House of Lords to rally support. He also urged the Bishops to become more vocal in defending the Deposited Book.[46] The Archbishop may have been too sanguine that the new Prayer Book would receive Parliamentary approval.[47] In a memorandum dictated early in 1928, a few weeks after the first rejection, Davidson recalled that there had been a 'curious variety and changeableness of opinion' on the Prayer Book question. He was nevertheless optimistic when introducing the measure in the House of Lords on 12 December, in a speech he rightly noted was 'not an ambitious speech in the sense of rhetoric or purple patches'.[48] The Archbishop repeated his view that the new Prayer Book did not represent a fundamental change in doctrine or practice, but was instead needed to overcome Party strife, which would in turn allow the Church of England to work more effectively. Hensley Henson, who was present in the House of Lords, thought the speech was poor, but patronisingly added that it was 'a notable achievement for an octogenarian' (Henson himself supported the revised Book on the grounds that change was needed to gain greater support among the clergy).[49] The debate in the Lords lasted several days and ended with a clear majority in favour. Davidson received numerous letters and telegrams of congratulations on the removal of a 'grave anxiety'. The King's Private Secretary noted that His Majesty was sure that the Commons would act in a similar way.[50]

The rejection of the Deposited Book in the House of Commons on 15 December seems to have come as a genuine shock to Davidson (like a number of other senior Anglicans he had thought that the Lords might be the less sympathetic of the two Houses of Parliament). Some of the notes of sympathy he received in the wake of the vote read almost like letters of condolence. The novelist John Buchan noted that 'the disastrous vote' was the product of a night on which 'Everything seemed to go wrong'.[51] The case for the new Prayer Book certainly seems to have been put poorly in the House of Commons. Davidson later wrote that he listened with 'increasing dismay' to the 'incredibly poor' speeches in support of the Book. William Bridgeman, First Lord of the Admiralty, 'absolutely muffed' his speech (he was an odd choice of speaker given that had no great knowledge of the subject). Hugh Cecil 'completely failed'. Baldwin spoke towards the end of the debate 'but it was not his exact subject'. The Archbishop ruefully acknowledged that Jix, by contrast, gave a powerful speech against the new Prayer Book. So too did Sir Thomas Inskip 'who wound up with a really clear and able speech'. The Prayer Book was eventually rejected by a majority of 33.[52] Davidson noted mournfully that the scenes of celebration among the Bill's opponents – many MPs leapt onto the benches waving their order papers – reflected the 'inflammatory character' of many of the arguments used by opponents of the revised Book.

The rejection of the new Prayer Book created an immediate crisis in Church-State relations. The House of Common's assertion of its authority seemed to reflect a profoundly Erastian understanding of Establishment, which many considered at odds with the true character of the British Constitution. Although indignation was loudest on the Anglo-Catholic wing of the Church, it also infuriated many who had been active in the Life and Liberty Movement. At a meeting of the Bishops on 19 December, sharp exchanges took place between those who believed that the Bishops would 'lose their self-respect' if they 'took this rebuff lying down' and others who thought it 'puerile' to challenge Parliament.[53] The press statement issued by the two Archbishops echoed Davidson's own ambivalence about the situation: 'It was within the right of the House of Commons to reject the Measure. On the other hand, mere acquiescence would be in our judgement inconsistent with the responsibilities of the Church as a spiritual society'.[54] The Archbishops also noted that the House of Bishops had already resolved to present a somewhat changed version of the Book for approval to the Church Assembly (and, in due course, to Parliament). It was a move taken in the face of calls from some clergy and lay people for a campaign of 'civil disobedience', in which the new Prayer Book would have been used as if it had received approval. Davidson himself noted privately that he still had qualms about supporting a Prayer Book that contained a cautious provision for Permanent Reservation.[55] He was nevertheless aware that any substantial concessions would alienate Anglo-Catholics, who had accepted the revised Book, and risk pulling apart the delicate coalition of support within the Church.

The decision by the House of Commons to reject the new Prayer Book was predictably followed by the appearance of numerous new pamphlets and a slew of letters to the press. Some echoed Edward Knox's vigorous claim that 'to accept the Deposited Book is to reinstate the Mass and the idolatrous worship of the consecrated elements'.[56] The League of Loyal Churchmen and Protestant Alliance rejoiced that 'the Archbishops and Bishops of the Church have now been arraigned before the House of Commons, the great Council of the Nation'.[57] Davidson himself received numerous petitions from groups like the Protestant Truth Society opposing the submission of a new version of the revised Book to the Church Assembly and Parliament. He was also sent many letters demanding, by contrast, that the Bishops should act firmly 'to vindicate and secure the Church's authority, in spiritual things at all cost'.[58] Davidson loathed the public furore on 'matters so sacred'. A few weeks before the new Prayer Book was reintroduced to the Church Assembly, with minor changes, he fretted about such subjects 'being bandied about by Parliamentarians and Church Associationists' of 'the very rough and secular type'.[59]

Davidson tried to ease the tensions by a round of quiet personal diplomacy. In the middle of January, he noted that he hoped to meet Joynson-Hicks and Inskip – who had led opposition to the new Prayer Book in the

House of Commons – 'to find out from them what it is they would really like to happen'.[60] A few days later he met Inskip, who was 'helpful' but loathe to give any definite commitments, a position echoed by 'Jix' several weeks later, after the Church Assembly had decided to endorse the new Prayer Book with a few minor changes.[61] Davidson's notes show that his greatest concern was that intransigence within Parliament might lead Anglo-Catholics to leave the Church of England as the Methodists had in the eighteenth century. There is little doubt that Davidson himself would have been inclined to make more concessions to Parliamentary opinion, particularly on Reservation, but Lang in particular warned against such an approach, believing that it would undermine the spiritual independence of the Church of England.

Davidson's concern about the crisis led him to write a short book, *The Prayer Book. Our Hope and Meaning*, which sought to calm the febrile situation by arguing that much of the controversy was misguided. The tone was deliberately informal, almost 'chatty', as the Archbishop set down the reasons why a new Prayer Book was needed. He carefully laid out his own position, noting that he understood both the emotions of those who wanted the Church of England to be untainted by 'medieval superstition', as well as others who wanted to keep sight of what was 'wholesome and helpful' in the Medieval Church. He acknowledged concerns about Reservation, whilst arguing it was necessary to respond to 'the growing desire for the very frequent reception of Holy Communion as contrasted with what was customary fifty years ago'.[62] He also defended the Bishops against the charge that they were determined to change the character of the Church of England. Davidson's words were clear, balanced, and written in a way designed to be accessible to a wide audience. They had little impact. On June 13 1928, the House of Commons again rejected the new Prayer Book, this time by an even greater majority than before. Davidson was present at the debate (which he believed was of a 'higher' tone than previously). The Archbishop was convinced that the 'No Popery' cry continued to resound in England, noting that whilst it was not altogether fair, he shared 'the indignation against the priests [. . .] who have no sense of England's traditional Protestantism'. He concluded rather mournfully, 'I do not think I have ever known in public life a situation which was so perplexing – every pathway in every direction seems to lead into a morass'.[63]

The rejection of the revised Prayer Book for a second time reinvigorated the sense of crisis. The Bishops issued a statement arguing that the Church should

> in the last resort [. . .] retain its inalienable right, in loyalty to our Lord and Saviour Jesus Christ, to formulate the Faith in Him and to arrange the expression of that Holy Faith in its forms of worship.[64]

Davidson received numerous letters, including one from Henson, arguing that spiritual independence was ultimately of greater importance than Establishment.[65] Temple believed that Davidson was trying to manage the crisis by ignoring the important points of 'principle' at stake – although unlike Henson he continued to believe in the merits of Establishment.[66] Davidson himself tellingly wrote that the House of Commons has 'departed, lamentably as it seems to me, from the reasonable spirit in which alone the balanced relationship of the Church and State in England can be satisfactorily and harmoniously carried out'.[67] He went on to complain that Parliament had wilfully 'traversed the declared desire of the Church's official and representative bodies'. Davidson nevertheless still warned against calls for drastic action, telling one correspondent that 'we shall I hope find quieter air soon',[68] though in the event the announcement of his resignation just a few weeks later meant that he was able to remove himself from the fray.

Davidson's failure to secure Parliamentary approval for the new Prayer Book inevitably cast a shadow over his final months at Canterbury. He had for 25 years dedicated much of his energy to holding together the fissiparous strands in the Church of England. To get the new Prayer Book approved by the Church Assembly with large majorities, in the summer of 1927, was a moment of triumph for him: a victory for compromise between those who held seemingly irreconcilable positions on questions of doctrine. What Davidson could not do, though, was translate the language of toleration into a political vernacular that would allow it to escape the charge that the Church of England was abandoning its historical character. The Archbishop may have underestimated the 'No Popery' instincts that erupted in the House of Commons at the end of 1927. He certainly underestimated the extent to which MPs would assert their right to legislate on spiritual matters.

Davidson was torn in deciding whether such an action represented a breach of the principle of Establishment. He was ready to admit that MPs had the right to make such a decision, but he also believed it was contrary to the subtle codes and understandings that had for centuries guided Church-State relations. The principle of Establishment was for Davidson part of the unwritten rules that formed the core of the British Constitution. The Archbishop believed that the Church of England had the right to exert its influence on social and political questions, but no right to insist that Parliament follow its lead. He was equally convinced that Parliament had a right to exercise control over certain aspects of the Church's corporate life, but no right to determine questions of doctrine. The House of Commons' rejection of the revised Prayer Book showed that such unwritten rules only had authority as long as they were acknowledged by those to whom they supposedly applied.

Notes

1. A.J.P. Taylor, *English History, 1914–1945* (Oxford: Clarendon Press, 1965), p. 259.
2. John Maiden, *National Religion and the Prayer Book Controversy, 1927–1928* (Woodbridge: Boydell and Brewer, 2009), p. 14 ff.
3. For a masterly account that acknowledges these ambiguities when trying to make sense of the development of Christianity in the Britain Isles, see Robbins, *England, Ireland, Scotland, Wales, passim*.
4. On the whole question of the 'decline' of the Church of England after 1918, see Brown, *Religion and Society in Twentieth-Century* Britain, p. 116 ff; Green, Passing of Protestant

England; S.J.D. Green, *Religion in the Age of Decline: Organisation and Experience in Industrial Yorkshire, 1870–1920* (Cambridge: Cambridge University Press, 1996).

5 For an argument along these lines, see Hugh Mcleod, 'Protestantism and British National Identity', in P. Van der Veer and H. Lehman (eds), *Nation and Religion: Perspectives on Europe and Asia* (Princeton, NJ: Princeton University Press, 1999), pp. 44–70 (esp. pp 51–3).
6 For an insightful discussion of the changing role of Establishment, and the changing boundaries of the State, see S.J.D. Green, 'Survival and Autonomy: On the Strange Fortunes and Peculiar Legacy of Ecclesiastical Establishment in the Modern British State, c 1920 to the Present Day', in S.J.D. Green and R.C. Whiting (eds), *The Boundaries of the State in Modern Britain* (Cambridge: Cambridge University Press, 1996), pp. 299–326.
7 For the role of Life and Liberty in fostering demands for the Enabling Bill, see Thompson, *Bureaucracy and Church Reform* 156 ff.
8 Bell, *Davidson*, Vol. 2, p. 966.
9 See, for example, *Times*, 27 November 1918, 5 December 1918; *Yorkshire Post and Leeds Intelligencer*, 30 November 1918.
10 *Report of Proceedings of the Representative Church Council*, Afternoon session of 25 February 1919.
11 D.P. 13. fos. 386–91, Davidson Memorandum, 2 March 1919 (quotation fo. 386).
12 *Times*, 31 March 1919 (Letter by Henson).
13 *Times*, 19 April 1919 (Letter by Temple).
14 *Times*, 9 June 1919 (Letter by Guttery).
15 Prestige, *Gore*, p. 423.
16 *Times*, 29 March 1919.
17 For the correspondence, see *Times*, 29 March 1919.
18 D.P. 13, fos. 392–5, Davidson Memorandum, 23 March 1919 (quotation fo. 392).
19 *Chronicle of Convocation: Convocation of Canterbury (Upper House)*, 6 May 1919.
20 *Parliamentary Debates (Lords)*, 3 June 1919, col. 980.
21 The following account draws heavily on David M. Thompson, 'The Politics of the Enabling Act', in Derek Baker (ed), *Studies in Church History* (Oxford: Basil Blackwell, 1975), pp. 383–92.
22 Knox, *Reminiscences of an Octogenarian*, p. 318.
23 D.P. 284, fos. 167–71, Davidson to Bishop of Oxford, September 1921.
24 *The Modern Churchman*, 9, 5–6 (1921).
25 See, for example, *Times*, 15 August 1921; 25 August 1921; 27 August 1921.
26 *Chronicle of Convocation: Convocation of Canterbury (Upper House)*, 15 February 1922
27 Prestige, *Gore*, p. 455.
28 Bell, *Davidson*, Vol. 2, p. 1,140.
29 *Chronicle of Convocation: Convocation of Canterbury (Upper House)*, 2 May 1922.
30 D.P. 284, fos. 190–91, Bishop of Oxford to Davidson, 8 December 1921.
31 For a useful edition of the Report, see G.W.H. Lampe (ed), *Doctrine in the Church of England: The 1938 Report* (London: SPCK, 1982).
32 Henson, *Retrospect*, Vol. 2, p. 151.
33 See, for example, the letters by Edward Knox (former Bishop of Manchester), 20 April 1923; Michael Furse (Bishop of St Albans), 24 April 1924. See, too, *The Times* editorial, 20 April 1920.
34 D.P. 15, fos. 99–111, Davidson Memorandum, 18 July 1926 (quotations fos. 99, 101, 102). For a somewhat bleaker memory of the discussions by the Archbishop of York, see Lockhart, *Lang*, p. 301.
35 D.P. 15, fos. 27–63, Davidson Memorandum, January 1926 (quotation fos. 58–9).
36 *Chronicle of Convocation: Convocation of Canterbury (Joint Sitting of Convocations of Canterbury and York)*, 7 February 1927.

37 *Chronicle of Convocation: Convocation of Canterbury (Joint Sitting of Convocations of Canterbury and York)*, 29 March 1927.
38 For the debates in the Church Assembly, including Davidson's speech, see *Church Assembly Reports of Proceedings*, 6–7 July 1927, pp. 96–196.
39 *Times*, 31 October 1926 (Letter by Davidson).
40 *Times*, 24 June 1927 (Letter by Knox). Knox, *Reminiscences*, pp. 306–7.
41 *Times,* 5 July 1927 (Letter by Joynson-Hicks).
42 *Times*, 26 March 1927 (Letter by H. Maurice Relton).
43 D.P. 454, fo. 47, W. Dudley Dixon to Davidson, 7 November 1927.
44 D.P. 454, fos. 114–15, Letter from Chairman of Northern Council of the Committee for the Maintenance of Truth and Faith to Davidson 29 November 1927.
45 For a positive review of Davidson's role at the Assembly, see Lockhart, *Lang*, p. 302.
46 Davidson Papers, 453 ff. 39–40, undated letter by Davidson to the Bishops.
47 For a different view, see Henson, *Retrospect*, Vol. 2, p. 163.
48 D.P. 16, fos. 52–103, Davidson Memorandum, 15 January 1928 (quotation fo. 56). For the speech, see *Parliamentary Debates (Lords)*, cols. 771–93.
49 Henson, *Retrospect*, Vol. 2, p. 164.
50 D.P. 454, fo. 152, Stamfordham to Davidson, 15 December 1927.
51 D.P. 454, fo. 164, Buchan to Davidson, 16 December 1927.
52 D.P. 16, fos. 52–103, Davidson Memorandum, 15 January 1928 (quotations fos. 61–2, 64–5). For Lang's broadly similar view of the debate, see Lockhart, *Lang*, p. 305.
53 Lambeth Palace, BM 8, fos. 174–75 (Meeting of Bishops, 19 December 1927).
54 *Times*, 19 December 1927. For the full text of the Statement see Documents Section 4.
55 For evidence that Davidson did push for more revisions in the wake of the first rejection of the Prayer Book by Parliament, see Iremonger, *Temple*, p. 353.
56 Rt Rev E.A. Knox, *Will the Deposited Book Restore Order in the Church: Some Startling Facts* (London: Church Book Room, 1928), p. 3.
57 D.P. 455, fo. 12.
58 D.P. 455, fo. 117, 'Anglo-Catholics and the Prayer Book'.
59 D.P. 16, fos. 52–103, Davidson Memorandum, 15 January 1928 (quotation fo. 81).
60 D.P. 16, fos. 52–103, Davidson Memorandum, 15 January 1928 (quotation fo. 89).
61 D.P. 16, fos. 104–7, Interview with Inskip, 18 January 1928; interview with Joynson-Hicks, 19 February 1928.
62 Randall Davidson, *The Prayer Book: Our Hope and Meaning* (London: Hodder and Soughton, 1928), ps. 21, 29. For a longer excerpt, see Documents Section 1.
63 D.P. 16, fos. 108–26, Davidson Memorandum, 17 June 1918 (quotations fos. 111, 114, 115).
64 *Times*, 3 July 1928.
65 D.P. 456, fos. 12–13, Henson to Davidson, 18 June 1928. See, too, Henson, *Retrospect*, Vol. 2, pp. 196–200; Chadwick, *Henson*, pp. 204–5.
66 Iremonger, *Temple*, pp. 355–59.
67 Bell, *Davidson*, Vol. 2, p. 1,353.
68 D.P. 456, fo. 88, Davidson to Talbot, 22 June 1928.

Assessment

Randall Davidson dismissed any suggestion that he resigned as Archbishop in response to the second rejection of the new Prayer Book, but there is little doubt that the controversies of the previous few months had taken their toll. His departure was greeted by, in George Bell's words, 'a quite extraordinary outburst of gratitude and affection on all sides'.[1] More than £17,000 was raised in a subscription that allowed Davidson and his wife to buy a house in Chelsea. In November 1928, he was given a peerage, allowing him to continue as a member of the House of Lords. The former Archbishop nevertheless found it 'intensely difficult' to adjust to his new life. The house in Cheyne Walk seemed small after Lambeth Palace, and his days were empty without the 'stimulus' of the 'daily round of work'.[2]

His retirement did not last long. By the early spring of 1930, Davidson's health was fading, and after a lengthy period in bed, he died on 25 May, and was buried four days later at Canterbury.[3] Bell alludes in his biography to an incident that took place just a few days before the former Archbishop's death. Davidson in one of his moments of lucidity pronounced from his sickbed the 'Blessing of God the Father, God the Son and God the Holy Ghost [be] upon you all'. His wife Edith asked if the blessing included her sister, Lucy Tait, to which her husband firmly responded 'Of course it was *all*'. Lucy Tait was for many years a difficult sister and sister-in-law. She had also been in a relationship with the widow of Archbishop Benson. Whether Davidson was referring to Lucy's irascible behaviour or her unorthodox relationship is unclear. But the story, told to Bell by someone who overheard the words from a neighbouring room, suggests that the former Archbishop was as generous spirited on his death-bed as he had been in life. Lucy Tait had lived with her sister and brother-in-law for long periods of time at Lambeth Palace. They also met regularly after she set up home in Sussex. It was perhaps a sign that Davidson's natural tolerance extended far beyond questions of doctrinal latitudinarianism. It also provides an insight into the gentleness of character which allowed the Archbishop to prove so effective over many years at preventing disagreements with those around him from descending into personal animosity.

The public reaction to the announcement of Davidson's death was unequivocal in its respect and affection. Cosmo Lang praised the Archbishop's 'singular fairness of mind'. Dean Inge described Davidson as 'a great ecclesiastical statesman'. *The Times* said that his death would leave 'a blank in national life', and went on to praise him for defending 'liberty of thought' throughout his archiepiscopate.[4] Political leaders in the House of Lords recalled the Archbishop's 'wise and far-seeing spirit of conciliation' along with his 'moderating influence'.[5] All these tributes focused primarily on Davidson's character and outlook. The same was true of the numerous testimonials sent to George Bell when he began the research for his biography a few months later. Edith Davidson was anxious that Bell should bring out her late husband's 'unselfconsciousness'. His secretary thought that Bell should emphasise Davidson's 'simplicity'. Other correspondents praised the former Archbishop for combining a 'great sense of the dignity and position of the Archbishop of Canterbury' with an informality that allowed him to mix with people from many backgrounds.[6] One of the few who took a more cautious line was the former Bishop of Manchester Edmund Knox who, whilst praising Davidson for his skill in dealing with people, noted that he had never understood the Archbishop's 'Churchmanship'. He added somewhat cuttingly that Davidson had always been 'led by circumstances' rather than 'far-reaching designs'. Knox told Bell that critics of the new Prayer Book had doubted whether Davidson was ready to enforce ecclesiastical discipline, and feared that he would allow Anglo-Catholic clergy to persist in practices that were not clearly authorised by the new Book.[7]

George Bell acknowledged in his discussion of the Prayer Book crisis that Davidson underestimated 'the keen passions on either side'. He also criticised the Archbishop for not making more effort to ensure that questions relating to 'the revision of Church services' were treated as a separate matter from 'the enforcement of ecclesiastical discipline'.[8] This was one of the few times that Bell criticised Davidson in his biography, and whereas there is a good deal of truth in his claim that the Archbishop underestimated 'the deep Protestantism of the English people', it is not clear what other path Davidson could have followed. Even with the benefit of hindsight, it is difficult to see how the debacle could have been avoided. The Bishops knew that discipline could only be restored if the Prayer Book was amended in ways that made it more acceptable to the large number of Anglo-Catholic clergy – but such changes were bound to be opposed by Anglicans who were suspicious of anything that threatened the reformed character of the Church of England. Davidson as ever sought to pursue a course that would accommodate different traditions and opinions. The fact that the new Prayer Book was approved overwhelmingly by the Church Assembly, which contained lay and clerical members from different wings of the Church, suggests that a measure of agreement *was* possible amongst those who were close enough to the situation to understand the need for compromise. But once the issue moved into the marketplace of press and Parliament, such subtleties were quickly lost, and positions were drawn which allowed little room for agreement. Davidson's attempts to build compromise within the National Church produced an outcome that was rejected by the appointed and self-appointed representatives of the nation.

There is a sense in which Davidson faced the perennial problem encountered by most Archbishops of Canterbury since the Reformation – and certainly since the rise of the Oxford Movement in the first part of the nineteenth century. The very idea of a comprehensive Church, tolerant of a range of beliefs and practices, inevitably raises the question of how to manage differences that threaten to create divisions in which (to quote Yeats) 'the centre cannot hold'. Davidson understood that any attempt to define too rigidly the boundaries of permitted belief and practice could make tensions worse and even threaten schism. And yet he knew, as well, that allowing too much elasticity might drain Anglicanism of any identity, and leave the Church of England as little more than a shell containing men and women of vastly different beliefs and values. The fact that the Church of England was an Established Church – its history bound up closely with conceptions of national character – also meant that differences over doctrine and ceremony were bound to resonate far beyond the Church itself. Davidson's cast of mind, as he freely admitted, was to focus on the concrete rather than the abstract. This helped to make him an effective administrator, but it sometimes left him adrift when dealing with complex questions that could not be disaggregated into purely 'technical' issues.

All this perhaps raises the question of what an Archbishop of Canterbury is 'for'. What skills do they need to carry out their work? And what personal attributes are essential if they are to be successful? Archbishop Davidson was certainly not a first-rate theologian like Michael Ramsey. Nor was he a creative thinker about the relationship between Christianity and society like William Temple. He was neither a charismatic preacher nor a prophetic figure pointing to the meaning of the Christian gospel *sub specie aeternitatis*. And nor would he have claimed to be any of these things. Davidson's modesty was deep-seated and genuine. But so, too, was his sense that his long career had given him greater knowledge of the temper and workings of the Church of England than any of his contemporaries. It is perhaps helpful to think of Davidson as a Realist – in two meanings of that elusive and over-used word. He was a Realist in the sense that he understood the complex pressures shaping and confining almost all aspects of the Church's work. Whenever he attempted to rein in enthusiasts – in areas ranging from the development of the ecumenical movement through to the promotion of social reform – he was typically motivated both by his innate caution and a sense that positive change was best-achieved through careful and patient work. His caution was temperamental, but it clothed itself in a half-articulated *credo* characterised by a quizzical scepticism about the hopes of those who (to use a nineteenth-century language) wanted to leap from the realm of necessity into the realm of freedom.

There was, too, a second sense in which Davidson can be thought of as a Realist. Davidson was instinctively doubtful about the possibility of the Church possessing a clear and unambiguous sense of the will of God. This is not to say that he was in some intellectual sense a proponent of what a later generation would come to call Neo-Orthodoxy. His outlook was rooted in a far more prosaic sense that ordinary Christians were duty-bound to think hard about how their faith should shape their everyday lives, whilst acknowledging that their own sense of what was right or wrong, in both the ecclesiastical and secular spheres, ought to be considered both tentative and fallible. It was this instinct that made it hard for Davidson to understand the passions and certainties which characterised many of those he had to work with. Yet it also provided a positive foundation for his commitment to maintaining the comprehensive character of the Church of England. Davidson's open-mindedness was founded on an acknowledgement that his own beliefs were not necessarily a correct expression of a single and authoritative understanding of Anglicanism. He recognised that a policy of tolerance represented the best way of avoiding division – but his commitment to tolerance was also informed by his instinctive view that definite claims on matters of belief could all too often represent little more than a hubristic certainty about things that were necessarily uncertain. It is this that makes an understanding of Davidson's character so important when trying to understand his time at Canterbury. His reluctance to set down clear boundaries on matters ranging from Reservation to creedal orthodoxy echoed his conviction that intelligent and well-informed men and women could have different views on such issues.

Whilst Davidson was at heart a Victorian, he understood that the Church of England had to respond to the major changes taking place in the first quarter of the twentieth century. He was throughout his archiepiscopate determined to maintain the Church of England's status as a National Church, but his commitment to working with the Nonconformist churches, particularly after 1918, was fostered by his recognition that they too represented an important voice in the religious life of the nation. Davidson was also quick to recognise that the Church of England could not ignore how such developments as the birth of an embryonic welfare state and the extension of the franchise were reshaping the character of British society. The Archbishop was most at home in a traditional world of 'Whigs' and 'Tories', where Government ministers made decisions untrammelled by the sentiments of the *demos*, and the rights of property were unquestioned by those in positions of power. He looked with scepticism on calls for radical social and economic reform whether they came from within or beyond the Church. Davidson nevertheless grasped that the tide of change could not be turned back either in politics or religion. He often noted that 'old men' should not try to obstruct developments that were deep-rooted and popular. It was for this reason that he was sharply critical of the activities of the 'diehards' during the Constitutional Crisis of 1909–11, condemning their reluctance to consider any reforms that might threaten established patterns of privilege. His intervention in the General Strike of 1926 was similarly designed to promote a settlement that would calm the eruption of a more brutal class politics. The Archbishop's approach to such questions was invariably informed by his conviction that sensible people should be able to agree as long as they put aside their narrow self-interest and committed themselves to the virtues of compromise. It was a thoroughly reasonable position – but one that failed to grasp how for many the passions of both secular and religious life were not susceptible to the mandate of reason.

All this perhaps sounds rather negative. But that is perhaps to fall into the trap of a heroic conception of history that privileges the dramatic and the transformative over the virtues of order and calm. Davidson's personality – his steadiness and his ability to maintain good relations even with those who disagreed with him – itself forms an important part of the narrative of his archiepiscopate and the history of the Church of England more broadly. For all the divisions revealed by the rejection of the new Prayer Book, the Church was able to weather the storm, and maintain in the years that followed the comprehensive character which Davidson had so valued. Even the briefest list of the turbulent priests and laymen with whom the Archbishop had to deal whilst at Canterbury – Gore, Halifax, Henson, Joynson-Hicks, Barnes, and so on – puts into perspective Davidson's achievement in maintaining as much harmony or at least grudging consensus as he did. There was real wisdom in his view that the flux of time could not be stopped, and that the Church of England had to be careful to avoid being left high and dry. And, in a similar vein, his warnings about the dangers of moving too quickly in areas ranging from relations with other churches through to social reform were grounded in a sober view of the constraints of history and politics. Davidson's sense of balance and proportion – dullness when viewed from another perspective – was an important factor both in maintaining unity within the Church of England and preserving its place in national life.

None of this is to suggest that Davidson did not himself have real 'enthusiasms'. He was deeply committed to building a greater sense of identity within the Anglican Communion. He believed that the Church of England had a duty to criticise some aspects of a British Empire even though the Empire itself fostered the growth of Christian mission. His commitment to building closer relations between the churches at home and abroad was deep-seated, and played a significant part in fostering the ecumenical renaissance of the inter-war years. Davidson was also passionately committed to an Anglican tradition which he valued in part precisely *because* it could not be reduced to a series of *dicta* on questions of doctrine and liturgy. There are indeed times when Davidson's writings and actions took on the colour of a species of 'Conservatism' which values history and practice more than reason and ideas. This is not to suggest that the shadows of Edmund Burke lurked in the recesses of his mind. The Archbishop's busy life and lack of real intellectual curiosity meant that he never tried to set his religious views – let alone his broader vision of life – in any philosophical setting. It would indeed be absurd to ascribe patterns and principles to Davidson's words and actions that he himself would not have recognised. And yet it is still possible to ascribe value to a wisdom that was rooted in a generosity of spirit and a shrewd, if at times bemused, acknowledgement of the frailties and passions of human beings.

The familiar jibe that Davidson was a 'courtier-priest', a product of archiepiscopal and royal patronage, was unfair (or at least incomplete). So too is the view that he was an ecclesiastical 'statesman' or – less positively – an ecclesiastical administrator. It is true that he was, at times, all these things. But he was also an effective diocesan Bishop, a regular and well-regarded preacher, and a tireless correspondent. Nor did Davidson's belief in consensus mean that he would not risk controversy and conflict, whether in publicly condemning the activities of the Black and Tans in Ireland, or privately taking Edward VII to task for his behaviour. Bishop Knox noted that one of Davidson's greatest gifts was his ability to disagree without allowing disagreement to degenerate into rancour and bitterness. But still more important, perhaps, was the Archbishop's prodigious appetite for work. When Davidson was still Bishop of Rochester, he drily told Archbishop Benson that the public thought the main duty of the Archbishop of Canterbury was to draw his salary. He may have feared that the same was true when he himself went to Canterbury, given that so much of his work took place behind the scenes, but few who knew Davidson's workload could ever have accused him of neglecting his duties. His dedication was instrumental in allowing him to keep abreast of developments both within and beyond the Church of England.

It was noted at the start of this book that biographies by their very nature tend to ascribe a significance and agency to their subject which is not always merited. Certainly, the history of the Church of England in the years between 1903 and 1928 is not the same as the history of Davidson's time as Archbishop of Canterbury. But even the most cursory excursion into the world of counter-factual history suggests that Davidson was an important figure, whether in helping to manage divisions within the Church, or in nudging it to adapt to a changing world whilst keeping intact a sense of its own place in history. It is hard to imagine that anyone else could have been as effective. The challenges Davidson faced during his time at Canterbury were immense. He 'solved' very few of them. But he did possess the character and attributes to guide his Church through some of the most turbulent times in its history. Davidson has largely slipped from public memory and, perhaps, even from the memory of the Church. His reputation has been eclipsed by other figures who seem to have left a more definite ecclesiastical footprint. Yet he was much more than a well-connected ecclesiastical administrator. Randall Davidson played an important role in the history of the Church of England, skilfully contributing to its development, and providing its members with a leadership characterised by the values of tolerance and service.

George Bell's biography of Davidson is not without its flaws, but its author knew the Archbishop well, and it is worth giving him the last word. Bell noted that there were two sorts of leader. The first aimed to 'drive forward as fast as they can, and will cry aloud to their followers to make haste after them'. The second kind of leader was one who, like Davidson, sought

> to discover the *communis sensus* of the society, and to use all the means in his power to give it the opportunity of expression. Such a leader will guide and will show the way, and he will teach and suggest, but he will not be likely to lift his voice from the housetops and to cry aloud to the laggards to come at full speed. He will realize the diversity of human nature, of the

material with which he has to deal, and will give it, or lead it to, the best and highest unity of which he believes it to be capable under the given conditions. His is the leadership of the Chairman or the Moderator. He will wish to keep the boat even, without endangering the passengers. He prefers peace and agreement before violence and confusion. He runs the risk of misrepresentation, and is unlikely to win great popular applause. But he is not on that account to be dismissed as an unsuitable kind of leader in dangerous and unsettled times.[9]

Notes

1 Bell, *Davidson*, Vol. 2, p. 1,364.
2 D.P. 16, fos. 226–38, Untitled Davidson Note, 5 January 1930 (quotations fos. 232, 233).
3 For a detailed description of Davidson's death, see Bell Papers 222, fos. 90–130 (notes compiled by Mary Mills).
4 *Times*, 26 May 1930.
5 *Parliamentary Debates (Lords)*, 27 May 1930, cols. 1066, 1068.
6 Bell Papers 226, fos. 271–75, Lavinia Talbot, 'Archbishop Davidson'.
7 Bell Papers 225, fos. 156–62, Knox, 'An Appreciation of Archbishop Davidson'.
8 Bell, *Davidson*, Vol. 2, p. 1,356.
9 Bell, *Davidson*, Vol. 2, p. 1,161.

Documents

The following documents and commentaries are divided into six sections, each designed to allow the reader to hear Archbishop's Davidson's voice for themselves, or in a few cases the voices of those with particular insights into his life and career. The intention is not to provide detailed critical commentaries, but rather to offer an insight into the range of Davidson's activities, along with his views on a host of ecclesiastical and secular questions. A few obvious misspellings and errors that appear in the original documents have been removed.

Some of the documents record the Archbishop's public statements (whether expressed verbally or in writing). Others are taken from his private correspondence. A significant number have been selected from the private memoranda Davidson wrote for his own use, and perhaps for posterity, which provide a vivid insight into his understanding of events and his own part in them. The Archbishop was not the most riveting of speakers. Nor was he the most succinct of authors. The documents nevertheless give a sense of Davidson's approach both to his archiepiscopal duties and his role as the most prominent figure in the worldwide Anglican Communion.

1 Archbishop Davidson's Anglicanism

Randall Davidson's Anglicanism was not based on an elaborate theological foundation, although he was deeply committed to the principle that intellectual inquiry could help to illuminate its character. The following documents show how Davidson's Anglicanism was distinguished by a fluid amalgam of historical understanding and scriptural reading, leavened with a practical wisdom that recognised how attempts to set down overly rigid doctrinal and liturgical boundaries could lead to division and potential schism. The Archbishop's reluctance to be prescriptive was prompted both by a shrewd desire to maintain the Church of England intact, as well as a genuine conviction that the Anglican inheritance was shaped by a constant but potentially fruitful tension over the permitted boundaries of a 'broad Church'.

> We lay emphasis upon the historic continuity of the Church's corporate and organic life. We stand accordingly for a sacramental, governmental,

ministerial and even ritual system which, with adaptation to local requirements, has come down to us from Apostolic days. We stand for the unfettered study of Holy Scripture and for its circulation in the vernacular tongue whatever it be. We stand for the liberty of private judgement in the interpretation of Holy Scripture and in matters of faith, combined, as regards our own members, with the definiteness of such actual *credenda* as are set forth in our Formularies. We stand for the right of the National Churches to a wide elasticity and variety in system, in ritual and in worship, combined with a general loyalty to the principles and usages which have come down to us from the past, and especially from the first six centuries. And lastly we stand for the principle of plainness, openness and simplicity in all formularies, usages, and services, so that every word may, so far as possible, be understood and followed by even the unlearned among our people.

Randall Thomas Davidson, *The Character and Call of the Church of England* (London, 1912), p. 46

Although Davidson had little sympathy for 'Ritualism', he was shrewd enough to recognise the dynamism of the Anglo-Catholic wing of the Church, and was determined to pursue a tolerant policy that acknowledged the energy and the convictions of its proponents. The Archbishop was anxious that the older generation of clergy should be careful not to oppose changes simply because they were uncomfortable with them. In a memorandum written in 1913, he noted,

No man with his eyes open can have any doubt that English religion finds natural expression nowadays in a more dramatic, aesthetic, symbolic form than was habitual a generation ago. It is not true to say that this is the outcome of the Oxford Movement. Scotch Presbyterians, or English Baptists, are quite as Protestant as they used to be, but their chapels, their windows, their anthems, their round collars and so on, betoken something which was certainly not drawn from Dr Pusey, but belongs to the general aestheticism of the time. As regards the Church of England this falls in with doctrinal changes, [such] as the emphasis on sacramental teaching, and the two combine to make ritual more popular, because it happens that the aesthetic tendency which is "in the air" harmonises with mediaevalism in doctrine, and the mediaevalists flatter themselves that reverent services, beautiful churches, fine music, and the rest, are due to the Oxford Movement, whereas they are much more due, as Newman and Pusey used to admit [. . .] to Sir Walter Scott. For old-fashioned Bishops and Deans to decry or gird against the love of ornate services is, in my view, both stupid and mischievous. I do think that the older men among us, of whom I am coming to be one, are right to speak pretty strongly against the incoming streams of false doctrine, because I do not feel by any means sure that that doctrine does correspond with the inevitable spirit of the time in matters religious. On the contrary there seem to me a good many evidences that thoughtful people are revolting against eg the mechanical theory of apostolic succession, or the denial of sacramental validity in Nonconformist Communions, or a crude Mariolatry, and so on. If this be so, the younger high churchmen, who are rightly protesting against those errors, have a right to the definite support of us older people. And we must take care not to weaken the old man's protest against doctrinal errors, which have grown since his early days, by mixing them up with changes partly aesthetic and partly in a larger sense doctrinal which are establishing their position indisputably as part of the new spirit of the Church in these latter days.

Thus the task belonging to old men in this twentieth century is one which needs a good deal of care for its due discharge [. . .] the rapidity of change during the last half-century has been far greater than in any half-century which preceded it. Thus there are more men of say 65 or 70 years old to-day than there used to be who find themselves quite out of touch with the opinions and ways of younger people, both in political and religious matters. We have got to try and counteract our consequent drawback by getting as far as possible an appreciative knowledge of, and sympathy with, the opinions which have a firm grip on the popular mind, so that any restraining influence or corrective force which we may exercise shall be used wisely, and not with a mere obstinate or stupid opposition, which by its very narrowness and unaccommodation may defeat its own end and render imperative what might otherwise be really useful power of bringing the weight of life's experiences, and the sobriety which comes with age to bear wholesomely upon the enthusiasm of younger men, regulating and guiding, but not thwarting them.

D.P. 12, fos. 320–24, Extracts from Archbishop Davidson Memorandum, 28 September 1913

In 1917, Davidson reflected in a private memorandum on his approach to ecclesiastical administration, seeking to articulate the principles and values which had guided him from the time he arrived at Canterbury.

Suppose someone were to ask me what, if expressed in a summary way, had, while Archbishop, been my aim as regards Church administration, I should find it a little difficult to answer categorically. I do not think that either at the start, or since, I have had before me a clearly defined purpose intended to be pursued *coute-que-coute* in face of opposition. On the other hand, I have had an under-lying and I think continuous policy, the outcome partly of my general way of looking at things, partly perhaps of my upbringing, and partly of my sense of what is needed in the Church of England to-day and of the opposite things which offend my sense of what is the will of God for us and for our Church.

If I were forced to put it in a single phrase, I suppose it might be described as a desire to assert in practice the thoughtful and deliberate comprehensiveness of the Church of England as contrasted with the clear-cut lines and fences of demarcation which mark the rulings of the Church of Rome, and the corresponding, though quite different, rulings of protesting sects in England, Scotland, America, and presumably Germany in the seventeenth century and since.

This comprehensiveness, as I understand and value it, is assertible in three directions, affecting severally our boundaries of legitimate doctrinal belief, our boundaries of would be denominational differences, our boundaries of legitimate ritual and devotional variety – this last including what become very nearly credal differences.

In all these fields it has, I think, been my earnest endeavour to cast the net wide and to be slow to draw its boundary line very rigidly. I venture to think that in the first two of these three my fourteen years of Archiepiscopate have been useful, and that I have personally contributed a good deal of the usefulness.

D.P. 12, fos. 327–28, Extracts from Archbishop Davidson Memorandum, January 1917

Davidson was for much of his time at Canterbury embroiled in conflicts over questions of doctrine. Some Bishops – most notably Charles Gore – believed that the Church of England should set down clear limits to the boundaries of permitted belief. Anglican Modernists like Hastings Rashdall and Hensley Henson by contrast questioned (or perhaps were seen to question) the historical truth of miracles and the bodily Resurrection of Christ. The decision by Lloyd George to recommend the appointment of Henson as Bishop of Hereford, in 1917, paved the way for sharp clashes amongst the clergy (and indeed beyond). Davidson worked hard to reconcile the two sides – a process he found both difficult and draining – but one he recognised as necessary to preserve the unity of the Church of England.

As soon as the newspapers announced as probable Henson's nomination, I received many communications, largely verbal. Hugh Cecil came to me in real alarm to say that the storm which would be created would be formidable, and he showed that he also thought that the storm would be right, although I could not ascertain that he had any first hand knowledge of Henson. Then Bishop Gore wrote one or two ominous letters, and finally sent me a copy of a letter he had circulated to all the Bishops of the Province, protesting against Henson's nomination, and definitely threatening to resign if the nomination was made. Then Winton [the Bishop of Winchester], on receiving this letter from Gore wrote a reply to me in which he challenged Gore's right thus to threaten resignation. He came the same day to see me, and wrote a long letter to Gore, declining to admit that Henson is in the proper sense a heretic, and speaking admirably as to the real position, namely that Henson is a voluble preacher, who speaks far over a wide field, and is apt to cross the circumference boundary, but that he has no intention of teaching heresy, and his false opinions are inferred from his silence rather than stated in his utterances. This letter Winton showed to me privately before sending it to Gore. Next day, Gore himself spent the evening and night at Lambeth, and talked things over fully. He felt, I think, that he had acted wrongly in the form of his circular letter to the Bishops, inasmuch as he had first stated his conclusion of resigning, and then wished for a conference with the Bishops [...] Gore admitted frankly that Henson is a firm believer in the Incarnation, but that Henson's belief in that great doctrine is accompanied by a disbelief in those miraculous events of the Human Ministry which Gore regards as essential to the Incarnation doctrine in its entirety. He was somewhat excited, though not to the degree I have often seen, but he passionately exclaimed – "It all turns, though you won't see it, on his disbelief in miracles as such. He believes our Lord had a human father, and that His Body rotted in the tomb. A man who believes that cannot, with my consent, be made a Bishop of the Province"...

On Wednesday, the 19th [December], Henson came to breakfast, and I had full talk with him. He was pleasant and friendly, but he disappointed me by his self-satisfaction, and his rather venomous denunciation of those who were opposing his appointment [...] He did not deny that he had long wished to be a Bishop, and I liked his frankness in that matter.

D.P. 13, fos. 228–30, Extracts from Archbishop Davidson Memorandum dictated at Lambeth Palace on Christmas Day 1917

During the 1920s, the dispute over the new Prayer Book became the focus for sharp disagreement on questions of doctrine and ritual, as well as triggering a crisis in relations between Church and State (see following section for documents). Following the decision by the House of Commons to reject the new Book, in December 1927, Davidson wrote a lengthy pamphlet arguing that the changes from the Book of Common Prayer were far less extensive than widely supposed. He also once again took the opportunity to emphasise that the Church of England had always included men and women of widely different beliefs.

I find no real difficulty myself in understanding the unqualified desire of my keenly Protestant brother to ensure that the Church of England shall be untainted with doctrines or usages which retain, as he thinks, some trace of what he describes as "the beggarly elements" of mediaeval superstition from which the Reformed Church of England shook herself free. Nor, on the other hand, do I fail to understand the contention of an equally devout brother who, as a convinced Anglo-Catholic, presses upon me the danger of forgetting how carefully the Church of England has abstained from severing herself from what was wholesome and helpful in the Church system of the Middle Ages. The Reformation, he says, freed us from Roman shackles and Roman abuses, but kept safe for us the best and soundest elements of the devotional life of pre-Reformation days. Each side is eloquent and earnest, but the gains and losses are depicted, on right and left, respectively, with a more lurid brush than I could use. There are, and always have been, widely different groups of thinkers within the Church, differing in thought, in devotion, and in usage.

I am a firm and convinced supporter of the deliberate comprehensiveness of the Church of England. For half a century, I have made it a subject of thought and prayer, and in these later years I have used opportunity of action. The more carefully that I read the history of the sixteenth and seventeenth centuries, along the hundred years during which the Reformation was in progress and the Church of England was taking its distinctive shape, the deeper has become my sympathy with the wisest of the reformers. They were bent on consolidating the central opinion of the Church of England, in freedom alike from Rome and from Geneva. But that was not all. To consolidate the central cohort was comparatively easy. But how were they to deal with those who stood on the margins? One set of men wanted to keep all the mediaevalism which could anyhow be made compatible with the loyalty to the reformed Church; the opposite set was eager to purge the Church wholly from all that could savour of mediaeval error. The problem for the reforming leaders was therefore how to retain as many on either wing as could, when their faith and principles were made clear, be rightly furnished with a standing-place within the Church of England. No one who has traced the course pursued by Cranmer and Hooker, and those who followed them, will doubt the wisdom and effectiveness of their endeavour.

The problem which those men had to grapple with is with us still. In providing a new Prayer Book we have perforce had to keep in our purview the vigorous Anglo-Catholic, the staunch Protestant, and the anxious inquirers whose liberalism is equally foreign to both these sections.

Randall Thomas Davidson, *The Prayer Book: Our Hope and Meaning* (1928), pp. 21–3

Davidson was, more than any previous Archbishop of Canterbury, committed to developing closer relations between the various provinces in the worldwide Anglican Communion. It is therefore not surprising that, in the year after he became Archbishop, Davidson accepted an invitation to visit North America. He arrived in Canada, where he gave numerous talks and sermons, before heading to the USA. Many of the talks Davidson gave in Canada reflected his belief that the destinies of the Anglican Communion and the British Empire were closely linked together. They also showed his confidence that Anglicanism could flourish even in settings where it was not the Established (or even numerically dominant) Church. Davidson took care to emphasise that he did not as Archbishop of Canterbury have any formal authority over the other provinces. He nevertheless believed that he was duty-bound to act as a 'pivot' connecting the worldwide Anglican Communion. He also believed that even the most far-flung provinces were inheritors of the distinct historic traditions of the Church of England. Davidson's views on the relationship between the Church of England and the other Anglican provinces is set down clearly in this address given in Montreal early in his visit to Canada.

> Brothers and friends, Most Reverend, Reverend, and Lay, I thank you from my heart for the addresses which have been read, addresses as remarkable for the quiet eloquence of their terms as for the earnestness and reality of their every thought. You have struck the very chord which was already vibrating in my heart to-day, the thankful recognition of the mutual relationship which, to the untold good of both, subsists between the Mother Church at home and her daughter in the great Dominion.
>
> May I very briefly and very simply give expression to two thoughts which I find astir in me to-night? The first is that the world, as the field of our Church's active life, is so much bigger than we used to think it of old. I can show you by a simple object-lesson what I mean. We have happily preserved in our archives at Lambeth not a few bundles, now collected into rather unwieldy scrap-books, containing what may almost be called accidental remnants or specimens of the correspondence, important or unimportant, conducted in some particular year by one or other of my Episcopal predecessors, say a hundred or two hundred or even three hundred years ago. The bundles are of a chance sort, obviously the accidental remains surviving from the letters of the time. But their accidental character has this value, that it enables you to have, as it were, a surprise peep into the sort of thing that was happening at Lambeth and the sort of things which were occupying attention there. Now dip into these bundles or scrap-books, say in the days of Moore and Manners-Sutton a hundred years ago, or in the days of Tillotson and Wake a hundred years before, or of Bancroft and Laud a hundred years before that, and you will find at all these epochs patent evidence of the same fact. The interest, the responsibilities, the "day's work" of the then Archbishop were almost wholly concerned with the Island of Great Britain [. . .] Now dip into the corresponding bundles of Lambeth correspondence at any time you like during the last twenty years, and you find the whole business, or rather the whole atmosphere, different – Canada, Australia, South Africa, India, in daily – literally daily – touch with Lambeth. And then, superadded to this, all the problems and ramifications of Missionary work far beyond the boundaries of even the Empire itself. One feels at once the necessity for something of the nature of a central pivot – a pivot which takes tangible shape as a man, an Archbishop, round whom the work may spin, and who, if he be nothing more, furnishes at the least (and this perforce) a point of common touch,

common information, common life. I am not speaking even indirectly of any question about jurisdiction, however shadowy. I am speaking about a pivot not a pope. But, truly, this at least is certain, that the world, as the common field of our Church's work, is far bigger than of old. That is one thought.

And another is this. How much smaller the world is than it used to be. Those very letter bundles to which I have alluded; how odd it reads to-day to find that every letter sent across the sea was sent in triplicate by such different ships as might be found, and if ever all three arrived it was a triumph worth recording. And then the time required and the practical uselessness and almost hopelessness of giving advice by letter when months must pass before the letter could arrive and twice the time perhaps before an answer could come to hand. Contrast that with to-day, say with my own presence here and yet my touch with facts at home, and you will realise how the thought presses on me to-night that the world is far smaller than my predecessors found it to be.

These thoughts would, I suppose, press in, whatever the distant part of the world might be. But here in Canada there is a thought, of course, which you give to us visitors which is peculiarly your own. It is the thought of the big beginnings in the midst of which we stand. We are so obviously in the centre of mighty foundation-works, and the buoyancy of hope almost dwarfs the wonder of the present vision. Big beginnings indeed they are, and beginnings which we may commit to God with a solemn thought of whereunto they will lead. Perhaps to me personally the wonder and the interest of great beginnings and of new foundings has a peculiar strength. It has been my lot during the last ten years to have successively, as the centre of my work, the two spots in England where our beginnings, the Church and the State, can be most marvellously studied. First at Winchester, with its memories of King Alfred, and of what he founded and planned in the very Wolvesey which still forms part of the Bishop's official heritage: Winchester, with its ancient County-Hall wherein the Parliaments of England were devised and sat: Winchester, with its memories of William of Wykeham and of what he did or rather founded for us all. And then, soaked in the memories or associations of those beginnings, I moved to Canterbury and find my home there. There where every stone seems voiceful. There, where Augustine thirteen hundred years ago was laying foundations strong, and wise, and deep: there, where Theodore fashioned our Church's system in so many ways; and Anselm and Stephen Langton and many more contributed each to some new start as the centuries rolled on. The thought – the recurrent thought – is overwhelming. How much turned, how much depended on those men in the making of England and of England's Church, and how mightily beginnings do matter for the world.

And just as on the puny rivulets of Stour or Itchen big beginnings found a place, so now on the great St Lawrence and on the flowing Ottawa we are allowed to watch, to share, to work for beginnings which are vaster far. Take Canada as one living whole, the illimitable West as well as the elder regions here in the East, and no portion I imagine of the round world can exceed, perhaps can match, its possibilities. The wisest prophets, the most far-seeing statesmen, bid us direct our eye hitherward. And for that – for that task, that hope, that accomplishment in the right way, you and we together are responsible [...] God bless and help you, friends and brothers, in so splendid an emprise.

> Randall Davidson, speech given in Montreal on
> 31 August 1904, in Randall Thomas Davidson,
> *The Christian Opportunity* (1904), pp. 43–50

2 The daily round: Archbishop Davidson at work

Davidson's belief that the Archbishop of Canterbury should be a 'pivot' for the Anglican Communion reflected his extensive experience of working at Lambeth Palace. Davidson was at the time of his appointment to Canterbury widely seen as an administrator rather than a theologian or scholar. Although the Archbishop made extensive use of his chaplains and secretarial staff, especially after 1918, he always attracted admiration for his hard work and attention to detail. The following account, published by a journalist who visited Lambeth Palace in 1908, gives some insight into Davidson's daily routine as well as the way he approached his duties as Archbishop.

> We all know [Archbishop Davidson's] round, cheerful, ruddy face, with the bright eyes and courteous smile, and the voice that has proved so formidable to the foes of the English Church during the past two years. He has been trained in the purple. Starting as chaplain to Archbishop Tait, marrying his early patron's daughter, a favourite spiritual counsellor of Queen Victoria, then Dean of Windsor, successively Bishop of Rochester and Winchester, he has mounted by easy and certain steps to the chair of St Augustine.
>
> This is his favourite home, and here in Lambeth Palace he lives for the greater part of the year, with few holidays. Since Archbishop Temple gave up Addington, the beloved home of Benson, the Primates of All England have had no country house. Dr Davidson has practically rebuilt the Archbishop's house at Canterbury – adding to that Mecca of Anglicanism a very beautiful dwelling-place – but he rarely resides there. Canterbury is too far from London to make a convenient national centre, and Archbishop Davidson takes his national duties very seriously. He is not content to be the Diocesan of Canterbury. He is above all things head of the Established Church – and therefore a statesman as well as an ecclesiastic – responsible for the government of England as well as the doctrines of the English Church. Living at Lambeth, he is in the heart of poor London, and he can keep his ears open to the cry for social reform – first heard in his old Rochester days. He has, indeed, grown to love South London, both as Bishop and Archbishop, and perhaps he has learnt the great lesson that the strongest man nowadays is the man who stays in one place. Perhaps all the more because they have no family, Dr and Mrs Davidson are great entertainers. Entertaining, in fact, is

part of the business of the Primate of All England, Lambeth Palace is always full, and its guest include visitors from the uttermost parts of the earth – colonial bishops, African and Indian missionaries, American Episcopalians, European Protestants. Several English bishops – Winchester and Hereford among them – have their home here when they are up in London. English churchmen of all kinds are welcomed there with that kindly personal interest which is perhaps Dr Davidson's finest trait. London Society (with a big S) often crosses the water; for the Davidsons have many friends in all spheres – politicians like Mr Balfour and Mr Asquith, literary men and women, and several members of the Royal Family. No wonder Englishmen love to go to Lambeth, for to dine here, looked down upon from the walls by those portraits, must be in itself an event – an experience.

Yet hospitality is but the silver lining to a life of arduous and unceasing toil. There are few lives so hard as those of our English Bishops, and none perhaps as those of an English Archbishop...

The present Archbishop works as hard as any [of his predecessors]. He has on his shoulders the immense Atlantean burden of the Churches – "well nigh not to be borne". To him come up, as through the trapdoor which opened into Olympus, all the complaints of the clergy – not a very resigned class of men. But that is not all. He takes his secular duties seriously. He attends the House of Lords regularly. Rightly or wrongly – I am not discussing politics here – he acts as the great civil protector of the Church, and a State personage who, in the order of precedence, comes next to the throne. He attempts – again, wild horses shall not drag from me an opinion whether successfully or unsuccessfully – to prove that a great ecclesiastic can be also a social reformer. He has, at any rate, the great quality of being open to advice and counsel: and those who are driven by the stern and arid laws of our party system into opposition and criticism, are gradually discovering that they have a very formidable man to deal with. Perhaps he has taken to heart the maxim of Cardinal Pole, still written on the walls of Lambeth: *Estote prudentes sicut serpentes et innocents sicut columbae* (Be ye wise as serpents and innocent as doves).

Harold Spender, 'The Primate of All England', *Pall Mall* **magazine, June 1908, pp. 656–68**

Davidson found his work harder to manage during his final decade at Canterbury, despite the invaluable support of George Bell and the other staff at Lambeth, and was forced to take increasingly lengthy holidays to ensure he was able to cope with the strain. Even ten years before he left Canterbury, he complained in a letter to the Bishop of Winchester that his workload was becoming unmanageable in both its scope and complexity.

> This is going to be rather a long letter, but I shall relieve my mind by writing it, and you will think it over, and we can talk about it when the opportunity comes.

Each time that I return, as I am now returning, to my work after a little holiday, the thought comes over me that it may be the last time one is grappling with these problems in the sort of way one does when they have accumulated for a fortnight or so, and I want to face up to them and to look at the whole wood, and not only at the trees, and to view the position and its responsibilities in the sort of way in which one would like to commend it and describe it in handing it on to a successor.

The real difficulty is keeping a reasonable proportion between the great things of first-rate importance, and the small things, quite necessary and important, but apt to multiply to the obscuring of the bigger. I suppose my "make" has always been to look at things in the concrete, and not abstractly. Part of the glamour and mystery and inspiration to me of a teacher like Westcott was that he looked at everything with a certain abstractedness, seeing the principles rather than worrying about the practical details when he was writing, though in action he was pretty good at details also.

I myself see few things clearly except in the concrete – that is what makes me a bad metaphysician, and perhaps a bad, and certainly an indifferent, Archbishop. Therefore let me come to the concrete. I this week have had to face a pile of things most of which belong to the last six or seven days only, for I attended to a good many while I was absent. When I look at this mass of subjects and feel, as one must, how much really depends on what I, individually, do and say about each, I am faced by the thought that we are trying to do an impossibility in leaving on the Archbishop's shoulders the responsibility for so many things which seem to be nobody else's business, except his, and yet when we consider how to contrive conciliar aid one is baffled as to how it can be done, or what sort of council would be workable and reasonably permanent and tolerable to Bishops at home and abroad and to Church folk generally.

D.P. 13, fos. 324–25, Extracts from a letter by Archbishop Davidson to the Bishop of Winchester, 15 September 1918

Many visitors to Lambeth Palace paid testimony to the kindness they experienced from the Archbishop and his wife. His approachability and lack of pomposity helped Davidson to win the trust of those he met. H. H. Montgomery, a former Bishop of Tasmania, recalled how Davidson's knack for creating a welcoming atmosphere was a significant factor in the success of the 1920 Lambeth Conference.

The [Lambeth] Conference of 1920 was notable for the fact that at length an Archbishop of Canterbury had been able to preside over two Lambeth Conferences. Before Davidson's reign it had come to be believed that this could never happen. Of course it simplified matters very much, for there was no detail with which Davidson was not familiar. Moreover, his character for fairness and his obvious distaste of being looked upon as a quasi-Patriarch made all Bishops come to Lambeth without misgivings. Once more the Archbishop permitted me to be a Secretary for this Conference. I had resigned my post as Secretary of S.P.G. [Society for the Propagation of the Gospel] and was therefore a free agent. At first I was the only Secretary, and in a sense the whole organization was in my hands till the session. But later the Bishop of Peterborough (Woods) was appointed as an English Diocesan Bishop, and he naturally took first place all through the Conference itself...

In this Conference, too, the work of the Hospitality Committee developed greatly. Not only was hospitality found for all the Bishops and their families, but for the first time a most successful attempt was made to entertain the wives of the Bishops while their husbands were in session. For six weeks, three days a week, entertainments were arranged or expeditions planned to places of interest in or near London. Historical houses, ancient Churches, city factories, Hampton Court, Richmond Park – all these and many other places were visited and tea provided for. A fleet of omnibuses stood ready on the appointed days outside the National Gallery. Evening receptions were given by famous London hostesses, and everything was done to make the Lambeth Conference of 1920 a time of pleasure as well as profit for the visitors from overseas. Several of the Bishops had brought children with them. For these, visits to the Zoo, to the King's stables at Buckingham Palace, and a large children's party at Bishopsbourne, Chiswick, were organized. So splendidly was all this work done that it added enormously to the success of the Conference.

Another development from former Conferences was the smoking! A large room on the third floor of Morton's Tower was made into a writing and smoking room. Right well was it utilized! The growth of smoking filled me with astonishment. I remember one wet, cold morning, as I was going to my office, I met coming down the stairs a solid, impenetrable mass of smoke! Moreover, one could hear above a roar of voices. It seemed as though there must have been a hundred Bishops all smoking and all talking together at the same time. Then, too, whenever the Conference adjourned, it was not uncommon to see 150 Bishops strolling about, nearly all smoking pipes. And I noticed that some of the most Evangelical Bishops were the greatest smokers. I used to wonder what the next development would be in 1930. Surely they will not smoke in the Conference itself!

**Quoted in M.M., *Bishop Montgomery: A Memoir*
(London: S.P.G. 1933), pp. 81–2**

3 Archbishop Davidson on social and political questions

Archbishop Davidson had been fascinated by politics since he served as Chaplain to Archbishop Tait. Throughout his time as Archbishop, Davidson met assiduously with political leaders, convinced that it gave him the opportunity to exert the Church of England's influence on a range of important matters. He also spoke regularly in the House of Lords. Davidson was acutely aware that the character of politics was changing in the early years of the twentieth century. The rise of the New Liberalism before 1914, and the subsequent development of the Labour Party, signalled the growth of mass political participation and a political agenda that focused extensively on social and economic questions. Yet although Davidson understood the significance of the change, he was never entirely at home in this new political landscape, instinctively preferring a more traditional 'Victorian' style of politics. His attitudes come through clearly in this 1913 memorandum.

> We are passing through a time of revolution – the revolution is of a peaceful sort, perhaps surprisingly so considering how complete is the change from old-fashioned ideas into a thoroughly democratic age, instinctively hostile to the old notions of feudalism and its outcomes, and rather suspicious of what we have been accustomed to regard as loyalty and patriotism and a proper historical pride. The change is large and deep-reaching. It is being brought about, like all changes, by the younger, not the older, generation. We have cause for thankfulness that the happening of so big a thing should be peaceable, and not bloodstained, but happening it certainly is. And the process which is afoot is probably not nearly completed, even in its immediate character. Phases or aspects of it are what people call Socialism, as the practical outcome of vehement democratic views, or "Lloyd-Georgism", as the anti-feudal swing of the pendulum, or Parliament Act Government, instead of the old constitutional theories. All these, and many other forms, are facts, not mere theoretical possibilities or dangers. They have come into our English system, political, social, industrial, and have come to stay. The political cries which arouse a popular meeting are quite different from the political cries which aroused the Radicals in our fathers' days. They give voice to what people are really thinking and promoting with a sure sense that it is the spirit of the age. At such a time it is futile and perhaps harmful, for the old generation to keep girding at it all as something necessarily pernicious and evil-intentioned. It is not evil-intentioned, perhaps it is not pernicious. Anyhow our wholesale girding at it all can do no manner of good towards moulding into better and safer shapes the tendencies which, whatever shape they assume, will certainly persist and hold their own. Examples of a practical sort are seen in the sort of blind and unconstructive opposition to Home Rule, without any endeavour to appreciate, or guide, or steady its advance; but with a merely grunting utterance that it is accursed and ought not to be. Another instance is seen in the change of Parliamentary modes and action from the old-fashioned ways which we regard as constitutionally well-established into new ways which we fear and dislike, because they are, as we think them, mere unintelligent mob law, and so we gird at it instead of recognising the tread and trying in the light of older traditions, and old men's instincts, to make the inevitable process a

safer one, and loyally to acquiesce in it as something which may doubtless be mischievous in the form it is taking, but is capable of taking a wholesomer form. Such is always, as it seems to me, the danger against which the older generation, which is running its last lap round the course, should be on its guard if it wants to be really helping the world Christianly to a better and a brighter future.

D.P. 12, fos. 317–20, Extracts from Archbishop Davidson Memorandum, 28 September 1913

Davidson's commitment to meeting decision-makers in the privileged world of dinner parties and clubs reflected his conviction that such a strategy would be most effective in allowing him to exert influence. The Archbishop was convinced that he was successful in influencing decisions on a range of political issues. Although he was by instinct happy to work behind the scenes, there were nevertheless occasions when he considered that he was not given due recognition for his efforts, even as he recognised that such a situation was probably unavoidable.

A further [. . .] example of what I meant by doing my work apart from what others could observe, is found in the friendship which I have so curiously sustained with leading men on both sides of politics for about thirty years. Meeting ministers and others frequently at Windsor I enlarged and augmented the sort of acquaintance with public people which Lambeth life implies. But I think mine has been a quite exceptional experience with regard to actual leaders. I knew Gladstone pretty closely. He stayed with us at Windsor, as we with him at Hawarden, and I saw him a great deal in connexion with many public things. When Archbishop Benson died at Hawarden, I spent a few days alone with him, having gone off to Hawarden on the night of the Sunday on which the Archbishop died, and stayed there until the funeral when I accompanied his body to Canterbury. This was a quite exceptional opportunity, and I had the advantage of discussing with him throughout entire days the public things on which I wanted to know his mind. Lord Salisbury I never knew intimately, but I saw even more of him that I did of Mr Gladstone. I stayed on different occasions at Hatfield, and Lord Salisbury was much at Windsor. I also had a great deal of intercourse with him in connexion with matters in the House of Lords wherein I was taking part. Lord Rosebery had been known to me for many years, and my friendship with him has been at more than one crisis of real intimacy. When he lef[t] office I was staying with him at Dalmeny, as we have done many times, and when Bishop of Winchester I always stayed at the Durdans when I had work near Epsom. I think he reposes genuine confidence in me. Arthur Balfour has also been a real personal friend. Frequent visits to Whittinghame, and much close intercourse during Education controversies, and at other times, lead me to feel that I really know his mind. Campbell-Bannerman I knew nothing of at first, but in the last year of his life when his wife died he made friends with me, and during his long illness before his death I paid regular visits to him daily for a week or two before the end. On these occasions he talked with absolute unreserve both of his colleagues and about public affairs. Asquith I have known intimately, ever since his marriage. I married him, and we have had many episodes of close intercourse in his joys and sorrows, e.g. when [Asquith's wife] Margot was gravely ill, and I saw her frequently with him, and since that time in connexion with all sorts of public matters, and he has talked to me with the utmost freedom. But it has not been only these five Prime Ministers. There has hardly been a member of a Cabinet on either side whom I have not known more or less, and some, e.g. James Bryce, Balfour of Burleigh, Dunedin, were very old friends, while among latter friendships I can count as genuine my intercourse with men like Morley, Halsbury, Loreburn, Haldane, Salisbury the younger, Grey, Londonderry, Alfred Lyttelton, George Hamilton, and a great many more. Lansdowne I have never known well, and Bonar Law I at present hardly know at all [. . .] It means a good deal in my judgement for the Church's good that the man who holds the Archbishop's position should have this kind of natural and friendly access to the men to whom is given the responsibility for the nation's affairs. It places not the Archbishop only, but the Church, in quite a different relation to public life in its religious and secular aspects.

D.P. 12, fos. 312–14, Extracts from Archbishop Davidson Memorandum, originally dictated in 1913 and amended in January 1917

Davidson probably overestimated his influence on members of the British political elite, although his views were listened to with respect and attention. There were nevertheless occasions when he played a significant role in his self-appointed mission to use his position as Head of the National Church to bridge political divisions on important questions. The following document shows Davidson acting as an intermediary between the Prime Minister Herbert Asquith and the Opposition leader Andrew Bonar Law during the crisis over Ireland in 1914.

> I reported to [Asquith] what had passed at my second interview with Bonar Law on Sunday afternoon. I had hoped to have done this the previous day (Monday), but failed to get an appointment as there was a Cabinet in the morning and the Army debate in both Houses in the afternoon; but I think on the whole it was better that I saw him in the quiet of Tuesday morning rather than in the heated atmosphere of the previous afternoon. I placed in his hands as the outcome of my talk with Bonar Law the Memorandum appended hereto. He discussed it a little with his usual point and lucidity, but not in any detail. He turned the conversation to Bonar Law's personality. He had always found him absolutely straight

and fair-minded, eminently lacking in 'distinction' (the word was mine, but he cordially acquiesced in it), but shrewd, capable, and honest. This last corresponded with what Bonar Law had himself said to me about Asquith as regards personal intercourse and dealings. Obviously the two men are well adapted to confer usefully and confidentially with one another. With regard to this Asquith remarked "It was never more apparent than in yesterday's debate. Bonar Law was capable, plodding, and clear; but when Balfour rose it was the difference between a racer and a cart-horse." Asquith asked again for an assurance from me that I had made it clear to Bonar Law that he (Asquith) was in no sense committed to make the proposal on behalf of his party even in private conversation with Bonar Law, but he still thought it afforded basis for discussion between them, and I think he welcomed rather more cordially than he wished me to see the suggestion that there should be a further conference between himself and Bonar Law. He said that so far as I was concerned he was very grateful to me for genuine help, but he did not think that at the moment I could do more, as he would now himself, after thinking matters over, communicate with Bonar Law. I asked whether I should tell Bonar Law so, and he cordially approved of my so doing.

D.P. 12, fos. 412–13, Extracts from Archbishop Davidson Memorandum on 'Interview with the Prime Minister at 10 Downing Street on Tuesday morning, March 24th 1914'

Davidson's early career flourished in part because of the patronage of Queen Victoria. He was by contrast never close to Edward VII. The Archbishop found George V more straightforward to deal with than his father – though he did not always trust his judgement. The Archbishop always believed that he had a duty to protect the monarchy from controversy and criticism. He did not always find the task an easy one. In 1918, at a time when anti-monarchical feeling was strong in Britain, Davidson met George V and described shortly afterwards in a private memorandum that he had told the King he could not

> keep back from him things which I heard people saying freely, and which they probably would not say to him, or to one of his immediate staff. The kind of things were [. . .] the fact that prominent public men outside Government service never saw the King at all, and while this was quite explicable and tolerable at a crisis of the war it could not rightly go on for years, for he would get out of touch with some of the very people whom he ought to know best. The King agreed that this was so, and that possibly he ought to do something. I pressed for small dinner parties pretty frequently, and rather scouted his lame excuses that he had too many papers and documents to read etc. I told him he could save reading documents by hearing from first-hand the sort of people who wrote them in newspapers and elsewhere. The Queen [who was there]

backed me up strongly, and finally, after a good deal of bickering about it, the King said "Very well. We will do it. I understand, but it will be much more difficult than you think and so on". Then I pressed for more publicity to be given to such things as the giving of decorations etc – why not before a few thousand people instead of in the Throne Room? [. . .] Then I urged his driving through the streets in a way which made him more conspicuous. He talked lamely about the mischief of too many horses at a time of economy, and of the length of time required for a carriage as compared with a motor and so on. I urged that no pomp was necessary, but an open carriage with two horses which would take seven or eight minutes more than a motor to go to some place in London that he was constantly visiting. The Queen complained that open carriages disturbed one's hair, but she obviously agreed completely that it was right [. . .] All this was the outcome of prolonged conversation, the King talking most of the time, and I succeeding only by great determination in getting in my remarks, and declining to be interrupted. I was outspoken and told him that I thought the thing really serious, and then his nicest side came out, and he was gratefully appreciative and most cordial.

D.P. 13, fos. 312–13, Extracts from Archbishop Davidson Memorandum, 12 May 1918

Davidson acknowledged that the Church had a responsibility to comment on questions of poverty and unemployment, but he was wary of demands for social and economic reform that took place outside the usual confines of Parliamentary politics. Nor did the Archbishop believe that widespread material deprivation was in itself evidence of the fundamental immorality of the existing social and economic order. This perspective put him at odds with some clergy in the years before the First World War, at a time when many were active in organisations such as the Christian Social Union. The following letter to the Rev F. L. Donaldson, in response to a request asking the Archbishop to meet a delegation of unemployed men who had marched from Leicester to London, captures Davidson's instinctive caution and dislike of public protest.

I have today received your letter of yesterday. I yield to no one in my appreciation of the difficulties of the present industrial conditions in many parts of England, and I have from my earliest days done my best to understand the practical questions which have from time to time arisen. But such study as I am able to give to these questions tends to deepen my sense of their difficulty, and of the danger which is incurred by attempting rough and ready solutions of far reaching and complicated economic problems. Few things would give me more satisfaction than to be able so to devote myself to a deeper study of economics as to learn how to co-operate more adequately in promoting the amendment of present hardships where such exist. But a man who, like myself, has to work for 16 or 17 hours a day in discharging his own more immediate responsibilities cannot hope to be able to give to these studies so much time as many others can.

I need hardly tell you how deeply I sympathise with those whom you represent in their present lack of employment. But I am bound to say that I fail at present to see what good I could hope to effect by receiving such a Deputation as you suggest, and I cannot help fearing that I might really do harm by raising hopes and expectations which I should have no power whatever of satisfying. If what is desired is merely that I should be in possession of a statement of facts respecting the scarcity of employment in certain midland towns, I honestly believe that I should master those facts better were I to study them in writing than I should by listening to a oral statement [...] I have no wish to throw any doubt upon what you describe as the sacredness and nobility of the cause. But in the ceaseless stress of other duties I must admit that I have not at present given to the details of this particular controversy such study as would justify me in making myself responsible for thus endorsing the representation of those who are coming to London to plead their cause, nor dare I hope to be able speedily to master the intricacies of the problem.

Archbishop Davidson, letter to F. L. Donaldson, 8 June 1905 (*The Times*, 13 June 1905)

Davidson continued to take a keen interest in political and social questions during the final decade of his archiepiscopate. Political leaders from all the main parties continued to meet with him regularly. Although the Church of England was far from being in decline after 1918, changes in the fabric of politics perhaps made the Archbishop a somewhat more peripheral figure than before. He nevertheless continued to take his political role seriously, speaking out on major questions of policy, and using his private access to leading politicians both to offer advice and to learn more about their plans.

I have been very regular in House of Lords attendance, and have been considering the rights and wrongs of it. I am clear on the whole that it is best to do as I have done and go practically every day when the House sits, for my room has been to a greater degree than ever before beset with people, public men, desiring interviews. All kinds of important people, on subjects political, international, and of course ecclesiastical, have been coming thither for talks, and I think it is not without value that I should put in an appearance at the House itself whenever anything of the least importance is happening. I have not made many important speeches, but numerically I think they have been fairly frequent. I have talked about Russia, about the Eastern Church; about Divorce; about East Africa (Kenya), and rather importantly about a very local matter, the Whitgift Hospital at Croydon which became the centre of acute controversy among historians, architects, aesthet[e]s, though indeed the thoughtful people were all on one side and we triumphed overwhelmingly.

D.P. 14, fos. 215–16, Extracts from Archbishop Davidson Memorandum, 12 August 1923

Davidson had little sympathy with the ideas on radical social and economic reform expressed after 1918 by younger clergy like William Temple and Dick Sheppard. Temple supported greater autonomy for the Church of England from Parliamentary control, in part to allow it to take a more critical stand on questions of social policy (whilst, perhaps paradoxically, believing that its Established character remained valuable in fostering a strong moral foundation for community life). The Archbishop, by contrast, continued to focus more on the Church's duty to comment on such traditional moral issues as marriage and divorce. He was nevertheless ready to acknowledge that economic questions could not be separated from questions of morality, even if he was seldom ready to think too deeply about the practical implications of such a position. His views come through in the following extract from a speech he made to Convocation in 1921, supporting a motion which called on members of the Church 'to do all in their power to spread a spirit of fellowship, by personal example, by consistent advocacy of justice between man and man, and not least by doing all in their power to relieve the distress caused by the widespread unemployment at the present time'.

> I heard it said yesterday that there was at this moment a great deal of disillusionment on the part of those concerned in the mining industry, especially the operatives, when compared with the hopes which were current, say, on Armistice Day, when everyone talked about the coming of a new England, and so on. Surely that disillusionment is not confined to the miners. Are we not finding it in every department of life that we are trying to re-create after the War? Wherever we turn in our social, our educational, even our religious reconstruction, we are finding ourselves disillusioned with regard to hopes which were strongly entertained and vigorously and rightly expressed at the time the Armistice was declared. I suppose that others, like myself, find themselves bewildered when they realise how different are the conditions with which we have to contend from those that we hoped might be brought about as a result of the War. We thought that the War was going to lead us into sunnier conditions and greater freedom, and we are disappointed.
>
> I am grateful to the Bishop of Truro for his reference to bygone controversies and for his reminder of how many of the arguments that are used to-day were used in circumstances which seem to us to have been unbelievably bad. Those arguments were not used merely by the obscurantists of the old-fashioned type, but by those who were regarded as the progressive

and enlightened men of the age. John Bright and Richard Cobden were strong opponents of the Factory Laws. They said they were wrong both economically and practically. These facts should be borne in mind when we try to shape for ourselves the policy that we ought now to be advocating or following in regard to these economic questions.

But there does emerge, I am quite certain, something larger and clearer as to the fundamental principles which we ought to be resting upon and which we can give effect to as Christians in dealing with these questions now. The strange thing is, when one looks upon those past days, that the men who used well-worn religious arguments in support of slavery, long hours of labour, the employment of little children in mines and factories, and many other questions, were deeply earnest Christians, who yet were absolutely blind to conditions which now seem to us so obvious. That is a useful thought for us to have in mind when thinking over things that want altering.

Personally, I am not in the least prepared to express an opinion upon the details of the plans of pooling and the rest. Some Bishops to-day have done so. Their knowledge may justify them. Mine certainly does not. It has been said that by passing this Resolution we shall be committing ourselves to this or that opinion upon the economic side of these subjects. When that was said I looked at the Resolution again and tried to find whether its actual words contained anything of the sort, because I am quite convinced in my own mind that I do not know enough to express an opinion on a technical matter of this kind, which is a subject of acute controversy between thoughtful men. But the Resolution does not seem to me to say anything of the kind. It simply throws us back on the principles which we all stand by, and which we have reiterated again and again.

Speech by Archbishop Davidson to the Upper House of Convocation (Canterbury) on 28 April 1921

Davidson's determination to use his position to seek agreement on controversial issues was demonstrated in the General Strike of May 1926. Although he criticised the Strike in a speech in the House of Lords on 5 May, two days later he signed an Appeal by Church leaders calling for both sides to make concessions, a decision that earned him considerable criticism from 'diehard' ministers. The Archbishop was clearly surprised at the response, most notably when Lord Reith at the BBC refused to broadcast the Appeal, and on 11 May, he secured a meeting with the Prime Minister at which he characteristically tried to smooth away the tensions whilst still gently urging caution on Baldwin.

I was afraid that he [Baldwin] might be drifting into the same position as other people and regard me as hostile to him and his whole policy and as having raised an antagonistic flag which I was prepared to nail to the mast and to regard him as stupidly hostile that he did not conform to what our Appeal on behalf of the Churches had said. I told him that was not my position and that we had very deliberately come to the conclusion we had formulated as a suggestion for the Government to consider, but that the responsibility must now be his as to whether or not they turn our suggestion down and go forward on what they believe to be a sounder and more excellent line. I pressed on him that the responsibility must be his and that we had definitely had our say. I showed him that I appreciated his difficulties as well as my own . . .

I took the opportunity of pressing a little upon him the distrust we have in the truculent and fighting attitude not of himself but of some of his colleagues. He did not in the least deny it and spoke of his difficulties as hourly very great. He took on the whole a rather more sanguine view of the situation from the Government point of view than I should be prepared to take at the present moment. We parted in the friendliest way.

D.P. 15, fo. 65, Archbishop Davidson
Memorandum, 11 May 1916

4 Archbishop Davidson on Church-State relations

Davidson was a strong believer in maintaining the Established character of the Church of England, which he saw as a defining feature of the British Constitution. It informed his views of the role of the National Church on questions of politics and social reform (see previous section). During the years before the First World War, the main challenge to the Established status of the Church came from Nonconformity, since many Nonconformist MPs expressed resentment about the Church of England's privileges. After the First World War, the main debates about the value of Establishment took place within the Church of England itself. Some leading figures in the Church, like Charles Gore, came to believe that Disestablishment would free the Church of England from State control. Others, like William Temple, continued to support Establishment, but believed that the Church needed greater freedom to provide an independent voice on questions of social justice. Davidson's defence of Establishment was rooted in his belief that it was sanctioned by tradition. The Archbishop also, though, recognised that the Church's privileges needed to be articulated in terms of their contribution to the welfare of the whole nation. In the following passage from his 1912 *The Character and Call of the Church of England*, Davidson argues that the parish system, with all its benefits, could only operate with the existence of an Established Church.

> Look, then, with me at what are some of the changes which "Disestablishment" pure and simple would bring about. I should unhesitatingly put first in importance, and in its effect upon the homes of people, the abolition of what we know as the parochial system. The idea of a "persona" or "parson" appointed for each parish in the land, as the resident and representative

man who is bound to have his home there, whoever else is absent, and to be at the call of every parishioner who wishes, in health or sickness, by day or night, to avail himself of his services – that idea goes, once for all, never to return. I do not, of course, mean that the old traditional use would instantly come to an end, or that people would immediately cease to look to the quarter to which they have always looked, or to find a general friend and counsellor in the man who, although no longer technically the "parson", would be a minister of Christ and, if money could somehow be found for his support, would still be resident in the parish. But there is a wide difference between a man's trying, with a sense of the responsibility attached to ministerial office, to carry on with kindness and goodwill a set of undefined duties which have ceased to be obligatory, and on the other hand the maintenance of a traditional and recognised rule which from time immemorial has been gladly and thankfully followed, and which is capable, if need be, of enforcement by authority. We have at present such a rule, supported by both Church and State – a rule which requires the continuous residence and the personal service of a duly appointed and qualified officer who has a recognised status and a defined authority in matters ecclesiastical within an accurately prescribed area, surrounded on every side by other areas prescribed with equal accuracy, each of them served by a religious officer with status and responsibilities corresponding to his own.

Randall Davidson, *The Character and Call of the Church of England* (1912), pp. 92–3

The sharp debates over the Disestablishment of the Church in Wales reflected a sense on both sides that such a move might represent a step towards the Disestablishment of the Church of England as well. Davidson had been sharply critical of calls for the Disestablishment of the Church in Wales from his time as Bishop of Rochester. He continued to express the same views whenever the question was raised during his time at Canterbury. His opposition was in the event unsuccessful, since the Liberal Government approved Disestablishment of the Welsh Church in 1914 (although it did not take effect until after the end of the war). Davidson's views are expressed clearly in the following extract from an address to Convocation, in a session discussing reports that the Liberal Government was planning to introduce a Bill to promote Welsh Disestablishment.

To one point in the Bishop of Southwark's speech I should like to refer. He quoted – not, I think, as adopting it – the opinion that Establishment hampers us somewhat in our protest against moral wrongs. The very opposite seems to me to be the fact. I believe we are better able to speak effectively on such questions on account of our established position, and those Nonconformist ministers who apply to us for Ordination usually, I am afraid, without effect, commonly allege this as one of the difficulties which led them to desire a change. On the present point – the Disestablishment of the

Church in Wales – I am quite clear that our duty, both to Church and realm, bids us oppose by every reasonable means what is proposed in the Government Bill. I am myself absolutely ready to do everything that in me lies to lead such opposition when the right moment comes. I am not clear that it has come at present. The Bishop of London tells me that he thinks everybody knows that the Bill is not going to be pushed forward. For myself I certainly do not know that [. . .] Nothing that we can do will affect the Second Reading of this Bill in the House of Commons if that be moved by the Government of the day; but subsequent stages will arise in one House or the other when our influence may be capable of being used with real effect. We intend so to use it. When the right time comes I shall myself be ready to show that such a measure as the Government proposes would do immense harm to religious life generally in the hills and valleys of Wales. There is now everywhere a resident ministry – often, it may be, ineffectively exercised, but speaking generally it is admirable – and to remove it would be a national disaster. This Bill would inevitably have that effect in many districts. I believe further that its passing would inflict a cruel wrong on the Welsh people. They are unaware of it now, but they would wake hereafter to realise the disaster which had occurred [. . .] I pass to another group of considerations. Some Churchmen say we are right to desire Welsh Disestablishment because it will remove a sense of grievance and irritation which had been engendered by the existence of an Established Church. Christian charity, we are told, bids us get rid of stumbling blocks. It bids us be content to "take joyfully the spoiling of our goods". But are they our goods? In my judgement these endowments belong not to us, but to our children and our children's children. We hold them in trust, and we dare not, for the sake of allaying what is, I hope, a temporary soreness, deprive those who come after us of the means of doing their work aright for the common good.

Archbishop Davidson address to the Upper House of Convocation (Canterbury), 5 May 1909

Davidson reacted cautiously to the creation of the Life and Liberty Movement in 1917. He was sceptical about its members' calls for greater freedom for the Church, particularly in a time of war, when politicians had little time to consider the minutiae of Parliamentary oversight of Church affairs. The Archbishop was also sceptical of the radical social views held by many members of Life and Liberty. His concerns were expressed in a letter he wrote to William Temple, the most influential figure in Life and Liberty, following the publication of a letter by Temple and others in *The Times* expressing determination 'to arouse the Church to a sense of its vital need, and to call on all who love it to demand for it the liberty which is essential to its life' (*Times*, 20 June 1917).

I waited until to-day in order that I might read your letter in the Press before replying to what you have privately written to me. . .

I am not I think apt to be over-sensitive or thin-skinned in matters of this sort, or to seek to evade a criticism which, however rough, may be most useful. But of course you are right when you say or imply in your private letter that by what is now published my own personal difficulties are greatly augmented. That is a comparatively small matter unless it hinders the cause which I, like you, have at heart. This I fear it may do, but I shall endeavour to prevent it as far as possible. There is nothing in the letter which could be called violent or rude. Pray feel quite relieved on that score.

I am looking forward keenly to the outcome of your missionary effort to awaken the sense of Churchmen generally to the need of changes. I am certain that in that policy you are right. It is what specially needs doing at present, and it is just what can at present be done. Where I think that you and others are mistaken is in your belief that we could with advantage to the cause of wise reform take steps at the present moment for propounding schemes in Parliament or committing thoughtful people who care about the Church's life to a particular and detailed policy. I am mixing for hours on most days in the week with the men prominent in our public life on whose aid we should have to rely if the changes we want were to be made, and I do not literally know one of them who would share your view as to the practicability of the forward push in an official way at the present moment when every thought and every ounce of energy is absorbed in England's struggle for its very life. This makes me absolutely certain that I have been right in advocating or insisting upon the necessity of our eschewing a policy of hustle and push in matters ecclesiastical during these months of daily and nightly strain upon the thoughts and time of every public man who is worthy of the name...

If the publication of your letter has the effect of stiffening convertible people into unconvertibleness by the irritation it causes, I shall feel that the responsibility is not mine, and, as I have told you, I shall try to prevent it. Of course it is a distress to me that things should be said which will I think be the reverse of helpful in the direction we all desire. I honestly fear that it may have that effect, and that, after all, is what matters.

Letter from Archbishop Davidson to William Temple, quoted in F. A. Iremonger, *William Temple, Archbishop of Canterbury: His Life and Letters* (London: Oxford University Press, 1948), pp. 247–48

Davidson's reluctance to demand legislative changes in the relationship between Church and State relaxed with the end of hostilities. He was happy to play a leading role in the passing of the 'Enabling Bill' that provided the Church of England with greater freedom from Parliamentary control. The Archbishop was sensitive enough to the concerns of some of the more Erastian-minded MPs and Lords to present the change merely as a question of good housekeeping. It was this line of argument that he pursued when proposing the Bill in the House of Lords in June 1919.

> The character and range of our proposal, as your Lordships all know, have been widely discussed and criticised, and I think somewhat strangely misunderstood, during the last few months. Its opponents – and there may be some of them in this House – decry in it perils which I think are either quite imaginary or are no greater than those which attend all brave and adventurous legislation. Those fears I altogether repudiate. As to its friends, I find a little difficulty in making my own all the hopes and ambitions which have found eloquent expression in the fine body of men and women who have advocated it. We owe them a real debt of gratitude for their public-spirited work in keeping the question constantly to the fore.
>
> I am going to try this afternoon, with such brevity as I can, to explain the origin and character of the Bill, to remove such misconceptions as are apparent, and to urge its appropriateness and usefulness at the present time. I think I can do this best by reminding your Lordships, in the first instance, of some familiar historical facts. Familiar as they are, their relevance, I think, as to what we are now doing, is often overlooked. May I say at once, in order to clear the ground, that we are not dealing at all with deeper spiritual things. Doctrines of our faith, the duties of the Christian ministry, the help we can render publicly or privately to the souls of men – these are spiritual fundamental things, the very essence of our work, and with them we are not dealing directly, or I think hardly even indirectly, in this Bill in any way. We are speaking here of the framework, the outer secular rules, within which our work has to be done. Such framework is needed by every law-abiding Christian community, whatever its character, but the Church of England framework has a distinctive and a peculiar relation to the State and to the national life...
>
> I hope that your Lordships will not misunderstand me. I am very far from thinking or regarding the Church of England as a branch of the Civil Service. I have heard this phrase used, and it is a most misleading one. Nevertheless the analogy holds good, because we are face to face to-day with abundant new problems, with all kinds of new activities, all kinds of aims and plans. I am myself having them every day in my life, and they correspond in their degree, or in their own way, to those kind of things in our civil life, and it is not unfair to say that we are put in the same sort of difficulty as a Government Office would be put in if it were told, "We cannot find Parliamentary time for doing the things everybody desires to see done." We want to be able to rise to our opportunities with our new populations, and we are asking your Lordships now to help us to do so.
>
> Possibly some one may think that I am rather imagining or exaggerating the difficulties, and that what really stands in the way is not the conditions that I have described but the stupidity, or the laziness, or the obscurantism, or the red tape which characterises ecclesiastics, especially Bishops,

and prevents them from doing perfectly well what they might do with the existing laws. I have heard that said; but, my Lords, it is absurdly untrue. And about this I hope that I shall not be regarded as egotistic if I say that I make no apology for claiming to speak with firsthand knowledge. It so happens, long before I held the office which I have now held for more than sixteen years, that I had to do with the central work of the Church of England, and it is now more than forty years since I first began to be behind the scenes, so to speak, and had to be in touch with the central forces that were day by day at work. I was in a humble capacity at first, still I had thorough knowledge and was completely abreast of what was taking place. Therefore I speak with real inside knowledge when I say that the difficulties to which I have referred have been steadily increasing and multiplying on our hands. Just as our attempted activities have multiplied, so the old hampering conditions have been constantly increasing. It is literally true that in our system of administration, which now-a-days is very varied and very far reaching, and which grows more wide and more exacting every year, I am brought up not every week but every day against the difficulties which hamper our power to serve the nation as thoroughly as we would. That is why I come to your Lordships to-day.

Speech by Archbishop Davidson in the House of Lords on the National Assembly of the Church of England (Powers) Bill, 3 June 1919

The rejection of the revised Prayer Book by the House of Commons came as a surprise to Davidson. Opponents of the new Book welcomed the decision as evidence of Parliament's determination to maintain the Protestant heritage of the Church of England. Supporters insisted that the Bishops should refuse to accept the decision and authorise use of the revised Book. A few days after the MPs had rejected the new Prayer Book, Archbishop Davidson and Archbishop Lang issued a statement designed to calm opinion, acknowledging the right the House of Commons to act, but asserting the Church's right to independence in spiritual matters.

> The rejection of the Prayer-Book Measure by a vote of the House of Commons has brought about a position of difficulty and anxiety in the life of the Church and nation. While exaggeration must be avoided, and there is certainly no ground for panic, it cannot be denied that the crisis is grave. It lays upon the Bishops a heavy burden of responsibility. The Church is entitled to look to them for counsel and guidance.
>
> For two days the Diocesan Bishops have met at Lambeth, and we can record with thankfulness that the unity which marked our long deliberations during the last two years has been maintained. It is impossible within a few days of the vote of the House of Commons to take a just measure of its significance and to determine the obligations which it imposes on the

Church. We have therefore found it necessary to adjourn till January 11 in order that we may have further time for thought and prayer.

Some word, however, of counsel and reassurance must at once be spoken. Accordingly, with the consent of the Bishops and after full consultation with them, we address this message to the Church.

It was within the right of the House of Commons to reject the Measure. On the other hand, mere acquiescence in its decision would be in our judgement inconsistent with the responsibilities of the Church as a spiritual society.

The Bishops fully recognize that there are circumstances in which it would be their duty to take action in accordance with the Church's inherent spiritual authority. We realize this duty, and are ready, if need be, to fulfil it. But we believe that the recent decision by the House of Commons was influenced by certain avoidable misunderstandings as to the character of the proposals before it, and we cannot, therefore, take the responsibility of accepting as final the vote of December 15.

The House of Bishops has accordingly resolved to re-introduce the Measure into the Church Assembly as soon as possible with such changes, and such changes only, as may tend to remove misapprehensions and to make clearer and more explicit its intentions and limitations.

For the meantime we make a most earnest appeal to the whole Church for that corporate loyalty by which alone it can meet the dangers and rise to the opportunities of this critical time. With all the authority which belongs to our office we ask that until the Deposited Book is fully authorized by the Church, no one shall avail himself of its provisions so as to make changes in the accustomed order of services or to introduce usages which would have been sanctioned by it. If any of the clergy have adopted usages which it would forbid, we ask them to be willing henceforth to discontinue such usages for the sake of the peace and unity of the Church. We make bold to believe that our fellow-Churchmen who have conscientiously opposed the Measure will do or say nothing now to increase our difficulties. At a time when, in a special degree, the well-being of the Church in this land for many generations may depend on this things we do, or refrain from doing, it is clear that self-restraint and self-sacrifice will be the truest proofs of loyalty, and calmness the highest form of courage.

During this Holy Season of Christmas let no hasty words or acts disturb its peace. Let the voices of controversy be hushed. Let us enter upon a New Year fraught with issues so grave in the spirit of united prayer. In these happenings God must have some purpose for His Church. May we have humility and faith to discern it, strength and stedfastness to obey it.

We believe that these very anxieties have set a new tide moving within the Church of England of eager and generous devotion. Let it raise and bear along with it a new love of loyalty as a thing in itself true and beautiful, a new care for unity and a new constraint of charity within the fellowship of Christ, a new zeal in the service of his Kingdom at home and abroad.

Then this tide may prove to be a means which God will use to cleanse and defend His Church.

Statement by the Archbishop of Canterbury and the Archbishop of York on the Prayer Book Crisis, 18 December 1927

5 The Archbishop, peace, and war

Throughout the nineteenth century, questions of war and peace were discussed far more widely amongst Nonconformists than Anglicans. This began to change early in the twentieth century, as senior figures in the Church of England began to focus more on various international initiatives designed to prevent war and reduce expenditure on armaments. Amongst these was the second Hague Conference of 1907, at which the major powers agreed to a series of measures including a system of voluntary arbitration to resolve conflict, along with recognition of the rights of neutral shipping in times of war. In a speech to Convocation before the Conference opened, Davidson praised such initiatives as an important mechanism for securing peace, but he also made it clear that he did not believe that the Church of England should endorse any kind of pacifism.

> It was calculated a few years ago – I have no means of knowing whether the calculation was accurate or not – that it was not impossible that in the event of a great conflagration among the States of Europe there might be no less than twenty millions of men in arms at one time. That may have been an exaggeration, but it was certainly a view widely held by intelligent men, and I have no reason to suppose that the possibilities are less to-day. And all these things are allied with conditions which science has brought about in the world's life, which tend to make our difficulties as peace-lovers greater rather than less, whatever be our sentiments or desires upon the subject. The facility of quick news, and, therefore, very often misleading news, is undoubtedly, I suppose, a grave peril in the conditions of modern life, and not least in international relations. The similar facility of the quick creation of public panic or public sentiment will readily be seen. It is difficult to exaggerate the importance (as an element of this problem) of the fact that it is possible now, in a way that was utterly impracticable a few years ago, to let literally millions of people be red-hot with ill-informed enthusiasm within an hour or two of the happening of some particular thing, perhaps incorrectly reported after all ... [I]t is at such an hour that the Hague Conference is again summoned, with the definite view of practical action. What is the relation of the Christian Church to that gathering, and to the action which may follow from it? There can be no subject on earth for which we, as Christians, ought to care, and and I think do care, more keenly than that.
>
> ... [The Church needs] To strive to bring home to the minds of those on whom our words have influence the responsibility that rests upon Christian men, as such, at a juncture like the present, for forcing upon everybody's

attention the need, the duty, and the possibility of the preservation of the world's peace . . .

Apply then in practice those sacred principles at the juncture which we have come to. Let us ourselves remember, and let us bid our people remember, this Hague Conference when it meets. Let us teach people to make it the subject of their prayers as well as their hopes; let us try to help the average man to bear his share of personal responsibility in a matter which does, of necessity, concern us every one. No one will say that by doing so we are for a moment deprecating action or co-operation for the defence of our national life and of our national interests, provided such defence is promoted and set forward in a legitimate way. In one sense, it is the very first duty of a Government as such, and of the nation whom that Government represents, so to act as to protect the rights of its own citizens, provided it realises at every step of the course that these rights are accompanied by duties and responsibilities. We are not, therefore, deprecating such action for home defence as tends to give evidence to everybody that we should be prepared, if need were, to defend ourselves effectively against aggression and wrong [. . .] But, with all that, we do want to foster, as Christians, that peace-loving temper, that attitude of mind towards those questions, towards the right of other men and nations, which will help everybody, amidst the complexity of the problems of international life, to look at them more as God would have us look at them, remembering not every man his own things only, but every man the things of others – other men and other nations too. Without that effort all that we are now trying to do in sending our great statesmen, our thinkers, and our diplomatists to discuss the world's peace at the Hague Conference would be frustrated. We look forward with hopefulness to the fact that men, prominent in the keenness that they have shown in public life for the Christian side of public duty, should be going there to discuss with wise and thoughtful statesmen from other lands both what is desirable and what is possible for the promotion of international peace.

Archbishop Davidson address to the Upper House of Convocation (Canterbury), 30 April 1907

Davidson believed in the justice of Britain's cause in the First World War. He worked hard to encourage the Church of England to respond both to the needs of soldiers at the Front and the civilian population at home. He nevertheless viewed the war as a tragedy rather than an occasion for an outpouring of jingoism. His wartime sermons and addresses were typically sombre, seldom dealing much with immediate military questions, but rather seeking to place them in a context of broader Christian reflection.

What is it that is happening? A war greater in area and scale, and more fearful in carnage, than any that has ever been since life on the round world began. Five months – no more – have passed since the first gun was fired, and already the list of men who were strong, healthy, capable, keen, five short months ago, and who are now stark in death, outnumbers anything of its kind in human history. And to reckon up the load of sheer blank sorrow in innumerable homes, and the actual but incidental war sufferings, short of death, or possibly worse than death, would baffle the power of any man. Put thus bluntly, it is all horrible beyond words. And to ignore or belittle its horribleness – its blackness – is to falsify plain facts. And yet, facing it all, I take deliberately my text, "The peace of God, which passeth all understanding, shall keep your hearts and minds through Christ Jesus"; and I maintain that if we note how these words find their place in St. Paul's letter, we shall see their absolute fitness to our thoughts to-day. They are the words, remember, of a manacled prisoner, broken in body, and lying in peril of death. What he says is, "Rejoice in the Lord alway; and again I say Rejoice. The Lord is at hand. In nothing be anxious; but in everything" – here comes our Intercession Day – "in everything by prayer and supplication with thanksgiving let your requests be made known unto God". And then, because of that, and through that, "the peace of God, which passeth all understanding, shall keep" (literally, shall "guard" or "garrison") "your hearts and minds through Christ Jesus".

If our Intercession Day is used aright, this – in the very midst of all the fearful and gruesome warring and death – must be the outcome: "The peace of God which passeth all understanding". It does "pass understanding". You cannot express it easily in terms of common talk. But, understood or not, it is there, or it can be there, and it will keep – will "guard" and "garrison" – your heart and mind against the evils, the horrors, which such a time might readily, perhaps naturally, bring. That surely is exactly our purpose and our hope in these prayers to-day. Consider with me for a few minutes what are the things from which heart and mind will thus be guarded by what that chained prisoner calls "the peace of God".

First of all there is simple fright or panic. The people who in hours of inevitable stress and danger are, as experience shews, least apt to give way to sheer helpless fright are those whose courage rests upon some definite faith, not on mere buoyancy or high spirit. They are the people whose trust in the care and guidance of our Father, however simple and even childlike it be, is also thoughtful and deliberate. About that fact there is not, I think, any doubt. It would be easy to give examples. It so happens that in modern English history at home we have little or no experience of anything which would give occasion to widespread fear among us civil folk in our own country. But records of the Indian Mutiny days, or of some vast accident or catastrophe by sea or land, have proved abundantly who are those who can best at such an hour be trusted. I do not underrate the nerve and coolness of hundreds of men and women who would claim no religious basis for their courage, but the power which belongs to or emerges from a thoughtful, definite, religious trustfulness has been proved a thousand times, from the days of the bloodstained Colosseum to these days of the shrapnelled trenches of the Aisne or the trampled banks of the Vistula.

Archbishop Davidson sermon *The Peace of God* **preached at St Paul's Cathedral 3 January 1915**

~~~~~

Archbishop Davidson was well aware that the passions raised by war could lead to greater cruelty and make it difficult to secure long-term peace. He was ready both privately and publicly to warn against reprisals by British forces that would increase the cycle of hatred. Davidson's view about the morality of using such weapons as poisonous gas was effectively rooted in the Christian understanding of Just War, derived from Augustine and Aquinas, even if he seldom used the language associated with the tradition. He accepted that Britain had right on its side in going to war (*jus ad bellum*). He did not believe that the use of poisonous gas, or the deliberate mass targeting of civilians, could be reconciled with the *jus in bello* – that is the conditions that should govern the actual conduct of fighting. His views emerge clearly in the following letter to the Asquith Prime Minister written in May 1915.

Dear Prime Minister,

May I write to you with frankness about a matter which is causing me the gravest concern. From what has been said both in Parliament and outside I gather that our authorities, military and civil, who have the responsibility for the conduct of the War are at present contemplating as a practical matter the question whether the conduct of our enemies in the barbarous employment of poisonous gas as a means of warfare ought to be met by corresponding action on the part of our own Army. I have not seen any official statement to the effect that this is definitely intended, but the words used both in Parliament and outside seem to show that it is at all events not out of the question. The infamous conduct of the German military authorities in deliberately organising this mode of warfare and the fact that it has been put into effective operation in defiance of every principle of international ethics has aroused a burning sense of indignation among all reasonable men. I am no soldier, but as a Christian citizen I try to understand the situation as it exists, and I confess that I was profoundly disquieted by indications that our own Army may be bidden to meet the new situation by itself adopting these inhuman tactics. I suppose that if anyone had suggested a few months ago that the British Army would use poisonous gas for creating fatal disease among its enemies, the notion would have been scouted as preposterous. What has happened to change our view? Nothing, so far as I know, except that our opponents have sunk to that level of misconduct in defiance of International Conventions and of the dictates of common humanity. Is the reason adequate? They have degraded the traditions of military honour and the good name of the German Army by adopting these vile practices. We can no doubt follow their example if we choose. If we adopt that line of reprisal (and this is a really important point) how far will the principle carry us? If they are poisoning the wells in South Africa, and perhaps ultimately in Belgium, are we forthwith to do the like? If so, can we retain self-respect on the part either of the Army or the Nation? It seems to me that International agreements for securing the honourable conduct of war would then be obliterated in a brutal rivalry as to the horrors which can be perpetrated by both sides. The result would be such a tangle that the world will soon be saying, and history will say hereafter, that there was nothing to choose between the nations who were at War and it would become a matter of small importance, and probably of disputed fact who it was who begun the general course of adopting these vile usages. That is how the matter strikes me. I have, as I say, no knowledge whatever of military matters and I may be making some blunder of thought, but I try as a Christian man to look fairly at these things, and I own that the vision of what may be about to happen disquiets me profoundly.

D.P. 366, fos. 192–94, Archbishop Davidson letter to Asquith, 7 May 1915

There were numerous attempts during the war to organise meetings between Christians from the various belligerent countries to work together to bring the war to a close. Davidson was sympathetic to the idea that the war in some sense represented a failure on the part of Christians to apply their faith to international affairs. He was nervous, though, of taking any action that might be seen to undermine Britain's war effort or place his Church in a difficult position at home. His doubts are clear in his response to Archbishop Söderblom of Uppsala who in 1918 sent invitations to churches across Europe calling them to send representatives to a conference to discuss ways of ending the war.

My Dear Archbishop and Friend,
[...] We appreciate to the full the importance of the invitation you extend to representatives of various Christian communions to meet at Upsala, or at Christiana, or even at Berne, for united prayer and for conference, not about the conditions of peace or about the International differences as such, but about the spirit which we desire as Christians to extend and deepen among the peoples of Europe. We note the information you give as to the bodies or persons to whom an invitation has been extended. The list is long and varied, and I observe that the Roman Catholic Church appears as one item though of course it is noted that its followers are in many lands and that the co-operation of different ecclesiastical leaders would be required if that branch of the Church Catholic is to be properly represented. I am myself particularly anxious that we should not in any way seem to underrate the importance of your proposal or the true spirit of loyalty to Our Lord and

Master Jesus Christ which underlies it. The value and significance of such a gathering, however, must in large measure depend on its constituent elements, and a meeting which consisted in great measure of representatives from the small and scattered denominations, Evangelical and Protestant, on the Continent of Europe without the great central Churches would not bear the character which you rightly desire such a Conference to have. If you are able to tell me that the invitation is accepted by the authorities of the Roman Catholic Church, that the Pope gives it his benediction, and that duly accredited Roman Catholic representatives from such countries as France, Italy, Austria, Spain, and the United States of America, will officially attend it, we should feel it to be both a privilege and a duty that the Church of England should bear its part. Similarly, we should desire to see duly accredited representatives from the Eastern Churches in Russia, in the Turkish Empire, and in Greece. We should not feel it to be possible to send representatives to a gathering which, while claiming to represent the organised forces of the Church of Christ in Europe (you even use the word Oecumenical), was without accredited spokesmen belonging to the Roman Catholic Church or belonging to the Orthodox Churches of the East. Upon that point therefore I ask you to give me reassurance and information before I could be justified in asking delegates belonging to the Church of England to attend in that capacity.

There is another point: In the careful arrangement which you have foreshadowed you suggest that the representatives of belligerent countries attending such a Conference should be lodged apart and should not, according to your plan, meet one another either for devotion or for conference, though each of them would meet representatives of the Neutral Powers. To me and to others whom I have consulted it seems impossible to anticipate that such an arrangement could work satisfactorily if the representatives of the belligerent countries are in the same place whether it be Upsala, Christiana or Berne, at the same time. The arrangement you contemplate would work more satisfactorily were the representatives of belligerent nations to meet the representatives of Neutral Powers in successive weeks, the opposing belligerent Powers not being represented in the town at the same time. This is a matter which would require careful consideration, but the principle to which I have already given expression – namely, that if we are to bear part in such a Conference it must be a Conference of the chief organised Christian communions – is the supreme question and is in our judgement vital to the true significance and usefulness of such a gathering.

D.P. 366, fos. 25–7, Archbishop Davidson letter to Archbishop Söderblom of Up[p]sala, 12 February 1918

Archbishop Davidson, like all Church leaders, supported the creation of the League of Nations, hoping that it would make a repetition of a global war impossible. He was sometimes privately sceptical about its prospects, but in public, he was anxious to praise the League, urging members of all the churches to offer their support. In September 1922, he gave a sermon at St Peter's Cathedral, in Geneva, ahead of the opening of the Third Assembly of the League. Davidson was unusually forthright in suggesting that the League represented an attempt to ensure that international relations were conducted according to Christian principles. His language was emotive and powerful. It may be that Davidson was simply adapting his language to the occasion. It was not, though, the only time the normally cautious Archbishop gave a glimpse of another side to his personality and his hopes (see the following section for an extract from his speech to the 1910 Edinburgh Conference). There was a prophetic aspect to Davidson's religious outlook even if he seldom displayed it in public.

> Brothers and Sisters – I am going to speak about the Kingdom of God among men. The League of Nations might, as I at least verily believe, go far towards making that a reality – an accepted reality – in our lifetime. Many of us are here in pursuance of a high resolve that it shall indeed come to pass . . .
>
> The League of Nations, though it touches only a portion of the field of Christian faith and life, can claim unhesitatingly, both for its purpose and its policy, the surest Christian sanction. Its key-note vibrates in harmony with the key-note of the Christian Faith itself, and the Christian Faith lies at the core of the progressive history of mankind. That plain statement, as a simple fact of history, will hardly be disputed by any competent man . . .
>
> If we consider what the League of Nations is for, what its covenant covers, what are its aims, its possibilities, its resolves, here, as the very kernel of Jesus Christ's teaching, it lies compact – 'The Kingdom of God and His righteousness'. It is nothing less than that. Promoting it, we take part in something which, in that fashion and on that scale, has never before been attempted among the sons of men. We believe in the Kingship of God as revealed by our Lord Himself for the governance of our conduct. We want nations loyally to conform to it as nations, not merely men as men. And that – are we not persuaded of it, or we should not be here? – that can come true. We mean, please God, that it shall. Look, then, at the words a little more closely. In the first place, we are to seek, in the large affairs of public as of private life, loyalty, fealty, to the 'Kingdom of God' as Christ put it before us. And next, in the handling of those affairs we are to seek God's righteousness – His rule, that is, of justice, of honest considerateness for others, of kind-heartedness, of self-denial for the common good . . .
>
> The mission of the Christian society is not exhausted. It is ours to revivify it now. Seek to bring about on earth the inward recognition everywhere of the great ideal, an enduring, advancing 'kingdom of God' absorbing the work of the generations and establishing a kingdom not made with hands, into which, in the sacred seer's words – the nations shall bring their glory and their honour, shall bring, that is, their theories, their ideals, their policies,

their heroes, as to a touchstone for testing their worth [...] There is in the peoples of Europe to-day, for all their divergencies and strifes, a higher level of average knowledge and intelligence. A better understanding – I will not say of one another, but about one another – is beginning to prevail. There is a little, just a little, less crass ignorance in one country of what people say and think in other countries. The elementary knowledge is the outcome in part of the Great War itself. The soil has been upturned. Right seed rightly sown could grow now more readily than ever before, and a common currency of thought, though not yet of opinion, is beginning surely to be perceptible. The hour is right for the husbandry of a League of Nations – ripe for the sowing and then for the growth and then for the garnering of popular thoughts unobtainable before...

Once let the Christian men and women upon earth, West and East, North and South, kneel to God side by side, stand shoulder to shoulder before men, to say what they mean shall happen, or rather, what shall not happen, in the round world again, and they are irresistible. Would to God that any words of mine to-day should help to rally that unconquerable force to pledge itself with one voice to the great emprise. Restless, invincible, yes, because it is the will of God and if we answer to that will there is none other than can stand. The Lord God Omnipotent reigneth. May the kingdoms of this world become the kingdoms of our Lord and of His Christ.

Extracts from Archbishop Davidson's sermon on 'The League of Nations', given in St Peter's Cathedral Geneva, 3 September 1922

6 Archbishop Davidson and the Ecumenical Movement

Although Davidson's early career was spent at the heart of the ecclesiastical and social establishments, at Lambeth Palace and Windsor respectively, his appointment as Bishop of Rochester provided him with insights into a very different world. After becoming Archbishop, Davidson was committed to establishing good relations with prominent Nonconformists, although the divisions over educational reform inevitably meant that relations were sometimes difficult. Davidson was also committed to promoting greater cooperation with Nonconformists in the missionary field. There was, however, something particularly startling about his address to the 1910 Edinburgh Missionary Conference, when the Archbishop appeared to suggest that success in the missionary field could transform relations between the churches and even hasten the coming of the Kingdom of God. His address is described here by a delegate to the Edinburgh Conference.

> [T]he first part of [Davidson's] address [...] was marked by gracious humility and brotherliness unfeigned. It revealed unmistakable and even passionate conviction that evangelisation is the paramount duty of the Church.

There were many orators on both sides of the Atlantic who would have impressed no one by calling that Conference one "which if men be weighed rather than counted has, I suppose, no parallel in the history of this or of other lands": but coming from a Scots statesman-ecclesiastic, with a merited reputation for sobriety of thought and word, it impressed. But it was the closing sentence that gave the unforgettable thrill: he was affirming with tremendous emphasis that "the place of missions in the life of the Church must be the central place, and none other: that is what matters"; and thus concluded: "Secure for that thought its true place, in our plans, our policy, our prayers; and then – why then, the issue is His, not ours. *But it may well be that, if that come true, there be* SOME STANDING HERE TONIGHT WHO SHALL NOT TASTE OF DEATH TILL THEY SEE THE KINGDOM OF GOD COME WITH POWER".
W.H.T. Gairdner, *Edinburgh 1910: an account and interpretation of the world missionary conference* **(Edinburgh, 1910), p. 43**

Davidson was more cautious in his response to the Kikuyu Conference, which caused sharp divisions within the Church of England, when news broke that two missionary Bishops in East Africa had attended an inter-denominational Communion Service. In a letter to Herbert Tugwell, Bishop of Western Equatorial Africa, he made it clear that whilst he had sympathy with those who believed that the Mission field provided a setting to ease denominational boundaries, such local initiatives had to take into view the wider implications.

I think I appreciate to the full the craving that good men working as Christian teachers in the midst of a huge heathen population must have for marking their unity in Christ and doing it in the most characteristic way of all. My whole instinct would be against any thwarting of such unifying action, and if we only had the Mission Field to consider I personally shld incline to encouragement rather than restraint, even though the action may in strict logic be difficult to defend. But our thoughts cannot be limited to the Mission Field. We are face to face with intense difficulties on the whole subject of Reunion and the indirect result of action taken in a particular Diocese may be considerable for good or ill. . .

It is quite certain that with our fuller inter-communication throughout the world and the wider organisation of our own Church the different parts of it are affected more than they used to be by what any one part does. Action taken in Australia or West Africa affects in a new degree Church controversies and discussions in, say, in Montreal, or Shanghai or London. This throws a heavier responsibility upon each group of workers in the Mission Field or elsewhere, inasumuch as what they do will now in a new degree complicate the issues of a discussion or a 'movement' thousands of miles away. I am persuaded that the policy laid down by the Edinburgh Conference and followed in its Continuation Committee is the policy which is likely in the long run to lead to a stronger and a wider union than can otherwise be brought about.

D.P. 266, fos. 86–9, Davidson to Bishop Herbert Tugwell, 25 November 1913

~~~~~

The First World War helped to foster growing determination across the churches to promote closer relations. The decision by the 1920 Lambeth Conference to issue 'An Appeal to All Christian People' raised enthusiasm both in Britain and abroad for the goal of Reunion. Davidson's commitment to building closer relations between the churches was deep-rooted, but he was also cautious about any attempts to anything like genuine Reunion, aware that such a process would create tensions within the Church of England. The following document shows how the Archbishop's positive view of 'ecumenism' in the abstract was more guarded when dealing with specific discussions with the leaders of other churches both at home and abroad.

> All these things came vividly home to us last year [during the discussions at the 1920 Lambeth Conference on the question of Reunion]. And as we thought and spoke and planned, our younger men saw visions and our older men dreamed dreams. Some of you know as I do how hard it is for an old man to recast the thoughts which he has treated as axioms for a score of years, to reconstruct the familiar architecture of his spiritual home. But we did try. It came home to us that we must, simply must, appeal to all Christian people that we should "consider our ways", and see whether a larger and a newly-devised unity might not be first a possibility, then a duty, then an element of power. And we found utterance in the "Appeal to all Christian People", which is in your hands. It has had a reception to which my long experience offers no parallel. It is sold by tens of thousands. You can read it in Latin, in Greek, in Spanish, in Portuguese, in Russian, in French, in Italian, in German, even in Esperanto, and its chord is vibrant. How oddly the utterance has been, I will not say misrepresented, here and there, but utterly misunderstood! It has been described as a programme – almost as an agenda-paper – or even, *mirabile dictu* – as an "ultimatum", instead of being a reverent attempt to give to our vision some coherent form, if only a cloud-shape. Ruskin has taught us in eloquent words how cloud-shapes seen in the heavens can be the source of the beautiful and the practical upon earth in structures fashioned by those who had gazed and learned. I suppose it is hardly necessary for me to go over with you afresh the terms of our Lambeth Appeal. It is now in everybody's hands.
>
> I have been trying simply to remind you of its breadth of origin and purpose, and its range of vision. We had, and have, in view, not solely, I think might say not even chiefly, our home differences and schismata, but Christendom as a whole. That means, as one great section, the Church of the Historic East, with its roots deep down in the earliest centuries – its

life dim and unfamiliar to most of us either in its history, or in its expansions and curtailments, or in its present trend, yet capable, as we are beginning eagerly to see, of new sympathies which may surprise us all [...] And more difficult far, the Historic West. We have never ceased to make it clear that we enter no portal of fellowship which has "submission" graven on its lintel – submission to what would be unendurable because it is untrue. About that we have no vestige of hesitation. And no part which we could possibly tread upon a reconciliation-road is at present even dimly in sight. Yet as we bow reverently before the Lord *"who maketh men to be of one mind in an house"*, and look onward into the unrolling of His purpose, I dare not myself quite say *Lasciate ogni speranza*, or hold it inconceivable that, in the providence of God, a truer light may some day dawn. So our vision cannot rightly, with regard to either East or West, take a constructive shape which would for ever render such an approach, even in the long last, unthinkable.

Archbishop of Canterbury, *An Address to the General Assembly of the Church of Scotland, May 31 1921* **(London, 1921)**

Davidson was sceptical about the value of the Malines Conversations set in motion by Lord Halifax in the early 1920s, doubting whether they could lead to any real understanding between the Church of England and the Church of Rome. He was also anxious that any developments that looked likely to create closer links with Rome would be bitterly opposed by many in the Church. The Archbishop nevertheless believed that following the Lambeth Appeal he could not refuse to give at least tacit approval to the talks between Halifax and Cardinal Mercier.

During the last few weeks there have been a good many matters of interest. The most important is the visit of Halifax, Armitage Robinson, and Frere to Malines to confer with Cardinal Mercier on the problem of Roman and Anglican relationship, or possible approach. The letters which are carefully preserved tell the beginning of the story more than a year ago. At that time the three Anglicans had no credentials from me but went on their own account, and without my official knowledge. It had come about through Halifax and his friend the Abbé Portal. I did know about it unofficially, and have a memorandum as to what took place at that time. This later matter had rather more of an official character, though we have been very guarded as to that. I insisted, as the dossier will show, upon securing that the Roman authorities should give at least as definite a credential to their representatives as we gave to ours, and accordingly Cardinal Mercier, after some indirect correspondence, wrote me a plain letter quoting the letter which he had received from the Vatican giving the Pope's benediction to the interview and conversations. We did not go a yard further than this, but it had a sufficiently official character to make it necessary that I should mention it to the Bishops at their recent meeting. This I did, and the Bishops, speaking generally, approved altogether of what had been done, the only critic being Henson of Durham, who when I pressed him had no suggestion to offer as to any other way of dealing with the subject than that which I had followed. The invitation to discuss matters had not come from me, but from Cardinal Mercier, and for me to have refused all cognisance of it in any way would have run counter to the whole principles on which we are trying to promote general Reunion, whether with Nonconformists or Easterns or Romans.

This last week the Conference which took place on Wednesday and Thursday, was recounted in two memoranda, one in French drawn by Mercier, one in English drawn by our men. They differ in character, but the statements are practically the same. They all signed the memoranda which thus have a much more for[m]al character than anything that went before. I think they have managed quite fairly and that Robinson and Frere have been eager not to give away the Anglican position in any respect. Halifax's attitude is somewhat different. He has for many years maintained that there is no difference in doctrine between the Churches of Rome and of England, and that it is only a matter of jurisdiction and Papal assumption which separates us, and he thinks that this could be readjusted so as to bring about union, though he admits the practical difficulty in view of popular feeling of a Protestant sort. On reading the memoranda I have felt anxious lest if they become public in their present form – a thing which we cannot regard as inconceivable, though perhaps improbable just now – they would be regarded as a betrayal by the Church of England of our whole position since the Reformation. This would be altogether unfair, for if the memoranda are carefully read it will be seen that nothing of the sort has been done. The appearance, however, is, I think, liable to be misleading in the view of people who read these things in a more popular way. I have accordingly to-day been preparing a letter to Armitage Robinson setting out from my point of view the true position of the discussions and calling attention to dangers lurking in the memoranda. This is not yet done, and I think I must show it to the Archbishop of York before actually sending it, though I may read it to Armitage in draft. He is now staying here. The whole matter may turn out to be of very great importance, though personally I think all will break down over the requirements which I regard as fundamental respecting the Papacy and its claims. If these be stated from any standpoint which I could accept, the Vatican would, I think, be bound to repudiate them absolutely and in that case the conversations, we cannot at present call them negotiations, would, I suppose, come abruptly to an end. This would deeply distress Halifax, who would regard me as having been quite unduly insistent on an Anti-Roman position. I do not think it would distress other people much, for there are very few sensible men who would really think that anything could come of such negotiations while matters stand as at present. The documents are of historic importance. I suppose nothing of the kind has happened since the days of Archbishop Wake – his communications with the Gallican Church, not with the Vatican.

D.P. 14, fos. 207–9, Extracts from Archbishop Davidson Memorandum, dictated 18 March 1923

Davidson had a lifelong interest in the Eastern churches. The turmoil in Russia and south-eastern Europe after 1918 created huge problems for the Eastern Churches, as their fate became increasingly bound up with the political changes taking place in the region. Davidson favoured building closer relations with the Christian East. He was nevertheless concerned by the over-enthusiasm of some Anglicans who believed that, in the wake of the 'Appeal to all Christian People', it might be possible to transform relations in the course of a few years. Davidson believed that any moves towards Reunion – or indeed any efforts simply to improve relations between the Church of England and the Churches of the East – could only take place slowly and with frank acknowledgement of the political and theological obstacles to such developments. The following two documents show both his support in principle for building closer relations with the Eastern churches – along with his recognition of the challenges involved. The first is taken from a speech to Canterbury Convocation in 1923.

> But among all the gleams of hope which are struggling into steadier light, none is vaster in its possibilities than are the questions which belong to our relation to the ancient Christian Churches of the East. On this question I desire to say something to you now.
>
> This is the first meeting of Convocation since a Declaration was given to the world by the chief authority of the Orthodox Church, and opportunity was offered for discussing it, a Declaration regarding their view of our position, and I think it most important that we should take in exactly what it is and what it means. I cannot even speak of the problem of the Eastern Churches just now without referring here in our larger gathering to what I referred to yesterday in the Upper House, the awful catastrophe of the sufferings by which our Christian brethren in the East are confronted just now, the scale of which, the gravity of it, the urgency of it, are incapable of exaggeration. Our knowledge of the details, such as it is, surely lays an obligation upon all of us that we should think about it, pray about it, and know about it as well as we may. . .
>
> For myself personally I began to handle the subject [of relations with the Eastern Churches] at Lambeth long ago – forty-six years ago – though in a very subordinate capacity. So that I am able to estimate the steady growth of intercourse between then and now, and the new flood of communication between the Churches of the East and ourselves. Especially is it so in our latter days. . .
>
> The Reports of the Lambeth Conferences of 1897 and 1908 each had full reports upon the problem which are well worth study to-day. And

now, in our immediate memory, the whole thing has bounded forward into prominence and importance and urgency by the events of the War. It is now four years since I appointed our Eastern Churches Committee, the outcome of a request of the Conference of 1908 to deal with these questions, and that Committee, presided over by Bishop Gore, has corresponding committees in the East itself, dealing with their relations with us. Constantinople, Moscow and Athens all have their own committees which are handling these questions.

Archbishop Davidson address to both Houses of Convocation (Canterbury), 16 February 1923

The second document is an extract from a private memorandum Davidson wrote in 1925, describing the visit of a number of senior clergy to Britain

We spent Easter at Wells – then came a spell of very heavy Lambeth work with a great many utterances of one kind & another – & very troublesome arrangements connected with the Eastern Patriarchs and Bishops who came to England for the Nicaean Celebration in Westminster Abbey on June 29th [1925]. I had to preach there and speak at different meetings and dinners at which the Easterns were welcomed and entertained, including a great luncheon at Lambeth. The whole arranging of this was very difficult, owing to what I regarded as the over-enthusiasm of some lovers and students of Eastern Church problems who failed to realise the way in which religious questions were complicated with & affected by political ambitions & schemes on the part of our Eastern guests. On the one hand I had to make it clear that I was entirely friendly to such endeavour as is practicable for drawing our Church into closer touch with Eastern Christians, yet feeling all the time that their mode of outlook and impact upon the world's life and its wrongs which need mending is at present widely different from our own and belongs really to another epoch than ours.

D.P. 15, fos. 27–8, Extracts from Archbishop Davidson Memorandum, January 1926

Davidson supported efforts to build closer relations between the Church of England and the Nonconformist churches after the First World War, although he left much of the work to the Archbishop of York, who took the leading role in a series of meetings on the subject. The following address by Davidson was delivered in Convocation in support of a Resolution to allow Bishops to authorise ministers who were not Episcopally ordained to preach in churches in their diocese *and* to allow their clergy on occasion to preach in 'the churches of such ministers'. Davidson supported the Resolution on the grounds that it would improve relations with the Nonconformist churches, but made clear his opposition to anything that smacked of 'general schemes of inter-communion or exchange of pulpits'. It reflected his habitual caution as well as his genuine commitment to improving relations between the churches.

> The Resolution is of a limited kind, dealing with one very limited range of practical action, but it is impossible not to allude for a moment to the larger question of which it forms a part – the general subject of the steps towards the reunion of the Church of Christ throughout the world. I agree with what was said yesterday by the Bishop of Worcester as to the inevitable falling of the temperature from that which prevailed in 1920. That was inevitable. We were then rightly warmed to enthusiasm on a great subject, and undoubtedly, as the Bishop of Worcester put it yesterday, the temperature then stood high. It has cooled, but, my lords, it is well that we should deal with the matter coolly. It is right that we should now be dealing with it with the calm consideration which comes from deliberation and time. But that does not in a whit diminish our resolve to give effect to what we have in mind. We did then, under the great impulse of those momentous weeks, if one may use the phrase without irreverence, mount up with wings as an eagle; we have now to walk and not faint. That is the difference; we are walking now with the result that we are not going to faint. We mean to carry out what we were then speaking of with the larger vision. Of course, difficulties emerged as we came down from the mount of vision to the plain of practical work. Those difficulties are not going to disappear; they are not going to grow less as we come to practical action. We shall find them in many respects even more formidable locally than they were centrally [...] Is the need for delay a strange thing? We are trying to attempt some healing of the disunion which has been a grave reality for long centuries of the Church's life. Could anybody for a moment suppose that that could be healed in a few weeks, or that the great rifts could be lightly plastered over? I shall have the privilege, I hope, in a few weeks' time of going to Scotland to speak to the General Assembly of the Church of Scotland and the General Assembly of the United Free Church. It is amazing to hear the quiet way in which some people seem to suppose that this means a great stride into a position of reunion between Anglicanism and Presbyterianism. What one hopes to do is this, to point out to the brethren there what is the vision which we seem to see of things that may, under the good hand of God, come about in the Church's life, and to suggest what seem to us some possible modes by which that vision can be brought into practical effect, and then to say to them: Do you share that? [...] One step at a time is all that we can or ought to attempt.
>
> **Address by Archbishop Davidson to the Upper House of Convocation (Canterbury), 27 April 1921**

Bibliography

A full list of the sources relevant to the life and times of Randall Davidson would fill an entire book. The sources listed here are those mentioned in the notes along with a small number of others that have been of particular value in the preparation of the manuscript. The Davidson Papers at Lambeth Palace Library have been by far the most important source of archival material used in this book. Other archival collections both at Lambeth Palace Library and elsewhere have also proved useful. Lambeth Palace Library also contains a host of published and archival material relating to developments in the Church of England during the first quarter of the century.

Archival sources

Bodleian Library Oxford
Herbert Asquith Papers
Stanley Baldwin Papers

Borthwick Institute for Archives (University of York)
Charles Lindley (First Viscount Halifax) Papers

British Library
Arthur Balfour Papers
Henry Campbell-Bannerman Papers

Lambeth Palace Library, London
George Bell Papers
Edward White Benson Papers
W. J. Birkbeck Papers
Randall Davidson Papers
J. A. Douglas Papers
William Temple Papers
Anglican and Eastern Churches Association Papers
Bishops' Meetings Minutes
Lambeth Conference Papers

Strozier Library (Florida State University Papers)
Stephen Graham Papers

Published documents

The Archbishop's Committee on Church and State: A Report with Appendices (London: SPCK, 1916). (Anonymous)
Christianity and Industrial Problems (London: SPCK, 1918).
The Chronicle of Convocation: Convocation of Canterbury
Church Assembly Reports of Proceedings
Doctrine in the Church of England: The 1938 Report (London: SPCK, 1982), ed. G.W.H. Lampe.
Documents Bearing on the Problems of Christian Unity and Fellowship, 1916–1920 (London: SPCK, 1920) ed. G.K.A. Bell.
Documents on Christian Unity, 1920–1924 (Oxford: Oxford University Press, 1924), ed. G.K.A. Bell.
The Six Lambeth Conferences, 1867–1920 (London: SPCK, 1929), ed. Randall Davidson.
Report of the Proceedings of the Representative Church Council

Newspapers and journals

Aberdeen Journal
Brooklyn Daily Eagle
Cambrian News
Cambridge Daily News
The Christian East
Church Times
Evening Dispatch
Evening Star
Guardian
Hartlepool Mail
The Inter-Ocean
Isle of Wight Observer
Manchester Guardian
The Modern Churchman
Morning Post
New York Times
Observer
Ottawa Journal
Pall Mall Gazette
Sheffield Daily Telegraph
The Times
Western Daily Press

Memoirs and other contemporary sources

Angell, Norman, *The Great Illusion: A Study of the Relation of Military Power to National Advantage* (London: William Heinemann, 1909).
Barber, Melanie (ed), 'Randall Davidson: A Partial Retrospective', in Stephen Taylor (ed), From Cranmer to Davidson: A Church of England Miscellany (Woodbridge: Boydell Press for the Church of England Record Society, 1999).
Begbie, Harold, *Painted Windows: A Study in Religious Personality* (London: Mills and Boon, 1922).

Bell, G.K.A. (ed), *The War and the Kingdom of God* (London: Longmans, 1915).
Benham, Revd Wm. Benham (ed), *Catherine and Craufurd Tait: A Memoir* (London: Palgrave Macmillan, 1879).
Benson, Arthur, *The Life of Edward White Benson, Sometime Archbishop of Canterbury*, 2 vols. (London: Macmillan, 1899).
Bowen, W.E., *Contemporary Ritualism: A Volume of Evidence* (London: Spottiswoode, 1902).
Bryce, James, *Studies in Contemporary Biography* (London: Macmillan, 1927).
Clayton, P.B., *Plain Tales from Flanders* (London: Longmans, 1929).
Clayton, P.B., *Tales of Talbot House* (London: Chatto and Windus, 1919).
Dark, Sidney, *Archbishop Davidson and the English Church* (New York: William and Morrow, 1929).
Davidson, Randall, *A Charge Delivered to the Clergy of the Diocese of Rochester* (London: Macmillan, 1984).
Davidson, Randall, *A Charge Delivered to the Clergy of Winchester, September-October 1899* (London: Macmillan, 1899).
Davidson, Randall, *The Christian Opportunity* (London: Macmillan, 1904).
Davidson, Randall, *Disestablishment: A Speech Delivered at a Meeting Held at the Corn Exchange at Rochester on June 8th 1893* (London, 1893).
Davidson, Randall, *The Education Controversy* (London: Warren and Son, 1902).
Davidson, Randall, *The Inheritance of a Great Name: A Sermon Preached in the Chapel of Harrow School on Founder's Day, October 11 1883* (London: Macmillan, 1883).
Davidson, Randall, *Kikuyu* (London: Macmillan, 1914).
Davidson, Randall, *Lambeth and Edinburgh: An Address to the General Assembly of the Church of Scotland* (London: SPCK, 1921).
Davidson, Randall, *Occasions* (London: Mowbray, 1925).
Davidson, Randall, *The Prayer Book: Our Hope and Meaning* (London: Hodder and Stoughton, 1928).
Davidson, Randall, *Quit You Like Men* (London: SPCK, 1915).
Davidson, Randall, *The Testing of a Nation* (London: Macmillan, 1919).
Davidson, Randall, *Three Sermons Preached in the Private Chapel of Windsor Castle* (London: Printed by Command of the Queen, 1884).
Davidson, Randall and Benham, William, *Life of Archibald Campbell Tait: Archbishop of Canterbury*, 2 vols. (London: Macmillan, 1891).
Frere, Walter, *Recollections of Malines* (London: Centenary Press, 1935).
Fry, T.C. (ed), *Why We Christians Believe in Christ: Bishop Gore's Lectures Shortened for Popular Use* (London: John Murray, 1904).
Gairdner, W.H.T., *Edinburgh 1910: An Account and Analysis of the Edinburgh Missionary Conference* (Edinburgh: Oliphant, Anderson and Ferrier, 1910).
Gibraltar, W.E., 'The Pan-Anglican Congress', *The Irish Church Quarterly*, 1, 4 (1908), pp. 274–90.
Graham, Edward, *The Harrow Life of Henry Montagu Butler* (London: Longman, Green & Co, 1903).
Graham, Stephen, *Part of the Wonderful Scene* (London: Collins, 1964).
Graham, Stephen, *A Private in the Guards* (London: Heinemann, 1928).
Haldane, Richard Burdon, *An Autobiography* (London: Hodder and Stoughton, 1929).
Halifax, Viscount, *A Call to Reunion* (London: Mowbray, 1922).
Henson, Herbert Hensley, *Letters of Herbert Hensley Henson*, ed. Evelyn Foley (London: SPCK, 1951).
Henson, Herbert Hensley, *Retrospect of an Unimportant Life*, 3 vols. (London: Oxford University Press, 1942–50).

Herbert, Charles, *Twenty-Five Years as Archbishop of Canterbury* (London: Wells Gardner, Darnton, 1929).
Inge, W.R., *Diary of a Dean: St Paul's 1911–1934* (London: Hutchinson, 1934).
Knox, Edward Arbuthnott, *Reminiscences of an Octogenarian, 1874–1934* (London: Hutchinson, 1935).
Knox, Rt. Rev E.A., *Will the Deposited Book Restore Order in the Church: Some Startling Facts* (London: Church Book Room, 1928).
The Letters of Queen Victoria, Series 2–3 (London: John Murray, 1926–30).
Latimer, R.S., *Under Three Tsars: Liberty of Conscience in Russia, 1856–1909* (London: Morgan and Scott, 1909).
Lodge, Oliver, *Raymond, or Life or Death* (New York: George Doran, 1916).
Macnutt, F.B. (ed), *The Church in the Furnace* (London: Macmillan, 1974).
Methuen, Charlotte (ed), 'Lambeth 1920: The Appeal to All Christian People: An Account by G.K.A. Bell and the Redactions of the Appeal', in Melanie Barber and Stephen Taylor with Gabriel Sewell (eds), *From the Reformation to the Permissive Society: A Miscellany in Celebration of the 400th Anniversary of Lambeth Palace Library* (Woodbridge: Boydell Press for the Church of England Record Society, 2010), pp. 521–64.
M.M., *Bishop Montgomery: A Memoir* (London: Society for the Propagation of the Gospel in Foreign Parts, 1933).
Montgomery, H.H, *Christian Missions in the Far East* (London: SPCK, 1905).
Montgomery, H.H., *The Relation of the Civil Government to Christian Missions* (London: SPG, 1910).
Montgomery, H.H., *Service Abroad* (London: Longmans, Green & Co, 1910).
Queen Victoria's Journal (www.queenvictoriasjournals.org/home.do)
Peake, A.S., *Prisoners of Hope: The Problem of the Conscientious Objector* (London: George Allen and Unwin, 1918).
Sandford, E.G. (ed), *Memoirs of Archbishop Temple by Seven Friends*, 2 vols. (London: Macmillan, 1906).
Scott Holland, Henry, *A Bundle of Memories* (London: Wells, Gardiner, Darnton, 1915).
Snape, Michael (ed), 'Archbishop Davidson's Visit to the Western Front, May 1916', in Melanie Barber, Stephen Taylor with Gabriel Sewell (eds), *From the Reformation to the Permissive Society: A Miscellany in Celebration of the 400th Anniversary of Lambeth Palace Library* (Woodbridge: Boydell Press for the Church of England Record Society, 2010), pp. 455–520.
Streeter, B.H. (ed), *Foundations: A Statement of Christian Belief in Terms of Modern Thought* (London: Macmillan, 1912).
Studdert-Kennedy, Geoffrey K., *The Hardest Part* (London: Hodder and Stoughton, 1918).
Waddel, Peter (ed), *Charles Gore: Radical Anglican* (Norwich: Canterbury Press, 2014).
Ward, Mrs Humphrey, *Daphne, or Marriage a La Mode* (London: Cassel, 1909).
Webb, Beatrice, *Break Up the Poor Law and Abolish the Workhouse (Being the Minority Report of the Poor Law Commission)* (London: Fabian Society, 1909).
Westcott, Arthur (ed), *Life and Letters of Brooke Foss Westcott*, 2 vols. (London: Macmillan, 1903).
Weston, Frank, *The Case Against Kikuyu: A Study in Vital Principles* (London: Longmans, 1914).
Winninton-Ingram, Arthur Foley, *The Church in a Time of War* (London: Wells, Gardner, Darnton, 1915).

Secondary sources

Arnstein, Walter L., 'Queen Victoria and Religion', in Gail Malmgreen (ed), *Religion in the Lives of English Women* (London: Croom Helm, 1986), pp. 88–128.

Bahlmann, Dudley W.R., 'Politics and Church Patronage in the Victorian Age', *Victorian Studies*, 22, 3 (1976), pp. 253–96.
Bailey, Charles E., 'The British Protestant Theologians in the First World War: Germanophobia Unleashed', *The Harvard Theological Review*, 77, 2 (1984), pp. 382–95.
Barry, F. Russell, *Mervyn Haigh* (London: SPCK, 1964).
Beaken, Robert, *Cosmo Gordon Lang: Archbishop in Church and Crisis* (London: I.B. Tauris, 2012).
Bebbington, D. W., *The Nonconformist Conscience: Chapel and Politics, 1870–1914* (London: Allen and Unwin, 1982).
Beckett, Ian, *The Army and the Curragh Incident* (London: Bodley Head for Army Records Society, 1986).
Bell, Duncan, *The Idea of Greater Britain: Empire and the Future of World Order, 1860–1900* (Princeton, NJ: Princeton University Press, 2007).
Bell, G.K.A., *Randall Davidson: Archbishop of Canterbury*, 2 vols. (London: Oxford University Press, 1938).
Bell, P.M.H., *Disestablishment in Ireland and Wales* (London: SPCK, 1969).
Bell, Stuart, 'Malign or Maligned: Arthur Winnington-Ingram, Bishop of London, in the First World War', *Journal for the History of Modern Theology / Zeitschrift für Neuerer Theologiegeschichte*, 20, 1 (2014), pp. 117–33.
Bentley, James, *Ritualism and Politics in Victorian Britain* (Oxford: Oxford University Press, 1978).
Bernstein, George Lurcy, *Liberalism and Liberal Politics in Edwardian England* (Boston: Allen and Unwin, 1986).
Bibbings, Lois, *Telling Tales About Men: Conceptions of Conscientious Objectors to Military Service During the First World War* (Manchester: Manchester University Press, 2009).
Birn, Donald, *The League of Nations Union, 1918–1945* (Oxford: Clarendon Press, 1981).
Blakely, Derek W., 'The Archbishop of Canterbury, the Episcopal Bench, and the Passing of the 1911 Parliament Act', *Parliamentary History*, 27, 1 (2008), pp. 141–54.
Bolt, Robert, *As Good as Gold, As Clever as the Devil: The Impossible Life of Mary Benson* (London: Atlantic Books, 2011).
Boulton, John, *Objection Overruled* (London: MacGibbon and Key, 1967).
Briggs, Asa, *The Birth of Broadcasting* (London: Oxford University Press, 1961).
Brown, Callum, *The Death of Christian Britain* (London: Routledge, 2001).
Brown, Callum, *Religion and Society in Twentieth-Century Britain* (London: Pearson, 2006).
Brown, Stewart J. and Nockles, Peter B. (eds), *The Oxford Movement: Europe and the Wider World, 1830–1930* (Cambridge: Cambridge University Press, 2014).
Canadine, David, *George V: The Unexpected King* (London: Allen Lane, 2014).
Carpenter, Edward, *Cantuar: The Archbishops in their Office* (London: Cassel, 1971).
Carpenter, James, *Gore: A Study in Liberal Catholic Thought* (London: Faith Press, 1960).
Carpenter, S.C., *Winnington-Ingram: The Biography of Arthur Foley Winnington-Ingram, Bishop of London, 1901–1939* (London: Hodder and Stoughton, 1949).
Ceadel, Martin, *Pacifism in Britain, 1914–1945: The Defining of a Faith* (Oxford: Oxford University Press, 1980).
Ceadel, Martin, *Semi-Detached Idealists: The British Peace Movement and International Relations, 1854–1945* (Oxford: Oxford University Press, 2000).
Chadwick, Owen, *Hensley Henson: A Study in the Friction Between Church and State* (Oxford: Clarendon Press, 1983).
Chadwick, Owen, *The Victorian Church*, 2 vols. (London: Adam and Charles Black, 1970).
Chandler, Andrew (ed), *The Church and Humanity: the Life and Work of George Bell, 1883–1958* (London: Routledge, 2012).

Chandler, Andrew, *George Bell. Bishop of Chichester: Church, State and Resistance in the Age of Dictatorship* (Grand Rapids, MI: William B. Eerdmans, 2016).
Clark, Christopher M., *The Sleepwalkers: How Europe went to War in 1914* (London: Penguin Books, 2013).
Clements, Keith, *Faith on the Frontier: A Life of J.H. Oldham* (London: Bloomsbury, 1999).
Currie, Robert et al (eds.), *Churches and Churchgoers: Patterns of Church Growth in the British Isles Since 1700* (Oxford: Oxford University Press, 1977).
Currie, Robert, 'Power and Principle: The Anglican Prayer Book Controversy, 1927–1930', *Church History*, 33, 2 (1964), pp. 192–205.
Dangerfield, George, *The Strange Death of Liberal England* (London: Constable, 1936).
Dick, John A., *The Malines Conversations Revisited* (Leuven: Leuven University Press, 1989).
Dowland, David, *Nineteenth-Century Anglican Theological Training: The Redbrick Challenge* (Oxford: Oxford University Press, 1997).
Edmondson, Charles, M. and Levis, R. Barry, 'Archbishop Randall Davidson, Russian Famine Relief, and the Fate of the Orthodox Clergy, 1917–1923', *Journal of Church and State*, 40, 3 (1998), pp. 619–37.
Edwards, David L., *Leaders of the Church of England, 1828–1978* (London: Hodder and Stoughton, 1978).
Evans, G.R., *Edward Hicks: Pacifist Bishop at War* (Oxford: Lion Books, 2014).
Fletcher, Sheila, *Maude Royden: A Life* (Oxford: Basil Blackwell, 1989).
Geffert, Bryn, *Eastern Orthodox and Anglicans: Diplomacy, Theology and the Politics of Interwar Ecumenism* (Notre Dame, IN: University of Notre Dame Press, 2010).
Gilbert, Alan D., *The Making of Post-Christian Britain: A History of the Secularisation of Modern Society* (London: Longmans, 1980).
Gilbert, Martin, *Winston S. Churchill*, 8 vols. (London: Heinemann, 1966–88).
Goldman, Lawrence, *The Life of R.H. Tawney: Socialism and History* (London: Bloomsbury, 2013).
Gordon-Taylor, Benjamin and Stebbing, Nicholas (eds), *Walter Frere: Scholar, Monk, Bishop* (Norwich: Canterbury Press, 2011).
Gouldstone, Timothy, *The Rise and Decline of Anglican Idealism in the Nineteenth Century* (Basingstoke: Palgrave Macmillan, 2005).
Green, S.J.D., *The Passing of Protestant England: Secularisation and Social Change, c. 1920–1960* (Cambridge: Cambridge University Press, 2012).
Green, S.J.D., *Religion in the Age of Decline: Organisation and Experience in Industrial Yorkshire, 1870–1920* (Cambridge: Cambridge University Press, 1996).
Green, S.J.D., 'Survival and Autonomy: On the Strange Fortunes and Peculiar Legacy of Ecclesiastical Establishment in the Modern British State, c 1920 to the Present Day', in S.J.D. Green and R.C. Whiting (eds), *The Boundaries of the State in Modern Britain* (Cambridge: Cambridge University Press, 1996), pp. 299–326.
Grimley, Matthew, *Citizenship, Community and the Church of England* (Oxford: Clarendon Press, 2004).
Haig, Alan, *The Victorian Clergy* (London: Croom Helm, 1984).
Haig, A.G.L., 'The Church, the Universities and Learning in Later Victorian England', *The Historical Journal*, 21, 9 (1986), pp. 187–201.
Hastings, Adrian, *A History of English Christianity, 1920–1985* (London: Fount, 1986).
Hattersley, Roy, *Borrowed Time: The Story of Britain Between the Wars* (London: Abacus, 2007).
Heeney, Brian, 'The Beginnings of Church Feminism: Women and the Councils of the Church of England, 1897–1919', *Journal of Ecclesiastical History*, 33, 1 (1982), pp. 89–109.

Hinchliff, Peter, *Frederick Temple, Archbishop of Canterbury: A Life* (Oxford: Clarendon Press, 1998).
Hinchliff, Peter, 'Frederick Temple, Randall Davidson and the Coronation of Edward VII', *Journal of Ecclesiastical History*, 48, 1 (1997), pp. 71–99.
Honeycutt, Dwight A., 'Motivations of a Political Activist: John Clifford and the Education Bill of 1902', *Journal of Church and State*, 32, 1 (1990), pp. 81–96.
Horne, John N. and Kramer, Alan, *German Atrocities, 1914: A History of Denial* (New Haven, NJ: Yale University Press, 2001).
Hubbard, Kate, *Serving Victoria: Life in the Royal Household* (London: Chatto and Windus, 2012).
Hughes, Michael, *Beyond Holy Russia: The Life and Times of Stephen Graham* (Cambridge: Open Book Publishers, 2014).
Hughes, Michael, *Conflict and Conscience: Methodism, Peace and War in the Twentieth Century* (London: Epworth Press, 2008).
Hughes, Michael, 'The English Slavophile: W.J. Birkbeck and Russia', *Slavonic and East European Review*, 82, 3 (2004), pp. 680–706.
Hynes, Samuel, *The Edwardian Turn of Mind* (Princeton, NJ: Princeton University Press, 1968).
Iremonger, F.A., *William Temple: Archbishop of Canterbury* (London: Oxford University Press, 1948).
Jasper, Ronald C.D., *George Bell, Bishop of Chichester* (Oxford: Oxford University Press, 1967).
Jenkins, Roy, *Asquith* (London: Collins, 1964).
Kent, John, *William Temple: Church, State and Society in Britain, 1880–1950* (Cambridge: Cambridge University Press, 1992).
Kuhn, William, *Democratic Royalism: The Transformation of the British Monarchy* (London: Palgrave Macmillan, 1996).
Laity, Paul, *The British Peace Movement, 1870–1914* (Cambridge: Cambridge University Press, 2002).
Link-Wieczorek, Ulrike, 'Mediating Anglicanism: Maurice, Gore, and Temple', in David Fergusson (ed), *The Blackwell Companion to Nineteenth-Century Theology* (Oxford: Blackwell, 2010), pp. 280–300.
Lockhart, J.G., *Charles Lindley, Viscount Halifax, 1885–1934* (London: The Centenary Press, 1936).
Lockhart, J.G, *Cosmo Gordon Lang* (London: Hodder and Stoughton, 1949).
Machin, G.I.T., *Churches and Social Issues in Twentieth-Century Britain* (Oxford: Clarendon Press, 1998).
Machin, G.I.T., *Politics and the Churches in Great Britain, 1869–1921* (Oxford: Clarendon Press, 1987).
Macmillan, Margaret, *Peacemakers: Six Months that Changed the World* (London: John Murray, 2003).
Madigan, Edward, *Faith Under Fire: Anglican Chaplains and the Great War* (London: Palgrave Macmillan, 2011).
Maiden, John, *National Religion and the Prayer Book Controversy, 1927–1928* (Woodbridge: Boydell Press, 2009).
Marrin, Albert, *The Last Crusade: The Church of England in the First World War* (Durham, NC: Duke University Press, 1974).
Maughan, Stephen, *Mighty England do Good* (Grand Rapids, MI: William B. Eerdmans, 2014).
Mayer, Arno, 'Domestic Causes of the First World War', in Leonard Krieger and Fritz Stern (eds), *The Responsibility of Power* (New York: Garden City, 1967), pp. 286–93.

Mcleod, Hugh, 'Protestantism and British National Identity', in Peter Van der Veer and Hartmut Lehman (eds), *Nation and Religion: Perspectives on Europe and Asia* (Princeton, NJ: Princeton University Press, 1999), pp. 44–70.

Methuen, Charlotte, 'Fulfilling Christ's Own Wish That We Should Be One': The Early Ecumenical Career of George Bell as Chaplain to the Archbishop of Canterbury and Dean of Canterbury', *Kirchliche Zeitgeschichte*, 21, 2 (2008), pp. 222–45.

Mews, Stuart, 'From Shooting to Shopping: Randall Davidson's Attitudes to Work, Rest, and Recreation', in Robert Norman Swanson (ed), *The Use and Abuse of Time in Christian History* (Woodbridge: Boydell and Brewer, 2002), pp. 385–99.

Mews, Stuart, 'Randall Davidson', in *Oxford Dictionary of National Biography*.

Middlemas, Keith and Barnes, John, *Baldwin: A Biography* (London: Weidenfeld and Nicolson, 1969).

Mills, Mary (M.C.S.M.), *Edith Davidson of Lambeth* (John Murray, 1938).

Morgan, D.H.J., 'The Social and Educational Background of Bishops – Continuities and Changes', *British Journal of Sociology*, 20, 3 (1969), pp. 295–310.

Munson, J.E.B., 'The Oxford Movement by the End of the Nineteenth Century: The Anglo-Catholic Clergy', *Church History*, 44, 3 (1975), pp. 382–95.

Murray, Bruce K., *The People's Budget 1909/10: Lloyd George and Liberal Politics* (Oxford: Oxford University Press, 1980).

Nockles, P.B., 'Lost Causes and. . . Impossible Loyalties: The Oxford Movement and the University', in M.G. Brock and M.C. Curthoys (eds), *The History of the University of Oxford* (Clarendon Press, 1997), Vol. VI, Part 2, pp. 195–207.

Nockles, Peter, *The Oxford Movement in Context: Anglican High Churchmanship, 1760–1857* (Cambridge: Cambridge University Press, 1997).

Norman, E.R., *Church and Society in England, 1770–1970: A Historical Study* (Oxford: Clarendon, 1976).

O'Day, Alan, *Irish Home Rule: 1867–1921* (Manchester: Manchester University Press, 1998).

Osborne, Charles E., *Life of Father Dolling* (London: Edward Arnold, 1903).

Otte, Thomas, *July Crisis: The World's Descent into War* (Cambridge: Cambridge University Press, 2014).

Overy, Richard, *The Morbid Age: Britain and the Crisis of Civilization, 1919–1939* (London: Penguin, 2010).

Park, Trevor, *Nolo Episcopari: A Life of C.J. Vaughan* (St Bees: St Bega Publications, 2013).

Pawley, Bernard and Pawley, Margaret, *Rome and Canterbury through Four Centuries* (London: Mowbray, 1974).

Peart-Binns, John S., *Herbert Hensley Henson: A Biography* (Cambridge: Lutterworth Press, 2013).

Philip, Rev Andrew, *The Ancestry of Randall Thomas Davidson DD, Archbishop of Canterbury* (London: Elliot Stock, 1903).

Plant, Raymond, *Philosophy, Politics and Citizenship: The Life and Thought of the British Idealists* (Oxford: Blackwell, 1984).

Powell, David, *The Edwardian Crisis, 1901–1914* (Basingstoke: Macmillan, 1996).

Prestige, G.L., *The Life of Charles Gore: A Great Englishman* (London: William Heinemann, 1935).

Pugh, D.H., 'The 1902 Education Act: the Search for Compromise', *British Journal of Educational Research*, 15, 2 (1968), pp. 164–78.

Rae, John, *Conscience and Politics* (London: Oxford University Press, 1970).

Raina, Peter, *Bishop Bell: The Greatest Churchman: A Portrait in Letters* (Peterborough: Churches Together in Britain and Ireland, 2006).

Ramsey, Michael, *An Era in Anglican Theology: From Gore to Temple* (Eugene, OR: Wipf and Stock, 1960).
Read, Anthony, *The World on Fire: 1919 and the Battle with Bolshevism* (London: Pimlico, 2009).
Read, Donald (ed), *Edwardian England* (New Brunswick, NJ: Rutgers University Press, 1982).
Robbins, Keith, *England, Ireland, Scotland, Wales: The Christian Church, 1900–2000* (Oxford: Oxford University Press, 2008).
Roberts, Andrew, *Salisbury: Victorian Titan* (London: Faber and Faber, 2010).
Rose, Jonathan, *The Edwardian Temperament* (Athens, OH: Ohio University Press, 1986).
Rouse, Ruth and Neill, Stephen Charles, *A History of the Ecumenical Movement, 1517–1948* (London: SPCK, 1967).
Salter, A.T.J., 'An Outline History of the Anglican & Eastern Churches Association', www.aeca.org.uk/articles/AECA_Outline_History.pdf.
Sherrington, G.E., 'The 1918 Education Act: Origins, Aims and Development', *British Journal of Educational Studies*, 24, 1 (1976), pp. 66–85.
Smith, H. Maynard, *Frank, Bishop of Zanzibar: Life of Frank Weston, D.D., 1871–1924* (London: SPCK, 1926).
Snape, Michael and Madigan, Edward (eds), *The Clergy in Khaki: New Perspectives on British Army Chaplaincy in the First World War* (Farnham: Ashgate, 2013).
Stephenson, Alan M.G., *Anglicanism and the Lambeth Conferences* (London: SPCK, 1978).
Stephenson, Alan M.G., *Rise and Decline of English Modernism: The Hulsean Lectures, 1979–80* (London: SPCK, 1984).
Taylor, A.J.P., *English History, 1914–1945* (Oxford: Clarendon Press, 1965).
Taylor, D.J., *Bright Young People: Rise and Fall of a Generation* (London: Vintage, 2008).
Taylor, Tony, 'Arthur Balfour and Educational Change: the Myth Revisited', *British Journal of Educational Studies*, 42, 4 (1994), pp. 133–49.
Thompson, E.P., *William Morris: Romantic to Revolutionary* (New York: Pantheon Books, 1997).
Turberfield, Alan, *John Scott Lidgett: Archbishop of Methodism?* (Peterborough: Epworth Press, 2003).
Webster, Peter, 'The Archbishop of Canterbury, the Lord Chamberlain and the Censorship of the Theatre, 1909–49', *Studies in Church History*, 48 (2012), pp. 437–48.
Wellings, Martin, *Evangelicals Embattled: Responses of Evangelicals to Ritualism, Darwinism and Theological Liberalism, 1890–1930* (Cumbria: Paternoster Press, 2003).
Wilkinson, Alan, *Christian Socialism: Scott Holland to Tony Blair* (London: SCM, 1998).
Wilkinson, Alan, *The Church of England and the First World War* (London: SPCK, 1978).
Wilkinson, Alan, *The Community of the Resurrection: A Centenary History* (London: SCM, 1992).
Williamson, Philip, 'National Days of Prayer: The Churches, the State and Public Worship in Britain, 1899–1957', *English Historical Review*, 128 (2013), pp. 323–66.
Williamson, Philip, *Stanley Baldwin: Conservative Leadership and National Values* (Cambridge: Cambridge University Press, 1999).
Winter, Jay, *Sites of Mourning, Sites of Memory* (Cambridge: Cambridge University Press, 1995).
Yelton, Michael, *Outposts of the Faith: Anglo-Catholicism in some Rural Parishes* (Norwich: Canterbury Press, 2009).
Zernov, Nicholas, *Orthodox Encounter: The Christian East and the Ecumenical Movement* (London: James Clarke and Co, 1961).

Index

Anglo-Catholic Conference (1923) 121
Apostles Creed 68
Apostolicae Curae 22, 115, 119
'Appeal to All Christian People' 112–15, 116, 119–20, 122–6
'Appeal to Evangelical Christians Abroad' 104
Aquinas, Thomas 203
Archbishop Davidson and the English Church (Dark) 1
Asquith, Herbert: constitutional crisis 38–41; with Davidson 182; government in wartime and 86–8; Irish Home Rule crisis 42–3, 187–8; letter from Davidson 203–4
Asquith, Margot 187
Augustine of Hippo, Saint 203

Balfour, Arthur J. 24, constitutional crisis 40–1; Davidson's relationship with 182, 186; educational reform 28–9, at Geneva 141; Home Rule crisis, 42; Licensing Bill 52–3; Parliament and Ritualism 62; in wartime 87
Barber, Melanie 7
Barker, Ernest 148
Barnes, E. W., Bishop of Birmingham 154
Beach, Michael Hicks 62
Begbie, Harold 1, 2
Bell, George, Chaplain to Davidson and later Bishop of Chichester: appointment as Davidson's Chaplain 104–5; biography of Davidson 1, 6, 7, 27, 171–2; on Davidson's handling of Enabling Bill 152; Davidson's invaluable support of 182; as Dean of Canterbury 126; drafts Archbishop's correspondence, 111; positive picture of Davidson's involvement in National Mission 98; reports Davidson's deathbed blessing 166–7; Reunion with other churches 116, 119; role in the discussions with Nonconformist churches 126
Benson, Edward, Bishop of Truro later Archbishop of Canterbury 2, 15–19, 21, 26, 49, 60, 106, 166, 171, 181, 186
Benson, Mary 2
Bermondsey Settlement 74
Bigge, Arthur, Lord Stamfordham 17, 21, 87, 137
Birrell, Augustine 37
Bishop Montgomery: A Memoir (M. M.) 184
Black and Tans 143, 171
Bonar Law, Andrew 42–3, 187–8
Bowen, W. E. 61
Bridgeman, William 132, 160
Bright, John 192
Brown, Callum 7, 48
Browne, Harold 15, 19
Brown, John 16–17, 88
Burge, Hubert, Bishop of Oxford 154–6
Burke, Edmund 170
Butler, Henry M. 11

Call to Reunion Arising out of Discussions with Cardinal Mercier, A (Halifax) 120
Campbell-Bannerman, Henry 36, 38
Carnegie, William, Canon of St Margaret's Westminster 105
Carpenter, William Boyd, Bishop of Ripon 18
Cecil, Hugh 36, 38, 53, 79, 81, 98, 160, 176
Cecil, Robert 103, 141
Chamberlain, Joseph 70
Character and Call of the Church of England, The (Davidson) 68, 173–4, 193–4
Charge Delivered to the Clergy of Rochester, A (Davidson) 22
Chavasse, Francis, Bishop of Liverpool 99

226 Index

Christian Opportunity, The (Davidson) 178–81
Christian Social Union (CSU) 20, 39, 51, 52, 67, 130, 181
Church Association 18, 117, 161
Church League for Women's Suffrage 48
Church of England: challenges during First World War 5; Church-State relations 101–3; Eastern Churches and 115–19; Nonconformist Churches and 123–6; internal tensions 4, 59; Kikuyu crisis 77–80; place in modern culture 6–7; relations with Roman Catholic Church 119–23; Reunion with Episcopal and non-Episcopal churches 124–6; role in World War I 85–106; status as National Church 22–3, 147–9, 169–70; tension between Nonconformist churches and 75–80, 105–6
Church Self-Government Council 149
Clifford, John 28, 35, 124
Cobden, Richard 192
Commission on Christian Doctrine 153–6
Conference on Christ and the Creeds (Cambridge, 1921) 154–5
Conference on Christian Politics, Economics and Citizenship (Birmingham, 1924) 105, 126
Conference on Faith and Order (Lausanne, 1927) 126
Congo Free State 46
Conrad, Joseph 46
conscription and conscientious objectors 92–4
constitutional crisis (1909–1911) 38–41
Creed in the Pulpit, The (Henson) 66, 100
Curragh Mutiny 42
Curzon, George N. 87, 118

Dark, Sidney 1
Darwin, Charles 3
Davidson, Edith 1, 13, 14, 20, 48, 51, 166, 167
Davidson, Henry 12
Davidson, Randall, Archbishop of Canterbury: address to both houses of Convocation on the Eastern churches 212–13; address to General Assembly of Church of Scotland 126, 209–10; addresses to Upper House of Convocation 68, 191–2, 194–5, 200–1, 213–14; Anglicanism 173–81; appointment to Canterbury 29; approach to ecclesiastical administration 175–6; assessment 166–72; biography by Bell 1–3, 6, 7, 27, 152, 171–2; birth 3, 10; as Bishop of Rochester 19–23, 51, 59, 74; as Bishop of Winchester 23–9, 59; on Bishops in Parliament 27; career during First World War 4–5, 85–110; career in years before appointment to Canterbury 4, 10–33; challenge of conscription 92–4; challenge of Modernism 64–9; challenge of social and economic reform 5, 130–46, 169–70, 184–93; challenge of Welsh Disestablishment 43–4, 194–5; challenges during first ten years at Canterbury in managing tensions within the Church of England 4, 59–84; *Character and Call of the Church of England, The* 68, 173–4, 193–4; *Charge Delivered to the Clergy of Rochester, A* 22; *Christian Opportunity, The* 178–81; Church-State relations 5, 147–65, 193–200; Commission on Christian Doctrine 153–6; constitutional crisis of 1909–11 38–41; criticisms of 2; as Dean of Windsor 15–19, 74; death 1, 3, 166; development of relations between the churches and its impact on peace-building in the First World War 103–6; early years 10–11; ecclesiastical discipline 60–4, 153–6; effect of the war on morals of civilian population 96–8; Enabling Bill and 149–53, 196–8; ethical challenge of war and 88–92; General Strike and 131–5; government in wartime and 86–8; at Harrow School 11; involvement in major political controversies 4, 34–58; Irish Home Rule crisis 42–3; Kikuyu crisis 60, 77–80, 114, 208; letter on League of Nations 103; letters on educational reform 35, 37; letter to Archbishop Söderblom on wartime relations between the churches 104, 204–5; letter to Asquith on use of poisonous gas 203–4; letter to Bishop of Winchester describing heavy work load, 182–3; letter to F. L. Donaldson 189–90 on unemployment; letter to Temple on Life and Liberty 195–6; letter to Tugwell on missionary activity in Africa 208–9; Malines Conversations 119–23; marriage laws 53, 131, 139–40, 144, 190; note on interview with Baldwin over General Strike 192–3; at Oxford 11–12; peace and war after 1918 200–7; *Peace of God* sermon 201–4; politics of educational reform and 35–8; Prayer

Book crisis and 5, 8, 126, 147–8, 151, 153, 156–63, 167, 170, 177–8, 198–200; *Prayer Book: Our Hope and Meaning, The* 162, 177–8; question of Sunday Observance 52–3; as Realist 168–9; relations with Eastern Churches after the First World War 115–19, 212–13; relations with Nonconformist churches before 1914 75–7; relations with the Nonconformist churches after the First World War 124–6; relations with Roman Catholic Church after the First World War 119–23; as Resident Chaplain at Lambeth Palace 12–15; retirement 166; Ritualism 4, 7, 8, 23–5, 59, 60–4; role in ecumenical movement 5, 111–29, 207–14; search for peace in 1918 103–6; sermon in St Peter's Cathedral Geneva, 205–7; shooting accident 11; speech at Albert Hall 44; speech in Caernarvon 43; speech in Croydon 44; speech in House of Lords 196–8; speech in Montreal 70, 178–81; speech in Toronto 70; statement on Prayer Book Crisis 198–200; on suffrage question 48–50; support for international arbitration 46; time in Dartford 12; at Trinity College 11; views on British Empire 47, 69–71, 142; visit to Canada 70; visit to United States 70–1; war at the Front and 94–6; wartime doctrinal controversies 98–101
Dibdin, Lewis 152
Dickens, Charles 3
Disestablishment of the Church in Wales 22, 34, 39, 43–4, 148, 194–5
divorce law 53, 131, 139–40, 144, 190
Dolling, Robert 24, 63
Dombey and Son (Dickens) 3
Donaldson, F. L. 50, 189–90
Douglas, J. A. 117
'Dreadnought' lobby 46
Dugdale, Blanche 24

Eastern Churches 74, 105, 113, 115–19, 205, 212–13
Eastern Churches Association 117
ecclesiastical discipline 60–4, 153–6
Ecumenical Patriarch at Constantinople 116
Edinburgh 1910: an account and interpretation of the world missionary conference (Gairdner) 207–8
Edinburgh Missionary Conference (1910) 75–8, 207–8

Education Act of 1870 27
Education Act of 1902 28, 35–8, 55, 75
Educational Act of 1918 140
Edward VII, King of the United Kingdom 25–6, 29, 37, 38, 40, 54, 88, 171
Eliot, T. S. 111
Enabling Bill 148, 149–53, 196–8
English Church Union (ECU) 61, 113, 117, 154–5
English Hymnal, The 64
Establishment: Church-State relations 5, 22, 101–2, 144, 193–4; growing scepticism about value of 148–51; hostility to principle of 64; Prayer Book crisis 161–3; principle of 14; role of Church of England in public life 130; value of 139

February Revolution (Russia, 1917) 87
Ferdinand, Franz 85
Figgis, J. N. 148
Fisher, H.A.L. 152
Foundations (Streeter) 67, 77
Free Church Council 124
Frere, Walter 52, 120, 124, 158, 210

Gairdner, W.H.T. 207–8
Gascoyne-Cecil, Robert, Lord Salisbury 17, 18, 19, 21, 23 26, 35
General Strike (1926) 69, 111, 131–5, 192–3
George V, King of the United Kingdom 38, 40, 54, 87–8, 96, 137, 188
Gladstone, William E. 15–16, 18, 36, 186
Gore, Charles, Bishop of Oxford: appointment of Henson as Bishop of Hereford (reaction) 100–1, 176–7; belief that Church of England heading for formal split 113; belief that Church of England would benefit from Disestablishment 148; chair of Eastern Churches Committee 118; Commission on Christian Doctrine 154–5; critical of prevailing economic system 51; as influential figure 8; Kikuyu crisis 78, 81; *Lux Mundi* essays edited by 18; opposition to Boer War 45; Prayer Book crisis 121; relationship with Davidson 65–8, 170; resigns as Bishop of Oxford 151; Reunion with other churches 118; Weston as protégé of 77
'Great Service for Protestants' (1924) 122
Green, Simon 7
Green, Thomas H. 11
Grey, Edward 27, 152
Grimley, Matthew 7, 148
Guttery, Arthur 151

Index

Haldane, Richard B. 36, 152
Harcourt, William 24–6
Hardie, Keir 50
Harrow School 11, 12, 51
Headlam, Arthur 117
Heart of Darkness (Conrad) 46
Henson, Hensley, Bishop of Hereford: appointment to Hereford 6, 99–102, 176–7; Church-State relations 148; Davidson saying Churchmen had right to express their views 50; Davidson's rebuke to 78; deploring prospect of 'any doctrinal pronouncement that would limit freedom of clergy to develop understanding of Christian belief 66–7; Enabling Bill 150; Lambeth conference 113; letter to Davidson on need to consider Disestablishment 162; Malines Conversations 120, 211; relationship with Davidson 170
Hicks, Edward, Bishop of Lincoln (and former Canon of Manchester) 44, 88, 105
Hoare, Samuel (Viscount Templewood) 115
Holland, Henry Scott 39, 52, 72

Incarnation and Incarnational Theology 6, 21, 68, 101, 177
Inge, William R., Dean of St Paul's Cathedral 64, 101, 167
international arbitration 46
Iremonger, F. A. 102, 196
Irish Home Rule crisis 4, 34, 42–3, 185

Joynson-Hicks, William 122, 134, 136, 159, 161, 170

Kent, John 7
Kidd, Beresford 121
Kikuyu crisis 60, 77–80, 114, 208–9
King, Edward, Bishop of Lincoln 18
Kipling, Rudyard 47, 70
Knollys, Francis 40
Knox, Edmund, Bishop of Manchester 38, 151, 153, 167

Lady Chatterley's Lover (Lawrence) 3
Lambeth Conferences 26–7, 69, 71–4, 78, 112–15, 124, 209–10
Lambeth Quadrilateral 113
Lang, Cosmo 76, 111, 113, 124, 126, 166–7
Lansbury, George 51
Lawrence, D. H. 3

Lawrence, William, Bishop of Massachusetts 70
League of Nations 103, 104, 105, 141–2, 205–7
Leopold II, King of Belgium 46
Leopold, Prince, Duke of Albany 16
Leo XIII, Pope 22, 119
Licensing Bill 52–3
Lidgett, J. Scott 45, 74, 75, 105, 125, 153
Life and Liberty Movement 101–2, 148, 149, 161, 195
Lloyd George, David: appointment of Henson as Bishop of Hereford 99–100, 176; in biography of Davidson by Bell 2; challenge of conscription 93; coalition government 136; constitutional crisis 38–9; educational reform 36; Enabling Bill 152; on German relations 85; industrial unrest 131; Irish Home Rule 143; mistress 96; replacing Asquith 87; using religion as way of mobilising support for political change 75
Loftus, Jane, Marchioness of Ely 15
Lux Mundi 18, 21, 65, 154

Maiden, John 147
Malines Conversations 22, 64, 112, 119–23, 125–6, 210
Mansfield College Oxford (1920 Conference between Anglicans and Nonconformists) 113
marriage laws 53, 131, 139, 140
Marx, Karl 52
Mercier, Désiré-Félicien-François-Joseph, Archbishop of Malines 119–21, 210–13
Metaxakis, Meletios 118
Mews, Stuart 7
Military Service Act of 1916 86
Milner, Alfred 47
Miracles in the New Testament (Thompson) 66
Modern Churchman, The 154
Modernism 5, 59, 64–9, 77, 79, 99, 100, 112, 155
Montgomery, H. H., (Secretary of the Society for the Propagation of the Gospel), 47, 72, 73, 78, 114, 183–4
Montgomery, Maud (M. M.) 184
More Leaves from the Journal of a Life in the Highlands (Victoria, Queen of Great Britain) 17
Morley, John 43
Morris, William 52
Mott, J. R. 75, 91

National Assembly of the Church of England 150
National Free Church Council 152
National Mission of Repentance and Hope, 97–8, 102, 132, 149
National Service League 46
Nestorian Assyrian Church 118
Nikaean Club 119
Nonconformists: churches at home and in the missionary field (before 1914) 74–80; educational reform 35–6; growing political influence of 36, 144; international politics 44; Liberal Party support 28; new social gospel of 39; relations between churches 105–6, 123–6, 207, 213–14; retreating to suburbs 22

Oldham, J. H. 75
Origin of Species (Darwin) 3
Oxford Movement 4, 11, 59, 168, 174

Paget, Francis, Bishop of Oxford 62, 66
Palmer, William W., Earl of Selborne 152
Pan-Anglican Congress (1908) 39, 71–4
Pankhurst, Emmeline 48
Parliament Act 39–41
Parliamentary crisis 4, 38–41
Patriarchates 116
Peel, W. G. 77
'People's Budget' 38
Percival, John 21, 99
Perks, Robert 125
Petty-Fitzmaurice, Henry, Lord Lansdowne 43, 103
Portal, Fernand 119
Powell, Enoch 147
Prayer Book crisis 5, 8, 121, 126, 147–8, 151, 153, 156–63, 167, 170, 177–8, 198–200
Prayer Book: Our Hope and Meaning, The (Davidson) 162, 177–8
Prayers for the Dead 99
'Primate of All England, The' (Spender) 181–2
Primitive Methodist Church 124
Primrose, Archibald, Lord Rosebery 21, 36, 186
Protestant Truth Society 161
Public Worship Regulation Act 14, 60, 61, 62

Ramsey, Michael 168
Rashdall, Hastings 64, 100, 154, 176
Reith, John 134, 138, 192

Representative Church Council (RCC) 102, 150–1
Reservation of the Sacrament 60, 99, 148, 151–2, 156, 157, 159, 161, 162, 169
Riley, Athelstan 61, 78, 80, 97–8
Ritualism 4, 7, 8, 14, 23–5, 59, 60–4, 65, 112, 136, 157, 159
Ritualistic Party 18
Robbins, Keith 7
Robinson, Armitage 120, 210–11
Rogers, J. Guiness 74
Roman Catholic Church 28, 74, 78, 80, 94, 113, 117, 119–23, 204–5
Roosevelt, Theodore 71
Royal Commission on Ecclesiastical Discipline 62–4, 153–6
Royal Commission on the Poor Laws 51
Royden, Maude 97
Russian Orthodox Church 45, 115–17

Sanday, William 67
Sheppard, Dick 143, 191
Simpson, Carnegie 124
Smith, Frederick E., Lord Birkenhead 152
Smyth, Ethel 48
Society for the Propagation of the Gospel 114
Söderblom, Nathan, Archbishop of Uppsala 104, 204–5
South Africa 47
South African War of 1899–1902 34
Spender, Harold 181–2
Spiritualism 99
Spurgeon, C. H. 74
Stephenson, Frances 96
Stockholm Conference on Life and Work (1925) 126
Streeter, B. H. 67, 77
Suffragette Movement 48–50
Sunday Observance 52–3, 75

Tait, Archibald, Archbishop of Canterbury 2, 4, 8, 12–15, 19, 22, 60–1, 74, 184
Tait, Craufurd 12, 14
Tait, Edith *see* Davidson, Edith
Tait, Lucy 2, 49, 166
Tawney, R. H. 5, 131, 132
Taylor, A. J. P. 147
Temple, Frederick, Archbishop of Canterbury 25–7, 28–9, 59, 66, 69, 181
Temple, William: Christian Social Union 39; Church-State relations 148, 191, 193; Davidson at odds with 5, 103; as

influential figure 8, 168; Life and Liberty Movement 101–2, 150, 195–6; National Mission 98; ordination 6, 66; part in shaping public opinion on Enabling Bill 152; views on role of State in shaping social and economic life 131, 133, 143–4
Tikhon of Moscow, Patriarch of Russian Orthodox Church 116–17
Trinity College 11
Tugwell, Herbert 208–9

Vaughan, Charles 12
Velimirović, Nikolai 105
Venizelos, Eleuthérios 118
Versailles Peace Treaty 85
Victoria, Queen of Great Britain 2, 15–17, 19, 25–6, 34, 54, 88, 181
Virgin Birth 66, 67, 100

War Memoirs (Lloyd George) 87
Wasteland, The (Eliot) 111
Webb, Beatrice 51
Wells, H. G. 34
Wells Theological College 104
Wesleyan Conference 124, 125
Westcott, Brooke Foss, Bishop of Durham 11, 16, 51
Weston, Frank, Bishop of Zanzibar 77–9, 81, 113
William Temple, Archbishop of Canterbury: His Life and Letters (Iremonger) 196
Willis, J. J. 77, 79
Winchester College Mission 24
Winnington-Ingram, Arthur, Bishop of London 86
women priests 97
Wood, Edward, Lord Halifax 21–2, 25, 36, 39, 61–2, 81, 100, 112, 170, 210–11